# Mastering Ansible
## *Third Edition*

Effectively automate configuration management and deployment challenges with Ansible 2.7

**James Freeman**
**Jesse Keating**

BIRMINGHAM - MUMBAI

# Mastering Ansible
## *Third Edition*

Copyright © 2019 Packt Publishing

All rights reserved. No part of this book may be reproduced, stored in a retrieval system, or transmitted in any form or by any means, without the prior written permission of the publisher, except in the case of brief quotations embedded in critical articles or reviews.

Every effort has been made in the preparation of this book to ensure the accuracy of the information presented. However, the information contained in this book is sold without warranty, either express or implied. Neither the authors, nor Packt Publishing or its dealers and distributors, will be held liable for any damages caused or alleged to have been caused directly or indirectly by this book.

Packt Publishing has endeavored to provide trademark information about all of the companies and products mentioned in this book by the appropriate use of capitals. However, Packt Publishing cannot guarantee the accuracy of this information.

**Commissioning Editor:** Vijin Boricha
**Acquisition Editor:** Meeta Rajani
**Content Development Editor:** Shubham Bhattacharya
**Technical Editor:** Sayali Thanekar
**Copy Editor:** Safis Editing
**Project Coordinator:** Nusaiba Ansari
**Proofreader:** Safis Editing
**Indexer:** Rekha Nair
**Graphics:** Jisha Chirayil
**Production Coordinator:** Tom Scaria

First published: November 2015
Second edition: March 2017
Third edition: March 2019

Production reference: 1220319

Published by Packt Publishing Ltd.
Livery Place
35 Livery Street
Birmingham
B3 2PB, UK.

ISBN 978-1-78995-154-7

www.packtpub.com

mapt.io

Mapt is an online digital library that gives you full access to over 5,000 books and videos, as well as industry leading tools to help you plan your personal development and advance your career. For more information, please visit our website.

# Why subscribe?

- Spend less time learning and more time coding with practical eBooks and Videos from over 4,000 industry professionals

- Improve your learning with Skill Plans built especially for you

- Get a free eBook or video every month

- Mapt is fully searchable

- Copy and paste, print, and bookmark content

# Packt.com

Did you know that Packt offers eBook versions of every book published, with PDF and ePub files available? You can upgrade to the eBook version at www.packt.com and as a print book customer, you are entitled to a discount on the eBook copy. Get in touch with us at customercare@packtpub.com for more details.

At www.packt.com, you can also read a collection of free technical articles, sign up for a range of free newsletters, and receive exclusive discounts and offers on Packt books and eBooks.

# Contributors

## About the authors

**James Freeman** is an accomplished IT consultant with over 20 years' experience in the technology industry. He has more than 5 years of first-hand experience of solving real-world enterprise problems in production environments using Ansible, frequently introducing Ansible as a new technology to businesses and CTOs for the first time. In addition, he has authored and facilitated bespoke Ansible workshops and training sessions, and has presented at both international conferences and meetups on Ansible.

> *I would like to thank my other half, Neeshia Jasmara, for her support, without which this book would probably never have happened; my sons, Sam and Jaedyn, for their continued patience while I have my head in a computer; and my employer, Quru, and especially our founder, Roland Whitehead, who have provided me with the opportunities that enabled me to write this book.*

**Jesse Keating** is an accomplished Ansible user, contributor, and presenter. He has been an active member of the Linux and open source community for over 15 years. He has first-hand experience involving a variety of IT activities, software development, and large-scale system administration. He has presented at numerous conferences and meetups, and has written many articles on a variety of topics.

# About the reviewer

**Timothy Rupp** has been working in various fields of computing for the last 15 years. He has held positions in cybersecurity and software engineering, as well as in the fields of cloud computing and DevOps.

He was first introduced to Ansible while at Rackspace. As part of the cloud engineering team, he made extensive use of a tool for deploying new capacity to the Rackspace public cloud. Since that introduction, he has contributed patches, provided support for, and presented on Ansible topics at local meetups.

While at F5 Networks, he led the development of F5's Ansible modules and became a core contributor to the Ansible project. Most recently, he has become reinvolved with cybersecurity in the financial sector.

# Packt is searching for authors like you

If you're interested in becoming an author for Packt, please visit authors.packtpub.com and apply today. We have worked with thousands of developers and tech professionals, just like you, to help them share their insight with the global tech community. You can make a general application, apply for a specific hot topic that we are recruiting an author for, or submit your own idea.

# Table of Contents

**Preface**   1

## Section 1: Ansible Overview and Fundamentals

**Chapter 1: The System Architecture and Design of Ansible**   9
- **Technical requirements**   9
- **Ansible version and configuration**   10
- **Inventory parsing and data sources**   11
  - Static inventory   12
  - Inventory ordering   13
  - Inventory variable data   14
  - Dynamic inventories   17
  - Runtime inventory additions   20
  - Inventory limiting   21
- **Playbook parsing**   24
  - Order of operations   24
  - Relative path assumptions   26
  - Play behavior directives   29
  - Execution strategies   30
  - Host selection for plays and tasks   31
  - Play and task names   32
- **Module transport and execution**   35
  - Module reference   35
  - Module arguments   36
  - Module blacklisting   37
  - Module transport and execution   38
    - Task performance   39
- **Variable types and location**   40
  - Variable types   40
  - Magic variables   42
- **Accessing external data**   43
- **Variable precedence**   43
  - Precedence order   44
  - Variable group priority ordering   45
  - Merging hashes   49
- **Summary**   50

**Chapter 2: Protecting Your Secrets with Ansible**   51
- **Technical requirements**   51
- **Encrypting data at rest**   52

*Table of Contents*

|  |  |
|---|---|
| Vault IDs and passwords | 53 |
| Things Vault can encrypt | 54 |
| Creating new encrypted files | 55 |
|     Password prompt | 56 |
|     Password file | 57 |
|     Password script | 58 |
| Encrypting existing files | 58 |
| Editing encrypted files | 60 |
| Password rotation on encrypted files | 62 |
| Decrypting encrypted files | 63 |
| Executing Ansible-playbook with encrypted files | 64 |
| **Mixing encrypted data with plain YAML** | **66** |
| **Protecting secrets while operating** | **69** |
| Secrets transmitted to remote hosts | 70 |
| Secrets logged to remote or local files | 70 |
| **Summary** | **72** |
| **Chapter 3: Ansible and Windows - Not Just for Linux** | **73** |
| **Technical requirements** | **73** |
| **Running Ansible from Windows** | **74** |
| Checking your build | 74 |
| Enabling WSL | 75 |
| Installing Linux under WSL | 75 |
| **Setting up Windows hosts for Ansible control** | **77** |
| System requirements for automation with Ansible | 77 |
| Enabling the WinRM listener | 78 |
| Connecting Ansible to Windows | 81 |
| **Handling Windows authentication and encryption** | **83** |
| Authentication mechanisms | 83 |
| A note on accounts | 86 |
| Certificate validation | 87 |
| **Automating Windows tasks with Ansible** | **89** |
| Picking the right module | 89 |
| Installing software | 91 |
| Extending beyond modules | 91 |
| **Summary** | **92** |
| **Chapter 4: Infrastructure Management for Enterprises with AWX** | **93** |
| **Technical requirements** | **94** |
| **Getting AWX up and running** | **94** |
| **Integrating AWX with your first playbook** | **98** |
| Defining a project | 99 |
| Defining an inventory | 101 |
| Defining credentials | 104 |
| Defining a template | 105 |
| **Going beyond the basics** | **108** |

[ ii ]

| | |
|---|---|
| Role-based access control (RBAC) | 108 |
| Organizations | 109 |
| Scheduling | 109 |
| Auditing | 110 |
| Surveys | 111 |
| Workflow templates | 112 |
| Notifications | 114 |
| **Summary** | **115** |

# Section 2: Writing and Troubleshooting Ansible Playbooks

## Chapter 5: Unlocking the Power of Jinja2 Templates — 119

| | |
|---|---|
| **Technical requirements** | **119** |
| **Control structures** | **120** |
| Conditionals | 120 |
| Inline conditionals | 122 |
| Loops | 124 |
| Filtering loop items | 125 |
| Loop indexing | 126 |
| Macros | 129 |
| Macro variables | 129 |
| name | 130 |
| arguments | 131 |
| defaults | 132 |
| catch_kwargs | 133 |
| catch_varargs | 134 |
| caller | 134 |
| **Data manipulation** | **137** |
| Syntax | 137 |
| Useful built-in filters | 138 |
| default | 139 |
| count | 139 |
| random | 139 |
| round | 140 |
| Useful Ansible provided custom filters | 140 |
| Filters related to task status | 140 |
| shuffle | 142 |
| Filters dealing with path names | 143 |
| basename | 143 |
| dirname | 144 |
| expanduser | 144 |
| Base64 encoding | 145 |
| Searching for content | 146 |
| Omitting undefined arguments | 148 |
| Python object methods | 149 |
| String methods | 149 |
| List methods | 150 |
| int and float methods | 151 |

[ iii ]

## Comparing values — 151
### Comparisons — 151
### Logic — 152
### Tests — 152
## Summary — 153

# Chapter 6: Controlling Task Conditions — 155
## Technical requirements — 156
## Defining a failure — 156
### Ignoring errors — 156
### Defining an error condition — 158
## Defining a change — 163
### Special handling of the command family — 164
### Suppressing a change — 167
## Error recovery — 168
### Using the rescue section — 168
### Using the always section — 171
### Handling unreliable environments — 174
## Iterative tasks with loops — 177
## Summary — 179

# Chapter 7: Composing Reusable Ansible Content with Roles — 181
## Technical requirements — 181
## Task, handler, variable, and playbook inclusion concepts — 182
### Including tasks — 182
#### Passing variable values to included tasks — 184
#### Passing complex data to included tasks — 187
#### Conditional task includes — 189
#### Tagging included tasks — 191
### Task includes with loops — 193
### Including handlers — 197
### Including variables — 199
#### vars_files — 199
#### Dynamic vars_files inclusion — 200
#### include_vars — 201
#### extra-vars — 204
### Including playbooks — 205
## Roles — 208
### Role structure — 208
#### Tasks — 208
#### Handlers — 209
#### Variables — 209
#### Modules and plugins — 209
#### Dependencies — 210
#### Files and templates — 210
#### Putting it all together — 211
### Role dependencies — 211

|  |  |
|---|---|
| Role dependency variables | 212 |
| Tags | 213 |
| Role dependency conditionals | 213 |
| Role application | 214 |
| Mixing roles and tasks | 216 |
| Role includes and imports | 219 |
| Role sharing | 219 |
| Ansible Galaxy | 220 |
| **Summary** | **226** |
| **Chapter 8: Troubleshooting Ansible** | **227** |
| Technical requirements | 227 |
| Playbook logging and verbosity | 227 |
| Verbosity | 228 |
| Logging | 228 |
| Variable introspection | 229 |
| Variable subelements | 232 |
| Subelements versus Python object method | 235 |
| Debugging code execution | 236 |
| Playbook debugging | 237 |
| Debugging local code | 239 |
| Debugging inventory code | 240 |
| Debugging playbook code | 244 |
| Debugging executor code | 246 |
| Debugging remote code | 249 |
| Debugging the action plugins | 253 |
| **Summary** | **254** |
| **Chapter 9: Extending Ansible** | **255** |
| Technical requirements | 255 |
| Developing modules | 256 |
| The basic module construct | 256 |
| Custom modules | 257 |
| Example – Simple module | 257 |
| Documenting a module | 260 |
| Providing fact data | 266 |
| The check mode | 267 |
| Supporting check mode | 267 |
| Handling check mode | 268 |
| Developing plugins | 269 |
| Connection-type plugins | 269 |
| Shell plugins | 269 |
| Lookup plugins | 270 |
| Vars plugins | 270 |
| Fact-caching plugins | 270 |
| Filter plugins | 270 |
| Callback plugins | 272 |

*Table of Contents*

>    Action plugins — 275
>    Distributing plugins — 275
>    **Developing dynamic inventory plugins** — 276
>      Listing hosts — 277
>      Listing host variables — 277
>      Simple inventory plugin — 278
>        Optimizing script performance — 283
>    **Contributing to the Ansible project** — 285
>      Contribution submissions — 285
>        The Ansible repository — 286
>        Executing tests — 286
>          Unit tests — 287
>          Integration tests — 288
>          Code-style tests — 290
>        Making a pull request — 291
>    **Summary** — 292

## Section 3: Orchestration with Ansible

**Chapter 10: Minimizing Downtime with Rolling Deployments** — 295
>    **Technical requirements** — 296
>    **In-place upgrades** — 296
>    **Expanding and contracting** — 299
>    **Failing fast** — 302
>      The any_errors_fatal option — 302
>      The max_fail_percentage option — 304
>      Forcing handlers — 307
>    **Minimizing disruptions** — 310
>      Delaying a disruption — 310
>      Running destructive tasks only once — 315
>    **Serializing single tasks** — 316
>    **Summary** — 319

**Chapter 11: Infrastructure Provisioning** — 321
>    **Technical requirements** — 321
>    **Managing cloud infrastructures** — 322
>      Creating servers — 323
>        Booting virtual servers — 324
>        Adding to runtime inventory — 328
>      Using OpenStack inventory sources — 331
>    **Managing a public cloud infrastructure** — 337
>    **Interacting with Docker containers** — 345
>      Building images — 346
>      Building containers without a Dockerfile — 349
>      Docker inventory — 353
>    **Ansible Container** — 357

[ vi ]

|   |   |
|---|---|
| Using ansible-container init | 360 |
| Using ansible-container build | 362 |
| Using ansible-container run | 364 |
| **Summary** | 367 |
| **Chapter 12: Network Automation** | **369** |
| **Technical requirements** | 370 |
| **Ansible for network management** | 370 |
| Cross-platform support | 370 |
| Configuration portability | 371 |
| Backup, restore, and version control | 371 |
| Automated change requests | 372 |
| **Handling multiple device types** | 372 |
| Researching your modules | 373 |
| Configuring your modules | 374 |
| Writing your playbooks | 374 |
| **Configuring Cumulus Networks switches with Ansible** | 375 |
| Defining our inventory | 376 |
| Practical examples | 377 |
| Best practices | 382 |
| Inventory | 382 |
| Gathering facts | 383 |
| Jump hosts | 384 |
| **Summary** | 385 |
| **Other Books You May Enjoy** | **387** |
| **Index** | **391** |

[ vii ]

# Preface

Welcome to *Mastering Ansible*, your guide to a collection of the most valuable advanced features and functionalities provided by Ansible, the automation and orchestration tool. This book will provide readers with the knowledge and skills required to truly understand how Ansible functions at a fundamental level. In turn, this will allow readers to master the advanced capabilities needed to tackle the complex automation challenges of today, and the future. Readers will gain knowledge of Ansible workflows, explore use cases for advanced features, troubleshoot unexpected behavior, extend Ansible through customization, and learn about many of the new and important developments in Ansible, especially around infrastructure and network provisioning.

## Who this book is for

This book is for Ansible developers and operators who have an understanding of the core elements and applications but are now looking to enhance their skills in applying automation using Ansible.

## What this book covers

Chapter 1, *The System Architecture and Design of Ansible*, looks at the ins and outs of how Ansible goes about performing tasks on behalf of an engineer, how it is designed, and how to work with inventory and variables.

Chapter 2, *Protecting Your Secrets with Ansible*, explores the tools available to encrypt data at rest and prevent secrets from being revealed at runtime.

Chapter 3, *Ansible and Windows - Not Just for Linux*, explores the integration of Ansible with Windows hosts to enable automation in cross-platform environments.

Chapter 4, *Infrastructure Management for Enterprises with AWX*, provides an overview of the powerful open source graphical management framework for Ansible known as AWX, and how this might be employed in an enterprise environment.

Chapter 5, *Unlocking the Power of Jinja2 Templates*, states the varied uses of the Jinja2 templating engine within Ansible and discusses ways to make the most out of its capabilities.

Preface

Chapter 6, *Controlling Task Conditions*, explains how to change the default behavior of Ansible to customize task error and change conditions.

Chapter 7, *Composing Reusable Ansible Content with Roles*, explains how to move beyond executing loosely-organized tasks on hosts, and instead to build clean, reusable, and self-contained code structures known as roles to achieve the same end result.

Chapter 8, *Troubleshooting Ansible*, takes you through the various methods that can be employed to examine, introspect, modify, and debug the operations of Ansible.

Chapter 9, *Extending Ansible*, covers the various ways in which new capabilities can be added to Ansible via modules, plugins, and inventory sources.

Chapter 10, *Minimizing Downtime with Rolling Deployments*, explains the common deployment and upgrade strategies in order to showcase the relevant Ansible features.

Chapter 11, *Infrastructure Provisioning*, examines cloud infrastructure providers and container systems in order to create an infrastructure to manage.

Chapter 12, *Network Automation*, describes the advancements in the automation of network device configuration using Ansible.

# To get the most out of this book

To follow the examples provided in this book, you will need access to a computer platform capable of running Ansible. Currently, Ansible can be run on any machine with Python 2.7 or Python 3 (versions 3.5 and higher) installed (Windows is supported for the control machine, but only through a Linux distribution running in the **Windows Subsystem for Linux (WSL)** layer available on newer versions—see Chapter 3, *Ansible and Windows - Not Just for Linux*, for details). Supported operating systems include (but are not limited to) Red Hat, Debian, Ubuntu, CentOS, macOS, and FreeBSD.

This book uses the Ansible 2.7.x.x series release. Ansible installation instructions can be found at https://docs.ansible.com/ansible/intro_installation.html.

Some examples use Docker version 1.13.1. Docker installation instructions can be found at https://docs.docker.com/install/.

A handful of examples in this book make use of accounts on both Amazon Web Services (AWS) and Microsoft Azure. More information about these services may be found at `https://aws.amazon.com` and `https://azure.microsoft.com` respectively. We also delve into management of OpenStack with Ansible, and the examples in this book were tested against a single "all-in-one" instance of Devstack, as per the instructions found here: `https://docs.openstack.org/devstack/latest/`.

Finally, the chapter on network device management makes use of Cumulus VX, version 3.7.3, in the example code—please see here for more information: `https://cumulusnetworks.com/products/cumulus-vx/`.

# Download the example code files

You can download the example code files for this book from your account at `www.packt.com`. If you purchased this book elsewhere, you can visit `www.packt.com/support` and register to have the files emailed directly to you.

You can download the code files by following these steps:

1. Log in or register at `www.packt.com`.
2. Select the **SUPPORT** tab.
3. Click on **Code Downloads & Errata**.
4. Enter the name of the book in the **Search** box and follow the onscreen instructions.

Once the file is downloaded, please make sure that you unzip or extract the folder using the latest version of:

- WinRAR/7-Zip for Windows
- Zipeg/iZip/UnRarX for Mac
- 7-Zip/PeaZip for Linux

The code bundle for the book is also hosted on GitHub at `https://github.com/PacktPublishing/Mastering-Ansible-Third-Edition`. In case there's an update to the code, it will be updated on the existing GitHub repository.

We also have other code bundles from our rich catalog of books and videos available at `https://github.com/PacktPublishing/`. Check them out!

# Preface

## Download the color images

We also provide a PDF file that has color images of the screenshots/diagrams used in this book. You can download it here: `https://www.packtpub.com/sites/default/files/downloads/9781789951547_ColorImages.pdf`.

## Code in Action

Visit the following link to check out videos of the code being run: `http://bit.ly/2HCcfRE`

## Conventions used

There are a number of text conventions used throughout this book.

`CodeInText`: Indicates code words in text, database table names, folder names, filenames, file extensions, pathnames, dummy URLs, user input, and Twitter handles. Here is an example: "Also, note that Ansible requires the `winrm` Python module installed to connect successfully."

A block of code is set as follows:

```
---
- name: Linux file example playbook
  hosts: all
  gather_facts: false
```

Any command-line input or output is written as follows:

```
sudo yum install python2-winrm
```

**Bold**: Indicates a new term, an important word, or words that you see onscreen. For example, words in menus or dialog boxes appear in the text like this. Here is an example: "Now, note the buttons along the top of the **Inventories** pane—**DETAILS**, **PERMISSIONS**, **GROUPS**, **HOSTS**, **SOURCES**, and **COMPLETED JOBS**."

Warnings or important notes appear like this.

*Preface*

 Tips and tricks appear like this.

# Get in touch

Feedback from our readers is always welcome.

**General feedback**: If you have questions about any aspect of this book, mention the book title in the subject of your message and email us at `customercare@packtpub.com`.

**Errata**: Although we have taken every care to ensure the accuracy of our content, mistakes do happen. If you have found a mistake in this book, we would be grateful if you would report this to us. Please visit `www.packt.com/submit-errata`, selecting your book, clicking on the Errata Submission Form link, and entering the details.

**Piracy**: If you come across any illegal copies of our works in any form on the Internet, we would be grateful if you would provide us with the location address or website name. Please contact us at `copyright@packt.com` with a link to the material.

**If you are interested in becoming an author**: If there is a topic that you have expertise in and you are interested in either writing or contributing to a book, please visit `authors.packtpub.com`.

# Reviews

Please leave a review. Once you have read and used this book, why not leave a review on the site that you purchased it from? Potential readers can then see and use your unbiased opinion to make purchase decisions, we at Packt can understand what you think about our products, and our authors can see your feedback on their book. Thank you!

For more information about Packt, please visit `packt.com`.

# Section 1: Ansible Overview and Fundamentals

In this section, we will explore the fundamentals of how Ansible works and establish a sound basis on which to develop playbooks and workflows.

The following chapters are included in this section:

Chapter 1, *The System Architecture and Design of Ansible*

Chapter 2, *Protecting Your Secrets with Ansible*

Chapter 3, *Ansible and Windows – Not Just for Linux*

Chapter 4, *Infrastructure Management for Enterprises with AWX*

# The System Architecture and Design of Ansible

This chapter provides a detailed exploration of the architecture and design of Ansible, and how it goes about performing tasks on your behalf. We will cover the basic concepts of inventory parsing and how data is discovered, and then proceed onto playbook parsing. We will take a walk through module preparation, transportation, and execution. Lastly, we will detail variable types and find out where the variables are located, their scope of use, and how precedence is determined when variables are defined in more than one location. All these things will be covered in order to lay the foundation for mastering Ansible!

In this chapter, we will cover the following topics:

- Ansible version and configuration
- Inventory parsing and data sources
- Playbook parsing
- Execution strategies
- Module transport and execution
- Variable types and locations
- Magic variables
- Variable precedence (and interchanging this with variable priority ordering)

## Technical requirements

Check out the following video to see the Code in Action:

```
http://bit.ly/2u1bmEl
```

## Ansible version and configuration

It is assumed that you have Ansible installed on your system. There are many documents out there that cover installing Ansible in a way that is appropriate to the operating system and version that you might be using. This book will assume use of Ansible version 2.7.x.x. To discover the version in use on a system where Ansible is already installed, make use of the version argument, that is, either `ansible` or `ansible-playbook`, as follows:

```
ansible-playbook --version
```

This command should give you an output that's similar to the following screenshot:

```
~/src/mastery> ansible-playbook -i mastery-hosts -c local names.yaml

PLAY [play with a not-mastery] *************************************************

TASK [set a variable] **********************************************************
ok: [localhost]

TASK [task with a defined variable] ********************************************
ok: [localhost] => {
    "msg": "I am mastery task"
}

PLAY [second play with a {{ task_var_name }}] **********************************

TASK [task with a {{ runtime_var_name }}] **************************************
ok: [localhost] => {
    "msg": "I am another mastery task"
}

PLAY RECAP *********************************************************************
localhost                  : ok=3    changed=0    unreachable=0    failed=0

~/src/mastery>
```

 Note that `ansible` is the executable for doing ad hoc one-task executions, and `ansible-playbook` is the executable that will process playbooks for orchestrating many tasks.

The configuration for Ansible can exist in a few different locations, where the first file found will be used. The search involves the following:

- `ANSIBLE_CFG`: This environment variable is used, provided it is set
- `ansible.cfg`: This is located in the current directory
- `~/.ansible.cfg`: This is located in the user's home directory
- `/etc/ansible/ansible.cfg`

Some installation methods may include placing a `config` file in one of these locations. Look around to check whether such a file exists and see what settings are in the file to get an idea of how Ansible operation may be affected. This book will assume that there are no settings in the `ansible.cfg` file that would affect the default operation of Ansible.

# Inventory parsing and data sources

In Ansible, nothing happens without an inventory. Even ad hoc actions performed on the localhost require an inventory, though that inventory may just consist of the localhost. The inventory is the most basic building block of Ansible architecture. When executing `ansible` or `ansible-playbook`, an inventory must be referenced. Inventories are either files or directories that exist on the same system that runs `ansible` or `ansible-playbook`. The location of the inventory can be referenced at runtime with the `--inventory-file` (`-i`) argument, or by defining the path in an Ansible `config` file.

Inventories can be static or dynamic, or even a combination of both, and Ansible is not limited to a single inventory. The standard practice is to split inventories across logical boundaries, such as staging and production, allowing an engineer to run a set of plays against their staging environment for validation, and then follow with the same exact plays run against the production inventory set.

Variable data, such as specific details on how to connect to a particular host in your inventory, can be included, along with an inventory in a variety of ways, and we'll explore the options available to you.

## Static inventory

The static inventory is the most basic of all the inventory options. Typically, a static inventory will consist of a single file in the `ini` format. Here is an example of a static inventory file describing a single host, `mastery.example.name`:

```
mastery.example.name
```

That is all there is to it. Simply list the names of the systems in your inventory. Of course, this does not take full advantage of all that an inventory has to offer. If every name were listed like this, all plays would have to reference specific hostnames, or the special built-in `all` group (which, as it suggests, contains all hosts in the inventory). This can be quite tedious when developing a playbook that operates across different environments within your infrastructure. At the very least, hosts should be arranged into groups.

A design pattern that works well is to arrange your systems into groups based on expected functionality. At first, this may seem difficult if you have an environment where single systems can play many different roles, but that is perfectly fine. Systems in an inventory can exist in more than one group, and groups can even consist of other groups! Additionally, when listing groups and hosts, it's possible to list hosts without a group. These would have to be listed first before any other group is defined. Let's build on our previous example and expand our inventory with a few more hosts and groupings as follows:

```
[web]
mastery.example.name

[dns]
backend.example.name

[database]
backend.example.name

[frontend:children]
web

[backend:children]
dns
database
```

What we have created here is a set of three groups with one system in each, and then two more groups, which logically group all three together. Yes, that's right; you can have groups of groups. The syntax used here is `[groupname:children]`, which indicates to Ansible's inventory parser that this group, going by the name of `groupname`, is nothing more than a grouping of other groups.

*Chapter 1*

The `children`, in this case, are the names of the other groups. This inventory now allows writing plays against specific hosts, low-level, role-specific groups, or high-level logical groupings, or any combination thereof.

By utilizing generic group names, such as `dns` and `database`, Ansible plays can reference these generic groups rather than the explicit hosts within. An engineer can create one inventory file that fills in these groups with hosts from a pre-production staging environment, and another inventory file with the production versions of these groupings. The playbook content does not need to change when executing on either a staging or production environment because it refers to the generic group names that exist in both inventories. Simply refer to the correct inventory to execute it in the desired environment.

# Inventory ordering

A new play-level keyword, `order`, was added to Ansible in version 2.4. Prior to this, Ansible processed the hosts in the order specified in the inventory file, and continues to do so by default, even in newer versions. However, the following values can be set for the order keyword for a given play, resulting in the processing order of hosts described as follows:

- `inventory`: This is the default option, and simply means Ansible proceeds as it always has, processing the hosts in the order specified in the `inventory` file
- `reverse_inventory`: This results in the hosts being processed in the reverse of the order specified in the inventory
- `sorted`: The hosts are processed in alphabetically sorted order by name
- `reverse_sorted`: The hosts are processed in reverse alphabetically sorted order
- `shuffle`: The hosts are processed in a random order, with the order being randomized on each run

> In Ansible, the alphabetical sorting used is otherwise known as lexicographical. In short this means that values are sorted as strings, with the strings being processed from left to right. Thus, say we have three hosts—`mastery1`, `mastery11`, and `mastery2`. In this list, `mastery1` comes first as the character as position 8 is a 1. Then comes `mastery11`, as the character at position 8 is still a 1, but now there is an additional character at position 9. Finally comes `mastery2`, as character 8 is a 2 and 2 comes after 1. This is important as numerically we know that 11 is greater than 2, but in this list `mastery11` comes before `mastery2`.

[ 13 ]

## Inventory variable data

Inventories provide more than just system names and groupings. Data pertaining to the systems can be passed along as well. This data may include the following:

- Host-specific data to use in templates
- Group-specific data to use in task arguments or conditionals
- Behavioral parameters to tune how Ansible interacts with a system

Variables are a powerful construct within Ansible and can be used in a variety of ways, not just those described here. Nearly every single thing done in Ansible can include a variable reference. While Ansible can discover data about a system during the setup phase, not all data can be discovered. Defining data with the inventory expands this. Note that variable data can come from many different sources, and one source may override another. Variable precedence order is covered later in this chapter.

Let's improve upon our existing example inventory and add to it some variable data. We will add some host-specific data, as well as group-specific data:

```
[web]
mastery.example.name ansible_host=192.168.10.25

[dns]
backend.example.name

[database]
backend.example.name

[frontend:children]
web

[backend:children]
dns
database

[web:vars]
http_port=88
proxy_timeout=5

[backend:vars]
ansible_port=314

[all:vars]
ansible_ssh_user=otto
```

In this example, we defined `ansible_host` for `mastery.example.name` to be the IP address of `192.168.10.25`. The `ansible_host` variable is a behavioral inventory variable, which is intended to alter the way Ansible behaves when operating with this host. In this case, the variable instructs Ansible to connect to the system using the IP address provided, rather than performing a DNS lookup on the name using `mastery.example.name`. There are a number of other behavioral inventory variables that are listed at the end of this section, along with their intended use.

Our new inventory data also provides group-level variables for the web and backend groups. The web group defines `http_port`, which may be used in an **NGINX** configuration file, and `proxy_timeout`, which might be used to determine **HAProxy** behavior. The backend group makes use of another behavioral inventory parameter to instruct Ansible to connect to the hosts in this group using port `314` for SSH, rather than the default of `22`.

Finally, a construct is introduced that provides variable data across all the hosts in the inventory by utilizing a built-in `all` group. Variables defined within this group will apply to every host in the inventory. In this particular example, we instruct Ansible to log in as the `otto` user when connecting to the systems. This is also a behavioral change, as the Ansible default behavior is to log in as a user with the same name as the user executing `ansible` or `ansible-playbook` on the control host.

Here is a table of behavior inventory variables and the behaviors they intend to modify:

| Inventory parameters | Behavior |
| --- | --- |
| `ansible_host` | This is the DNS name or or the Docker container name which Ansible will initiate a connection to. |
| `ansible_port` | Specifies the port number that Ansible will use to connect to the inventory host, if not the default value of 22. |
| `ansible_user` | Specifies the username that Ansible will connect to the inventory host with, regardless of the connection type. |
| `ansible_ssh_pass` | Used to provide Ansible with the password for authentication to the inventory host in conjunction with ansible_user. |
| `ansible_ssh_private_key_file` | Used to specify which SSH private key file will be used to connect to the inventory host, if not using the default one or ssh-agent. |
| `ansible_ssh_common_args` | This defines SSH arguments to append to the default arguments for `ssh`, `sftp`, and `scp`. |
| `ansible_sftp_extra_args` | Used to specify additional arguments that will be passed to the sftp binary when called by Ansible. |
| `ansible_scp_extra_args` | Used to specify additional arguments that will be passed to the scp binary when called by Ansible. |

# The System Architecture and Design of Ansible

| | |
|---|---|
| `ansible_ssh_extra_args` | Used to specify additional arguments that will be passed to the ssh binary when called by Ansible. |
| `ansible_ssh_pipelining` | This setting uses a Boolean to define whether SSH pipelining should be used for this host. |
| `ansible_ssh_executable` | This setting overrides the path to the SSH executable for this host. |
| `ansible_become` | This defines whether privilege escalation (`sudo` or otherwise) should be used with this host. |
| `ansible_become_method` | This is the method to use for privilege escalation, and can be one of `sudo`, `su`, `pbrun`, `pfexec`, `doas`, `dzdo`, or `ksu`. |
| `ansible_become_user` | This is the user to become through privilege escalation. |
| `ansible_become_pass` | This is the password to use for privilege escalation. |
| `ansible_sudo_pass` | This is the sudo password to use (this is insecure; we strongly recommend using `--ask-sudo-pass`). |
| `ansible_connection` | This is the connection type of the host. Candidates are `local`, `smart`, `ssh`, `paramiko`, `docker`, or `winrm` (more on this later in the book). The default is `smart` in any modern Ansible distribution (this detects whether the SSH feature `ControlPersist` is supported and, if so, uses `ssh` as the connection type, falling back to `paramiko` otherwise). |
| `ansible_docker_extra_args` | Used to specify the extra argument that will be passed to a remote Docker daemon on a given inventory host. |
| `ansible_shell_type` | Used to determine the shell type on the inventory host(s) in question. Defaults to sh-style syntax, but can be set to csh or fish to work with systems that use these shells. |
| `ansible_shell_executable` | Used to determine the shell type on the inventory host(s) in question. Defaults to sh-style syntax, but can be set to csh or fish to work with systems that use these shells. |
| `ansible_python_interpreter` | This is used to manually set the path to Python on a given host in the inventory. For example some distributions of Linux have more than one Python version installed, and it is important that the correct one is set. For example, a host might have both /usr/bin/python27 and /usr/bin/python3, and this is used to define which one will be used. |
| `ansible_*_interpreter` | Used for any other interpreted language that Ansible might depend upon (e.g. Perl or Ruby). Replaces the interpreter binary with the one specified. |

# Dynamic inventories

A static inventory is great, and enough for many situations. But there are times when a statically written set of hosts is just too unwieldy to manage. Consider situations where inventory data already exists in a different system, such as **LDAP**, a cloud computing provider, or an in-house **configuration management database** (CMDB) (inventory, asset tracking, and data warehousing) system. It would be a waste of time and energy to duplicate that data and, in the modern world of on-demand infrastructure, that data would quickly grow stale or disastrously incorrect.

Another example of when a dynamic inventory source might be desired is when your site grows beyond a single set of playbooks. Multiple playbook repositories can fall into the trap of holding multiple copies of the same inventory data, or complicated processes have to be created to reference a single copy of the data. An external inventory can easily be leveraged to access the common inventory data stored outside of the playbook repository to simplify the setup. Thankfully, Ansible is not limited to static inventory files.

A dynamic inventory source (or plugin) is an executable that Ansible will call at runtime to discover real-time inventory data. This executable may reach out into external data sources and return data, or it can just parse local data that already exists but may not be in the Ansible inventory `ini` format. While it is possible, and easy, to develop your own dynamic inventory source, which we will cover in a later chapter, Ansible provides a number of example inventory plugins, including, but not limited to, the following:

- OpenStack Nova
- Rackspace Public Cloud
- DigitalOcean
- Linode
- Amazon EC2
- Google Compute Engine
- Microsoft Azure
- Docker
- Vagrant

Many of these plugins require some level of configuration, such as user credentials for EC2 or authentication endpoint for OpenStack Nova. Since it is not possible to configure additional arguments for Ansible to pass along to the inventory script, the configuration for the script must either be managed via an `ini` config file read from a known location, or environment variables read from the shell environment used to execute `ansible` or `ansible-playbook`. Note also that sometimes, external libraries are required for these inventory scripts to function.

*The System Architecture and Design of Ansible*

When `ansible` or `ansible-playbook` is directed at an executable file for an inventory source, Ansible will execute that script with a single argument, `--list`. This is so that Ansible can get a listing of the entire inventory in order to build up its internal objects to represent the data. Once that data is built up, Ansible will then execute the script with a different argument for every host in the data to discover variable data. The argument used in this execution is `--host <hostname>`, which will return any variable data specific to that host.

The inventory scripts are too numerous to go through each in detail in this book. However, to demonstrate the process, we will work through the use of the EC2 dynamic inventory. The dynamic inventory scripts officially included with Ansible can be found on Github:

`https://github.com/ansible/ansible/tree/devel/contrib/inventory`

On browsing this directory system, we can see there is an `ec2.py` and associated example configuration file, `ec2.ini`. Download these onto your system and make the Python file executable:

```
~> curl -O https://raw.githubusercontent.com/ansible/ansible/devel/contrib/inventory/ec2.py
  % Total    % Received % Xferd  Average Speed   Time    Time     Time  Current
                                 Dload  Upload   Total   Spent    Left  Speed
100 73063  100 73063    0     0   102k      0 --:--:-- --:--:-- --:--:--  102k
~> curl -O https://raw.githubusercontent.com/ansible/ansible/devel/contrib/inventory/ec2.ini
  % Total    % Received % Xferd  Average Speed   Time    Time     Time  Current
                                 Dload  Upload   Total   Spent    Left  Speed
100  9529  100  9529    0     0  28118      0 --:--:-- --:--:-- --:--:-- 28109
~> chmod +x ec2.py
~>
```

If we take a look at the comments at the top of `ec2.py`, we can see it tells us that we need the `Boto` library installed. Installing this will depend on your operating system and Python environment, but on CentOS 7 (and other EL7 variants), it could be done with the following:

```
~> sudo yum -y install python-boto
Loaded plugins: fastestmirror
Loading mirror speeds from cached hostfile
 * base: mirror.sov.uk.goscomb.net
 * epel: mirror.1000mbps.com
 * extras: repo.uk.bigstepcloud.com
 * updates: anorien.csc.warwick.ac.uk
Package python-boto is obsoleted by python2-boto, trying to install python2-boto
-2.45.0-3.el7.noarch instead
Resolving Dependencies
--> Running transaction check
---> Package python2-boto.noarch 0:2.45.0-3.el7 will be installed
```

Now, take a look at the `ec2.ini` file, and edit it as appropriate. You can see that your AWS credentials could go into this file, but it is not recommended for security reasons. For this example, we will simply specify them using environment variables, and then run our dynamic inventory script with the `--list` parameter, as discussed in the previous screenshot. Doing so yields the following:

```
~> export AWS_ACCESS_KEY_ID='XXXXXXXXXXXXXXXXXXXX'
~> export AWS_SECRET_ACCESS_KEY='xxxxxxxxxxxxxxxxxxxxxxxxxxxxxxxxxxxxxxxx'
~> ./ec2.py --list
{
  "_meta": {
    "hostvars": {
      "xx.xxx.xxx.xx": {
        "ansible_host": "xx.xxx.xxx.xx",
        "ec2__in_monitoring_element": false,
```

Voila! We have a listing of our current AWS inventory, along with a glimpse into the host variables for the discovered hosts. Note that, of course, the full output is far more complete than this.

With the AWS inventory in place, you could use this right away to run a single task or entire playbook against this dynamic inventory. For example, to use the ping module to check Ansible connectivity to all hosts in the inventory, you could run the following command:

```
ansible -i ec2.py all -m ping
```

This, of course, is just one example. However, if you follow this process for other dynamic inventory providers, you should get them working with ease.

In Chapter 9, *Extending Ansible*, we will develop our own custom inventory plugin to demonstrate how they operate.

## Runtime inventory additions

Just like static inventory files, it is important to remember that Ansible will parse this data once, and only once, per `ansible` or `ansible-playbook` execution. This is a fairly common stumbling point for users of cloud dynamic sources, where frequently, a playbook will create a new cloud resource and then attempt to use it as if it were part of the inventory. This will fail, as the resource was not part of the inventory when the playbook launched. All is not lost though! A special module is provided that allows a playbook to temporarily add an inventory to the in-memory inventory object, the `add_host` module.

The `add_host` module takes two options, `name` and `groups`. The `name` should be obvious; it defines the hostname that Ansible will use when connecting to this particular system. The `groups` option is a comma-separated list of groups to add this new system to. Any other option passed to this module will become the host variable data for this host. For example, if we want to add a new system, name it `newmastery.example.name`, add it to the `web` group, and instruct Ansible to connect to it by way of IP address `192.168.10.30`. This will create a task resembling the following:

```
- name: add new node into runtime inventory
  add_host:
    name: newmastery.example.name
    groups: web
    ansible_host: 192.168.10.30
```

This new host will be available to use, by way of the name provided, or by way of the web group, for the rest of the `ansible-playbook` execution. However, once the execution has completed, this host will not be available unless it has been added to the inventory source itself. Of course, if this were a new cloud resource created, the next `ansible` or `ansible-playbook` execution that sourced inventory from that cloud would pick up the new member.

# Inventory limiting

As mentioned earlier, every execution of `ansible` or `ansible-playbook` will parse the entire inventory it has been directed at. This is even true when a limit has been applied. A limit is applied at runtime by making use of the `--limit` runtime argument to `ansible` or `ansible-playbook`. This argument accepts a pattern, which is basically a mask to apply to the inventory. The entire inventory is parsed, and at each play, the limit mask supplied further limits the host pattern listed for the play.

Let's take our previous inventory example and demonstrate the behavior of Ansible with and without a limit. If you recall, we have the special group, `all`, that we can use to reference all the hosts within an inventory. Let's assume that our inventory is written out in the current working directory in a file named `mastery-hosts`, and we will construct a playbook to demonstrate the host on which Ansible is operating. Let's write this playbook out as `mastery.yaml`:

```
---
- name: limit example play
  hosts: all
  gather_facts: false

  tasks:
    - name: tell us which host we are on
      debug:
        var: inventory_hostname
```

The debug module is used to print out text, or values of variables. We'll use this module a lot in this book to simulate actual work being done on a host.

Now, let's execute this simple playbook without supplying a limit. For simplicity's sake, we will instruct Ansible to utilize a local connection method, which will execute locally rather than attempting to SSH to these non-existent hosts.

*The System Architecture and Design of Ansible*

Let's take a look at the following screenshot:

```
~/src/mastery> ansible-playbook -i mastery-hosts -c local mastery.yaml

PLAY [limit example play] ***************************************************

TASK [tell us which host we are on] *****************************************
ok: [backend.example.name] => {
    "inventory_hostname": "backend.example.name"
}
ok: [mastery.example.name] => {
    "inventory_hostname": "mastery.example.name"
}

PLAY RECAP ******************************************************************
backend.example.name       : ok=1    changed=0    unreachable=0    failed=0
mastery.example.name       : ok=1    changed=0    unreachable=0    failed=0

~/src/mastery>
```

As we can see, both hosts, `backend.example.name` and `mastery.example.name`, were operated on. Let's see what happens if we supply a limit, specifically to limit our run to frontend systems only:

```
~/src/mastery> ansible-playbook -i mastery-hosts -c local --limit frontend mastery.yaml

PLAY [limit example play] ***************************************************

TASK [tell us which host we are on] *****************************************
ok: [mastery.example.name] => {
    "inventory_hostname": "mastery.example.name"
}

PLAY RECAP ******************************************************************
mastery.example.name       : ok=1    changed=0    unreachable=0    failed=0

~/src/mastery>
```

We can see that only `mastery.example.name` was operated on this time. While there are no visual clues that the entire inventory was parsed, if we dive into the Ansible code and examine the inventory object, we will indeed find all the hosts within, and see how the limit is applied every time the object is queried for items.

It is important to remember that regardless of the host's pattern used in a play, or the limit supplied at runtime, Ansible will still parse the entire inventory set during each run. In fact, we can prove this by attempting to access the host variable data for a system that would otherwise be masked by our limit. Let's expand our playbook slightly and attempt to access the `ansible_port` variable from `backend.example.name`:

```yaml
---
- name: limit example play
  hosts: all
  gather_facts: false

  tasks:
    - name: tell us which host we are on
      debug:
        var: inventory_hostname

    - name: grab variable data from backend
      debug:
        var: hostvars['backend.example.name']['ansible_port']
```

We will still apply our limit, which will restrict our operations to just `mastery.example.name`:

```
~/src/mastery> ansible-playbook -i mastery-hosts -c local --limit frontend mastery.yaml

PLAY [limit example play] ************************************************

TASK [tell us which host we are on] **************************************
ok: [mastery.example.name] => {
    "inventory_hostname": "mastery.example.name"
}

TASK [grab variable data from backend] ***********************************
ok: [mastery.example.name] => {
    "hostvars['backend.example.name']['ansible_port']": "314"
}

PLAY RECAP ***************************************************************
mastery.example.name       : ok=2    changed=0    unreachable=0    failed=0

~/src/mastery>
```

We have successfully accessed the host variable data (by way of group variables) for a system that was otherwise limited out. This is a key skill to understand, as it allows for more advanced scenarios, such as directing a task at a host that is otherwise limited out. Delegation can be used to manipulate a load balancer to put a system into maintenance mode while being upgraded without having to include the load balancer system in your limit mask.

## Playbook parsing

The whole purpose of an inventory source is to have systems to manipulate. The manipulation comes from playbooks (or, in the case of Ansible ad hoc execution, that is, simple single-task plays). You should already have a basic understanding of playbook construction, so we won't spend a lot of time covering that; however, we will delve into some specifics of how a playbook is parsed. Specifically, we will cover the following:

- Order of operations
- Relative path assumptions
- Play behavior keys
- Host selection for plays and tasks
- Play and task names

## Order of operations

Ansible is designed to be as easy as possible for a human to understand. The developers strive to strike the best balance of human comprehension and machine efficiency. To that end, nearly everything in Ansible can be assumed to be executed in a top-to-bottom order; that is, the operation listed at the top of a file will be accomplished before the operation listed at the bottom of a file. Having said that, there are a few caveats, and even a few ways to influence the order of operations.

A playbook has only two main operations it can accomplish. It can either run a play, or it can include another playbook from somewhere on the filesystem. The order in which these are accomplished is simply the order in which they appear in the playbook file, from top to bottom. It is important to note that while the operations are executed in order, the entire playbook and any included playbooks are completely parsed before any executions. This means that any included playbook file has to exist at the time of the playbook parsing. They cannot be generated in an earlier operation. This is specific to playbook inclusions, and not necessarily to task inclusions that may appear within a play, which will be covered in a later chapter.

Within a play, there are a few more operations. While a playbook is strictly ordered from top to bottom, a play has a more nuanced order of operations. Here is a list of the possible operations and the order in which they will happen:

- Variable loading
- Fact gathering
- The `pre_tasks` execution
- Handlers notified from the `pre_tasks` execution
- Roles execution
- Tasks execution
- Handlers notified from roles or tasks execution
- The `post_tasks` execution
- Handlers notified from the `post_tasks` execution

Here is an example play with most of these operations shown:

```
---
- hosts: localhost
  gather_facts: false

  vars:
    - a_var: derp

  pre_tasks:
    - name: pretask
      debug:
        msg: "a pre task"
      changed_when: true
      notify: say hi

  roles:
    - role: simple
      derp: newval

  tasks:
    - name: task
      debug:
        msg: "a task"
      changed_when: true
      notify: say hi
```

```
post_tasks:
  - name: posttask
    debug:
      msg: "a post task"
    changed_when: true
    notify: say hi
```

Regardless of the order in which these blocks are listed in a play, the order detailed in the previous code block is the order in which they will be processed. Handlers (the tasks that can be triggered by other tasks that result in a change) are a special case. There is a utility module, `meta`, which can be used to trigger handler processing at a specific point:

```
- meta: flush_handlers
```

This will instruct Ansible to process any pending handlers at that point before continuing on with the next task or next block of actions within a play. Understanding the order and being able to influence the order with `flush_handlers` is another key skill to have when there is a need for orchestrating complicated actions, where things such as service restarts are very sensitive to order. Consider the initial rollout of a service.

The play will have tasks that modify `config` files and indicate that the service should be restarted when these files change. The play will also indicate that the service should be running. The first time this play happens, the `config` file will change and the service will change from not running to running. Then, the handlers will trigger, which will cause the service to restart immediately. This can be disruptive to any consumers of the service. It would be better to flush the handlers before a final task to ensure the service is running. This way, the restart will happen before the initial start, so the service will start up once and stay up.

## Relative path assumptions

When Ansible parses a playbook, there are certain assumptions that can be made about the relative paths of items referenced by the statements in a playbook. In most cases, paths for things such as variable files to include, task files to include, playbook files to include, files to copy, templates to render, and scripts to execute, are all relative to the directory where the file referencing them resides. Let's explore this with an example playbook and directory listing to show where the files are:

- The directory structure is as follows:

```
.
├── a_vars_file.yaml
```

```
├── mastery-hosts
├── relative.yaml
└── tasks
    ├── a.yaml
    └── b.yaml
```

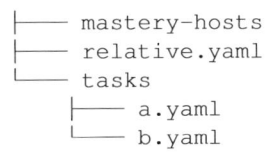

- The content of `a_vars_file.yaml` is as follows:

  ```
  ---
  something: "better than nothing"
  ```

- The content of `relative.yaml` is as follows:

  ```
  ---
  - name: relative path play
    hosts: localhost
    gather_facts: false
    vars_files:
        - a_vars_file.yaml

    tasks:
      - name: who am I
        debug:
          msg: "I am mastery task"
      - name: var from file
        debug:
          var: something

      - include: tasks/a.yaml
  ```

- The content of `tasks/a.yaml` is as follows:

  ```
  ---
  - name: where am I
    debug:
      msg: "I am task a"

  - include: b.yaml
  ```

- The content of `tasks/b.yaml` is as follows:

  ```
  ---
  - name: who am I
    debug:
      msg: "I am task b"
  ```

*The System Architecture and Design of Ansible*

Execution of the playbook is shown as follows:

```
~/src/mastery> ansible-playbook -i mastery-hosts -c local relative.yaml

PLAY [relative path play] ************************************************

TASK [who am I] **********************************************************
ok: [localhost] => {
    "msg": "I am mastery task"
}

TASK [var from file] *****************************************************
ok: [localhost] => {
    "something": "better than nothing"
}

TASK [where am I] ********************************************************
ok: [localhost] => {
    "msg": "I am task a"
}

TASK [who am I] **********************************************************
ok: [localhost] => {
    "msg": "I am task b"
}

PLAY RECAP ***************************************************************
localhost                  : ok=4    changed=0    unreachable=0    failed=0

~/src/mastery>
```

We can clearly see the relative references to paths and how they are relative to the file referencing them. When using roles, there are some additional relative path assumptions; however, we'll cover that in detail in a later chapter.

# Play behavior directives

When Ansible parses a play, there are a few directives it looks for in order to define various behaviors for a play. These directives are written at the same level as the `hosts:` directive. Here is a description of the subset of the keys that can be used:

- `any_errors_fatal`: This Boolean directive is used to instruct Ansible to treat any failure as a fatal error to prevent any further tasks from being attempted. This changes the default, where Ansible will continue until all the tasks are complete or all the hosts have failed.
- `connection`: This string directive defines which connection system to use for a given play. A common choice to make here is local, which instructs Ansible to do all the operations locally, but with the context of the system from the inventory.
- `gather_facts`: This Boolean directive controls whether or not Ansible will perform the fact-gathering phase of the operation, where a special task will run on a host to uncover various facts about the system. Skipping fact gathering, when you are sure that you do not need any of the discovered data, can be a significant time-saver in a larger environment.
- `max_fail_percentage`: This number directive is similar to `any_errors_fatal`, but is more fine-grained. This allows you to define just what percentage of your hosts can fail before the whole operation is halted.
- `no_log`: This is a Boolean to control whether or not Ansible will log (to the screen and/or a configured `log` file) the command given or the results received from a task. This is important if your task or return deals with secrets. This key can also be applied to a task directly.
- `port`: This is a number directive to define what port SSH (or an other remote connection plugin) should use to connect unless otherwise configured in inventory data.
- `remote_user`: This is a string directive that defines which user to log in with on the remote system. The default is to connect as the same user that `ansible-playbook` was started with.
- `serial`: This directive takes a number and controls how many systems Ansible will execute a task on before moving to the next task in a play. This is a drastic change from the normal order of operation, where a task is executed across every system in a play before moving to the next. This is very useful in rolling update scenarios, which will be detailed in later chapters.

- `become`: This is a Boolean directive used to configure whether privilege escalation (`sudo` or otherwise) should be used on the remote host to execute tasks. This key can also be defined at a task level. Related directives include `become_user`, `become_method`, and `become_flags`. These can be used to configure how the escalation will occur.
- `strategy`: This directive sets the execution strategy to be used for the play.

Many of these keys will be used in example playbooks through this book.

> For a full list of available play directives, see the online documentation at https://docs.ansible.com/ansible/latest/reference_appendices/playbooks_keywords.html#play.

## Execution strategies

With the release of Ansible 2.0, a new way to control play execution behavior was introduced: strategy. A strategy defines how Ansible coordinates each task across the set of hosts. Each strategy is a plugin, and two come with Ansible – linear and free. The linear strategy, which is the default strategy, is how Ansible has always behaved. As a play is executed, all the hosts for a given play execute the first task.

Once all are complete, Ansible moves to the next task. The serial directive can create batches of hosts to operate in this way, but the base strategy remains the same. All the targets for a given batch must complete a task before the next task is executed. The free strategy breaks from this traditional behavior. When using the free strategy, as soon as a host completes a task, Ansible will execute the next task for that host, without waiting for any other hosts to complete.

This will happen for every host in the set, for every task in the play. The hosts will complete the tasks as fast as each are able to, minimizing the execution time of each specific host. While most playbooks will use the default linear strategy, there are situations where the free strategy would be advantageous; for example, upgrading a service across a large set of hosts. If the play has numerous tasks to perform the upgrade, which starts with shutting down the service, then it would be more important for each host to suffer as little downtime as possible.

Allowing each host to independently move through the play as fast as it is able to will ensure that each host is down only for as long as necessary. Without using free, the entire set will be down for as long as the slowest host in the set takes to complete the tasks.

> As the free strategy does not coordinate task completion across hosts, it is not possible to depend on the data that is generated during a task on one host to be available for use in a later task on a different host. There is no guarantee that the first host will have completed the task that generates the data.

Execution strategies are implemented as a plugin and, as such, custom strategies can be developed to extend Ansible behavior. Development of such plugins is beyond the scope of this book.

## Host selection for plays and tasks

The first thing that most plays define (after a name, of course) is a host pattern for the play. This is the pattern used to select hosts out of the inventory object to run the tasks on. Generally, this is straightforward; a host pattern contains one or more blocks indicating a host, group, wildcard pattern, or regex to use for the selection. Blocks are separated by a colon, wildcards are just an asterisk, and regex patterns start with a tilde:

```
hostname:groupname:*.example:~(web|db)\.example\.com
```

Advanced usage can include group index selection or even ranges within a group:

```
webservers[0]:webservers[2:4]
```

Each block is treated as an inclusion block; that is, all the hosts found in the first pattern are added to all the hosts found in the next pattern, and so on. However, this can be manipulated with control characters to change their behavior. The use of an ampersand allows an inclusion selection (all the hosts that exist in both patterns). The use of an exclamation point allows exclusion selection (all the hosts that exist in the previous patterns but are NOT in the exclusion pattern):

```
webservers:&dbservers  # Hosts must exist in both webservers and dbservers
groups
webservers:!dbservers  # Hosts must exist in webservers but not dbservers
groups
```

Once Ansible parses the patterns, it will then apply restrictions, if any. Restrictions come in the form of limits or failed hosts. This result is stored for the duration of the play, and it is accessible via the `play_hosts` variable. As each task is executed, this data is consulted and an additional restriction may be placed upon it to handle serial operations. As failures are encountered, be it a failure to connect or a failure in executing tasks, the failed host is placed in a restriction list so that the host will be bypassed in the next task.

If, at any time, a host selection routine gets restricted down to zero hosts, the play execution will stop with an error. A caveat here is that if the play is configured to have a `max_fail_precentage` or `any_errors_fatal` parameter, then the playbook execution stops immediately after the task where this condition is met.

## Play and task names

While not strictly necessary, it is a good practice to label your plays and tasks with names. These names will show up in the command-line output of `ansible-playbook` and will show up in the log file if `ansible-playbook` is directed to log to a file. Task names also come in handy to direct `ansible-playbook` to start at a specific task and to reference handlers.

There are two main points to consider when naming plays and tasks:

- Names of plays and tasks should be unique
- Beware of what kind of variables can be used in play and task names

Naming plays and tasks uniquely is a best practice in general that will help to quickly identify where a problematic task may reside in your hierarchy of playbooks, roles, task files, handlers, and so on. Uniqueness is more important when notifying a handler or when starting at a specific task. When task names have duplicates, the behavior of Ansible may be non-deterministic, or at least non-obvious.

With uniqueness as a goal, many playbook authors will look to variables to satisfy this constraint. This strategy may work well, but authors need to take care as to the source of the variable data they are referencing. Variable data can come from a variety of locations (which we will cover later in this chapter), and the values assigned to variables can be defined at a variety of times. For the sake of play and task names, it is important to remember that only variables for which the values can be determined at playbook parse time will parse and render correctly. If the data of a referenced variable is discovered via a task or other operation, the variable string will be displayed as unparsed in the output. Let's look at an example playbook that utilizes variables for play and task names:

```
---
- name: play with a {{ var_name }}
  hosts: localhost
  gather_facts: false

  vars:
  - var_name: not-mastery

  tasks:
  - name: set a variable
    set_fact:
      task_var_name: "defined variable"

  - name: task with a {{ task_var_name }}
    debug:
      msg: "I am mastery task"

- name: second play with a {{ task_var_name }}
  hosts: localhost
  gather_facts: false

  tasks:
  - name: task with a {{ runtime_var_name }}
    debug:
      msg: "I am another mastery task"
```

*The System Architecture and Design of Ansible*

At first glance, you might expect at least `var_name` and `task_var_name` to render correctly. We can clearly see `task_var_name` being defined before its use. However, armed with our knowledge that playbooks are parsed in their entirety before execution, we know better:

```
~/src/mastery> ansible-playbook -i mastery-hosts -c local names.yaml

PLAY [play with a not-mastery] ************************************************

TASK [set a variable] *********************************************************
ok: [localhost]

TASK [task with a defined variable] *******************************************
ok: [localhost] => {
    "msg": "I am mastery task"
}

PLAY [second play with a {{ task_var_name }}] *********************************

TASK [task with a {{ runtime_var_name }}] *************************************
ok: [localhost] => {
    "msg": "I am another mastery task"
}

PLAY RECAP ********************************************************************
localhost                  : ok=3    changed=0    unreachable=0    failed=0

~/src/mastery>
```

As we can see in the previous screenshot, the only variable name that is properly rendered is `var_name`, as it was defined as a static play variable.

# Module transport and execution

Once a playbook is parsed and the hosts are determined, Ansible is ready to execute a task. Tasks are made up of a name (optional, but nonetheless important, as described previously), a module reference, module arguments, and task control directives. A later chapter will cover task control directives in detail, so we will only concern ourselves with the module reference and arguments.

## Module reference

Every task has a module reference. This tells Ansible which bit of work to carry out. Ansible is designed to easily allow for custom modules to live alongside a playbook. These custom modules can be wholly new functionality, or they can replace modules shipped with Ansible itself. When Ansible parses a task and discovers the name of the module to use for a task, it looks into a series of locations in order to find the module requested. Where it looks also depends on where the task lives, whether in a role or not.

If a task is in a role, Ansible will first look for the module within a directory tree named `library` within the role the task resides in. If the module is not found there, Ansible looks for a directory named `library` at the same level as the main playbook (the one referenced by the `ansible-playbook` execution). If the module is not found there, Ansible will finally look in the configured library path, which defaults to `/usr/share/ansible/`. This library path can be configured in an Ansible `config` file, or by way of the `ANSIBLE_LIBRARY` environment variable.

This design, allowing modules to be bundled with roles and playbooks, allows for the addition of functionality or the reparation of problems quickly and easily.

## Module arguments

Arguments to a module are not always required; the help output of a module will indicate which models are required and which are not. Module documentation can be accessed with the `ansible-doc` command as follows:

```
~/src/mastery> ansible-doc debug | cat -
> DEBUG    (/usr/lib/python2.7/site-packages/ansible/modules/utilities/logic/debug.py)

        This module prints statements during execution and can be
        useful for debugging variables or expressions without
        necessarily halting the playbook. Useful for debugging
        together with the 'when:' directive. This module is also
        supported for Windows targets.

  * note: This module has a corresponding action plugin.

OPTIONS (= is mandatory):

- msg
        The customized message that is printed. If omitted, prints a
        generic message.
        [Default: Hello world!]

- var
        A variable name to debug.  Mutually exclusive with the 'msg'
        option.
        [Default: (null)]

- verbosity
        A number that controls when the debug is run, if you set to 3
        it will only run debug when -vvv or above
        [Default: 0]
        version_added: 2.1


NOTES:
      * This module is also supported for Windows targets.

AUTHOR: Dag Wieers (@dagwieers), Michael DeHaan
        METADATA:
          status:
          - stableinterface
          supported_by: core


EXAMPLES:
# Example that prints the loopback address and gateway for each host
- debug:
    msg: "System {{ inventory_hostname }} has uuid {{ ansible_product_uuid }}"
```

> This command was piped into `cat` to prevent shell paging from being used.

Arguments can be templated with **Jinja2**, which will be parsed at module execution time, allowing for data discovered in a previous task to be used in later tasks; this is a very powerful design element.

Arguments can be supplied in a `key=value` format, or in a complex format that is more native to YAML. Here are two examples of arguments being passed to a module showcasing the two formats:

```yaml
- name: add a keypair to nova
  os_keypair: cloud={{ cloud_name }} name=admin-key wait=yes

- name: add a keypair to nova
  os_keypair:
    cloud: "{{ cloud_name }}"
    name: admin-key
    wait: yes
```

Both formats will lead to the same result in this example; however, the complex format is required if you wish to pass complex arguments into a module. Some modules expect a list object or a hash of data to be passed in; the complex format allows for this. While both formats are acceptable for many tasks, the complex format is the format used for the majority of examples in this book.

## Module blacklisting

Starting with Ansible 2.5, it is now possible for system administrators to blacklist Ansible modules that they do not wish to be available to playbook developers. This might be for security reasons, to maintain conformity, or even to avoid the use of deprecated modules.

The location for the module blacklist is defined by the `plugin_filters_cfg` parameter found in the defaults section of the Ansible configuration file. By default, it is disabled, and the suggested default value is set to `/etc/ansible/plugin_filters.yml`.

The format for this file is, at present, very simple—it contains a version header to allow for the file format to be updated in future, and a list of modules to be filtered out. For example, one of the currently deprecated modules to be completely removed in Ansible 2.11 is `sf_account_manager` (see https://docs.ansible.com/ansible/latest/porting_guides/porting_guide_2.7.html#deprecation-notices). Thus, to prevent anyone from using this internally, the `plugin_filters.yml` file would look like this:

```
---
filter_version:'1.0'
module_blacklist:
  # Deprecated - to be removed in 2.11
  - sf_account_manager
```

Although useful in helping to ensure high-quality Ansible code is maintained, this functionality is, at the time of writing, limited to modules, and cannot be extended to anything else, such as roles.

## Module transport and execution

Once a module is found, Ansible has to execute it in some way. How the module is transported and executed depends on a few factors; however, the common process is to locate the module file on the local filesystem and read it into memory, and then add in the arguments passed to the module. Then, the boilerplate module code from core Ansible is added to the file object in memory. This collection is compressed, Base64-encoded, and then wrapped in a script. What happens next really depends on the connection method and runtime options (such as leaving the module code on the remote system for review).

The default connection method is `smart`, which most often resolves to the `ssh` connection method. With a default configuration, Ansible will open an SSH connection to the remote host, create a temporary directory, and close the connection. Ansible will then open another SSH connection in order to write out the wrapped ZIP file from memory (the result of local module files, task module arguments, and Ansible boilerplate code) into a file within the temporary directory that we just created and close the connection.

Finally, Ansible will open a third connection in order to execute the script and delete the temporary directory and all its contents. The module results are captured from `stdout` in the JSON format, which Ansible will parse and handle appropriately. If a task has an `async` control, Ansible will close the third connection before the module is complete, and SSH back into the host to check the status of the task after a prescribed period until the module is complete or a prescribed timeout has been reached.

## Task performance

The previous description of how Ansible connects to hosts results in three connections to the host for every task. In a small environment with a small number of tasks, this may not be a concern; however, as the task set grows and the environment size grows, the time required to create and tear down SSH connections increases. Thankfully, there are a couple of ways to mitigate this.

The first is an SSH feature, `ControlPersist`, which provides a mechanism to create persistent sockets when first connecting to a remote host that can be reused in subsequent connections to bypass some of the handshaking required when creating a connection. This can drastically reduce the amount of time Ansible spends on opening new connections. Ansible automatically utilizes this feature if the host platform where Ansible is run from supports it. To check whether your platform supports this feature, check the SSH man page for `ControlPersist`.

The second performance enhancement that can be utilized is an Ansible feature called pipelining. Pipelining is available to SSH-based connection methods and is configured in the Ansible configuration file within the `ssh_connection` section:

```
[ssh_connection]
pipelining=true
```

This setting changes how modules are transported. Instead of opening an SSH connection to create a directory, another to write out the composed module, and a third to execute and clean up, Ansible will instead open an SSH connection on the remote host. Then, over that live connection, Ansible will pipe in the zipped composed module code and script for execution. This reduces the connections from three to one, which can really add up. By default, pipelining is disabled.

Utilizing the combination of these two performance tweaks can keep your playbooks nice and fast even as you scale your environment. However, keep in mind that Ansible will only address as many hosts at once as the number of forks Ansible is configured to run. Forks are the number of processes Ansible will split off as a worker to communicate with remote hosts. The default is five forks, which will address up to five hosts at once. Raise this number to address more hosts as your environment size grows by adjusting the `forks=` parameter in an Ansible configuration file, or by using the `--forks` (`-f`) argument with `ansible` or `ansible-playbook`.

# Variable types and location

Variables are a key component of the Ansible design. Variables allow for dynamic play content and reusable plays across different sets of an inventory. Anything beyond the most basic of Ansible use will utilize variables. Understanding the different variable types and where they can be located, as well as learning how to access external data or prompt users to populate variable data, is one of the keys to mastering Ansible.

## Variable types

Before diving into the precedence of variables, we must first understand the various types and subtypes of variables available to Ansible, their location, and where they are valid for use.

The first major variable type is **inventory variables**. These are the variables that Ansible gets by way of the inventory. These can be defined as variables that are specific to `host_vars`, to individual hosts, or applicable to entire groups as `group_vars`. These variables can be written directly into the inventory file, delivered by the dynamic inventory plugin, or loaded from the `host_vars/<host>` or `group_vars/<group>` directories.

These types of variables might be used to define Ansible behavior when dealing with these hosts or site-specific data related to the applications that these hosts run. Whether a variable comes from `host_vars` or `group_vars`, it will be assigned to a host's `hostvars`, and it can be accessed from the playbooks and template files. Accessing a host's own variables can be done just by referencing the name, such as `{{ foobar }}`, and accessing another host's variables can be accomplished by accessing `hostvars`; for example, to access the `foobar` variable for `examplehost`: `{{ hostvars['examplehost']['foobar'] }}`. These variables have global scope.

The second major variable type is **role variables**. These are variables specific to a role and are utilized by the role tasks – however, it should be noted that once a role has been added to a playbook, its variables are generally accessible throughout the rest of the playbook, including from within other roles. In most simple playbooks, this won't matter, as the roles are typically run one at a time, but it is worth remembering this as playbook structure gets more complex—otherwise, unexpected behavior may result from variables being set within a different role!

These variables are often supplied as a **role default**, which are meant to provide a default value for the variable but can easily be overridden when applying the role. When roles are referenced, it is possible to supply variable data at the same time, either by overriding role defaults or creating wholly new data. We'll cover roles in depth in a later chapter. These variables apply to all hosts on which the role is executed and can be accessed directly, much like a host's own `hostvars`.

The third major variable type is **play variables**. These variables are defined in the control keys of a play, either directly by the `vars` key or sourced from external files via the `vars_files` key. Additionally, the play can interactively prompt the user for variable data using `vars_prompt`. These variables are to be used within the scope of the play and in any tasks or included tasks of the play. The variables apply to all hosts within the play and can be referenced as if they are `hostvars`.

The fourth variable type is **task variables**. Task variables are made from data discovered while executing tasks or in the fact-gathering phase of a play. These variables are host-specific and are added to the host's `hostvars` and can be used as such, which also means they have global scope after the point in which they were discovered or defined. Variables of this type can be discovered via `gather_facts` and **fact modules** (modules that do not alter state but rather return data), populated from task return data via the `register` task key or defined directly by a task making use of the `set_fact` or `add_host` modules. Data can also be interactively obtained from the operator using the `prompt` argument to the `pause` module and registering the result:

```
- name: get the operators name
  pause:
    prompt: "Please enter your name"
  register: opname
```

The **extra variables**, or `extra-vars` type, are variables supplied on the command line when executing `ansible-playbook` via `--extra-vars`. Variable data can be supplied as a list of `key=value` pairs, a quoted piece of JSON data, or a reference to a YAML-formatted file with variable data defined within:

```
--extra-vars "foo=bar owner=fred"
--extra-vars '{"services":["nova-api","nova-conductor"]}'
--extra-vars @/path/to/data.yaml
```

Extra variables are considered global variables. They apply to every host and have scope throughout the entire playbook.

## Magic variables

In addition to the previously listed variable types, Ansible offers a set of variables that deserve their own special mention – **magic variables**. These are variables that are always set when a playbook is run without them having to be explicitly created. Their names are always reserved and should not be used for other variables.

Magic variables are used to provide information about the current playbook run to the playbooks themselves and are extremely useful as Ansible environments become larger and more complex. For example, if one of your plays needs information about which groups the current host is in, the `group_names` magic variable returns a list of these. Similarly, if you need to configure the hostname for a service using Ansible, the `inventory_hostname` magic variable will return the current hostname as it is defined in the inventory. A simple example of this would be as follows:

```yaml
---
- name: demonstrate magic variables
  hosts: all
  gather_facts: false

  tasks:
    - name: tell us which host we are on
      debug:
        var: inventory_hostname

    - name: tell us which groups we are in
      debug:
        var: group_names
```

Whilst it is beyond the scope of this book to go into detail on each and every single magic variable, it is important to know of their existence. Imagine, for example, setting up the hostnames on a new set of Linux servers from a blank template. The `inventory_hostname` magic variable provides us with the hostname we need directly from the inventory, without the need for another source of data (or, for example, a connection to the **CMDB**). Similarly, accessing `groups_names` allows us to define which plays should be run on a given host within a single playbook – perhaps, for example, installing **NGINX** if the host is in the `webservers` group. In this way, Ansible code can be made more versatile and efficient, and hence, these variables deserve a special mention.

> A full list of magic variables is available here: https://docs.ansible.com/ansible/latest/reference_appendices/special_variables.html

# Accessing external data

Data for role variables, play variables, and task variables can also come from external sources. Ansible provides a mechanism to access and evaluate data from the **control machine** (the machine running `ansible-playbook`). The mechanism is called a **lookup plugin**, and a number of them come with Ansible. These plugins can be used to look up or access data by reading files, generate and locally store passwords on the Ansible host for later reuse, evaluate environment variables, pipe data in from executables, access data in the `Redis` or `etcd` systems, render data from template files, query `dnstxt` records, and more. The syntax is as follows:

```
lookup('<plugin_name>', 'plugin_argument')
```

For example, to use the `mastery` value from `etcd` in a debug task, execute the following command:

```
- name: show data from etcd
  debug:
    msg: "{{ lookup('etcd', 'mastery') }}"
```

Lookups are evaluated when the task referencing them is executed, which allows for dynamic data discovery. To reuse a particular lookup in multiple tasks and reevaluate it each time, a playbook variable can be defined with a lookup value. Each time the playbook variable is referenced, the lookup will be executed, potentially providing different values over time.

# Variable precedence

As you learned in the previous section, there are several major types of variables that can be defined in a myriad of locations. This leads to a very important question: what happens when the same variable name is used in multiple locations? Ansible has a precedence for loading variable data, and thus it has an order and a definition to decide which variable will win. Variable value overriding is an advanced usage of Ansible, so it is important to fully understand the semantics before attempting such a scenario.

## Precedence order

Ansible defines the precedence order as follows, with those closest to the top of the list winning. Note that this can change from release to release, and has changed quite significantly since Ansible 2.4 was released, so it is worth reviewing, especially when upgrading your Ansible environment:

1. Extra vars (from the command line) always wins
2. include parameters
3. Role (and include_role) parameters
4. Variables defined with set_facts, and those created with the register task directive
5. include_vars
6. Task vars (only for the specific task)
7. Block vars (only for the tasks within the block)
8. Role vars (defined in main.yml in the vars subdirectory of the role).
9. Play vars_files
10. Play vars_prompt
11. Play vars
12. Host facts (and also cached set_facts)
13. host_vars playbook
14. host_vars inventory
15. Inventory file (or script) defined host vars
16. group_vars playbook
17. group_vars inventory
18. group_vars/all playbook
19. group_vars/all inventory
20. Inventory file (or script) defined group vars
21. Role defaults
22. Command-line values (for example, -u REMOTE_USER)

> Ansible releases a porting guide with each release that details the changes you will need to make to your code in order for it to continue functioning as expected. It is important to review these as you upgrade your Ansible environment – the guides may be found here: https://docs.ansible.com/ansible/latest/porting_guides/porting_guides.html.

# Variable group priority ordering

The previous list of priority ordering is obviously helpful when writing Ansible playbooks, and, in most cases, it is apparent that variables should not clash. For example, a task `var` clearly wins over a play `var`, and all tasks and indeed plays are unique. Similarly, all hosts in the inventory will be unique, so again, there should be no clash of variables with the inventory either.

There is, however, one exception to this – inventory groups. A one-to-many relationship exists between hosts and groups, and, as such, any given host can be a member of one or more groups. Let's suppose that the following code is our inventory file by way of example:

```
[frontend]
host1.example.com
host2.example.com

[web:children]
frontend

[web:vars]
http_port=80
secure=true

[proxy]
host1.example.com

[proxy:vars]
http_port=8080
thread_count=10
```

Here, we have two hypothetical frontend servers, `host1.example.com` and `host2.example.com`, in the `frontend` group. Both hosts are `children` of the `web` group, which means they are assigned the inventory `group_vars` `http_port=80`. `host1.example.com` is also a member of the `proxy` group, which has an identically named variable but with a different assignment: `http_port=8080`.

Both of these variable assignments are at the inventory `group_vars` level, and so the order of precedence does not define a winner. So what happens in this case?

The answer is, in fact, predictable and deterministic. The `group_vars` assignments are done in alphabetical order of the group names (Refer to the tip box mentioned in the section *Inventory ordering*), with the last loaded group overriding all preceding variable values that coincide.

## The System Architecture and Design of Ansible

This means any competing variables from `mastery2` will win over the other two groups. Those from the `mastery11` then take precedence of those from the `mastery1` group, so please be mindful of this when creating group names!

In our example, when the groups are processed in alphabetical order, `web` comes after `proxy`, and so the `group_vars` assignments from `web` that coincide with those from any previously processed groups will win. Let's run the previous inventory file through this example playbook to take a look at the behavior:

```
---
- name: group variable priority ordering example play
  hosts: all
  gather_facts: false

  tasks:
    - name: show assigned group variables
      vars:
        msg: |
            http_port:{{ hostvars[inventory_hostname]['http_port'] }}
            thread_count:{{ hostvars[inventory_hostname]['thread_count'] | default("undefined") }}
            secure:{{ hostvars[inventory_hostname]['secure'] }}
      debug:
        msg: "{{ msg.split('\n') }}"
```

When run, we get the following output:

```
~/src/mastery> ansible-playbook -i priority-hosts -c local priorityordering.yaml


PLAY [group variable priority ordering example play] ******************************

TASK [show assigned group variables] **********************************************
ok: [host1.example.com] => {
    "msg": [
        "http_port:8080",
        "thread_count:10",
        "secure:true",
        ""
    ]
}
ok: [host2.example.com] => {
    "msg": [
        "http_port:80",
        "thread_count:undefined",
        "secure:true",
        ""
    ]
}

PLAY RECAP ************************************************************************
host1.example.com          : ok=1    changed=0    unreachable=0    failed=0
host2.example.com          : ok=1    changed=0    unreachable=0    failed=0

~/src/mastery>
```

As expected, the value assigned to the `http_port` variable for both hosts in the inventory is `80`. However, what if this behavior is not desired? Suppose we want the value of `http_port` from the proxy group to take priority. It would be painful to have to rename the group and all associated references to it to change the alphanumerical sorting of the groups (though this would work!). The good news is that Ansible 2.4 introduced the `ansible_group_priority` group variable, which can be used for just this eventuality. If not explicitly set, this variable defaults to `1`, leaving the rest of the inventory file unchanged.

## The System Architecture and Design of Ansible

Let's set this as follows:

```
[proxy:vars]
http_port=8080
thread_count=10
ansible_group_priority=10
```

Now, when we run the same playbook, note how the value assigned to `http_proxy` has changed, whilst all variable names that were not coincidental behave exactly as before:

```
~/src/mastery> ansible-playbook -i priority-hosts -c local priorityordering.yaml

PLAY [group variable priority ordering example play] ********************

TASK [show assigned group variables] ********************
ok: [host1.example.com] => {
    "msg": [
        "http_port:8080",
        "thread_count:10",
        "secure:true",
        ""
    ]
}
ok: [host2.example.com] => {
    "msg": [
        "http_port:80",
        "thread_count:undefined",
        "secure:true",
        ""
    ]
}

PLAY RECAP ********************
host1.example.com          : ok=1    changed=0    unreachable=0    failed=0
host2.example.com          : ok=1    changed=0    unreachable=0    failed=0

~/src/mastery>
```

As your inventory grows with your infrastructure, be sure to make use of this feature to gracefully handle any variable assignment collisions between your groups.

# Merging hashes

In the previous section, we focused on the precedence in which variables will override each other. The default behavior of Ansible is that any overriding definition for a variable name will completely mask the previous definition of that variable. However, that behavior can be altered for one type of variable; the hash. A hash variable (a dictionary, in Python terms) is a dataset of keys and values. Values can be of different types for each key, and can even be hashes themselves for complex data structures.

In some advanced scenarios, it is preferable to replace just one bit of a hash or add to an existing hash rather than replacing the hash altogether. To unlock this ability, a configuration change is necessary in the Ansible `config` file. The configuration entry is `hash_behavior`, which either takes the value `replace` or `merge`. A setting of `merge` will instruct Ansible to merge or blend the values of two hashes when presented with an override scenario, rather than assume the default of `replace`, which will completely replace the old variable data with the new data.

Let's walk through an example of the two behaviors. We will start with a hash loaded with data and simulate a scenario where a different value for the hash is provided as a higher-priority variable.

This is the starting data:

```
hash_var:
  fred:
    home: Seattle
    transport: Bicycle
```

This is the new data loaded via `include_vars`:

```
hash_var:
  fred:
    transport: Bus
```

With the default behavior, the new value for `hash_var` will be as follows:

```
hash_var:
  fred:
    transport: Bus
```

However, if we enable the `merge` behavior, we will get the following result:

```
hash_var:
  fred:
    home: Seattle
    transport: Bus
```

There are even more nuances and undefined behaviors when using merge and, as such, it is strongly recommended to only use this setting if absolutely necessary.

## Summary

While the design of Ansible focuses on simplicity and ease of use, the architecture itself is very powerful. In this chapter, we covered key design and architecture concepts of Ansible, such as version and configuration, playbook parsing, module transport and execution, variable types and locations, and variable precedence.

You learned that playbooks contain variables and tasks. Tasks link bits of code called modules with arguments, which can be populated by variable data. These combinations are transported to selected hosts from inventory sources provided. The fundamental understanding of these building blocks is the platform on which you can build a mastery of all things Ansible!

In the next chapter, you will learn how to secure secret data while working with Ansible.

# Protecting Your Secrets with Ansible

Secrets are meant to stay secret. Whether they are login credentials to a cloud service or passwords to database resources, they are secret for a reason. Should they fall into the wrong hands, they can be used to discover trade secrets, customers' private data, create infrastructure for nefarious purposes, or worse. All of which could cost you or your organization a lot of time, money, and headaches! When the second edition of this book was published, it was only possible to encrypt your sensitive data in external Vault files, and all data had to exist entirely in either an encrypted or unencrypted form. It was also only possible to use one single Vault password per playbook run, meaning it was not possible to segregate your secret data and use different passwords for items of different sensitivities. All that has now changed, with multiple Vault passwords permissible at playbook runtime, as well as the possibility of embedding encrypted strings in otherwise plain YAML files.

In this chapter, we will describe how to take advantage of these new features, and thus keep your secrets safe with Ansible, by covering the following topics:

- Encrypting data at rest
- Mixing encrypted data with plain YAML
- Protecting secrets while operating

## Technical requirements

Check out the following video to see the Code in Action:

`http://bit.ly/2HIteAS`

# Encrypting data at rest

As a configuration management system or an orchestration engine, Ansible has great power. To wield that power, it is necessary to entrust secret data to Ansible. An automation system that prompts the operator for passwords at each connection is not very efficient. To maximize the power of Ansible, secret data has to be written to a file that Ansible can read and from which it can utilize the data.

This creates a risk, though! Your secrets are sitting there on your filesystem in plain text. This is a physical and digital risk. Physically, the computer could be taken from you and pored over for secret data. Digitally, any malicious software that can break the boundaries set upon it is capable of reading any data to which your user account has access. If you utilize a source control system, the infrastructure that houses the repository is just as much at risk.

Thankfully, Ansible provides a facility to protect your data at rest. That facility is Vault. This facility allows for encrypting text files so that they are stored at rest in an encrypted format. Without the key or a significant amount of computing power, the data is indecipherable.

The key lessons to learn when dealing with encrypting data at rest include the following:

- Valid encryption targets
- Securing differing data with multiple passwords and Vault IDs
- Creating new encrypted files
- Encrypting existing unencrypted files
- Editing encrypted files
- Changing the encryption password on files
- Decrypting encrypted files
- Encrypting data inline in an otherwise unencrypted YAML file (for example, a playbook)
- Running `ansible-playbook` referencing encrypted files

# Vault IDs and passwords

Before the release of Ansible 2.4, it was only possible to use one Vault password at a time. Whilst you could have multiple secrets for multiple purposes stored in a number of locations, only one password could be used. This was obviously fine for smaller environments, but as the adoption of Ansible has grown, so has the requirement for better and more flexible security options. For example, we have already discussed the potential for Ansible to manage both a development and production environment through the use of groups in the inventory. It is realistic to expect that these environments would have different security credentials. Similarly, you would expect core network devices to have different credentials to servers. In fact, it is good security practice to do so.

Given this, it seems unreasonable to then protect any secrets under a single master password using Vault. Ansible 2.4 introduced the concept of Vault IDs as a solution, and whilst at present, the old single password commands are all still valid, it is recommended to use Vault IDs when working with Ansible on the command line. Each Vault ID must have one single password associated with it, but multiple secrets can share the same ID.

Ansible Vault passwords can come from one of the following three sources:

- A user-entered string, which Ansible will prompt for when it is required
- A flat text file containing the Vault password in plain unencrypted text (obviously, it is vital this file is kept secure!)
- An executable that fetches the password (for example, from a credential management system) and outputs it on a single line for Ansible to read

The syntax for each of these three options is broadly similar. If you only have one Vault credential and hence aren't using IDs, you would therefore enter the following line to run a playbook and prompt for the Vault password:

```
ansible-playbook --vault-id @prompt playbook.yaml
```

If you want to obtain the Vault password from a text file, you would run the following command:

```
ansible-playbook --vault-id /path-to/vault-password-text-file playbook.yaml
```

Finally, if you are using an executable script, you would run the following command:

```
ansible-playbook --vault-id /path-to/vault-password-script.py playbook.yaml
```

If you are working with IDs, simply add the ID in front of the password source, followed by the @ character—if your ID for your Vault is `prod`, for example, the three preceding examples become the following:

```
ansible-playbook --vault-id prod@prompt playbook.yaml
ansible-playbook --vault-id prod@/path-to/vault-password-text-file playbook.yaml
ansible-playbook --vault-id prod@/path-to/vault-password-script.py playbook.yaml
```

Multiple combinations of these can be combined into one command, as follows:

```
ansible-playbook --vault-id prod@prompt testing@/path-to/vault-password-text-file playbook.yaml
```

We will use the `vault-id` command line options throughout the rest of this chapter.

## Things Vault can encrypt

The Vault feature can be used to encrypt any **structured data** used by Ansible. This can either be almost any YAML (or JSON) file that Ansible uses during its operation, or even a single variable within an otherwise unencrypted YAML file, such as a playbook or role. Examples of encrypted files that Ansible can work with include:

- `group_vars/` files
- `host_vars/` files
- `include_vars` targets
- `vars_files` targets
- `--extra-vars` targets
- Role variables
- Role defaults
- Task files
- Handler files
- Source files for the `copy` module

If a file can be expressed in YAML and read by Ansible, or if a file is to be transported with the `copy` module, it is a valid file for encryption in Vault. Because the entire file will be unreadable at rest, care should be taken to not be overzealous in picking which files to encrypt. Any source control operations with the files will be done with the encrypted content, making it very difficult to peer-review.

As a best practice, the smallest possible amount of data should be encrypted, which may even mean moving some variables into a file all by themselves. It is for this reason that Ansible 2.3 added the `encrypt_string` feature to `ansible-vault`, allowing for individual secrets to be placed inline with otherwise unencrypted YAML, saving the user from encrypting the entire file. We will cover this later in the chapter.

## Creating new encrypted files

To create new files, Ansible provides a new program, `ansible-vault`. This program is used to create and interact with Vault-encrypted files. The subcommand to create encrypted files is `create`, as shown in the following screenshot:

```
~/src/mastery> ansible-vault create --help
Usage: ansible-vault create [options] file_name

encryption/decryption utility for Ansible data files

Options:
  --ask-vault-pass      ask for vault password
  --encrypt-vault-id=ENCRYPT_VAULT_ID
                        the vault id used to encrypt (required if more than
                        vault-id is provided)
  -h, --help            show this help message and exit
  --new-vault-id=NEW_VAULT_ID
                        the new vault identity to use for rekey
  --new-vault-password-file=NEW_VAULT_PASSWORD_FILE
                        new vault password file for rekey
  --vault-id=VAULT_IDS  the vault identity to use
  --vault-password-file=VAULT_PASSWORD_FILES
                        vault password file
  -v, --verbose         verbose mode (-vvv for more, -vvvv to enable
                        connection debugging)
  --version             show program's version number and exit

 See 'ansible-vault <command> --help' for more information on a specific
command.
~/src/mastery>
```

[ 55 ]

*Protecting Your Secrets with Ansible*

To create a new file, you'll need to know two things ahead of time. The first is the password `ansible-vault` will be using to encrypt the file, and the second is the filename itself. Once provided with this information, `ansible-vault` will launch a text editor (as defined in the `EDITOR` environment variable). Once you save the file and exit the editor, `ansible-vault` will use the supplied password as a key to encrypt the file with the AES256 cipher.

Let's walk through a few examples of creating encrypted files. First, we'll create one and be prompted for a password, then we will provide a `password` file, and lastly, we'll create an executable to deliver the password.

## Password prompt

Getting `ansible-vault` to request a password from the user at runtime is the easiest way to get started with Vault creation, so let's go through a simple example and create a Vault containing a variable we want to encrypt. Take a look at the following screenshot:

```
~/src/mastery> ansible-vault create --vault-id @prompt secrets.yaml
New vault password (default):
Confirm vew vault password (default):
```

Once the passphrase is entered, our editor opens and we're able to put content into the file, as shown in the following screenshot:

```
---
my_secret: is_safe
~
~
~
:wq
```

> On my system, the configured editor is Vim. Your system may be different, and you may need to set your preferred editor as the value for the `EDITOR` environment variable.

Now, we save the file. If we try to read the contents, we'll see that they are in fact encrypted, with a small header hint for Ansible to use later, as shown in the following screenshot:

```
~/src/mastery> cat secrets.yaml
$ANSIBLE_VAULT;1.1;AES256
6664393663353431623261316534663738306331323036376532326235366264613566613664 3434
363539633037376463643236656436396616164313232330a633637323966623661623432643532
613565643332643830633233531643263656623462623233337366432326464373235376463313835
37646466656136388620a655366353431663165343366643965346335653730633636313132386162
3831303230663132383434633238396539303466632653466353832393136633306333
~/src/mastery>
```

As you can see from the headers, `AES256` is used for Vault encryption at present, meaning that as long as you use a good password when creating your Vault, your data is very secure.

## Password file

To use `ansible-vault` with a password file, you first need to create such a file. Simply echoing a password into a file can do this. Once complete, you can now reference this file when calling `ansible-vault` to create another encrypted file, as shown in the following screenshot:

```
~/src/mastery> echo "my long password" > password_file
~/src/mastery> ansible-vault create --vault-id ./password_file more_secrets.yaml
```

Just as when being prompted for a password, the editor will open and data can be written.

## Password script

This last example uses a password script. This is useful for designing a system where a password can be stored in a central system for storing credentials and shared with contributors to the playbook tree. Each contributor could have his or her own password to the shared credentials store, where the Vault password would be retrieved from. Our example will be far more straightforward: just a simple output to STDOUT with a password. This file will be saved as `password.sh`. The file needs to be marked as an executable for Ansible to treat it as such, as shown in the following screenshot:

```
~/src/mastery> vim password.sh
~/src/mastery> cat password.sh
#!/bin/sh
echo "a long password"
~/src/mastery> chmod +x password.sh
~/src/mastery> ansible-vault create --vault-id ./password.sh even_more_secrets.yaml
```

Try this for yourself and see how it works—you should find that `ansible-vault` creates a Vault with the password `a long password`, as written to STDOUT by the script. You could even try editing using the following command:

```
ansible-vault edit --vault-id @prompt even_more_secrets.yaml
```

You should now see enter `a long password` when prompted—and you can now edit the Vault successfully!

## Encrypting existing files

The previous examples all dealt with creating new encrypted files using the `create` subcommand. But what if we want to take an established file and encrypt it? A subcommand exists for this as well. It is named `encrypt`, as shown in the following screenshot:

*Chapter 2*

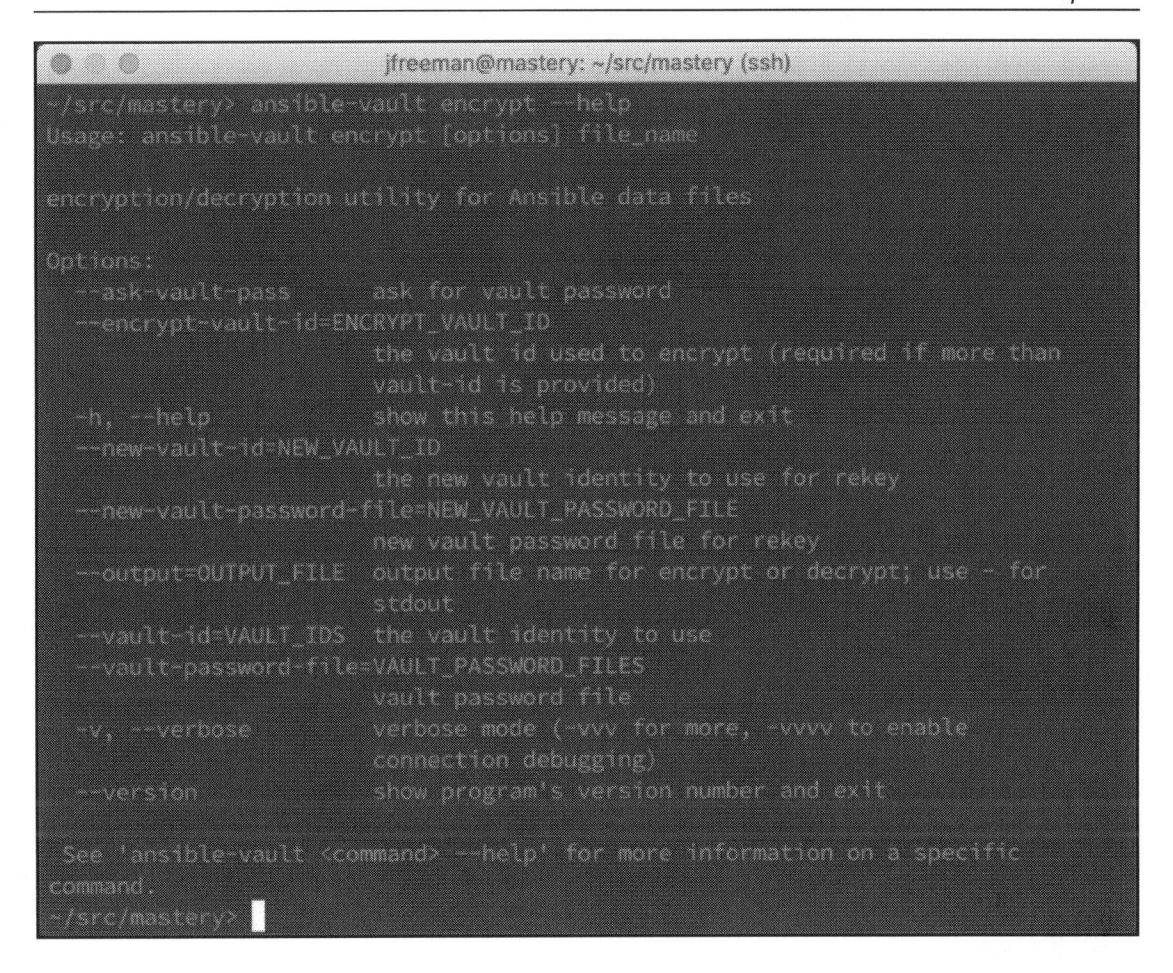

```
~/src/mastery> ansible-vault encrypt --help
Usage: ansible-vault encrypt [options] file_name

encryption/decryption utility for Ansible data files

Options:
  --ask-vault-pass      ask for vault password
  --encrypt-vault-id=ENCRYPT_VAULT_ID
                        the vault id used to encrypt (required if more than
                        vault-id is provided)
  -h, --help            show this help message and exit
  --new-vault-id=NEW_VAULT_ID
                        the new vault identity to use for rekey
  --new-vault-password-file=NEW_VAULT_PASSWORD_FILE
                        new vault password file for rekey
  --output=OUTPUT_FILE  output file name for encrypt or decrypt; use - for
                        stdout
  --vault-id=VAULT_IDS  the vault identity to use
  --vault-password-file=VAULT_PASSWORD_FILES
                        vault password file
  -v, --verbose         verbose mode (-vvv for more, -vvvv to enable
                        connection debugging)
  --version             show program's version number and exit

See 'ansible-vault <command> --help' for more information on a specific
command.
~/src/mastery>
```

As with `create`, `encrypt` expects a `password` (or `password` file or executable) and the path to a file. Once the appropriate password is received, an editor opens up, this time with our original content in plain text already visible to us.

> **TIP** Note that the file to be encrypted must already exist.

[ 59 ]

Let's demonstrate this by encrypting an existing file we have from `Chapter 1`, *The System Architecture and Design of Ansible*, called `a_vars_file.yaml`, as shown in the following screenshot:

```
~/src/mastery> cat a_vars_file.yaml
---
something: "better than nothing"
~/src/mastery> ansible-vault encrypt --vault-id ./password.sh a_vars_file.yaml
Encryption successful
~/src/mastery> cat a_vars_file.yaml
$ANSIBLE_VAULT;1.1;AES256
39363234666234353062386337303935666632363638373639396336663134636235653631616134
33623262376339303636363930633338353930383037333650a633265663163333635393303036
61313331646262383736396133376233376461663063366132616466376636653935373431623264
34633238333737383830a346332323335653539613531333635336333346331326531343737393638
32346635663439643230326335383139303835623631386430383136353631323364346265363837
32353032666536646233393433666164313330353736563313065
~/src/mastery>
```

In this example, we can see the file contents before and after the call to `encrypt`, where after the contents are indeed encrypted. Unlike the `create` subcommand, `encrypt` can operate on multiple files, making it easy to protect all the important data in one action. Simply list all the files to be encrypted, separated by spaces.

> Attempting to encrypt already-encrypted files will result in an error.

# Editing encrypted files

Once a file has been encrypted with `ansible-vault`, it cannot be directly edited. Opening the file in an editor would result in the encrypted data being shown. Making any changes to the file would damage the file and Ansible would be unable to read the contents correctly. We need a subcommand that will first decrypt the contents of a file, allow us to edit those contents, and then encrypt the new contents before saving it back to the file. Such a subcommand exists in `edit`, as shown in the following screenshot:

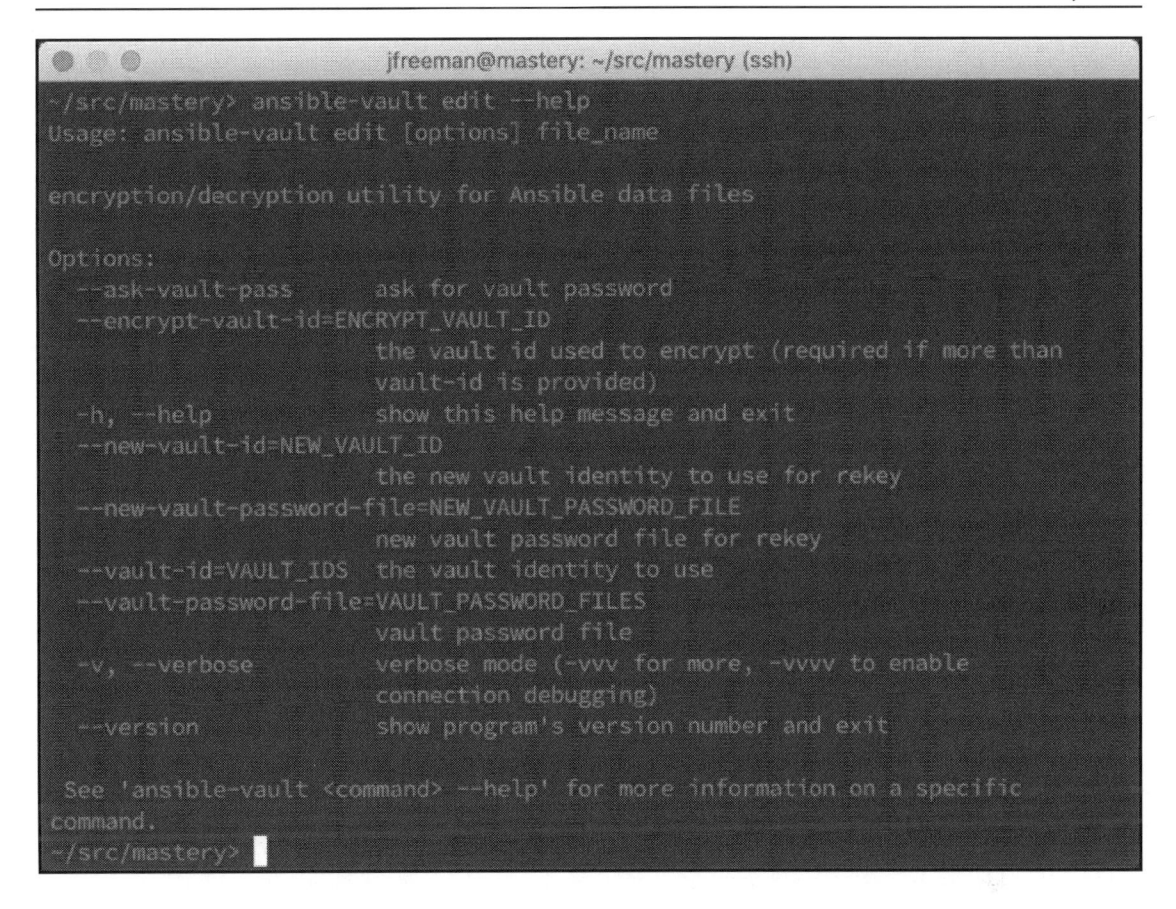

```
~/src/mastery> ansible-vault edit --help
Usage: ansible-vault edit [options] file_name

encryption/decryption utility for Ansible data files

Options:
  --ask-vault-pass      ask for vault password
  --encrypt-vault-id=ENCRYPT_VAULT_ID
                        the vault id used to encrypt (required if more than
                        vault-id is provided)
  -h, --help            show this help message and exit
  --new-vault-id=NEW_VAULT_ID
                        the new vault identity to use for rekey
  --new-vault-password-file=NEW_VAULT_PASSWORD_FILE
                        new vault password file for rekey
  --vault-id=VAULT_IDS  the vault identity to use
  --vault-password-file=VAULT_PASSWORD_FILES
                        vault password file
  -v, --verbose         verbose mode (-vvv for more, -vvvv to enable
                        connection debugging)
  --version             show program's version number and exit

 See 'ansible-vault <command> --help' for more information on a specific
command.
~/src/mastery>
```

As we've already seen, our editor opens up with our content in plain text visible to us. All of our familiar `vault-id` options are back, as before, as well as the file to edit. As such, we can now edit the file we just encrypted using the following command:

```
~/src/mastery> ansible-vault edit --vault-id ./password.sh a_vars_file.yaml
```

*Protecting Your Secrets with Ansible*

Notice that `ansible-vault` opens our editor with a temporary file as the file path. The editor will save this, and then `ansible-vault` will encrypt it and move it to replace the original file, as shown in the following screenshot:

```
---
something: "better than nothing"
~
~
"/tmp/tmpVvcJBK.yaml" 2L, 39C
```

The temporary file you can see in the editor window (`/tmp/tmpVvcJBK.yaml`) will be removed once the file is successfully encrypted by `ansible-vault`.

## Password rotation on encrypted files

Over time, as contributors come and go, it is a good idea to rotate the password used to encrypt your secrets. Encryption is only as good as the protection of the password. `ansible-vault` provides a subcommand that allows us to change the password named `rekey`, as shown in the following screenshot:

```
~/src/mastery> ansible-vault rekey --help
Usage: ansible-vault rekey [options] file_name

encryption/decryption utility for Ansible data files

Options:
  --ask-vault-pass      ask for vault password
  --encrypt-vault-id=ENCRYPT_VAULT_ID
                        the vault id used to encrypt (required if more than
                        vault-id is provided)
  -h, --help            show this help message and exit
  --new-vault-id=NEW_VAULT_ID
                        the new vault identity to use for rekey
  --new-vault-password-file=NEW_VAULT_PASSWORD_FILE
                        new vault password file for rekey
  --vault-id=VAULT_IDS  the vault identity to use
  --vault-password-file=VAULT_PASSWORD_FILES
                        vault password file
  -v, --verbose         verbose mode (-vvv for more, -vvvv to enable
                        connection debugging)
  --version             show program's version number and exit

See 'ansible-vault <command> --help' for more information on a specific
command.
~/src/mastery>
```

The `rekey` subcommand operates much like the `edit` subcommand. It takes in an optional password, file, or executable, and one or more files to `rekey`. You then need to use the `--new-vault-id` to define the new password (and ID if required), which again can be through a prompt, file, or executable. Let's `rekey` our `even_more_secrets.yaml` file in the following example, and add the `dev` ID to it:

```
~/src/mastery> ansible-vault rekey --vault-id password.sh --new-vault-id dev@./password_file even_more_secrets.yaml
Rekey successful
~/src/mastery>
```

Remember that all the encrypted files **with the same ID** need to have a matching key. Be sure to `rekey` all the files with the same ID at the same time.

## Decrypting encrypted files

If at some point, the need to encrypt data files goes away, `ansible-vault` provides a subcommand that can be used to remove encryption for one or more encrypted files. This subcommand is (surprisingly) named `decrypt`, as shown in the following screenshot:

```
~/src/mastery> ansible-vault decrypt --help
Usage: ansible-vault decrypt [options] file_name

encryption/decryption utility for Ansible data files

Options:
  --ask-vault-pass      ask for vault password
  -h, --help            show this help message and exit
  --new-vault-id=NEW_VAULT_ID
                        the new vault identity to use for rekey
  --new-vault-password-file=NEW_VAULT_PASSWORD_FILE
                        new vault password file for rekey
  --output=OUTPUT_FILE  output file name for encrypt or decrypt; use - for
                        stdout
  --vault-id=VAULT_IDS  the vault identity to use
  --vault-password-file=VAULT_PASSWORD_FILES
                        vault password file
  -v, --verbose         verbose mode (-vvv for more, -vvvv to enable
                        connection debugging)
  --version             show program's version number and exit

See 'ansible-vault <command> --help' for more information on a specific
command.
~/src/mastery>
```

*Protecting Your Secrets with Ansible*

Once again, we have our familiar `--vault-id` options and then one or more file paths to decrypt. Let's decrypt the file we created earlier using our `password` file, as shown in the following screenshot:

```
~/src/mastery> cat more_secrets.yaml
$ANSIBLE_VAULT;1.1;AES256
34316362386332626264663732613733623966663761633630633338626233316532326464313436
66666265323065613637313839323432626536316334660a323938343539386338643033333634
39623861316534363663383766396234316464356431653664646630363039323335613130316335
34323133332663763340a303866636653437343630333831653537363931313836163564393637343
366138373438646365393937356164663731366623334306164356562643839656466
~/src/mastery> ansible-vault decrypt --vault-id ./password_file more_secrets.yaml
Decryption successful
~/src/mastery> cat more_secrets.yaml
---
my_secret2: is_also_safe
~/src/mastery>
```

In the next section, we will see how to execute Ansible-playbook with encrypted files.

## Executing Ansible-playbook with encrypted files

To make use of our encrypted content, we need to be able to inform `ansible-playbook` how to access any encrypted data it might encounter. Unlike `ansible-vault`, which exists solely to deal with file encryption or decryption, `ansible-playbook` is more general-purpose, and it will not assume it is dealing with encrypted data by default. Luckily, all of our familiar `--vault-id` parameters from the previous examples work just the same in `ansible-playbook` as they do in `ansible-vault`. Ansible will hold the provided passwords and IDs in memory for the duration of the playbook execution.

Let's now create a simple playbook named `show_me.yaml` that will print out the value of the variable inside of `a_vars_file.yaml`, which we encrypted in a previous example, as follows:

```
---
- name: show me an encrypted var
  hosts: localhost
  gather_facts: false
```

```
    vars_files:
      - a_vars_file.yaml

    tasks:
      - name: print the variable
        debug:
          var: something
```

Now, let's run the playbook and see what happens. Note how we use the `--vault-id` parameter in exactly the same way as we did with `ansible-vault`; continuity is maintained between the two binaries, so you are able to apply everything you learned earlier in the chapter about using `--vault-id`. Take a look at the following screenshot:

```
~/src/mastery> ansible-playbook -i mastery-hosts --vault-id test@./password.sh inline.yaml

PLAY [inline secret variable demonstration] ************************************

TASK [print the secure variable] ***********************************************
ok: [localhost] => {
    "my_secret": "secure_password"
}

PLAY RECAP *********************************************************************
localhost                  : ok=1    changed=0    unreachable=0    failed=0

~/src/mastery>
```

As you can see, the playbook runs successfully and prints out the unencrypted value of the variable, even though the source variable file we included was an Ansible Vault. Naturally, you wouldn't print a secret value to the Terminal in a real playbook run, but this demonstrates how easy it is to access data from a Vault.

# Mixing encrypted data with plain YAML

Before the release of Ansible 2.3, secure data had to be encrypted in a separate file. For the reasons we discussed earlier, it is desirable to encrypt as little data as possible. This is now possible (and also saves the need for too many individual files as part of a playbook) through the use of the `encrypt_string` subcommand of `ansible-vault`, which produces an encrypted string that can be placed into an Ansible YAML file. Let's start with the following basic playbook as an example:

```yaml
---
- name: inline secret variable demonstration
  hosts: localhost
  gather_facts: false

  vars:
    my_secret: secure_password

  tasks:
    - name: print the secure variable
      debug:
        var: my_secret
```

When we run the preceding code, it should work as shown in the following screenshot:

```
~/src/mastery> ansible-playbook -i mastery-hosts inline.yaml

PLAY [inline secret variable demonstration] *************************

TASK [print the secure variable] ************************************
ok: [localhost] => {
    "my_secret": "secure_password"
}

PLAY RECAP **********************************************************
localhost                  : ok=1    changed=0    unreachable=0    failed=0

~/src/mastery>
```

Now, obviously, it is not clever to leave a secure password in plain text like this. So, rather than leave it like this, we will encrypt it using the `encrypt_string` subcommand of `ansible-vault`, as follows:

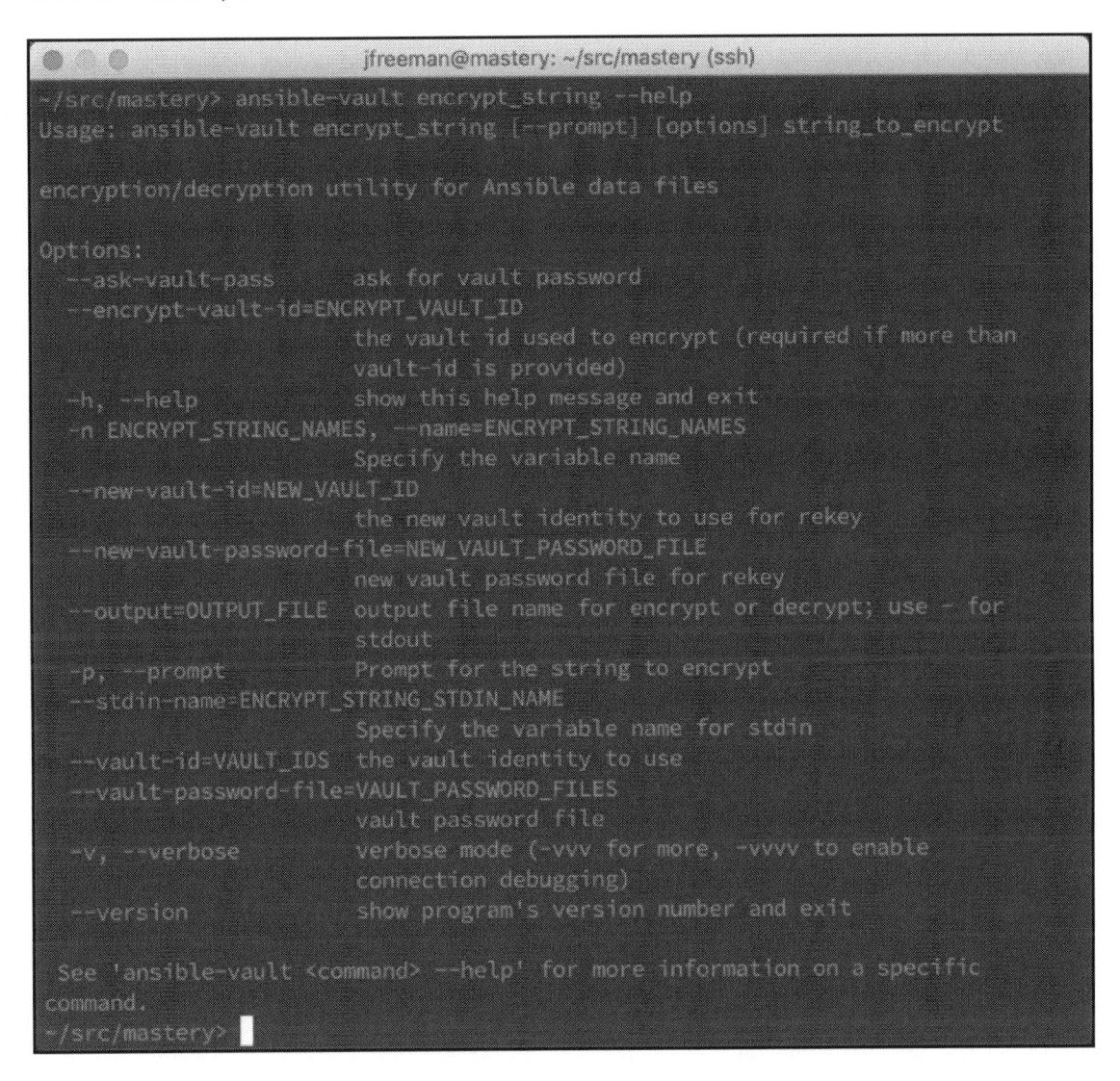

```
~/src/mastery> ansible-vault encrypt_string --help
Usage: ansible-vault encrypt_string [--prompt] [options] string_to_encrypt

encryption/decryption utility for Ansible data files

Options:
  --ask-vault-pass      ask for vault password
  --encrypt-vault-id=ENCRYPT_VAULT_ID
                        the vault id used to encrypt (required if more than
                        vault-id is provided)
  -h, --help            show this help message and exit
  -n ENCRYPT_STRING_NAMES, --name=ENCRYPT_STRING_NAMES
                        Specify the variable name
  --new-vault-id=NEW_VAULT_ID
                        the new vault identity to use for rekey
  --new-vault-password-file=NEW_VAULT_PASSWORD_FILE
                        new vault password file for rekey
  --output=OUTPUT_FILE  output file name for encrypt or decrypt; use - for
                        stdout
  -p, --prompt          Prompt for the string to encrypt
  --stdin-name=ENCRYPT_STRING_STDIN_NAME
                        Specify the variable name for stdin
  --vault-id=VAULT_IDS  the vault identity to use
  --vault-password-file=VAULT_PASSWORD_FILES
                        vault password file
  -v, --verbose         verbose mode (-vvv for more, -vvvv to enable
                        connection debugging)
  --version             show program's version number and exit

See 'ansible-vault <command> --help' for more information on a specific
command.
~/src/mastery>
```

*Protecting Your Secrets with Ansible*

So, if we wanted to create an encrypted block of text for our variable called `my_secret` with the encrypted string `secure_password`, using the test Vault ID and the `password.sh` script we created earlier for the password, we would run the following:

```
~/src/mastery> ansible-playbook -i mastery-hosts --vault-id test@./password.sh inline.yaml

PLAY [inline secret variable demonstration] ***********************************

TASK [print the secure variable] **********************************************
ok: [localhost] => {
    "my_secret": "secure_password"
}

PLAY RECAP ********************************************************************
localhost                  : ok=1    changed=0    unreachable=0    failed=0

~/src/mastery>
```

We can now copy and paste that output into our playbook, ensuring our variable is no longer human-readable, as shown in the following screenshot:

```
~/src/mastery> cat inline.yaml
---
- name: inline secret variable demonstration
  hosts: localhost
  gather_facts: false

  vars:
    my_secret: !vault |
          $ANSIBLE_VAULT;1.2;AES256;test
          39356563643564643764626332356638383931646661313735646138346263346661316163386435
          66316235313366376335663634616464633833313438366630a383336353335333333431
          6535313662
          31373938613834643062366165323731653730666356231336533626630323336376133
          6532363166
          65343038396465393103930653639363763383331613130333636563623232393862
          3632376165
          3533
  tasks:
    - name: print the secure variable
      debug:
          var: my_secret
~/src/mastery>
```

However, when we run the preceding while specifying the appropriate `--vault-id`, the information can be accessed just as any other Vault data can, as shown in the following screenshot:

```
~/src/mastery> ansible-playbook -i mastery-hosts --vault-id test@./password.sh inline.yaml

PLAY [inline secret variable demonstration] ****************************

TASK [print the secure variable] ***************************************
ok: [localhost] => {
    "my_secret": "secure_password"
}

PLAY RECAP *************************************************************
localhost                  : ok=1    changed=0    unreachable=0    failed=0

~/src/mastery>
```

Note that the playbook runs exactly as it did the first time we tested it, when all the data was open for the world to see. Now, however, we have successfully mixed our encrypted data with an otherwise unencrypted YAML playbook. Next, we will delve deeper into some of the operational aspects of running playbooks in conjunction with Ansible Vault.

## Protecting secrets while operating

In the previous section of this chapter, we covered how to protect your secrets at rest on the filesystem. However, that is not the only concern when operating Ansible with secrets. That secret data is going to be used in tasks as module arguments, loop inputs, or any number of other things. This may cause the data to be transmitted to remote hosts, logged to local or remote log files, or even displayed onscreen. This section of the chapter will discuss strategies for protecting your secrets during operation.

[ 69 ]

## Secrets transmitted to remote hosts

As we learned in Chapter 1, *The System Architecture and Design of Ansible,* Ansible will combine module code and arguments and write this out to a temporary directory on the remote host. This means your secret data is transferred over the wire *and* written to the remote filesystem. Unless you are using a connection plugin other than SSH or SSL-encrypted winrm, the data over the wire is already encrypted, preventing your secrets from being discovered by simple snooping. If you are using a connection plugin other than SSH, be aware of whether or not data is encrypted while in transit. Using any connection method that is not encrypted is strongly discouraged.

Once the data is transmitted, Ansible may write this data out in clear form to the filesystem. This can happen if pipelining (which we learned about in Chapter 1, *The System Architecture and Design of Ansible*) is not in use, or if Ansible has been instructed to leave remote files in place via the ANSIBLE_KEEP_REMOTE_FILES environment variable. Without pipelining, Ansible will write out the module code, plus arguments, into a temporary directory that is to be deleted upon execution. Should there be a loss of connectivity between writing out the file and executing it, the file will be left on the remote filesystem until manually removed. If Ansible is explicitly instructed to keep remote files in place, then, even if pipelining is enabled, Ansible will write out and leave a remote file in place. Care should be taken with these options when dealing with highly sensitive secrets, even though typically, only the user Ansible logs in as on the remote host (or becomes via privilege escalation) should have access to the leftover file. Simply deleting anything in the ~/.ansible/tmp/ path for the remote user will suffice to clean secrets.

## Secrets logged to remote or local files

When Ansible operates on a host, it will attempt to log the action to syslog (if verbosity level three or more is used). If this action is being done by a user with appropriate rights, it will cause a message to appear in the syslog file of the host. This message includes the module name and the arguments passed along to that command, which could include your secrets. To prevent this from happening, a play and task key exists, named no_log. Setting no_log to true will prevent Ansible from logging the action to syslog.

Ansible can also be instructed to log its actions locally. This is controlled either through log_path in the Ansible config file, or through an environment variable called ANSIBLE_LOG_PATH. By default, logging is off and Ansible will only log to STDOUT. Turning logging on in the config file causes Ansible to log its activities to the file defined in the config setting log_path.

Alternatively, setting the `ANSIBLE_LOG_PATH` variable to a path that can be written to by the user running `ansible-playbook` will also cause Ansible to log actions to this path. The verbosity of this logging matches that of the verbosity shown onscreen. By default, no variables or return details are displayed onscreen. With a verbosity level of one (-v), return data is displayed onscreen (and potentially in the local `log` file). With verbosity turned up to level three (-vvv), the input parameters may also be displayed. Since this can include secrets, the `no_log` setting applies to the onscreen display as well. Let's take our previous example of displaying an encrypted secret and add a `no_log` key to the task to prevent showing its value, as follows:

```yaml
---
- name: show me an encrypted var
  hosts: localhost
  gather_facts: false

  vars_files:
    - a_vars_file.yaml

  tasks:
    - name: print the variable
      debug:
        var: something
      no_log: true
```

If we execute this playbook, we should see that our secret data is protected, as shown in the following screenshot:

```
~/src/mastery> ansible-playbook -i mastery-hosts --vault-id password.sh showme.y
aml -v
Using /etc/ansible/ansible.cfg as config file

PLAY [show me an encrypted var] ************************************************

TASK [print the variable] ******************************************************
ok: [localhost] => {"censored": "the output has been hidden due to the fact that
 'no_log: true' was specified for this result"}

PLAY RECAP *********************************************************************
localhost                  : ok=1    changed=0    unreachable=0    failed=0

~/src/mastery>
```

As you can see, Ansible censored itself to prevent showing sensitive data.

> The `no_log` key can be used as a directive for a play, a role, a block, or a task.

## Summary

In this chapter, we covered how Ansible can deal with sensitive data effectively and securely, harnessing the latest Ansible features, including securing differing data with different passwords, and mixing encrypted data with plain YAML. We have also shown how this data is stored at rest and how this data is treated when utilized, and that with a little care and attention, Ansible can keep your secrets secret.

You learned how to use the `ansible-vault` tool to protect sensitive data by creating and editing encrypted files, modifying them, and the variety of methods available for providing the Vault password, including prompting the user, obtaining the password from a file, and running a script to retrieve it. You also learned how to mix encrypted strings with plain YAML files, and how this simplifies playbook layout. Finally, you learned the operational aspects of using Ansible Vaults, thus preventing Ansible from leaking data to `remote log` files or onscreen displays.

In our next chapter, we will explore how the power of Ansible is now available for Windows hosts, and how to harness this.

# 3
# Ansible and Windows - Not Just for Linux

A great deal of the work on Ansible has been performed on Linux OSes; indeed, the previous two editions of this book were based entirely around the use of Ansible in a Linux-centric environment. However, most environments are not like that, and, at the very least, are liable to have at least some Microsoft Windows server and desktop machines. Since the second edition of this book was published, a lot of work has gone into Ansible to create a really robust cross-platform automation tool that is equally at home in both a Linux data center and a Windows data center. There are fundamental differences in the way Windows and Linux hosts operate, of course, and so it should come as no surprise that there are some fundamental differences between the way in which Ansible automates tasks on Linux, and how it automates tasks on Windows. We will cover those fundamentals in this chapter, in order to give you a rock solid foundation to start automating your Windows tasks with Ansible, specifically covering the following areas:

- Running Ansible from Windows
- Setting up Windows hosts for Ansible control
- Handling Windows authentication and encryption
- Automating Windows tasks with Ansible

## Technical requirements

Check out the following video to see the Code in Action:

```
http://bit.ly/2Jtvz5u
```

# Running Ansible from Windows

If you browse the official installation documentation for Ansible, you will find a variety of instructions for most mainstream Linux variants, Solaris, macOS, and FreeBSD. You will note, however, that there is no mention of Windows. The good news is that, if you are running recent versions of Windows 10 or Windows Server 2016, installing and running Ansible is now incredibly easy thanks to **Windows Subsystem for Linux (WSL)**. This technology allows Windows users to run unmodified Linux distributions on top of Windows without the complications or overheads of a virtual machine, and, as such, this lends itself perfectly to running Ansible, as it can be installed and run with ease.

> The official Ansible installation documentation can be found at https://docs.ansible.com/ansible/latest/installation_guide/intro_installation.html.

## Checking your build

WSL is only available on specific builds of Windows, as follows:

- Windows 10—version 1607 (build 14393) or later:
    - Note that you will need build 16215 or later if you want to install Linux through the Microsoft Store
    - Only 64-bit versions of Windows 10 are supported
- Windows Server 2019—version 1709 (build 16237) or later

You can easily check your build and version number in PowerShell by running the following command:

```
systeminfo | Select-String "^OS Name","^OS Version"
```

If you are running an earlier version of Windows, running Ansible is still possible, either through a virtual machine or via Cygwin. However, these methods are beyond the scope of this book.

## Enabling WSL

Once you have verified your build, enabling WSL is easy. Simply open PowerShell as an administrator and run the following command:

```
Enable-WindowsOptionalFeature -Online -FeatureName Microsoft-Windows-Subsystem-Linux
```

Once the installation completes successfully, you will be able to select and install your preferred Linux distribution. A number are available, but for running Ansible, it makes sense to choose one of those listed in the official Ansible installation instructions, such as Debian or Ubuntu.

## Installing Linux under WSL

If you have a recent enough build of Windows 10, then installing your preferred Linux is as easy as opening the Microsoft Store and searching for it. For example, search for Ubuntu and you should find it easily. This is displayed in the following screenshot:

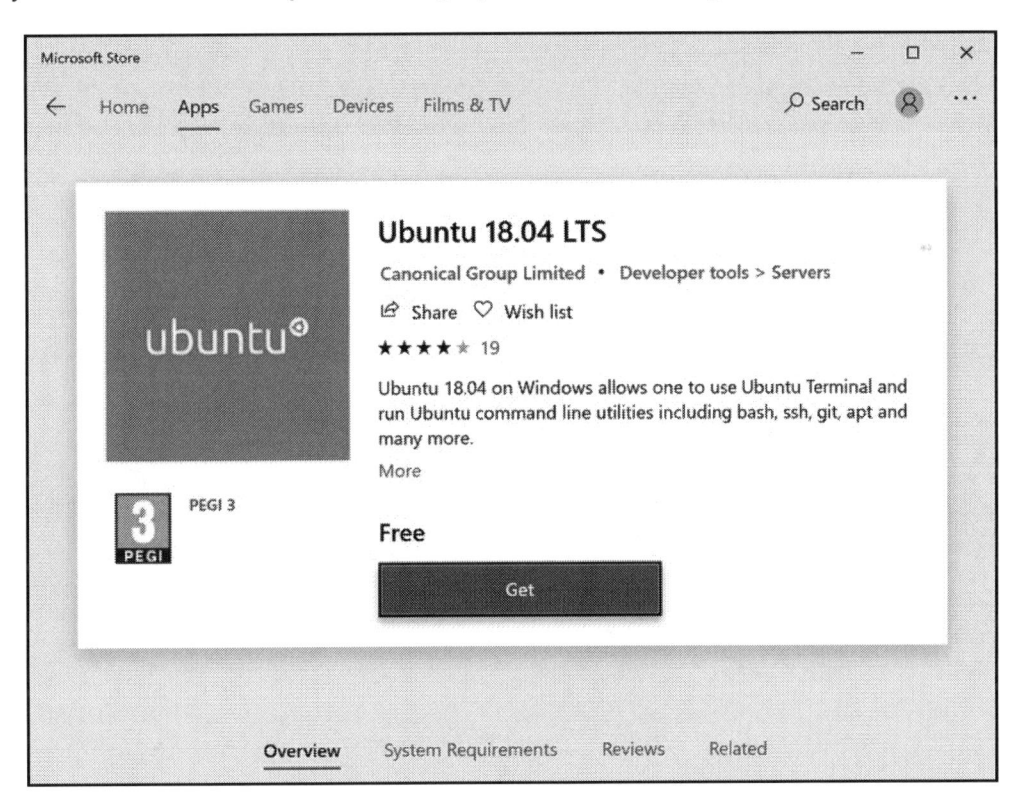

Click on the **Get** button and wait for the installation to complete. If you are running Windows 10, but a build earlier than 16215, or indeed Windows Server 2019, then the installation of Linux is a slightly more manual process. First of all, download your preferred Linux distribution from Microsoft—for example, Ubuntu can be downloaded using the following PowerShell command:

```
Invoke-WebRequest -Uri https://aka.ms/wsl-ubuntu-1804 -OutFile Ubuntu.appx
-UseBasicParsing
```

Once successfully downloaded, unzip the `Ubuntu.appx` file—this can be unzipped to any location provided that it is on the system (boot) drive, normally `C:`. If you want to keep your Linux distribution private, it can be unzipped somewhere within your profile directory, otherwise you can unzip the file anywhere on the system drive. For example, the following PowerShell commands would unzip the archive into `C:\WSL\`:

```
Rename-Item Ubuntu.appx Ubuntu.zip
Expand-Archive Ubuntu.zip C:\WSL\Ubuntu
```

Once completed, you can launch your newly-installed Linux distribution using the executable named after the distribution itself. In the case of our Ubuntu example, you would run the following:

```
C:\WSL\Ubuntu\ubuntu.exe
```

The first time you run your newly installed Linux distribution, whether it was installed through the Microsoft Store or installed manually, it will initialize itself. As part of this process, it will ask you to create a new user account. Please note that this account is independent of your Windows username and password, so be sure to remember the password you set here! You will need it every time you run commands through `sudo` (for example), although, as with any Linux distribution, you can customize this behavior through `/etc/sudoers` if you wish. This is demonstrated in the following screenshot:

Congratulations! You now have Linux running under WSL. From here, you should follow the standard installation process for Ansible, and you can run it from your Linux subsystem just as you would on any other Linux box.

# Setting up Windows hosts for Ansible control

So far, we have talked about running Ansible itself from Windows. This is helpful, especially in a corporate environment where perhaps Windows end user systems are the norm. However, what about actual automation tasks? The good news is that automation of Windows with Ansible does not require WSL. One of Ansible's core premises is to be agentless, and that remains true for Windows as for Linux. Just as it is fair to assume that almost any modern Linux host will have SSH access enabled, most modern Windows hosts have a remote management protocol built in, called WinRM. For security reasons, this technology is disabled by default, and so, in this part of the book, we walk through the process for enabling and securing WinRM for remote management with Ansible.

# System requirements for automation with Ansible

The use of WinRM means a wide array of support for Windows versions new and old—under the hood, just about any Windows version that supports the following will work:

- PowerShell 3.0
- .NET 4.0

In practice, this means that the following Windows versions can be supported, provided the preceding requirements are met:

- **Desktop**: Windows 7 SP1, 8.1, and 10
- **Server**: Windows Server 2008 SP2, 2008 R2 SP1, 2012, 2012 R2, 2016, and 2019

Note that the older OSes listed previously (such as Windows 7 or Server 2008) did not ship with .NET 4.0 or PowerShell 3.0, and these will need to be installed before they can be used with Ansible. Note that newer versions of PowerShell are supported, and, equally, there may be security patches for .NET 4.0. Given that, in a business environment, there are likely to be policies and procedures already in place for this kind of thing, incorporating the older OSes listed previously is beyond the scope of this text.

> **TIP:** A bug exists in WinRM under PowerShell 3.0 that limits the memory available to the service, which, in turn, can cause some Ansible commands to fail. This is resolved by ensuring KB2842230 is applied to all hosts running PowerShell 3.0.

## Enabling the WinRM listener

Once all the system requirements have been met, as detailed previously, the task that remains is to enable the WinRM listener. With this achieved, we can actually run Ansible tasks against the Windows host itself! WinRM can run over both HTTP, and HTTPS protocols, and, while it is quickest and easiest to get up and running over plain HTTP, this leaves you vulnerable to packet sniffers and the potential for sensitive data to be revealed on the network. This is especially true if basic authentication is being used. By default, and perhaps unsurprisingly, Windows does not allow remote management with WinRM over HTTP or using basic authentication.

Sometimes, basic authentication is sufficient (for example, in a development environment), and if it is to be used, then we definitely want to enable HTTPS as the transport for WinRM! However, later in the chapter, we will look at Kerberos authentication, which is preferable, and also enables the use of domain accounts. For now though, to demonstrate the process of connecting Ansible to a Windows host with a modicum of security, we will enable WinRM over HTTPS using a self-signed certificate, and enable basic authentication to allow us to work with the local `Administrator` account.

For WinRM to function over HTTPS, there must exist a certificate that has the following:

- A `CN` matching the hostname
- `Server Authentication (1.3.6.1.5.5.7.3.1)` in the **Enhanced Key Usage** field

Ideally, this should be generated by a central **certificate authority** (**CA**) to prevent man-in-the-middle attacks and such—more on this later. For the sake of simplicity, we will generate a self-signed certificate. Run the following command in PowerShell to generate a suitable certificate:

```
New-SelfSignedCertificate -CertStoreLocation Cert:\LocalMachine\My -DnsName
"$env:computername" -FriendlyName "WinRM HTTPS Certificate" -NotAfter (Get-
Date).AddYears(5)
```

> The `New-SelfSignedCertificate` command is only available on newer versions of Windows—if it is not available on your system, consider using the automated PowerShell script provided by Ansible available at `https://raw.githubusercontent.com/ansible/ansible/devel/examples/scripts/ConfigureRemotingForAnsible.ps1`.

This should yield something like the following—make a note of the certificate thumbprint, as you will need it later:

```
Administrator: Windows PowerShell
PS C:\Users\Administrator> New-SelfSignedCertificate -CertStoreLocation Cert:\LocalMachine\My -DnsName $env:computername -FriendlyName "WinRM HTTPS Certificate" -NotAfter (Get-Date).AddYears(5)

   PSParentPath: Microsoft.PowerShell.Security\Certificate::LocalMachine\My

Thumbprint                                Subject
----------                                -------
7CB312B9009E596652974C7FC3912363AF5BF016  CN=WIN-2NJFMROMNBD

PS C:\Users\Administrator>
```

With the certificate in place, we can now set up a new WinRM listener with the following command:

```
New-Item -Path WSMan:\Localhost\Listener -Transport HTTPS -Address * -CertificateThumbprint <thumbprint of certificate>
```

When successful, that command sets up a WinRM HTTPS listener on port `5986` with the self-signed certificate we generated earlier. To test this setup, we need to perform two more steps—open up this port on the firewall, and enable basic authentication so that we can test using the local `Administrator` account. This is achieved with the following two commands:

```
New-NetFirewallRule -DisplayName 'WinRM HTTPS Management' -Profile Domain,Private -Direction Inbound -Action Allow -Protocol TCP -LocalPort 5986

Set-Item -Path "WSMan:\localhost\Service\Auth\Basic" -Value $true
```

# Ansible and Windows - Not Just for Linux

You should see output from the previous commands as follows:

```
Administrator: Windows PowerShell

PS C:\Users\Administrator> New-Item -Path WSMan:\Localhost\Listener -Transport HTTPS -Address * -CertificateThumbprint
CB312B9009E596652974C7FC3912363AF5BF016

Creates a new Listener item.
This command creates a new Listener item.
Do you want to continue?
[Y] Yes  [N] No  [S] Suspend  [?] Help (default is "Y"): y


   WSManConfig: Microsoft.WSMan.Management\WSMan::localhost\Listener

Type            Keys                              Name
----            ----                              ----
Container       {Transport=HTTPS, Address=*}      Listener_1305953032


PS C:\Users\Administrator> New-NetFirewallRule -DisplayName "WinRM HTTPS Management" -Profile Domain,Private -Direction
Inbound -Action Allow -Protocol TCP -LocalPort 5986

Name                   : {a21b1711-ab50-4baf-89a7-26735dbc71f5}
DisplayName            : WinRM HTTPS Management
Description            :
DisplayGroup           :
Group                  :
Enabled                : True
Profile                : Domain, Private
Platform               : {}
Direction              : Inbound
Action                 : Allow
EdgeTraversalPolicy    : Block
LooseSourceMapping     : False
LocalOnlyMapping       : False
Owner                  :
PrimaryStatus          : OK
Status                 : The rule was parsed successfully from the store. (65536)
EnforcementStatus      : NotApplicable
PolicyStoreSource      : PersistentStore
PolicyStoreSourceType  : Local

PS C:\Users\Administrator> Set-Item -Path "WSMan:\localhost\Service\Auth\Basic" -Value $true
PS C:\Users\Administrator>
```

These commands have been broken out individually to give you an idea of the process involved in setting up a Windows host for Ansible connectivity. For automated deployments, and systems where New-SelfSignedCertificate isn't available, consider using the ConfigureRemotingForAnsible.ps1 script available on the official Ansible GitHub account here:

https://raw.githubusercontent.com/ansible/ansible/devel/examples/scripts/ConfigureRemotingForAnsible.ps1

This script performs all the steps we completed previously (and more), and can be downloaded and run in PowerShell as follows:

```
$ansibleconfigurl =
"https://raw.githubusercontent.com/ansible/ansible/devel/examples/scripts/C
onfigureRemotingForAnsible.ps1"

$ansibleconfig = "$env:temp\ConfigureRemotingForAnsible.ps1"
```

```
(New-Object -TypeName System.Net.WebClient).DownloadFile($ansibleconfigurl,
$ansibleconfig)

powershell.exe -ExecutionPolicy ByPass -File $ansibleconfig
```

There are many other ways to roll out the required configuration of WinRM for Ansible, including via Group Policy—however, this section sufficiently outlines the steps involved for successful future rollout.

## Connecting Ansible to Windows

Once WinRM is configured, getting Ansible talking to Windows is fairly straightforward, provided you bear two caveats in mind—it expects to use the SSH protocol, and if you don't specify a user account, it will attempt to use the same user account that Ansible is being run under to connect. This is almost certainly not going to work with a Windows username.

Also, note that Ansible requires the `winrm` Python module installed to connect successfully. This is not always installed by default, so it is worth testing for it on your Ansible system before you start working with Windows hosts. If it's not present, you will see something like the error shown in the following screenshot:

If you see this error, you will need to install the module before proceeding any further. There may be a prepackaged version available for your OS—for example, on CentOS 7, you can install it with the following command:

```
sudo yum install python2-winrm
```

If a packaged version is not available, install it directly from `pip` using the following command:

```
sudo pip install "pywinrm>=0.3.0"
```

Once this is complete, we can test to see whether our earlier WinRM configuration work was successful. For SSH-based connectivity, there is an Ansible module called `ping`, which performs a full end-to-end test to ensure connectivity, successful authentication, and a usable Python environment on the remote system. Similarly, there exists a module called `win_ping`, which performs an analogous test on Windows.

In my test environment, I would prepare an inventory as follows to connect to my newly configured Windows host:

```
[windows]
192.168.81.150

[windows:vars]
ansible_user=Administrator
ansible_password="password"
ansible_port=5986
ansible_connection=winrm
ansible_winrm_server_cert_validation=ignore
```

Note the connection specific variables beginning `ansible_` that are being set in the `windows:vars` section of the playbook. At this stage, they should be fairly self-explanatory, as they were covered earlier in the book, but, in particular, note the `ansible_winrm_server_cert_validation` variable, which needs to be set to ignore when working with self-signed certificates. Obviously, in a real-world example, you would not leave the `ansible_password` parameter in clear text—it would either be placed in an Ansible vault, or prompted for upon launch using the `--ask-pass` parameter.

> Certificate-based authentication is also possible with WinRM, which carries with it more or less the same benefits and risks as SSH key-based authentication.

Using the previous inventory (with appropriate changes for your environment such as hostname/IP addresses and authentication details), we can run the following command to test connectivity:

```
ansible -i windows-hosts -m win_ping all
```

If all goes well, you should see some output like the following:

```
jfreeman@mastery: ~/src/mastery (ssh)
~/src/mastery> ansible -i windows-hosts -m win_ping all
192.168.81.150 | SUCCESS => {
    "changed": false,
    "ping": "pong"
}
~/src/mastery>
```

That completes a successful end-to-end setup of an Ansible host to a Windows one! From such a setup, you can author and run playbooks just as you would on any other system, except that you must work with Ansible modules that specifically support Windows. Next, we will work on improving the security of our connection between Ansible and Windows, before finally moving on to some examples of Windows playbooks.

# Handling Windows authentication and encryption

Now that we have established the basic level of connectivity required for Ansible to perform tasks on a Windows host, let's dig deeper into the authentication and encryption side of things. In the earlier part of the chapter, we used the basic authentication mechanism with a local account. While this is fine in a testing scenario, what happens in a domain environment? Basic authentication only supports local accounts, so clearly we need something else here. We also chose not to validate the SSL certificate (as it was self-signed), which again, is fine for testing purposes, but is not best practice in a production environment. In this section, we will explore options for improving the security of our Ansible communications with Windows.

## Authentication mechanisms

Ansible, in fact, supports five different Windows authentication mechanisms as follows:

- **Basic**: Supports local accounts only
- **Certificate**: Supports local accounts only, conceptually similar to SSH key-based authentication
- **Kerberos**: Supports AD accounts
- **NTLM**: Supports both local and AD accounts
- **CredSSP**: Supports both local and AD accounts

It is worth noting that Kerberos, NTLM, and CredSSP all provide message encryption over HTTP, which improves security. However, we have already seen how easy it is to set up WinRM over HTTPS, and WinRM management over plain HTTP is not enabled by default anyway, so we will assume that the communication channel is already encrypted. WinRM is a SOAP protocol meaning it must run over a transport layer such as HTTP or HTTPS. To prevent remote management commands being intercepted on the network, it is best practise to ensure WinRM runs over the HTTPS protocol.

Of these authentication methods, the one that interests us most is Kerberos. Kerberos (for the purpose of this chapter) effectively supersedes NTLM for Ansible authentication against Active Directory accounts. CredSSP provides another mechanism, but there are also security risks relating to the interception of clear-text logons on the target host that are best understood before it is deployed—in fact, it is disabled by default.

Before we move on to configuring Kerberos, a brief note about certificate authentication. Although initially, this might seem appealing, as it is effectively passwordless, current dependencies in Ansible mean that the private key for the certificate authentication must be unencrypted on the Ansible automation host. In this regard, it is actually more secure (and wiser) to place the password for either a basic or Kerberos authentication session in an Ansible vault. We have already covered basic authentication, and so we will focus our efforts on Kerberos here.

As Kerberos authentication only supports Active Directory accounts, it is assumed that the Windows host to be controlled by Ansible is already joined to the domain. It is also assumed that WinRM over HTTPS has already been set up, as discussed earlier in the chapter.

With these requirements in place, the first thing we have to do is install a handful of Kerberos-related packages on the Ansible host itself. The exact packages will depend upon your chosen OS, but on CentOS 7, it would look like this:

```
sudo yum -y install python-devel krb5-devel krb5-libs krb5-workstation
```

On Ubuntu 16.04, you would install the following packages:

```
sudo apt-get install python-dev libkrb5-dev krb5-user
```

> Package requirements for Kerberos support on a wider range of OSes are available on the Ansible documentation for Windows Remote Management: https://docs.ansible.com/ansible/latest/user_guide/windows_winrm.html.

In addition to these packages, we also need to install the `pywinrm[kerberos]` Python module. Availability of this will vary—on CentOS 7, it is not available as an RPM, so we need to install it through `pip` as follows:

```
sudo yum install python-pip gcc
sudo pip install pywinrm[kerberos]
```

> Note that `gcc` is needed by `pip` to build the module—this can be removed afterward if no longer required.

Next, ensure that your Ansible server can resolve your **Active Directory** (**AD**)-related DNS entries. The procedure for this will vary according to the OS and network architecture, and so is beyond the scope of this book—suffice to say, your Ansible controller must be able to resolve your domain controller and related entries for the rest of this procedure to work.

With DNS in place, next, add your domain to `/etc/krb5.conf`. For example, my test domain is `mastery.example.com`, and my domain controller is `WIN-2NJFMR0MNBD.mastery.example.com`, so the bottom of my `/etc/krb5.conf` looks like this:

```
[realms]
MASTERY.EXAMPLE.COM = {
  kdc = WIN-2NJFMR0MNBD.mastery.example.com
}

[domain_realm]
.mastery.example.com = MASTERY.EXAMPLE.COM
```

Note the capitalization—this is important! Test your Kerberos integration using the `kinit` command with a known domain user account. Here is an example using the Domain Administrator for my test domain:

```
~/src/mastery> kinit Administrator@MASTERY.EXAMPLE.COM
Password for Administrator@MASTERY.EXAMPLE.COM:
~/src/mastery> klist
Ticket cache: KEYRING:persistent:1000:1000
Default principal: Administrator@MASTERY.EXAMPLE.COM

Valid starting       Expires              Service principal
01/09/2019 13:44:10  01/09/2019 23:44:10  krbtgt/MASTERY.EXAMPLE.COM@MASTERY.EXAMPLE.COM
        renew until 01/16/2019 13:44:08
~/src/mastery>
```

Finally, let's create a Windows host inventory—note that it is almost identical to the one we used in our basic authentication example; only this time, we have specified the Kerberos domain after the username:

```
[windows]
192.168.81.150

[windows:vars]
ansible_user=administrator@MASTERY.EXAMPLE.COM
ansible_password="password"
ansible_port=5986
ansible_connection=winrm
ansible_winrm_server_cert_validation=ignore
```

Now, we can test connectivity just like before:

```
~/src/mastery> ansible -i windows-hosts -m win_ping all
192.168.81.150 | SUCCESS => {
    "changed": false,
    "ping": "pong"
}
~/src/mastery>
```

Success! The previous result shows successful end-to-end connectivity with Windows, including successful authentication, and access to the WinRM subsystem.

## A note on accounts

By default, WinRM is configured to only allow management by members of the local Administrators group on a given Windows host. This does not have to be the administrator account itself—we have used this here for demonstration purposes. It is possible to enable the use of less privileged accounts for WinRM management, but their use is likely to prove limited, as most Ansible commands require a degree of privileged access. Should you wish to have a less privileged account available to Ansible via WinRM, run the following command on the host:

```
winrm configSDDL default
```

Running this command opens a Windows dialog box. Use this to add and grant (as a minimum) the Read and Execute privileges to any user or group you wish to have WinRM remote management capabilities.

# Certificate validation

So far, we have been ignoring the self-signed SSL certificates used in WinRM communication—obviously, this is less than ideal, and it is quite straightforward to get Ansible to validate SSL certificates if they are not self-signed.

The easiest way to do this if your Windows machines are members of a domain is to use **Active Directory Certificate Services (ADCs)**—however, most businesses will have their own certification process in place through ADCS, or another third-party service. It is assumed, in order to proceed with this section, that the Windows host in question has a certificate generated for remote management, and that the CA certificate is available in Base64 format.

Just as we did earlier on the Windows host, you will need to set up an HTTPS listener, but this time using the certificate signed by your CA. You can do so (if not already completed) using a command such as the following:

```
Import-Certificate -FilePath .\certnew.cer -CertStoreLocation
Cert:\LocalMachine\My
```

Naturally, replace the `FilePath` certificate with the one that matches the location of your own certificate. If you need to, you can delete any previously created HTTPS WinRM listener with the following command:

```
winrm delete winrm/config/Listener?Address=*+Transport=HTTPS
```

Then, using the thumbprint from the imported certificate, create a new listener:

```
New-Item -Path WSMan:\Localhost\Listener -Transport HTTPS -Address * -CertificateThumbprint <thumbprint of certificate>
```

Now to the Ansible controller. The first thing to do is to import the CA certificate for the WinRM listener into the CA bundle for your OS. The method and location for this will vary between OSes, but, on CentOS 7, you can place the Base64-encoded CA certificate in `/etc/pki/ca-trust/source/anchors/`.

Once this has been done, run the following commands:

```
update-ca-trust enable
update-ca-trust extract
```

# Ansible and Windows - Not Just for Linux

Finally, we need to tell Ansible where to find the certificate. By default, Ansible uses the Python Certifi module and will use the default path for this unless we tell it otherwise. This process updates the CA bundle, located in `/etc/pki/ca-trust/extracted/pem/tls-ca-bundle.pem`, and luckily, we can tell Ansible where to find this in the inventory file. Note the two further changes to the inventory file as shown in the following code—first of all, we have now specified the full hostname for the Windows host rather than the IP address, as the inventory hostname must match the `CN` on the certificate for full validation to occur. Also, we have removed the `ansible_winrm_server_cert_validation` line, which means all SSL certificates are now implicitly validated:

```
[windows]
WIN-2NJFMR0MNBD.mastery.example.com

[windows:vars]
ansible_user=administrator@MASTERY.EXAMPLE.COM
ansible_password="password"
ansible_port=5986
ansible_connection=winrm
ansible_winrm_ca_trust_path=/etc/pki/ca-trust/extracted/pem/tls-ca-bundle.pem
```

If we run our ping test again, we should now see SUCCESS:

```
~/src/mastery> ansible -i windows-hosts -m win_ping all
/usr/lib/python2.7/site-packages/urllib3/connection.py:362: SubjectAltNameWarning: Certificate for win-2njfmr0mnbd.mastery.example.com has no `subjectAltName`, falling back to check for a `commonName` for now. This feature is being removed by major browsers and deprecated by RFC 2818. (See https://github.com/shazow/urllib3/issues/497 for details.)
  SubjectAltNameWarning
WIN-2NJFMR0MNBD.mastery.example.com | SUCCESS => {
    "changed": false,
    "ping": "pong"
}
~/src/mastery>
```

Obviously, we could improve our certificate generation to remove the `subjectAltName` warning, but for now, this demonstrates Ansible connectivity to Windows, with Kerberos authentication to a domain account and full SSL validation. So far, in demonstrating this, we have only used the Ansible `win_ping` module to test connectivity. While Windows playbooks for Ansible could occupy a complete book on their own, let's wrap up the chapter with some simple example playbooks.

# Automating Windows tasks with Ansible

A full list of the Windows modules for Ansible is available at the following link, and it must be noted that, although you can use all the familiar Ansible constructs with Windows hosts such as `vars`, `handlers`, and `blocks`, you must use Windows-specific modules when defining tasks:

https://docs.ansible.com/ansible/latest/modules/list_of_windows_modules.html

In this part of the chapter, we will run through a few simple examples of Windows playbooks to highlight a few of the things you need to know when writing playbooks for Windows.

# Picking the right module

If you were running Ansible against a Linux server, and wanted to create a directory and then copy a file into it, you would use the `file` and `copy` Ansible modules, in a playbook that looks something like the following:

```yaml
---
- name: Linux file example playbook
  hosts: all
  gather_facts: false

  tasks:
    - name: Create temporary directory
      file:
        path: /tmp/mastery
        state: directory
    - name: Copy across a test file
      copy:
        src: mastery.txt
        dest: /tmp/mastery/mastery.txt
```

However, on Windows, this playbook would fail to run, as the `file` and `copy` modules are not compatible with WinRM. As a result, an equivalent playbook to perform the same task, but on Windows, would look like this:

```yaml
---
- name: Windows file example playbook
  hosts: all
  gather_facts: false

  tasks:
```

```yaml
    - name: Create temporary directory
      win_file:
        path: 'C:\Mastery Test'
        state: directory
    - name: Copy across a test file
      win_copy:
        src: ~/src/mastery/mastery.txt
        dest: 'C:\Mastery Test\mastery.txt'
```

Note the following differences between the two playbooks:

- `win_file` and `win_copy` are used in place of the `file` and `copy` modules for Windows.
- It is recommended in the documentation for the `win_file` and `win_copy` modules to use a backslash (\) when dealing with remote (Windows paths).
- Continue to use forward slashes (/) on the Linux host.
- Use single quotes (not double quotes) to quote paths that contain spaces.

It is always important to consult the documentation for the individual modules used in your playbooks. For example, reviewing the documentation for the `win_copy` module documentation, it recommends using the `win_get_url` module for large file transfers because the WinRM transfer mechanism is not very efficient.

Also note that, if a filename contains certain special characters (for example, square braces), they need to be escaped using the PowerShell escape character, `. For example, the following task would install the `c:\temp\setupdownloader_[aaff].exe` file:

```yaml
    - name: Install package
      win_package:
        path: 'c:\temp\setupdownloader_`[aaff`].exe'
        product_id: {00000000-0000-0000-0000-000000000000}
        arguments: /silent /unattended
        state: present
```

There are many other Windows modules that should suffice to complete your Windows playbook needs, and, combined with these tips, you would get the end results you need, quickly and with ease.

## Installing software

Most Linux systems (and indeed other Unix variants) have a native package manager that makes it easy to install a wide variety of software. The `chocolatey` package manager makes this possible for Windows, and the Ansible `win_chocolatey` module makes installing software in an unattended manner with Ansible simple.

> **TIP**: You can explore the `chocolatey` repository and find out more about it at https://chocolatey.org.

For example, if you wanted to roll out Adobe's Acrobat Reader across an estate of Windows machines, you could use either the `win_copy` or `win_get_url` modules to distribute the installer, and then the `win_package` module to install it. However, the following code would perform the same task with less code:

```
- name: Install Acrobat Reader
  win_chocolatey:
    name: adobereader
    state: present
```

Discussing the `chocolatey` packaging system in greater depth is beyond the scope of this book, but it deserves mention because of the ease of package installation and management it brings to the Windows platform.

## Extending beyond modules

Just as on any platform, there may come a time when the exact functionality required is not available from a module. Although writing a custom module (or modifying an existing one) are viable solutions to this, sometimes, a more immediate solution is required. To this end, the `win_command` and `win_shell` modules come to the rescue—these can be used to run literal PowerShell commands on Windows. Many examples are available in the official Ansible documentation, but the following code, for example, would create the `C:\Mastery` directory using PowerShell:

```
- name: Create a directory using PowerShell
  win_shell: New-Item -Path C:\Mastery -ItemType Directory
```

We could even revert to the traditional `cmd` shell for this task:

```
- name: Create a directory using cmd.exe
  win_shell: mkdir C:\MasteryCMD
  args:
    executable: cmd
```

With these pointers, it should be possible to create the desired functionality in just about any Windows environment.

# Summary

Ansible handles Windows hosts as effectively as Linux (and other Unix) ones. In this chapter, we covered both how to run Ansible from a Windows host, and how to integrate Windows hosts with Ansible for automation, including the authentication mechanisms, encryption, and even the basics of Windows specific playbooks.

You have learned that Ansible can run from a recent build of Windows that supports WSL, and how to achieve this. You have also learned how to set up Windows hosts for Ansible control, and to secure this with Kerberos authentication and encryption. Finally, you learned the basics of authoring Windows playbooks, including finding the correct modules for use with Windows hosts, escaping special characters, creating directories and copy files for the host, installing packages, and even running raw shell commands on the Windows host with Ansible. This is a sound foundation on which you will be able to build out the Windows playbooks needed to manage your own estate of Windows hosts.

In the next chapter, we will cover the effective management of Ansible in the enterprise with AWX.

# 4
# Infrastructure Management for Enterprises with AWX

It is clear that Ansible is an incredibly powerful and versatile automation tool, lending itself well to managing an entire estate of servers and network devices. Mundane, repetitive tasks can be made repeatable and straightforward with ease, hence a great deal of time can be saved! Obviously, this is of great benefit in a corporate environment, but this power comes at a price. If everyone has their own copy of Ansible on their own machines, how do you know who ran what and when? How do you ensure that all playbooks are correctly stored and version-controlled? Indeed, how do you prevent the proliferation of superuser-level access credentials across your organization while benefiting from the power of Ansible?

The answer to these questions comes in the form of **AWX**, an open source enterprise management system for Ansible. AWX is the open source, upstream version of the commercial Ansible Tower software available from Red Hat, and it offers virtually the same features and benefits, but without the support or stable release cycle that Red Hat offers. It must be said that AWX could warrant its own book, but in this chapter, we hope to give you enough information to get up and running with the basics of AWX, and the thirst for further exploration, should you so desire.

We will cover the following in this chapter:

- Getting AWX up and running
- Integrating AWX with your first playbook
- Going beyond the basics

# Technical requirements

Check out the following video to see the Code in Action:

http://bit.ly/2JsHFeR

# Getting AWX up and running

Before we get stuck into installing AWX, it is worth briefly exploring what AWX is, and indeed isn't. AWX is a tool to be employed alongside Ansible. It does not duplicate or replicate, in any way, the features of Ansible—indeed, when Ansible playbooks are run from AWX, the `ansible-playbook` binary is being called behind the scenes. Rather, AWX should be considered a complementary tool that adds the following benefits, on which many enterprises depend:

- **Rich role-based access control (RBAC)**
- Integration with centralized login services (for example, LDAP or Active Directory)
- Secure credential management
- Auditability
- Accountability
- Lower barrier to entry for new operators
- Improved management of playbook version control

Most of the AWX code runs in a set of Docker containers, which makes it straightforward to deploy in most environments. However, as further proof that AWX is a complementary tool to Ansible, it is installed using the `ansible-playbook` command!

Given the use of Docker containers, it is possible to run AWX in OpenShift or other Kubernetes environments—however, for the sake of simplicity here, we will get started by installing it on a single Docker host. Before you proceed any further, you should ensure that your chosen host has the following:

- Docker, fully installed and working
- The `docker-py` module for your version of Python
- Access to Docker Hub
- Ansible 2.4 or newer
- Git 1.8.4 or newer

With these tools in place, we start simply by cloning the AWX repository from GitHub to the host on which it is to be installed:

`git clone https://github.com/ansible/awx.git`

> **TIP**: The previous command will clone the latest development release of AWX—if you want to clone one of the releases, browse the *Releases* section of the repository and check out the desired version: https://github.com/ansible/awx/releases.

Now, change into the installer directory under the cloned repository:

`cd awx/installer`

By now, the contents of this directory should be familiar to you—we have an inventory file, and a playbook on which to install AWX! Edit the inventory file before proceeding any further—as you will see, there are many variables that can be configured, and most of them are well documented in the comments on the inventory file. As a bare minimum to get started, I recommend setting the following variables:

| Variable name | Recommended value |
|---|---|
| admin_password | This is the default password for the admin user—you will need this the first time you log in, so be sure to set it to something memorable and secure! |
| pg_password | This is the password for the backend PostgreSQL database—be sure to set it to something unique and secure. |
| postgres_data_dir | This is the directory on the local filesystem where the PostgreSQL container will store its data—it defaults to a directory under /tmp which, on most systems, will be automatically cleaned up on a regular basis. This often destroys the PostgreSQL database, so set it to something safe (for example, /var/lib/awx/pgdocker). |
| project_data_dir | For uploading playbooks manually to AWX without the need for a version control system, the playbooks must sit somewhere on the filesystem. To prevent having to copy them into a container, this variable maps the local folder specified to the required one inside a container. For the examples in this book, we will use the default (the /var/lib/awx/projects folder). |
| rabbitmq_password | This is the password for the backend RabbitMQ service—be sure to set it to something unique and secure. |
| secret_key | This is the secret key used to encrypt credentials in the PostgreSQL database. It must be the same between upgrades of AWX, so be sure to store it somewhere secure as it will need to be set in future AWX inventories. Make this something long and secure. |

# Infrastructure Management for Enterprises with AWX

You will, by now, have spotted that the previous file contains many secret values that lend themselves well to being stored in a Vault, but are in fact stored in the clear in the inventory file. It is assumed that you will delete the previous inventory once installation is complete, and **it is highly recommended you do so**!

Once the inventory is edited to your satisfaction, simply run the following command to install AWX:

```
sudo ansible-playbook -i inventory install.yml
```

That's all there is to it—when the playbook run finishes, the installation process is complete. If this is the first time you have installed AWX, you might need to give the system a few minutes to settle as the Docker containers start up and database schema is created. Once this completes, however, you will be able to log into AWX. Note here that the AWX web interface (and indeed the API) run unencrypted using HTTP on port 80. It is left up to the individual enterprise to configure SSL access to AWX—the easiest way to do this is to firewall off port 80 from the outside world, and put an SSL offloading setup in front of it. This could be a load balancer, reverse proxy, or even the venerable `stunnel` utility. For example, if we have installed AWX on CentOS 7, we could perform the following process:

1. First of all, let's install NGINX (note that this requires that the EPEL repository is installed and enabled for CentOS 7):

   ```
   sudo yum install nginx
   ```

2. Next, we're going to need an SSL certificate for NGINX to use. If you have one, copy the certificate and associated private key to the following locations:
   - Certificate: `/etc/pki/tls/certs/mastery.example.com.crt`
   - Private key: `/etc/pki/tls/private/mastery.example.com.key`

   If you don't have an SSL certificate, you can easily generate a self-signed one to complete this example using the following command:

   ```
   openssl req -x509 -nodes -newkey rsa:4096 -keyout
   /etc/pki/tls/private/mastery.example.com.key -out
   /etc/pki/tls/certs/mastery.example.com.crt -days 3650 -subj
   "/C=GB/CN=mastery.example.com"
   ```

3. Tailor the details to match your system—for example, `/CN=mastery.example.com` is the common name of the certificate, and should match the hostname of the AWX system.

4. Once your certificate is in place, create the /etc/nginx/conf.d/awx.conf file with the following contents:

```
server {
  listen 443 ssl;
  server_name mastery.example.com;

ssl on;
  ssl_certificate /etc/pki/tls/certs/mastery.example.com.crt;
  ssl_certificate_key
/etc/pki/tls/private/mastery.example.com.key;

location / {
  proxy_pass http://127.0.0.1:80;
  proxy_set_header Host $host;
  proxy_set_header X-Real-IP $remote_addr;
  proxy_set_header X-Forwarded-Proto $scheme;
  proxy_set_header X-Forwarded-For $proxy_add_x_forwarded_for;

  }
}
```

5. Now we will edit /etc/nginx/nginx.conf and change the lines telling it to listen on port 80 to another port that we are not using—one of the Docker containers created earlier will be listening on port 80 already, so the nginx service won't start if we don't reassign this. Here's an example:

```
server {
  listen 81 default_server;
  listen [::]:81 default_server;
```

6. Enable and start the service:

```
sudo systemctl enable nginx.service
sudo systemctl start nginx.service
```

7. Finally, we will open up port 443 on the local firewall to allow this traffic in:

```
sudo firewall-cmd --permanent --add-service=https
sudo firewall-cmd --reload
```

Now we have a fully configured AWX service, and users should be able to access it using SSL! As discussed, there are many ways to enable SSL encryption of the AWX service, and the previous code should be used as an example only.

When you first log into AWX, you will be presented with a dashboard screen and a menu bar down the left-hand side. It is through this menu bar that we will explore AWX and perform our first configuration work. Equally, it is worth noting that when AWX is first installed, some example content is populated to help you get up to speed quicker. Feel free to explore the demo content as the examples are different to those given in this book.

Let's get started on getting our first playbook integrated and running with AWX.

## Integrating AWX with your first playbook

There is a basic four-stage process involved in getting a playbook to run from AWX, and once this is understood, it paves the way for more advanced usage and fuller integration in an enterprise environment. In this part of the chapter, we will master these four stages in order to get to the stage where we can run our first simple playbook, and this will give us the building blocks to move forwards with AWX in confidence. The four stages are as follows:

1. Define a project.
2. Define an inventory.
3. Define credentials.
4. Define a template.

The first three stages can be performed in any order, but the template mentioned in the final stage pulls together the three previously-created facets, and so, it must be defined last. Also, note that there does not need to be a one-to-one relationship between these items—several templates can be created from one project, as is also the case for inventories and credentials.

Before we get started, we need a simple playbook for use in our examples as we go through this part of the chapter. First of all, on the AWX host, create a folder for the project—if you used the recommended path suggested earlier in the chapter, this will be `/var/lib/awx/projects`.

Every locally hosted project must have its own folder, so let's create one here:

```
sudo mkdir /var/lib/awx/projects/mastery
```

Now place the following example code into this folder as `example.yaml`:

```
---
- name: AWX example playbook
  hosts: all
  gather_facts: false

  tasks:
    - name: Create temporary directory
      file:
        path: /tmp/mastery
        state: directory

    - name: Create a file with example text
      lineinfile:
        path: /tmp/mastery/mastery.txt
        line: 'Created with Ansible Mastery!'
        create: yes
```

With this done, we can proceed to defining a project.

# Defining a project

A project, in AWX terms, is a simply a collection of Ansible playbooks grouped together. These collections of playbooks are often retrieved from a **Source Control Management** (**SCM**) system, and indeed, this is the recommended way to host Ansible playbooks in an enterprise. Using an SCM means that everyone is working from the same version of code, and all changes are tracked—all elements that are vital in an enterprise environment.

With regards to the grouping of playbooks, there is no right or wrong way to organize projects, so this is very much up to the teams involved. Put simply, one project links to one repository, and so where it makes sense for multiple playbooks to live in one repository, it would make sense for them to live in one project within AWX.

For the sake of simplicity, it is also possible to store Ansible playbooks locally. This is useful when testing or when starting out, and we will utilize this capability in our example here.

Logging into the AWX interface using the **admin** account, click on the **projects** link on the left-hand menu bar. Then click on the green + button near the top right of the window—this creates a new blank project for us.

For now, we not need to worry about all the fields (more on some of these later)—however, we now need to configure the following:

| Field Name | Value | Notes |
| --- | --- | --- |
| NAME | `Mastery Examples` | A unique name to distinguish the project from the others. |
| SCM TYPE | `Manual` | Refers to the source of the playbook code—note the other options available in the drop-down list. `Manual` refers to playbooks on the local disk. |
| PLAYBOOK DIRECTORY | `mastery` | This is the name of the directory we defined earlier in the chapter, and put our `example.yaml` file in. |

The end result should look something like this:

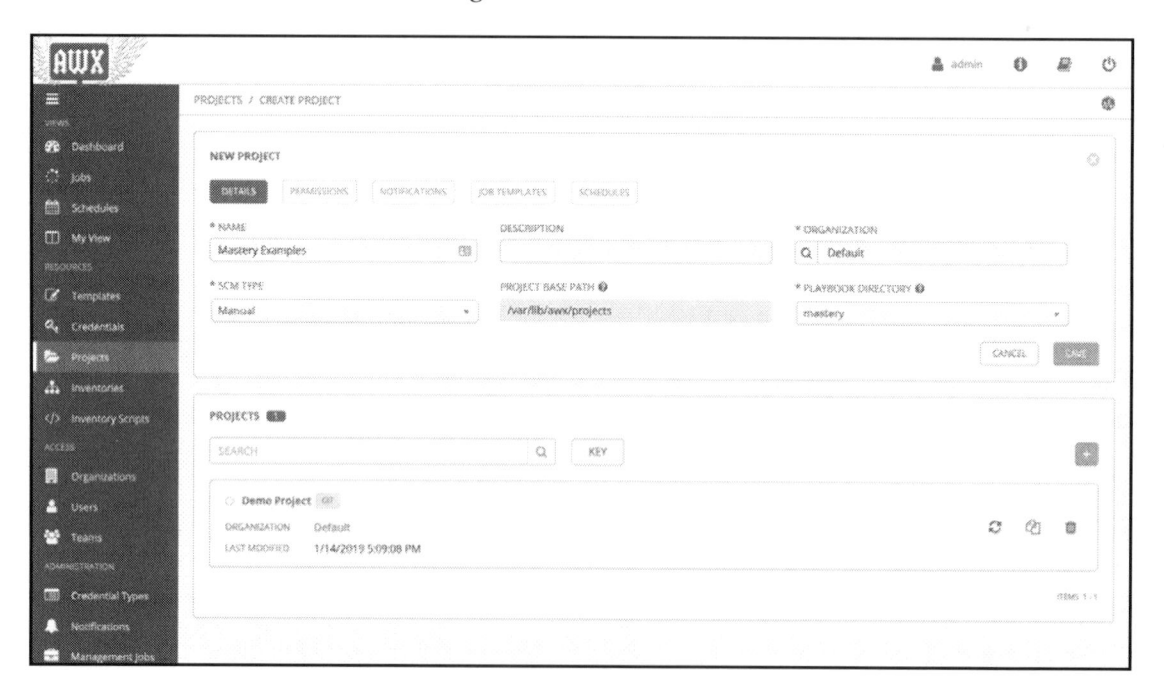

Click the green **SAVE** button to store your edits. That's it—you have defined your first Project in AWX! From here, we can define an inventory.

# Defining an inventory

Inventories in AWX work exactly the same as inventories that we worked with earlier on the command line. They can be static or dynamic, can consist of groups and/or individual hosts, and can have variables defined on a global per group or per host basis—we are now simply defining them through a user interface.

Click on the **Inventories** item on the left-hand menu bar. As with projects, we want to define something new, so click on the green + button near the top right of the window and a drop-down list will appear. Select **Inventory** from this list.

When the **NEW INVENTORY** definition screen appears, enter a name for the inventory (for example, `Mastery Demo`), and then click the green **SAVE** button.

> **TIP**: You must save your blank inventory before you can start defining hosts or groups.

When this is completed, you should have a screen that looks something like this:

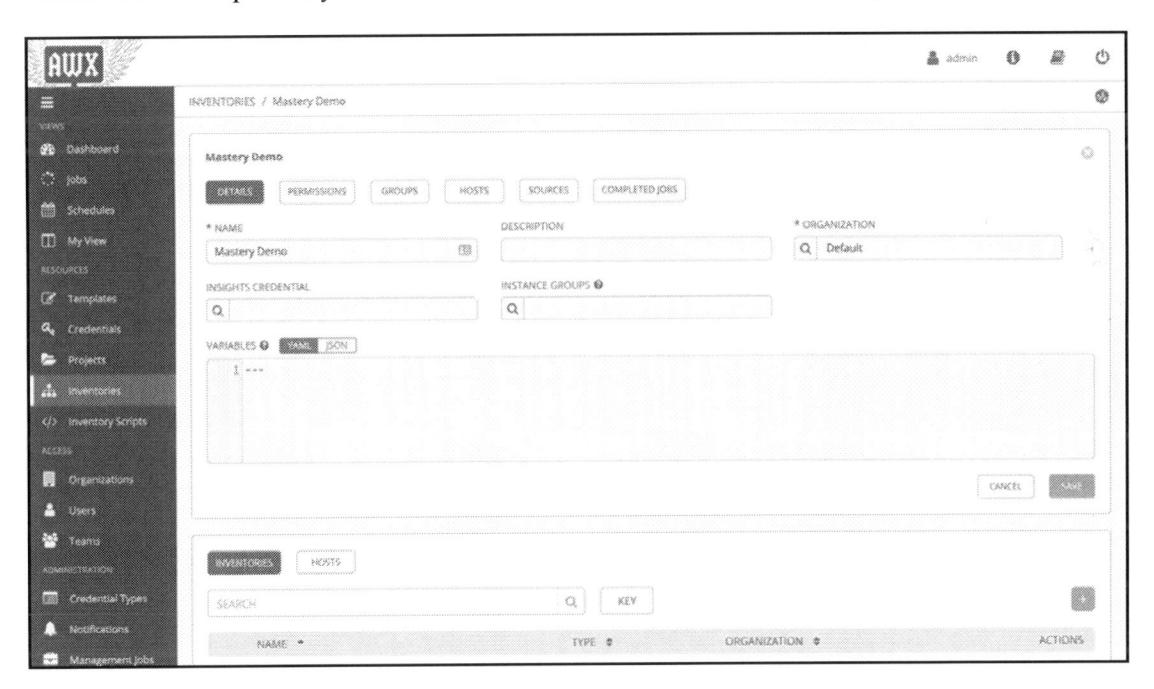

*Infrastructure Management for Enterprises with AWX*

Now, note the buttons along the top of the inventories pane—**DETAILS, PERMISSIONS, GROUPS, HOSTS, SOURCES,** and **COMPLETED JOBS**. You will find buttons like these on almost every pane in the AWX user interface and, indeed, we saw them when we defined our first project earlier (we just didn't need to use them at that stage). These work just like tabs, and clicking on each will load new contents into the pane for the appropriate configuration work to take place.

Keeping our example simple, we will define one host in a group to run our example playbook against. Click on the **GROUPS** tab button, and then click on the green + to add a new group. Give the group a name and click **SAVE**, as shown in the following screenshot:

Now click on the **HOSTS** tab button, and then click on the green + and select new host from the drop-down menu. Enter the IP address of your AWX host into the **HOST NAME** field and click **SAVE**—the end result should look something like this:

*Chapter 4*

[Screenshot of AWX Create Host interface]

> **TIP**: The **VARIABLES** box seen on most of the inventory screens expects variables to be defined in YAML or JSON format, and not the INI format we used on the command line. Where earlier we had defined variables such as `ansible_ssh_user=james`, we would now enter `ansible_ssh_user: james` if the YAML mode is selected.

Well done! You've just created your first inventory in AWX. If we were to create this inventory on the command line, it would look like this:

```
[Mastery Group]
192.168.81.149
```

It might be simple, but it paves the way for us to run our first playbook. Next, let's look at the concept of credentials in AWX.

# Defining credentials

One of the ways in which AWX lends itself to an enterprise is the secure storage of credentials. Ansible, given its nature and typical use cases, is often given the "keys to the kingdom" in the form of SSH keys or passwords that have root or other administrative level privileges. Even if encrypted in a Vault, the user running the playbook will have the encryption password and hence can obtain the credentials. Obviously, this may not be a desirable scenario, having many people with uncontrolled access to administrator credentials, but luckily for us, AWX solves this issue.

Let's take a simple example—suppose my test host, which we defined the inventory for previously, has a `root` password of `Mastery123!`. How do we store this securely?

First of all, navigate to the **Credentials** menu item, and then click the green + as we have done previously to create something new. Give the credential an appropriate name (for example, `Mastery Login`) and then click on the magnifying glass next to the **CREDENTIAL TYPE** field. You will see that there are many different credential types that AWX can store, and for a machine login, such as ours, we want to select the `Machine` type. Once the credential type is set, you will see that the screen changes and fields appropriate to creating a machine credential have appeared. We could define the login based on the SSH key and various other parameters, but in our simple example, we will simply set the **USERNAME** and **PASSWORD** to the appropriate values:

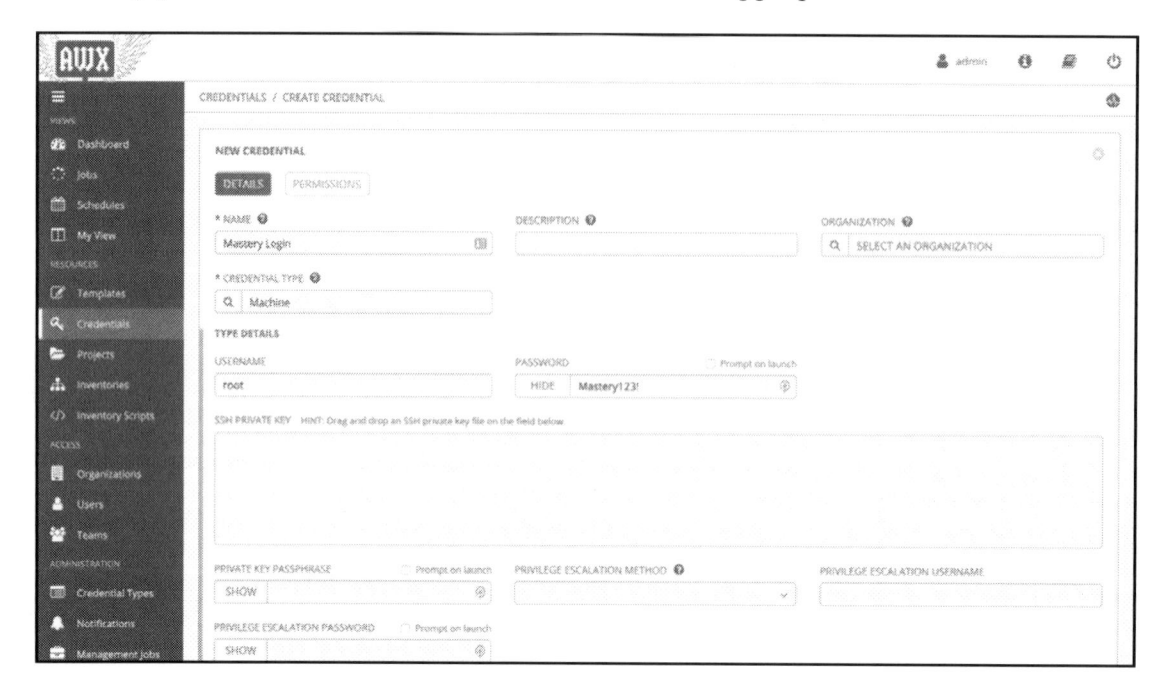

Now, **SAVE** the credential. As soon as it is saved, you will note that the password disappears and is replaced by the string `ENCRYPTED`. It is now impossible to retrieve the password (or SSH key, or other sensitive data) through the AWX user interface—you will notice that you can **REPLACE** the existing value, but cannot see it. The only way to get the credential would be to get both connectivity to the backend database, and the encryption key used at the time of installation. As discussed earlier, these should be secured elsewhere, and so, as long as AWX operators are not given root access to the AWX machine itself, the credentials remain secure and under control.

In this way, AWX has protected your sensitive access data in a manner not totally dissimilar to Ansible Vault (note that Ansible Vault remains a command-line tool and, although Vault data can be used in playbooks in AWX exactly as it can when Ansible is used on the command line, Vault creation and modification remains a command-line activity). Now, let's proceed to the final step necessary to run our first ever playbook from AWX—defining a template.

## Defining a template

A job template—to give it its full name—is a way of pulling together all the previously-created configuration items, along with any other required parameters, to run a given playbook against an inventory. Think of it as defining how you would run `ansible-playbook` if you were on the command line.

Let's dive right in and create our template by carrying out the following steps:

1. Click on **Templates** from the left-hand menu.
2. Click on the green + to create a new template.
3. Select **Job Template** from the drop-down list.
4. As a minimum to run our first job, you will need to define the following fields on the **NEW JOB TEMPLATE** screen:

| Field name | Values | Notes |
|---|---|---|
| NAME | `Mastery Template` | A unique name for the job template to identify it. |
| JOB TYPE | `Run` | The default here is `Run`, which is exactly what we want to do. We could also select **Check**, which runs the playbook using the defined parameters, without making any changes on the inventory hosts. |
| INVENTORY | `Mastery Demo` | Click on the magnifying glass icon in this field, and then select the inventory you created earlier in this process. |

| PROJECT | Mastery Examples | Click on the magnifying glass icon in this field and select the project we created earlier in this chapter, containing our example playbook. |
|---|---|---|
| PLAYBOOK | example.yaml | Once the **PROJECT** field is populated, the **PLAYBOOK** drop-down menu is automatically populated with a list of all files with the `*.yaml` or `*.yml` extension, which were found in the **PROJECT** source. Note that if your project was linked to an SCM, this list will be blank. |
| CREDENTIAL | Mastery Login | Click on the magnifying glass icon in this field and select the credential we created earlier. |

This should result in a screen that looks something like this:

With all the fields populated, as in the previous screenshot, click on the **SAVE** button. Congratulations! You are now ready to run your first playbook from AWX. To do so, navigate back to the list of **Templates** and click on the small rocket ship-icon to the right of our newly created template. Immediately upon doing so, you will see the job execute, and will see the output from `ansible-playbook` that we are familiar with from the command line, as shown in the following screenshot:

Chapter 4

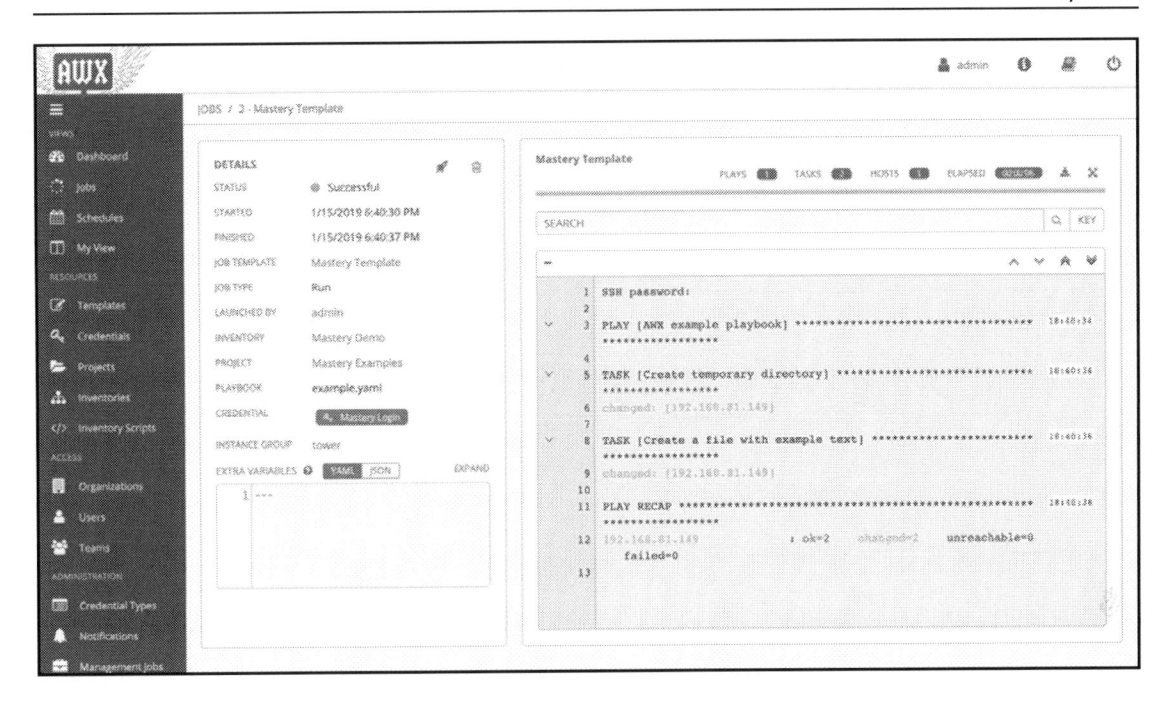

On the left-hand side of the **JOBS** screen, you can see the **DETAILS** pane, where all the fundamental parameters we defined earlier are listed, such as **PROJECT** and **JOB TEMPLATE**, along with useful information for auditing purposes, such as which user the job was **LAUNCHED BY**, and times that the job **STARTED** and **FINISHED**. On the right-hand side, you can see the raw output from `ansible-playbook`. You can access the **JOBS** screen any time by clicking on the **Jobs** menu item on the menu bar, and browsing all jobs that have been run—this is excellent for auditing the various activities that AWX has been orchestrating, especially in a large multi-user environment.

While there is much more that AWX is capable of, these fundamental stages are central to most of the tasks you will want to perform in AWX. Therefore, gaining an understanding of their usage and sequence is a good start to learning how to use AWX. In the next section, we will take a look at some of the more advanced things you can do with AWX.

## Going beyond the basics

We have now covered the basics necessary to run your first playbook from AWX, and indeed, the basics required for most Ansible automation from within this environment, although we can't possibly cover all the advanced features AWX has to offer in a single chapter. In this section, we will highlight a few of the more advanced facets to explore if you wish to learn more about AWX.

## Role-based access control (RBAC)

So far, we have only looked at using AWX from the perspective of the built-in `admin` user. Of course, one of AWX's features is RBAC, and this is achieved by the use of **users** and **teams**. A team is basically a group of users, and users can be a member of one or more teams.

Both users and teams can be created manually in the AWX user interface, or through integration with an external directory service, such as LDAP or Active Directory. In the case of directory integration, teams would most likely be mapped to groups within the directory.

The RBAC's within AWX are rich; for example, a given user can be given the **ADMIN** role within one team, and either **MEMBER** or **READ** roles in another.

User accounts themselves can be set up as **System Administrators**, **Normal Users**, or **System Auditors**.

In addition to this, as we stepped through the basic setup part of this chapter, you will have noticed the tab buttons on just about every page of the AWX user interface. Among these, there is almost always a tab called **PERMISSIONS**, which allows true fine-grained access control to be achieved.

For example, a given user of the **Normal User** type could be given the **ADMIN** role within their assigned **Team**. However, they can then be assigned the **READ** role on a given **Project**, which superseded the more general **ADMIN Team** role. So, when they log in, they can see the **Project** in question, but can't change it or execute any tasks; for example, an update from SCM.

> As a general rule of thumb, more specific privileges supersede less specific ones. So, those at a **Project** level will take precedence over those at a **Team** or **User** level. Note that, for items where no **Permission** is specified via either a **User** or their **Team**, that person will not even see that item when logged into the user interface. The only exception to these rules are **System Administrators**, who can see everything and perform any action. Assign this type to **User** accounts sparingly!

There is a great deal to explore when it comes to RBAC, and, once you get the hang of it, it is easy to create secure and tightly-locked-down deployments of AWX where everyone has just the right amount of access.

## Organizations

AWX contains a top-level configuration item called an **organization**. This is a collection of **inventories, projects, job templates**, and **teams** (which, in turn, are a grouping of **users**). Hence, if you have two distinct parts of an enterprise that have entirely different requirements but still require the use of AWX, they can share a single AWX instance without the need for overlapping configuration in the user interface by virtue of organizations.

While users of the system administrator type have access to all organizations, normal users will only see the organizations and associated facets, and they are a really powerful way of segregating access to the differing parts of an enterprise deployment of AWX.

By way of example, when we created our inventory earlier in the chapter, you will notice that we ignored the **ORGANIZATION** field (which was set to default—the only organization that exists on a new AWX install). If we were to create a new organization called Mastery, then anyone who was not a member of this organization would be unable to see this inventory, regardless of the permissions or privileges they have (the exception to this being the system administrator user type, which can see everything).

## Scheduling

Some AWX configuration items, such as projects (which may need to update from an SCM), or job templates (which perform a specific task), may need to be run on a regular basis. Having a powerful tool such as AWX, but then requiring operators to log in regularly to perform routine tasks, would be pointless, so AWX has built-in scheduling.

On the definition page for any **Project** or **Templates**, simply look for the **Schedules** tab button, and you then have a rich range of scheduling options available to you—the following screenshot shows an example of scheduling for the job template we created earlier:

Note the variety of options available to you for scheduling—we have scheduled this job to run every two days, and end after five runs. A detailed breakdown of the schedule is shown at the bottom of the screenshot, in order to help you ensure that it is fit for your needs.

# Auditing

One of the risks of running Ansible on the command line is that once a particular task has been run, its output is lost forever. It is, of course, possible to turn on logging for Ansible; but in an enterprise, this would need to be enforced, and this would be difficult with lots of operators having root access to a given Ansible machine, be it their own laptop or a server somewhere. Thankfully, as we saw in our earlier example, AWX stores not only the details of who ran what tasks and when, but also stores all the output from the `ansible-playbook` tasks. In this way, compliance and auditability are achieved for enterprises wishing to use Ansible.

Simply navigate to the **Jobs** menu item, and a list of all previously run jobs (that the user has permission to see) will be shown. It is even possible to repeat previously completed jobs directly from this screen simply by clicking on the rocket-ship icon next to the job in question. Note that this immediately launches the job with the same parameters it was launched with last time!

The following screenshot shows the job history for our demo AWX instance being used for this book:

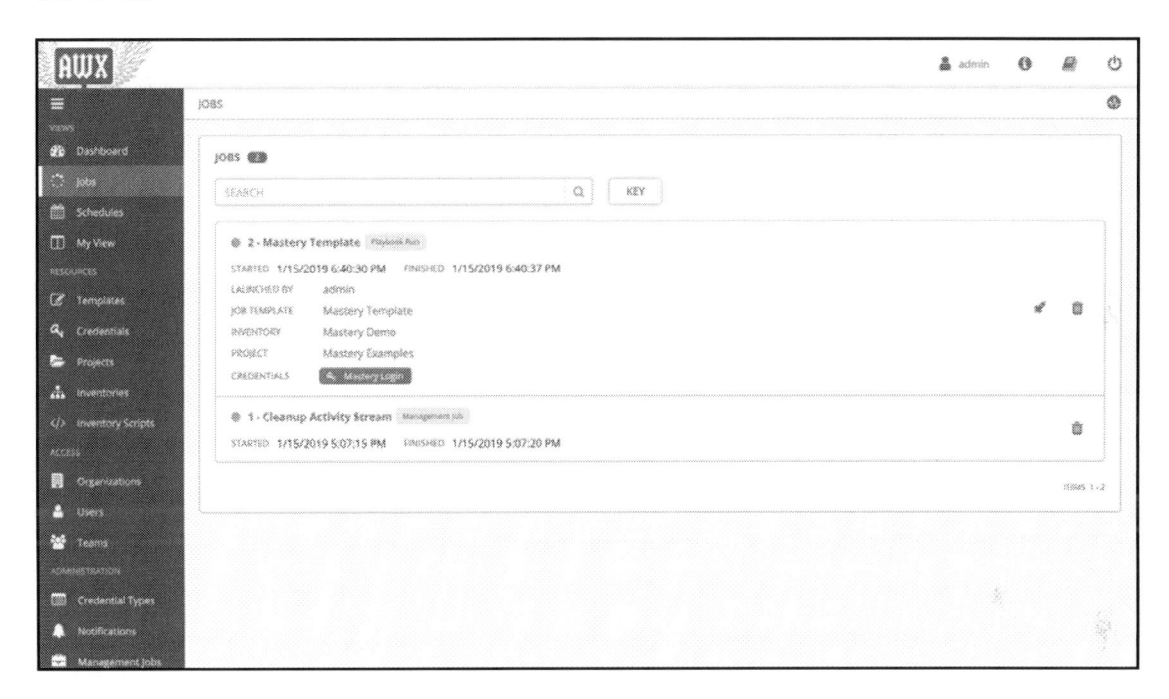

The previous screenshot shows an example of the jobs screen, taken from a recently-configured AWX instance built for this book. In the screenshot, you can clearly see the job that was run previously.

# Surveys

Sometimes, when launching a job template, it is not possible (or desirable) to define all information up front. While it is perfectly possible to define parameters using variables in the AWX user interface, this is not always desirable, especially if you don't wish to give a user the privileges to edit a job template, only to run it.

[ 111 ]

# Infrastructure Management for Enterprises with AWX

Surveys provide the answer to this, and on any job template you have created you will find a tab button at the top marked **ADD SURVEY**. A survey is essentially a questionnaire (hence the name!) defined by an administrator, where simple user input validation is performed, and then, once accepted, the entered values are stored in Ansible variables.

For example, if we wanted to capture the `http_port` variable value for a job template when it is run, we could create a survey as follows:

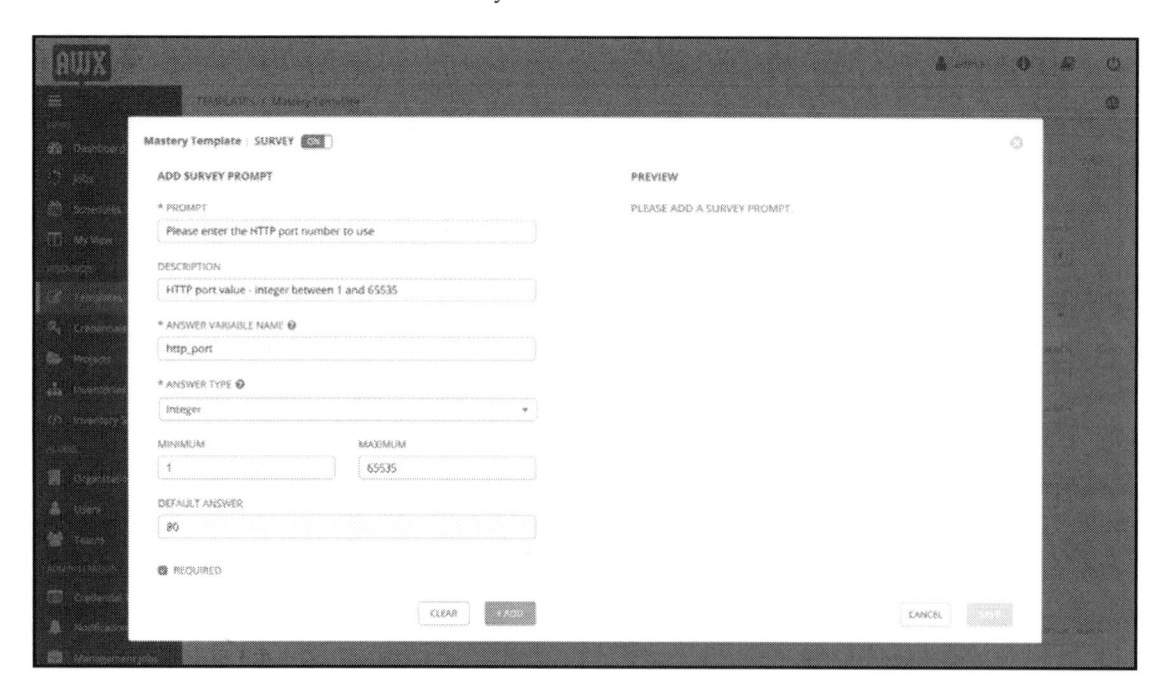

Now, when the playbook is run, the user is prompted to enter a value, and AWX ensures it is an integer in the specified range. A sensible default is also defined.

## Workflow templates

Playbook runs, especially from AWX, can be complex. For example, it might be desirable to update a project from SCM and any dynamic inventories first. We might then run a job template to roll out some updated code. If it fails, however, it would almost certainly be desirable to roll back any changes (or take other remedial action). When you click on our now familiar green + for adding a new template, you will see two options in the drop-down menu—job template (which we have already worked with), and workflow template.

Once all the required fields are filled in for the new workflow template and it is saved, you will be able to click on the **WORKFLOW VISUALIZER** tab button. This effectively builds up a simple flow, from left to right, of tasks for AWX to perform. For example, the following screenshot shows a workflow where, initially, our demo project is synchronized with its SCM.

If that step succeeds (denoted by the green link to the next block), the demo job template is run. If that in turn succeeds, then the mastery template is run. If any of the preceding steps fail, then the workflow stops there, though an **On Failure** action can be defined at any stage. Workflows, again, are an advanced discussion beyond the scope of this book, but their presence is worthy of note and further investigation. An example is shown in the following screenshot:

In this way, we can powerfully build up multi-step workflows, taking intelligent action after each stage, depending on whether it succeeded or not.

## Notifications

As you have stepped through the AWX user interface, you will have noticed that most screens have a tab button called **NOTIFICATIONS**. AWX has the ability to integrate with many popular communication platforms, such as Slack, IRC, Pagerduty, and even good old-fashioned email (this list is not exhaustive). Once the configuration for a given platform is defined through the user interface, **NOTIFICATIONS** can then be sent when specific events occur.

For example, the following screenshot shows our previously configured mastery template set up to email a given recipient list on the event that its execution fails. On success, no notification is given (though this can be turned on, of course!):

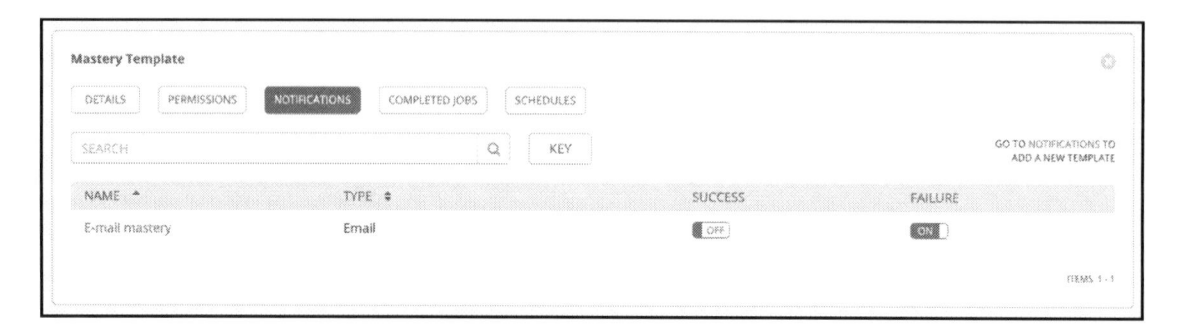

All **NOTIFICATIONS** defined in AWX appear in the **NOTIFICATIONS** tab—they do not have to be added once defined. It is simply up to the user to turn the **SUCCESS** and **FAILURE** notifications **ON** or **OFF** for each notification service.

# Summary

That concludes our whistle-stop tour of AWX. In this chapter, we showed that AWX is easy to install and configure once you know the core four-step process involved, and how to build on this with features such as surveys, notifications, and workflows.

You learned that AWX is easy to install (in fact, it installs with Ansible itself!), and how to add SSL encryption to it. You then built on this with an understanding of how the platform works, and how to go from a fresh install to building out projects, inventories, credentials, and templates to run Ansible jobs. There are many additional features that build on this, which were covered in the final part of this chapter in order to help you build a robust enterprise management system for Ansible.

From here, we will return to the Ansible language and look at the benefits of the Jinja2 templating system.

# Section 2: Writing and Troubleshooting Ansible Playbooks

In this section, you will gain a solid understanding of how to write robust, versatile playbooks, suitable for use in a wide variety of use cases and environments.

The following chapters are included in this section:

Chapter 5, *Unlocking the Power of Jinja2 Templates*

Chapter 6, *Controlling Task Conditions*

Chapter 7, *Composing Reusable Ansible Content with Roles*

Chapter 8, *Troubleshooting Ansible*

Chapter 9, *Extending Ansible*

# 5
# Unlocking the Power of Jinja2 Templates

Manipulating configuration files by hand is a tedious and error-prone task, and equally, performing pattern matching to make changes to existing files is risky, and ensuring that the patterns are reliable and accurate is a time-consuming task. Whether you are using Ansible to define configuration file content, to perform variable substitution in tasks, evaluate conditional statements, or beyond, templating comes into play with nearly every Ansible playbook. In fact, given the importance of this task, it could be said that templating is the lifeblood of Ansible.

The templating engine that was employed by Ansible is Jinja2, a modern and designer-friendly templating language for Python. Jinja2 deserves a book all of its own, but in this chapter, we will cover some of the more common usage patterns of Jinja2 templating in Ansible to get you started, and give you a taste for the power this can bring to your playbooks. In this chapter, we will cover the following topics:

- Control structures
- Data manipulation
- Comparisons

## Technical requirements

Check out the following video to see the Code in Action:

```
http://bit.ly/2TOvvlo
```

# Control structures

In Jinja2, a control structure refers to statements in a template that control the flow of the engine parsing the template. These structures include, but are not limited to, conditionals, loops, and macros. Within Jinja2 (assuming the defaults are in use), a control structure will appear inside blocks of `{% ... %}`. These opening and closing blocks alert the Jinja2 parser that a control statement is provided instead of a normal string or variable name.

## Conditionals

A conditional within a template creates a decision path. The engine will consider the conditional and choose from two or more potential blocks of code. There is always a minimum of two: a path if the conditional is met (evaluated as `true`), and either an explicitly defined else path if the conditional is not met (evaluated as `false`), or alternatively, an implied `else` path consisting of an empty block.

The statement for conditionals is the `if` statement. This statement works much the same as it does in Python. An `if` statement can be combined with one or more optional `elif` with an optional final `else`, and unlike Python, requires an explicit `endif`. The following example shows a config file template snippet combining both regular variable replacement and an `if else` structure:

```
setting = {{ setting }}
{% if feature.enabled %}
feature = True
{% else %}
feature = False
{% endif %}
another_setting = {{ another_setting }}
```

In this example, the `feature.enabled` variable is checked to see if it exists, and is not set to `False`. If this is `True`, then the text `feature = True` is used; otherwise, the text `feature = False` is used. Outside of this control block, the parser does the normal variable substitution for the variables inside the curly braces. Multiple paths can be defined by using an `elif` statement, which presents the parser with another test to perform should the previous tests equate to `False`.

To demonstrate rendering the template, we'll save the example template as `demo.j2` and then make a playbook named `template-demo.yaml` that defines the variables in use, and then uses a template lookup as part of a pause task to display the rendered template on the screen:

```
---
- name: demo the template
  hosts: localhost
  gather_facts: false
  vars:
    setting: a_val
    feature:
      enabled: true
    another_setting: b_val
  tasks:
    - name: pause with render
      pause:
        prompt: "{{ lookup('template', 'demo.j2') }}"
```

Executing this playbook will show the rendered template on screen while waiting for input. We can simply press *Enter* to complete the playbook:

```
~/src/mastery> ansible-playbook -i mastery-hosts template-demo.yaml

PLAY [demo the template] ************************************************

TASK [pause with render] ************************************************
[pause with render]
setting = a_val

feature = True

another_setting = b_val
:
ok: [localhost]

PLAY RECAP **************************************************************
localhost                  : ok=1    changed=0    unreachable=0    failed=0

~/src/mastery>
```

*Unlocking the Power of Jinja2 Templates*

If we were to change the value of `feature.enabled` to `False`, the output would be slightly different, as shown in the following screenshot:

```
~/src/mastery> ansible-playbook -i mastery-hosts template-demo.yaml

PLAY [demo the template] ****************************************************

TASK [pause with render] ****************************************************
[pause with render]
setting = a_val

feature = False

another_setting = b_val
:
ok: [localhost]

PLAY RECAP ******************************************************************
localhost                  : ok=1    changed=0    unreachable=0    failed=0

~/src/mastery>
```

As we can see from these simple tests, Jinja2 provides a very simple, yet powerful way of defining data through conditionals in a template.

## Inline conditionals

`if` statements can be used inside of inline expressions. This can be useful in some scenarios where additional new lines are not desired. Let's construct a scenario where we need to define an API as either `cinder` or `cinderv2`, as shown in the following code:

```
API = cinder{{ 'v2' if api.v2 else '' }}
```

This example assumes that `api.v2` is defined as Boolean `True` or `False`. Inline `if` expressions follow the syntax of `<do something> if <conditional is true> else <do something else>`. In an inline `if` expression, there is an implied `else`; however, that implied `else` is meant to be evaluated as an undefined object, which will normally create an error. We protect against this by defining an explicit `else`, which renders a zero-length string.

Let's modify our playbook to demonstrate an inline conditional. This time, we'll use the debug module to render the simple template, as follows:

```
---
- name: demo the template
  hosts: localhost
  gather_facts: false
  vars:
    api:
      v2: true
  tasks:
    - name: pause with render
      debug:
        msg: "API = cinder{{ 'v2' if api.v2 else '' }}"
```

Execution of the playbook will show the following template being rendered:

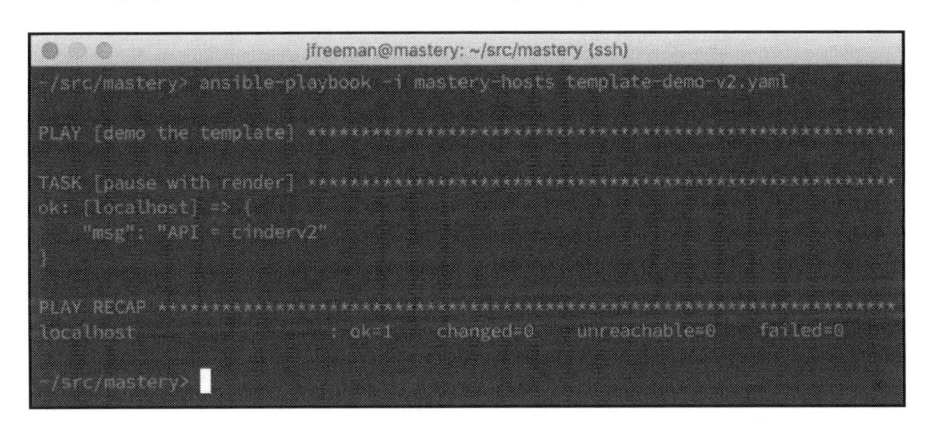

```
~/src/mastery> ansible-playbook -i mastery-hosts template-demo-v2.yaml

PLAY [demo the template] ************************************************

TASK [pause with render] ************************************************
ok: [localhost] => {
    "msg": "API = cinderv2"
}

PLAY RECAP **************************************************************
localhost                  : ok=1    changed=0    unreachable=0    failed=0

~/src/mastery>
```

Changing the value of `api.v2` to `false` leads to a different result, as shown in the following screenshot:

```
~/src/mastery> ansible-playbook -i mastery-hosts template-demo-v2.yaml

PLAY [demo the template] ************************************************

TASK [pause with render] ************************************************
ok: [localhost] => {
    "msg": "API = cinder"
}

PLAY RECAP **************************************************************
localhost                  : ok=1    changed=0    unreachable=0    failed=0

~/src/mastery>
```

In this way, we can create very concise, but powerful code that defines values based on an Ansible variable, as we have seen here.

## Loops

A loop allows you to build dynamically created sections in template files, and is useful when you know you need to operate on an unknown number of items in the same way. To start a loop control structure, the `for` statement is used. Let's look at a simple way to loop over a list of directories where a fictional service might find data:

```
# data dirs
{% for dir in data_dirs -%}
data_dir = {{ dir }}
{% endfor -%}
```

> **TIP**: By default, in Ansible 2.7.5, the `{% %}` blocks print an empty line when the template is rendered. This may not be desirable in our output, and luckily, we can trim this by ending the block with `-%}` instead. See the Jinja2 documentation at http://jinja.pocoo.org/docs/2.10/templates/#whitespace-control for more details.

In this example, we will get one `data_dir =` line per item within the `data_dirs` variable, assuming that `data_dirs` is a list with at least one item in it. If the variable is not a list (or other iterable type) or is not defined, an error will be generated. If the variable is an iterable type, but is empty, then no lines will be generated. Jinja2 allows for the reacting to this scenario, and also allows substituting in a line when no items are found in the variable via an `else` statement. In the following example, assume that `data_dirs` is an empty list:

```
# data dirs
{% for dir in data_dirs -%}
data_dir = {{ dir }}
{% else -%}
# no data dirs found
{% endfor -%}
```

We can test this by modifying our playbook and template file again. We'll update `demo.j2` with the earlier template content and make use of a prompt in our playbook again:

```
---
- name: demo the template
  hosts: localhost
  gather_facts: false
  vars:
    data_dirs: []
```

[ 124 ]

```
tasks:
  - name: pause with render
    pause:
      prompt: "{{ lookup('template', 'demo-for.j2') }}"
```

Running our playbook will show the following result:

```
~/src/mastery> ansible-playbook -i mastery-hosts template-demo-for.yaml

PLAY [demo the template] ****************************************************

TASK [pause with render] ****************************************************
[pause with render]
# data dirs
# no data dirs found
:
ok: [localhost]

PLAY RECAP ******************************************************************
localhost                  : ok=1    changed=0    unreachable=0    failed=0

~/src/mastery>
```

We can see that the `else` statement in the `for` loop handled the empty `data_dirs` list gracefully, exactly as we would wish for in a playbook run.

## Filtering loop items

Loops can be combined with conditionals, as well. Within the loop structure, an `if` statement can be used to check a condition using the current loop item as part of the conditional. Let's extend our example and prevent the user of this template from accidentally using / as a `data_dir` (actions performed on the root directory of a filesystem can be dangerous, especially if they're performed recursively):

```
# data dirs
{% for dir in data_dirs -%}
{% if dir != "/" -%}
data_dir = {{ dir }}
{% endif -%}
{% else -%}
# no data dirs found
{% endfor -%}
```

The preceding example successfully filters out any `data_dirs` item that is /, but takes more typing than should be necessary. Jinja2 provides a convenience that allows you to filter loop items easily as part of the `for` statement. Let's repeat the previous example using this convenience:

```
# data dirs
{% for dir in data_dirs if dir != "/" -%}
data_dir = {{ dir }}
{% else -%}
# no data dirs found
{% endfor -%}
```

Not only does this structure require less typing, but it also correctly counts the loops, which we'll learn about in the next section.

## Loop indexing

Loop counting is provided for free, yielding an index of the current iteration of the loop. As variables, this can be accessed in a few different ways. The following table outlines the ways they can be referenced:

| Variable | Description |
| --- | --- |
| `loop.index` | The current iteration of the loop (1 indexed) |
| `loop.index0` | The current iteration of the loop (0 indexed) |
| `loop.revindex` | The number of iterations until the end of the loop (1 indexed) |
| `loop.revindex0` | The number of iterations until the end of the loop (0 indexed) |
| `loop.first` | Boolean `True` if the first iteration |
| `loop.last` | Boolean `True` if the last iteration |
| `loop.length` | The number of items in the sequence |

Having information related to the position within the loop can help with logic around what content to render. Considering our previous examples, instead of rendering multiple lines of `data_dir` to express each data directory, we could instead provide a single line with comma-separated values. Without having access to loop iteration data, this would be difficult, but by using this data, it can be fairly easy. For the sake of simplicity, this example assumes a trailing comma after the last item is allowed, and that white space (new lines) between items is also allowed:

```
# data dirs
{% for dir in data_dirs if dir != "/" -%}
{% if loop.first -%}
data_dir = {{ dir }},
```

```
    {% else -%}
    {{ dir }},
    {% endif -%}
{% else -%}
# no data dirs found
{% endfor -%}
```

The preceding example made use of the `loop.first` variable to determine whether it needed to render the `data_dir =` part, or if it just needed to render the appropriately spaced padded directory. By using a filter in the `for` statement, we get a correct value for `loop.first`, even if the first item in `data_dirs` is the undesired `/`. To test this, we'll once again modify `demo-for.j2` with the updated template and modify `template-demo-for.yaml` to define some `data_dirs`, including one of `/`, which should be filtered out:

```
---
- name: demo the template
  hosts: localhost
  gather_facts: false
  vars:
    data_dirs: ['/', '/foo', '/bar']
  tasks:
    - name: pause with render
      pause:
        prompt: "{{ lookup('template', 'demo-for.j2') }}"
```

Now, we can execute the playbook and see our rendered content, as follows:

```
~/src/mastery> ansible-playbook -i mastery-hosts template-demo-for.yaml

PLAY [demo the template] ****************************************************

TASK [pause with render] ****************************************************
[pause with render]
# data dirs
data_dir = /foo,
/bar,
:
ok: [localhost]

PLAY RECAP ******************************************************************
localhost                  : ok=1    changed=0    unreachable=0    failed=0

~/src/mastery>
```

If in the preceding example trailing commas were not allowed, we could utilize inline `if` statements to determine whether we're done with the loop and render commas correctly, as shown in the following example:

```
# data dirs.
{% for dir in data_dirs if dir != "/" -%}
{% if loop.first -%}
data_dir = {{ dir }}{{ ',' if not loop.last else '' }}
{% else -%}
          {{ dir }}{{ ',' if not loop.last else '' }}
{% endif -%}
{% else -%}
# no data dirs found
{% endfor -%}
```

Using inline `if` statements allows us to construct a template that will only render a comma if there are more items in the loop that passed our initial filter. Once more, we'll update `demo-for.j2` with the earlier content and execute the playbook:

```
~/src/mastery> ansible-playbook -i mastery-hosts template-demo-for.yaml

PLAY [demo the template] ****************************************************

TASK [pause with render] ****************************************************
[pause with render]
# data dirs.
data_dir = /foo,
          /bar
:
ok: [localhost]

PLAY RECAP ******************************************************************
localhost                  : ok=1    changed=0    unreachable=0    failed=0

~/src/mastery>
```

The output is much the same as before, except this time, our template evaluates whether to place a comma after each value of `dir` in the loop using the inline `if`, removing the stray comma at the end of the final value.

# Macros

The astute reader will have noticed that, in the previous example, we had some repeated code. Repeating code is the enemy of any developer, and thankfully, Jinja2 has a way to help! A macro is like a function in a regular programming language; it's a way to define a reusable idiom. A macro is defined inside a `{% macro ... %}` ... `{% endmacro %}` block and has a name, and can take zero or more arguments. Code within a macro does not inherit the namespace of the block calling the macro, so all arguments must be explicitly passed in. Macros are called within curly brace blocks by name, and with zero or more arguments passed in via parentheses. Let's create a simple macro named `comma` to take the place of our repeating code:

```
{% macro comma(loop) -%}
{{ ',' if not loop.last else '' }}
{%- endmacro -%}
# data dirs.
{% for dir in data_dirs if dir != "/" -%}
{% if loop.first -%}
data_dir = {{ dir }}{{ comma(loop) }}
{% else -%}
          {{ dir }}{{ comma(loop) }}
{% endif -%}
{% else -%}
# no data dirs found
{% endfor -%}
```

Calling comma and passing it in the loop object allows the macro to examine the loop and decide whether a comma should be omitted or not.

## Macro variables

Macros have access to any positional or keyword argument passed along when calling the macro. Positional arguments are arguments that are assigned to variables, based on the order they are provided, while keyword arguments are unordered, and explicitly assign data to variable names. Keyword arguments can also have a default value if they aren't defined when the macro is called. Three additional special variables are available:

- varargs
- kwargs
- caller

*Unlocking the Power of Jinja2 Templates*

The `varargs` variable is a holding place for additional unexpected positional arguments that are passed along to the macro. These positional argument values will make up the `varargs` list.

The `kwargs` variable is the same as `varargs`; however, instead of holding extra positional argument values, it will hold a hash of extra keyword arguments and their associated values.

The `caller` variable can be used to call back to a higher level macro that may have called this macro (yes, macros can call other macros).

In addition to these three special variables, there are a number of variables that expose internal details regarding the macro itself. These are a bit complicated, but we'll walk through their usage one by one. First, let's take a look at a short description of each variable:

- `name`: The name of the macro itself
- `arguments`: A tuple of the names of the arguments the macro accepts
- `defaults`: A tuple of the default values
- `catch_kwargs`: A Boolean that will be defined as `true` if the macro accesses (and thus accepts) the `kwargs` variable
- `catch_varargs`: A Boolean that will be defined as `true` if the macro accesses (and thus accepts) the `varargs` variable
- `caller`: A Boolean that will be defined as `true` if the macro accesses the `caller` variable (and thus may be called from another macro)

Similar to a class in Python, these variables need to be referenced via the name of the macro itself. Attempting to access these macros without prepending the name will result in undefined variables. Now, let's walk through and demonstrate the usage of each of them.

## name

The `name` variable is actually very simple. It just provides a way to access the name of the macro as a variable, perhaps for further manipulation or usage. The following template includes a macro that references the name of the macro to render it in the output:

```
{% macro test() -%}
{{ test.name }}
{%- endmacro -%}
{{ test() }}
```

Let's say we were to create demo-macro.j2 with this template and the following template-demo-macro.yaml playbook:

```
---
- name: demo the template
  hosts: localhost
  gather_facts: false
  vars:
    data_dirs: ['/', '/foo', '/bar']
  tasks:
    - name: pause with render
      pause:
        prompt: "{{ lookup('template', 'demo-macro.j2') }}"
```

We would get the following output:

```
~/src/mastery> ansible-playbook -i mastery-hosts template-demo-macro.yaml

PLAY [demo the template] ****************************************************

TASK [pause with render] ****************************************************
[pause with render]
test
:
ok: [localhost]

PLAY RECAP ******************************************************************
localhost                  : ok=1    changed=0    unreachable=0    failed=0

~/src/mastery>
```

As we see from this test run, our template simply rendered with the macro name and nothing else, just as expected.

## arguments

The arguments variable is a tuple of the arguments the macro accepts. These are the explicitly defined arguments, not the special kwargs or varargs. Our previous example would have rendered an empty tuple (), so let's modify it to get something else:

```
{% macro test(var_a='a string') -%}
{{ test.arguments }}
{%- endmacro -%}
{{ test() }}
```

[ 131 ]

Rendering this template will result in the following output:

```
~/src/mastery> ansible-playbook -i mastery-hosts template-demo-macro.yaml

PLAY [demo the template] ************************************************

TASK [pause with render] ************************************************
[pause with render]
('var_a',)
:
ok: [localhost]

PLAY RECAP **************************************************************
localhost                  : ok=1    changed=0    unreachable=0    failed=0

~/src/mastery>
```

In this example, we can clearly see that our template rendered with the name of the arguments that the macro accepts (and not their values).

## defaults

The `defaults` variable is a tuple of the default values for any keyword arguments the macro explicitly accepts. Let's change our macro to display the default values as well as the arguments:

```
{% macro test(var_a='a string') -%}
{{ test.arguments }}
{{ test.defaults }}
{%- endmacro -%}
{{ test() }}
```

Rendering this version of the template will result in the following output:

```
~/src/mastery> ansible-playbook -i mastery-hosts template-demo-macro.yaml

PLAY [demo the template] ************************************************

TASK [pause with render] ************************************************
[pause with render]
('var_a',)
('a string',)
:
ok: [localhost]

PLAY RECAP **************************************************************
localhost                  : ok=1    changed=0    unreachable=0    failed=0

~/src/mastery>
```

Here, we can see that the template rendered with both the names, and this time, the default values of the arguments were accepted by the macro.

## catch_kwargs

This variable is only defined if the macro itself accesses the `kwargs` variable to catch any extra keyword arguments that might have been passed along. Without accessing the `kwargs` variable, any extra keyword arguments in a call to the macro will result in an error when rendering the template. Likewise, accessing `catch_kwargs` without also accessing `kwargs` will result in an undefined error. Let's modify our example template again so that we can pass along extra `kwargs`:

```
{% macro test() -%}
{{ kwargs }}
{{ test.catch_kwargs }}
{%- endmacro -%}
{{ test(unexpected='surprise') }}
```

The rendered version of this template will be as follows:

```
jfreeman@mastery: ~/src/mastery (ssh)
~/src/mastery> ansible-playbook -i mastery-hosts template-demo-macro.yaml

PLAY [demo the template] ************************************************

TASK [pause with render] ************************************************
[pause with render]
{'unexpected': 'surprise'}
True
:
ok: [localhost]

PLAY RECAP **************************************************************
localhost                  : ok=1    changed=0    unreachable=0    failed=0

~/src/mastery>
```

As we can see from this output, the template does not error when an unexpected variable is passed to it, and instead enabled us to access the unexpected value(s) that were passed.

# Unlocking the Power of Jinja2 Templates

## catch_varargs

Much like `catch_kwargs`, this variable exists if the macro accesses the `varargs` variable. Modifying our example once more, we can see this in action:

```
{% macro test() -%}
{{ varargs }}
{{ test.catch_varargs }}
{%- endmacro -%}
{{ test('surprise') }}
```

The template's rendered result will be as follows:

```
~/src/mastery> ansible-playbook -i mastery-hosts template-demo-macro.yaml

PLAY [demo the template] ******************************************************

TASK [pause with render] ******************************************************
[pause with render]
('surprise',)
True
:
ok: [localhost]

PLAY RECAP ********************************************************************
localhost                  : ok=1    changed=0    unreachable=0    failed=0

~/src/mastery>
```

Again, we can see that we were able to catch and render the unexpected value that was passed to the macro, rather than returning an error on render, as would have happened if we hadn't used `catch_varargs`.

## caller

The `caller` variable takes a bit more explaining. A macro can call out to another macro. This can be useful if the same chunk of the template will be used multiple times, but part of the inside changes more than what could easily be passed as a macro parameter. The `caller` variable isn't exactly a variable; it's more of a reference back to the call to get the contents of that calling macro.

Let's update our template to demonstrate its usage:

```
{% macro test() -%}
The text from the caller follows: {{ caller() }}
{%- endmacro -%}
{% call test() -%} This is text inside the call {% endcall -%}
```

The rendered result will be as follows:

```
~/src/mastery> ansible-playbook -i mastery-hosts template-demo-macro.yaml

PLAY [demo the template] ****************************************************

TASK [pause with render] ****************************************************
[pause with render]
The text from the caller follows:
This is text inside the call
:
ok: [localhost]

PLAY RECAP ******************************************************************
localhost                  : ok=1    changed=0    unreachable=0    failed=0

~/src/mastery>
```

A call to a macro can still pass arguments to that macro; any combination of arguments or keyword arguments can be passed. If the macro utilizes varargs or kwargs, then extras of those can be passed along as well. Additionally, a macro can pass arguments back to the caller too! To demonstrate this, let's create a larger example. This time, our example will generate a file that's suitable for an Ansible inventory:

```
{% macro test(group, hosts) -%}
[{{ group }}]
{% for host in hosts -%}
{{ host }} {{ caller(host) }}
{%- endfor -%}
{%- endmacro -%}
{% call(host) test('web', ['host1', 'host2', 'host3']) -%}
ssh_host_name={{ host }}.example.name ansible_sudo=true
{% endcall -%}
{% call(host) test('db', ['db1', 'db2']) %}
ssh_host_name={{ host }}.example.name
{% endcall -%}
```

Once rendered, the result will be as follows:

```
~/src/mastery> ansible-playbook -i mastery-hosts template-demo-macro.yaml

PLAY [demo the template] ************************************************

TASK [pause with render] ************************************************
[pause with render]
[web]
host1 ssh_host_name=host1.example.name ansible_sudo=true
host2 ssh_host_name=host2.example.name ansible_sudo=true
host3 ssh_host_name=host3.example.name ansible_sudo=true
[db]
db1
ssh_host_name=db1.example.name
db2
ssh_host_name=db2.example.name
:
ok: [localhost]

PLAY RECAP **************************************************************
localhost                  : ok=1    changed=0    unreachable=0    failed=0

~/src/mastery>
```

We called the `test` macro twice, once per group we wanted to define. Each group had a subtly different set of `host` variables to apply, and those were defined in the call itself. We saved typing by having the macro call back to the caller, passing along the `host` from the current loop.

Control blocks provide programming power inside of templates, allowing template authors to make their templates efficient. The efficiency isn't necessarily in the initial draft of the template; instead, the efficiency really comes into play when a small change to a repeating value is needed.

# Data manipulation

While control structures influence the flow of template processing, another tool exists to modify the contents of a variable. This tool is called a filter. Filters are the same as small functions, or methods, that can be run on the variable. Some filters operate without arguments, some take optional arguments, and some require arguments. Filters can be chained together as well, where the result of one filter action is fed into the next filter and the next. Jinja2 comes with many built-in filters, and Ansible extends these with many custom filters that are available to you when using Jinja2 within templates, tasks, or any other place Ansible allows templating.

# Syntax

A filter is applied to a variable by way of the pipe symbol |, followed by the name of the filter, and then any arguments for the filter inside parentheses. There can be a space between the variable name and the pipe symbol, as well as a space between the pipe symbol and the filter name. For example, if we wanted to apply the lower filter (which makes all the characters lowercase) to the my_word variable, we would use the following syntax:

```
{{ my_word | lower }}
```

Because the lower filter does not take any arguments, it is not necessary to attach an empty parentheses set to it. If we use a different filter that requires arguments, this all changes. Let's use the replace filter, which allows us to replace all occurrences of a substring with another substring. In this example, we want to replace all occurrences of the substring no with yes in the answers variable:

```
{{ answers | replace('no', 'yes') }}
```

Applying multiple filters is accomplished by simply adding more pipe symbols and more filter names. Let's combine both replace and lower to demonstrate the syntax:

```
{{ answers | replace('no', 'yes') | lower }}
```

We can easily demonstrate this with a simple play that uses the debug command to render the line:

```
---
- name: demo the template
  hosts: localhost
  gather_facts: false
  vars:
```

```
    answers: "no so YES no"
tasks:
  - name: debug the template
    debug:
      msg: "{{ answers | replace('no', 'yes') | lower }}"
```

Now, we can execute the playbook and provide a value for answers at runtime, as shown in the following code:

```
~/src/mastery> ansible-playbook -i mastery-hosts template-demo-filters.yaml

PLAY [demo the template] ************************************************

TASK [debug the template] ***********************************************
ok: [localhost] => {
    "msg": "yes so yes yes"
}

PLAY RECAP **************************************************************
localhost                  : ok=1    changed=0    unreachable=0    failed=0

~/src/mastery>
```

As we can see here, our variable has had all instances of the word no replaced with yes, and the letters are now all lower case.

## Useful built-in filters

A full list of the filters that are built into Jinja2 can be found in the Jinja2 documentation. At the time of writing this book, there are over 45 built-in filters, which is too many to describe here. To get you started, however, we'll take a look at some of the more commonly used filters.

> **TIP**: If you want to look at the list of all available filters, the Jinja2 documentation for the current version (as available at the time of writing) may be found here: `http://jinja.pocoo.org/docs/2.10/templates/#list-of-builtin-filters`.

## default

The `default` filter is a way to provide a default value for an otherwise undefined variable, which will prevent Ansible from generating an error. It is shorthand for a complex `if` statement, checking if a variable is defined before trying to use it with an `else` clause to provide a different value. Let's look at two examples that render the same thing. One uses the `if/else` structure, while the other uses the `default` filter:

```
{% if some_variable is defined -%}
{{ some_variable }}
{% else -%}
default_value
{% endif -%}

{{ some_variable | default('default_value') }}
```

The rendered result of each of these examples is the same; however, the example using the `default` filter is much quicker to write and easier to read.

While `default` is very useful, proceed with caution if you are using the same variable in multiple locations. Changing a default value can become a hassle, and it may be more efficient to define the variable with a default at the play or role level.

## count

The `count` filter will return the length of a sequence or hash. In fact, `length` is an alias of `count` to accomplish the same thing. This filter can be useful for performing any sort of math around the size of a set of hosts, or any other case where the count of some set needs to be known. Let's create an example where we set a `max_threads` configuration entry to match the count of hosts in the play:

```
max_threads: {{ play_hosts | count }}
```

This provides us with a nice, concise way of getting the number of hosts contained within the `play_hosts` variable, and assigning the answer to the `max_threads` variable.

## random

The `random` filter is used to make a random selection from a sequence. Let's use this filter to delegate a task to a random selection from the `db_servers` group:

```
name: backup the database
  shell: mysqldump -u root nova > /data/nova.backup.sql
```

*Unlocking the Power of Jinja2 Templates*

```
    delegate_to: "{{ groups['db_servers'] | random }}"
    run_once: true
```

Here, we can easily delegate this task to a single member of the `db_servers` group, picked at random using our filter.

## round

The `round` filter exists to round a number. This can be useful if you need to perform floating-point math, and then turn the result into a rounded integer. The `round` filter takes optional arguments to define a precision (default of 0) and a rounding method. The possible rounding methods are common (rounds up or down, and the default), `ceil` (always round up), and `floor` (always round down). In this example, we'll chain two filters together to commonly round a math result to zero precision, and then turn that into an integer:

```
{{ math_result | round | int }}
```

Therefore, if the `math_result` variable was set to `3.4`, the output of the previous filter chain would be `3`.

# Useful Ansible provided custom filters

While there are many filters provided with Jinja2, Ansible includes some additional filters that playbook authors may find particularly useful. Again, there are more than we can go into in this book, but we'll outline a few key ones here.

> **TIP**: These custom filters in Ansible change often between releases, and are worth reviewing, especially if you make heavy use of them. A full list of the custom Ansible filters is available here: `https://docs.ansible.com/ansible/latest/user_guide/playbooks_filters.html`.

## Filters related to task status

Ansible tracks task data for each task. This data is used to determine if a task has failed, resulted in a change, or was skipped altogether. Playbook authors can register the results of a task, and in previous versions of playbooks, would have used filters to check the tasks' status. This has been deprecated; however, it deserves a mention here because, while the previous method of using these filters will still work in Ansible 2.7, support will be removed completely in 2.9, and so it is important to transition over now.

Previously, you would have used a conditional with a filter like this:

```
when: derp | success
```

This should now be written as follows:

```
when: derp is success
```

Let's see this in action in an Ansible 2.9 compliant playbook in the following code:

```
---
- name: demo the filters
  hosts: localhost
  gather_facts: false
  tasks:
    - name: fail a task
      debug:
        msg: "I am not a change"
      register: derp
    - name: only do this on change
      debug:
        msg: "You had a change"
      when: derp is changed
    - name: only do this on success
      debug:
        msg: "You had a success"
      when: derp is success
```

The output is shown in the following screenshot:

*Unlocking the Power of Jinja2 Templates*

As we can see, our `debug` statement resulted in `success`, and so we skipped the task to be run on a `change`, and executed the one to be run on `success`.

## shuffle

Similar to the `random` filter, the `shuffle` filter can be used to produce randomized results. Unlike the `random` filter, which selects one random choice from a list, the `shuffle` filter will shuffle the items in a sequence and return the full sequence:

```
---
- name: demo the filters
  hosts: localhost
  gather_facts: false
  tasks:
    - name: shuffle the cards
      debug:
        msg: "{{ ['Ace', 'Queen', 'King', 'Deuce'] | shuffle }}"
```

The output is shown in the following screenshot:

```
~/src/mastery> ansible-playbook -i mastery-hosts template-demo-filters.yaml

PLAY [demo the filters] ************************************************

TASK [shuffle the cards] ***********************************************
ok: [localhost] => {
    "msg": [
        "Ace",
        "Deuce",
        "Queen",
        "King"
    ]
}

PLAY RECAP *************************************************************
localhost                  : ok=1    changed=0    unreachable=0    failed=0

~/src/mastery>
```

As expected, we see the whole list returned, but with the order shuffled.

## Filters dealing with path names

Configuration management and orchestration frequently refer to path names, but often only part of the path is desired. For example, perhaps we need the full path to a file but not the filename itself. Or, perhaps we need to extract just the filename from a full path, ignoring the directories preceding it. Ansible provides a few filters to help with precisely these tasks, and will be described in the following sections.

### basename

Let's say we have a requirement to work with just the filename from a full path. Obviously, we could perform some complex pattern matching to do this, but often this results in code that is not easy to read, and can be difficult to maintain. Luckily, Ansible provides a filter specifically for extracting the filename from a full path, as we shall demonstrate. In this example, we will use the `basename` filter to extract the filename from a full path:

```yaml
---
- name: demo the filters
  hosts: localhost
  gather_facts: false
  tasks:
    - name: demo basename
      debug:
        msg: "{{ '/var/log/nova/nova-api.log' | basename }}"
```

The output is shown in the following screenshot:

```
~/src/mastery> ansible-playbook -i mastery-hosts template-demo-filters.yaml

PLAY [demo the filters] ****************************************************

TASK [demo basename] *******************************************************
ok: [localhost] => {
    "msg": "nova-api.log"
}

PLAY RECAP *****************************************************************
localhost                  : ok=1    changed=0    unreachable=0    failed=0

~/src/mastery>
```

Here, we can see that just the filename was returned from the full path, as desired.

## dirname

The inverse of basename is dirname. Instead of returning the final part of a path, dirname will return everything, except the final part. Let's change our previous play to use dirname and rerun it:

```
~/src/mastery> ansible-playbook -i mastery-hosts template-demo-filters.yaml

PLAY [demo the filters] ************************************************

TASK [demo basename] ***************************************************
ok: [localhost] => {
    "msg": "/var/log/nova"
}

PLAY RECAP *************************************************************
localhost                  : ok=1    changed=0    unreachable=0    failed=0

~/src/mastery>
```

We now have just the path of our variable, which could be extremely useful elsewhere in our playbook.

## expanduser

Often, paths to various things are supplied with a user shortcut, such as ~/.stackrc. However, some tasks may require the full path to the file. Rather than the complicated command and register calls, the expanduser filter provides a way to expand the path to the full definition. In this example, the username is jfreeman:

```
---
- name: demo the filters
  hosts: localhost
  gather_facts: false
  tasks:
    - name: demo filter
      debug:
        msg: "{{ '~/.stackrc' | expanduser }}"
```

The output is shown in the following screenshot:

```
~/src/mastery> ansible-playbook -i mastery-hosts template-demo-filters.yaml

PLAY [demo the filters] ************************************************

TASK [demo filter] *****************************************************
ok: [localhost] => {
    "msg": "/home/jfreeman/.stackrc"
}

PLAY RECAP *************************************************************
localhost                  : ok=1    changed=0    unreachable=0    failed=0

~/src/mastery>
```

We have successfully expanded the path here, which could be useful for creating configuration files or performing other file operations that might need an absolute rather than a relative path name.

## Base64 encoding

When reading content from remote hosts, such as with the `slurp` module (used to read file content from remote hosts into a variable), the content will be Base64 encoded. To decode such content, Ansible provides a `b64decode` filter. Similarly, if running a task that requires Base64 encoded input, regular strings can be encoded with the `b64encode` filter.

Let's read content from the `derp` file, as shown in the following code:

```
---
- name: demo the filters
  hosts: localhost
  gather_facts: false
  tasks:
    - name: read file
      slurp:
        src: derp
      register: derp
    - name: display file content (undecoded)
      debug:
        var: derp.content
    - name: display file content (decoded)
      debug:
        var: derp.content | b64decode
```

# Unlocking the Power of Jinja2 Templates

The output is shown in the following screenshot:

```
~/src/mastery> cat << EOF > derp
\ Ansible is great
\ EOF
~/src/mastery> ansible-playbook -i mastery-hosts template-demo-filters.yaml

PLAY [demo the filters] ********************************************************

TASK [read file] ***************************************************************
ok: [localhost]

TASK [display file content (undecoded)] ****************************************
ok: [localhost] => {
    "derp.content": "QW5zaWJsZSBpcyBncmVhdAo="
}

TASK [display file content (decoded)] ******************************************
ok: [localhost] => {
    "derp.content | b64decode": "Ansible is great\n"
}

PLAY RECAP *********************************************************************
localhost                  : ok=3    changed=0    unreachable=0    failed=0

~/src/mastery>
```

Here, we can see that we successfully read the small file we created into a variable's, and that we can see the variable contents in the Base64 encoded form (remember that this encoding was performed by the `slurp` module). We can then decode it using a filter to see the original file contents.

## Searching for content

It is relatively common in Ansible to search a string for a substring. In particular, the common administrator task of running a command and grepping the output for a particular key piece of data is a reoccurring construct in many playbooks. While it's possible to replicate this with a shell task to execute a command, and pipe the output into `grep`, and use careful handling of `failed_when` to catch `grep` exit codes, a far better strategy is to use a command task, `register` the output, and then utilize the Ansible provided regex filters in later conditionals.

Let's look at two examples: one using the shell, pipe, `grep` method, and another using the search test:

```
- name: check database version
  shell: neutron-manage current | grep juno
  register: neutron_db_ver
  failed_when: false
- name: upgrade db
  command: neutron-manage db_sync
  when: neutron_db_ver | failed
```

The preceding example works by forcing Ansible to always see the task as successful, but assumes that if the exit code from the shell is non-zero, then the string `juno` was not found in the output of the neutron-manage command. This construct is functional but complex to read, and could mask real errors from the command. Let's try again using the `search` test.

As we stated previously regarding task status, using search on a string in Ansible is considered as a test, and is deprecated. Although it might read slightly odd, to be compliant with Ansible 2.9 and later versions, we must use the keyword `is` in place of the pipe when using `search` in this context:

```
- name: check database version
  command: neutron-manage current
  register: neutron_db_ver
- name: upgrade db
  command: neutron-manage db_sync
  when: not neutron_db_ver.stdout is search('juno')
```

What we are saying here is, run the task named `upgrade db` when `neutron_db_ver.stdout` does not contain the string `juno`. Once you get used to the concept of `when: not ... is`, you can see that this version is much cleaner to follow and does not mask errors from the first task.

The `search` filter searches a string and will return `True` if the substring is found anywhere within the input string. If an exact complete match is desired instead, the `match` filter can be used. Full Python regex syntax can be utilized inside the `search`/`match` string.

# Omitting undefined arguments

The `omit` variable takes a bit of explaining. Sometimes, when iterating over a hash of data to construct task arguments, it may be necessary to only provide some arguments for some of the items in the hash. Even though Jinja2 supports in-line `if` statements to conditionally render parts of a line, this does not work well in an Ansible task. Traditionally, playbook authors would create multiple tasks, one for each set of potential arguments passed in, and use conditionals to sort the loop members between each task set. A recently added magic variable named `omit` solves this problem when used in conjunction with the `default` filter. The `omit` variable will remove the argument the variable was used with altogether.

To illustrate how this works, let's consider a scenario where we need to install a set of Python packages with `pip`. Some of the packages have a specific version, while others do not. These packages are in a list of hashes named `pips`. Each hash has a `name` key and potentially a `ver` key. Our first example utilizes two different tasks to complete the installs:

```
- name: install pips with versions
  pip: name={{ item.name }} version={{ item.ver }}
  with_items: pips
  when: item.ver is defined
- name: install pips without versions
  pip: name={{ item.name }}
  with_items: pips
  when: item.ver is undefined
```

This construct works, but the loop is iterated twice, and some of the iterations will be skipped in each task. The following example collapses the two tasks into one, and utilizes the `omit` variable:

```
- name: install pips
  pip: name={{ item.name }} version={{ item.ver | default(omit) }}
  with_items: pips
```

This example is shorter, cleaner, and doesn't generate extra skipped tasks.

# Python object methods

Jinja2 is a Python-based template engine, and so Python object methods are available within templates. Object methods are methods, or functions, which are directly accessible by the variable object (typically a `string`, `list`, `int`, or `float`). A good way to think about this is as follows: if you were writing Python code and could write the variable, then a period, then a method call, then you would have access to do the same in Jinja2. Within Ansible, only methods that return modified content or a Boolean are typically used. Let's explore some common object methods that might be useful in Ansible.

## String methods

String methods can be used to return new strings or a list of strings that have been modified in some way or to test the string for various conditions and return a Boolean. Some useful methods are as follows:

- `endswith`: Determines if the string ends with a substring
- `startswith`: Same as `endswith`, but from the start
- `split`: Splits the string on characters (default is space) into a list of substrings
- `rsplit`: The same as `split`, but starts from the end of the string and works backwards
- `splitlines`: Splits the string at newlines into a list of substrings
- `upper`: Returns a copy of the string all in uppercase
- `lower`: Returns a copy of the string all in lowercase
- `capitalize`: Returns a copy of the string with just the first character in uppercase

We can create a simple playbook that will utilize some of these methods in a single task:

```
---
- name: demo the filters
  hosts: localhost
  gather_facts: false
  tasks:
    - name: string methods
      debug:
        msg: "{{ 'foo bar baz'.upper().split() }}"
```

*Unlocking the Power of Jinja2 Templates*

The output is shown in the following screenshot:

```
~/src/mastery> ansible-playbook -i mastery-hosts template-demo-objects.yaml

PLAY [demo the filters] ************************************************

TASK [string methods] **************************************************
ok: [localhost] => {
    "msg": [
        "FOO",
        "BAR",
        "BAZ"
    ]
}

PLAY RECAP *************************************************************
localhost                  : ok=1    changed=0    unreachable=0    failed=0

~/src/mastery>
```

As these are object methods, we need to access them with dot notation, rather than with a filter via `|`.

## List methods

Most of the methods Ansible provides relating to lists perform modifications on the list itself. However, there are two list methods that are useful when working with lists, especially when loops become involved. These two functions are `index` and `count`, and their functionality is described as follows:

- `index`: Returns the first index position of a provided value
- `count`: Counts the items in the list

These can be incredibly useful when iterating through a list in a loop, as it allows positional logic to be performed and appropriate actions to be taken, given our position in the list as we work through it. This is common in other programming languages, and fortunately, Ansible also provides this.

[ 150 ]

## int and float methods

Most `int` and `float` methods are not useful for Ansible. Sometimes, our variables are not exactly in the format we want them in. However, instead of defining more and more variables that slightly modify the same content, we can make use of Jinja2 filters to do the manipulation for us in the various places that require that modification. This allows us to stay efficient with the definition of our data, preventing many duplicate variables and tasks that may have to be changed later.

## Comparing values

Comparisons are used in many places with Ansible. Task conditionals are comparisons. Jinja2 control structures such as `if/elif/else` blocks, `for` loops, and `macros` often use comparisons; some filters use comparisons as well. To master Ansible's usage of Jinja2, it is important to understand what comparisons are available.

## Comparisons

Like most languages, Jinja2 comes equipped with the standard set of comparison expressions you would expect, which will render a Boolean `true` or `false`.

The expressions in Jinja2 are as follows:

| Expression | Definition |
|---|---|
| == | `True` if two objects are equal |
| != | `True` if two objects are not equal |
| > | `True` if the left-hand side is greater than the right-hand side |
| < | `True` if the left-hand side is less than the right-hand side |
| >= | `True` if the left-hand side is greater than, or equal to the right-hand side |
| <= | `True` if the left-hand side is less than, or equal to the right-hand side |

If you have written comparison operations in almost any other programming language (usually in the form of an `if` statement), these should all seem very familiar. Jinja2 maintains this functionality in templates, allowing for the same powerful comparison operations you would expect in conditional logic from any good programming language.

## Logic

Sometimes, performing a single comparison operation on its own is not enough—perhaps we might want to perform an action if two comparisons evaluate to `true` at the same time. Alternatively, we might want to perform an operation only if a comparison is not true. Logic in Jinja2 helps group two or more comparisons together, allowing for the formation of complex conditions from simple comparisons. Each comparison is referred to as an operand, and the logic that's used to bind these together into complex conditionals is given in the following list:

- `and`: Returns `true` if the left and the right operand are true
- `or`: Returns `true` if the left or the right operand is true
- `not`: Negates an operand
- `()`: Wraps a set of operands together to form a larger operand

## Tests

A test in Jinja2 is used to see if a variable matches certain well-defined criteria, and we have come across this already in this chapter in certain specific scenarios. The `is` operator is used to initiate a test. Tests are used any place a Boolean result is desired, such as with `if` expressions and task conditionals. There are many built-in tests, but we'll highlight a few of the particularly useful ones, as follows:

- `defined`: Returns `true` if the variable is defined
- `undefined`: The opposite of `defined`
- `none`: Returns `true` if the variable is defined, but the value is none
- `even`: Returns `true` if the number is divisible by 2
- `odd`: Returns `true` if the number is not divisible by 2

To test whether a value is not something, simply use `is not`.

We can create a playbook to demonstrate some of these value comparisons:

```
---
- name: demo the logic
  hosts: localhost
  gather_facts: false
  vars:
    num1: 10
    num3: 10
  tasks:
```

```yaml
- name: logic and comparison
  debug:
    msg: "Can you read me?"
  when: num1 >= num3 and num1 is even and num2 is not defined
```

The output is shown in the following screenshot:

```
~/src/mastery> ansible-playbook -i mastery-hosts template-demo-comparisons.yaml

PLAY [demo the logic] ****************************************************

TASK [logic and comparison] **********************************************
ok: [localhost] => {
    "msg": "Can you read me?"
}

PLAY RECAP ***************************************************************
localhost                  : ok=1    changed=0    unreachable=0    failed=0

~/src/mastery>
```

Here, we can see that our complex conditional evaluated as `true`, and so the debug task was executed.

## Summary

Jinja2 is a powerful language that is used extensively by Ansible. Not only is it used to generate file content, it is also used to make portions of a playbook dynamic. Mastering Jinja2 is vital to creating and maintaining elegant and efficient playbooks and roles.

In this chapter, we learned how to build simple templates with Jinja2 and render them from an Ansible playbook. We learned how to make effective use of control structures, to manipulate data, and even perform comparisons and tests on variables to both control the flow of Ansible playbooks (keeping the code lightweight and efficient) and create and manipulate data without the need for duplicate definitions, or excessive numbers of variables.

In the next chapter, we will explore Ansible's capability in more depth to define what constitutes a change or failure for tasks within a play.

# 6
# Controlling Task Conditions

Ansible is a system for running tasks on one or more hosts, and ensuring that operators understand whether changes have occurred (and indeed whether any issues were encountered). As a result, Ansible tasks result in one of four possible statuses: `ok`, `changed`, `failed`, or `skipped`. These statuses perform a number of important functions.

From the perspective of an operator running an Ansible playbook, they provide oversight of the Ansible run that completed—whether anything changed or not, and whether there were any failures that need addressing. In addition, they determine the flow of the playbook—for example, if a task results in a `changed` status, a handler might be triggered in the playbook.

Similarly, if a task results in a `failed` status, the default behavior of Ansible is not to attempt any further tasks on that host. Tasks can also make use of conditionals that check the status of previous tasks to control operations. As a result, these statuses, or task conditions, are central to just about everything Ansible does, and it is important to understand how to work with them and hence control the flow of a playbook—especially, for example, in a failure condition.

In this chapter, we'll explore this in detail, focusing specifically on the following topics:

- Controlling what defines a failure
- Recovering gracefully from a failure
- Controlling what defines a change
- Iterating over a set of tasks using loops

# Technical requirements

Check out the following video to see the Code in Action:

http://bit.ly/2TUkO03

# Defining a failure

Most modules that ship with Ansible have differing criteria for what constitutes an error. An error condition is highly dependent upon the module and what the module is attempting to accomplish. When a module returns an error, the host will be removed from the set of available hosts, preventing any further tasks or handlers from being executed on that host. Furthermore, the `ansible-playbook` binary (or other Ansible executable) will exit with a nonzero exit code to indicate failure. However, we are not limited by a module's opinion of what an error is. We can ignore errors or redefine an error condition.

## Ignoring errors

A task condition, named `ignore_errors`, is used to ignore errors. This condition is a Boolean, meaning that the value should be something Ansible understands to be `true`, such as `yes`, `on`, `true`, or `1` (string or integer).

To demonstrate how to use `ignore_errors`, let's create a playbook where we attempt to query a web server that doesn't exist. Typically, this would be an error, and if we don't define `ignore_errors`, we get the default behavior, that is, the host will be marked as failed and no further tasks will be attempted on that host. Create a new playbook called `error.yaml` as follows to look further at this behavior:

```
---
- name: error handling
  hosts: localhost
  gather_facts: false

  tasks:
  - name: broken website
    uri:
      url: http://notahost.nodomain
```

Running the task as is will give us the following error:

```
~/src/mastery> ansible-playbook -i mastery-hosts error.yaml

PLAY [error handling] ************************************************

TASK [broken website] ************************************************
fatal: [localhost]: FAILED! => {"changed": false, "content": "", "msg": "Status code was -1 and not [200]: Request failed: <urlopen error [Errno -2] Name or service not known>", "redirected": false, "status": -1, "url": "http://notahost.nodomain"}
        to retry, use: --limit @/home/jfreeman/src/mastery/error.retry

PLAY RECAP ***********************************************************
localhost                  : ok=0    changed=0    unreachable=0    failed=1

~/src/mastery>
```

Now, let's imagine that we didn't want Ansible to stop here, and instead we wanted it to continue. We can add the `ignore_errors` condition to our task like this:

```
- name: broken website
  uri:
    url: http://notahost.nodomain
  ignore_errors: true
```

This time, when we run the playbook, our error will be ignored, as we can see here:

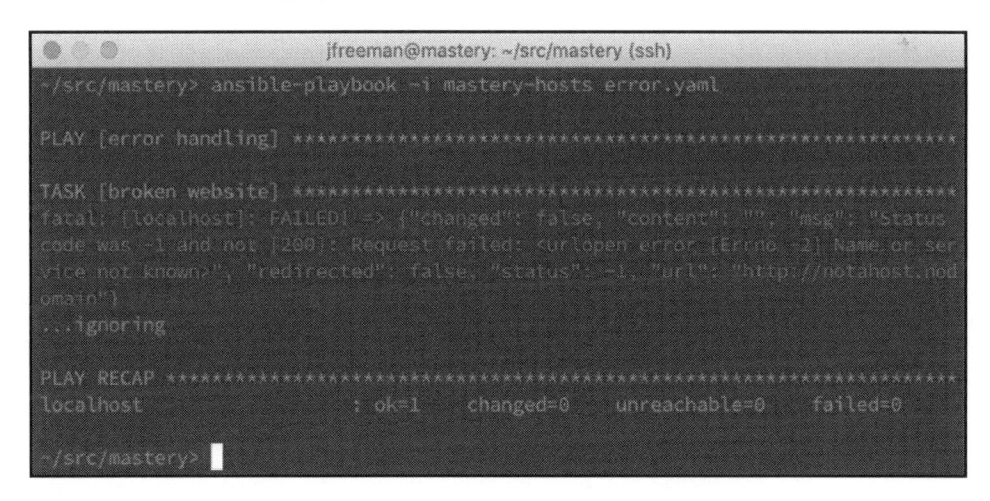

```
~/src/mastery> ansible-playbook -i mastery-hosts error.yaml

PLAY [error handling] ************************************************

TASK [broken website] ************************************************
fatal: [localhost]: FAILED! => {"changed": false, "content": "", "msg": "Status code was -1 and not [200]: Request failed: <urlopen error [Errno -2] Name or service not known>", "redirected": false, "status": -1, "url": "http://notahost.nodomain"}
...ignoring

PLAY RECAP ***********************************************************
localhost                  : ok=1    changed=0    unreachable=0    failed=0

~/src/mastery>
```

Any further tasks for that host will still be attempted and the playbook does not register any failed hosts.

# Defining an error condition

The `ignore_errors` condition is a bit of a blunt instrument. Any error generated from the module used by the task will be ignored. Furthermore, the output, at first glance, still appears like an error, and may be confusing to an operator attempting to discover a real failure. A more subtle tool is the `failed_when` condition. This condition is more like a fine scalpel, allowing a playbook author to be very specific as to what constitutes an error for a task. This condition performs a test to generate a Boolean result, much like the `when` condition. If the condition results in a Boolean `true`, the task will be considered a failure. Otherwise, the task will be considered successful.

The `failed_when` condition is quite useful when used in combination with the `command` or `shell` module and registering the result of the execution. Many programs that are executed can have detailed nonzero exit codes that mean different things. However, these Ansible modules all consider an exit code of anything other than 0 to be a failure. Let's look at the `iscsiadm` utility. This utility can be used for many things related to iSCSI. For the sake of a demonstration, we'll replace our `uri` module in `error.yaml` and attempt to discover any active `iscsi` sessions:

```
- name: query sessions
  command: /sbin/iscsiadm -m session
  register: sessions
```

If this were to be run on a system where there were no active sessions, we'd see output like this:

> **TIP**: The `iscsiadm` tool may not be installed by default, in which case you will get a different error to the preceding one. On our CentOS 7 test machine, it was installed using the following command: `sudo yum install iscsi-initiator-utils`.

We can just use the `ignore_errors` condition, but that would mask other problems with `iscsi`, so instead of this, we want to instruct Ansible that an exit code of 21 is acceptable. To that end, we can make use of the registered variable to access the `rc` variable, which holds the return code. We'll make use of this in a `failed_when` statement:

```
- name: query sessions
  command: /sbin/iscsiadm -m session
  register: sessions
  failed_when: sessions.rc not in (0, 21)
```

We simply stated that any exit code other than 0 or 21 should be considered a failure. Let's see the new output after this modification:

```
~/src/mastery> ansible-playbook -i mastery-hosts error.yaml -v
Using /etc/ansible/ansible.cfg as config file

PLAY [error handling] ********************************************************

TASK [query sessions] ********************************************************
changed: [localhost] => {"changed": true, "cmd": ["/sbin/iscsiadm", "-m", "sess
ion"], "delta": "0:00:00.003955", "end": "2019-02-18 20:25:08.426058", "failed_wh
en_result": false, "msg": "non-zero return code", "rc": 21, "start": "2019-02-18
 20:25:08.422103", "stderr": "iscsiadm: No active sessions.", "stderr_lines": ["
iscsiadm: No active sessions."], "stdout": "", "stdout_lines": []}

PLAY RECAP *******************************************************************
localhost                  : ok=1    changed=1    unreachable=0    failed=0

~/src/mastery>
```

The output now shows no error, and, in fact, we see a new data key in the results—`failed_when_result`. This shows whether our `failed_when` statement rendered `true` or `false`; it was `false` in this case.

[ 159 ]

## Controlling Task Conditions

Many command-line tools do not have detailed exit codes. In fact, most typically use 0 for success and one other nonzero code for all failure types. Thankfully, the `failed_when` statement is not just limited to the exit code of the application; it is a free-form Boolean statement that can access any sort of data required. Let's look at a different problem, one involving `git`. We'll imagine a scenario where we want to ensure that a particular branch does not exist in a `git` checkout. This task assumes a `git` repository checked out in the `/srv/app` directory. The command to delete a `git` branch is `git branch -D`. Let's have a look at the following code snippet:

```
- name: delete branch bad
  command: git branch -D badfeature
  args:
    chdir: /srv/app
```

> The `command` and `shell` modules use a different format for providing module arguments. The command itself is provided in free form, while module arguments go into an `args` hash.

If we start with just this command, we'll get an error, an exit code of 1, if the branch does not exist:

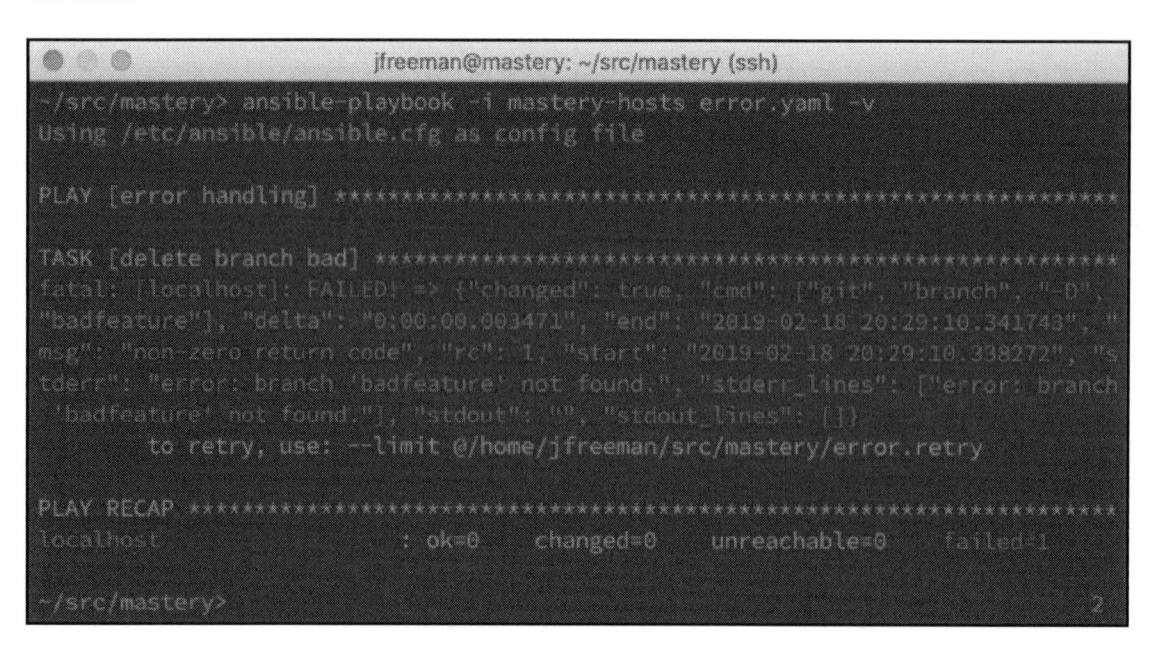

```
~/src/mastery> ansible-playbook -i mastery-hosts error.yaml -v
Using /etc/ansible/ansible.cfg as config file

PLAY [error handling] **********************************************************

TASK [delete branch bad] *******************************************************
fatal: [localhost]: FAILED! => {"changed": true, "cmd": ["git", "branch", "-D", "badfeature"], "delta": "0:00:00.003471", "end": "2019-02-18 20:29:10.341743", "msg": "non-zero return code", "rc": 1, "start": "2019-02-18 20:29:10.338272", "stderr": "error: branch 'badfeature' not found.", "stderr_lines": ["error: branch 'badfeature' not found."], "stdout": "", "stdout_lines": []}
        to retry, use: --limit @/home/jfreeman/src/mastery/error.retry

PLAY RECAP *********************************************************************
localhost                  : ok=0    changed=0    unreachable=0    failed=1

~/src/mastery>
```

As you can see, the error was not handled gracefully, and the play for localhost has been aborted.

> We're using the `command` module to easily demonstrate our topic despite the existence of the `git` module. When dealing with Git repositories, the `git` module should be used instead.

Without the `failed_when` and `changed_when` conditions, we would have to create a two-step task combo to protect ourselves from errors:

```
- name: check if branch badfeature exists
  command: git branch
  args:
    chdir: /srv/app
  register: branches
- name: delete branch bad
  command: git branch -D badfeature
  args:
    chdir: /srv/app
  when: branches.stdout is search('badfeature')
```

In the scenario where the branch doesn't exist, running these tasks looks as follows:

```
~/src/mastery> ansible-playbook -i mastery-hosts error.yaml -v
Using /etc/ansible/ansible.cfg as config file

PLAY [error handling] ********************************************************

TASK [check if branch badfeature exists] *************************************
changed: [localhost] => {"changed": true, "cmd": ["git", "branch"], "delta": "0:00:00.003240", "end": "2019-02-18 20:33:58.777764", "rc": 0, "start": "2019-02-18 20:33:58.774524", "stderr": "", "stderr_lines": [], "stdout": "* master", "stdout_lines": ["* master"]}

TASK [delete branch bad] *****************************************************
skipping: [localhost] => {"changed": false, "skip_reason": "Conditional result w
as False"}

PLAY RECAP *******************************************************************
localhost                  : ok=1    changed=1    unreachable=0    failed=0

~/src/mastery>
```

## Controlling Task Conditions

While the task set is functional, it is not efficient. Let's improve upon this and leverage the `failed_when` functionality to reduce the two tasks to one:

```
- name: delete branch bad
  command: git branch -D badfeature
  args:
    chdir: /srv/app
  register: gitout
  failed_when:
    - gitout.rc != 0
    - not gitout.stderr is search('branch.*not found')
```

> Multiple conditions that would normally be joined with `and` can instead be expressed as list elements. This can make playbooks easier to read and logic issues easier to find.

We check the command return code for anything other than `0` and then use the search filter to search the `stderr` value with a regex `branch.*not found`. We use the Jinja2 logic to combine the two conditions, which will evaluate to an inclusive `true` or `false` option:

```
~/src/mastery> ansible-playbook -i mastery-hosts error.yaml -v
Using /etc/ansible/ansible.cfg as config file

PLAY [error handling] ************************************************

TASK [delete branch bad §] *******************************************
changed: [localhost] => {"changed": true, "cmd": ["git", "branch", "-D", "badfea
ture"], "delta": "0:00:00.003175", "end": "2019-02-18 20:37:40.300397", "failed_
when_result": false, "msg": "non-zero return code", "rc": 1, "start": "2019-02-1
8 20:37:40.297222", "stderr": "error: branch 'badfeature' not found.", "stderr_l
ines": ["error: branch 'badfeature' not found."], "stdout": "", "stdout_lines":
[]}

PLAY RECAP ***********************************************************
localhost                  : ok=1    changed=1    unreachable=0    failed=0

~/src/mastery>
```

This demonstrates how we can redefine failure in an Ansible playbook, and gracefully handle conditions that would otherwise disrupt a play. We can also redefine what Ansible sees as a change, and we will look at this next.

# Defining a change

Similar to defining a task failure, it is also possible to define what constitutes a changed task result. This capability is particularly useful with the `command` family of modules (`command`, `shell`, `raw`, and `script`). Unlike most other modules, the modules of this family do not have an inherent idea of what a change may be. In fact, unless otherwise directed, these modules only result in `failed`, `changed`, or `skipped`. There is simply no way for these modules to assume a changed condition versus unchanged.

The `changed_when` condition allows a playbook author to instruct a module on how to interpret a change. Just like `failed_when`, `changed_when` performs a test to generate a Boolean result. Frequently, the tasks used with `changed_when` are commands that will exit nonzero to indicate that no work is needed to be done, so, often, authors will combine `changed_when` and `failed_when` to fine-tune the task result evaluation.

In our previous example, the `failed_when` condition caught the case where there was no work to be done but the task still showed a change. We want to register a change on the exit code 0, but not on any other exit code. Let's expand our example task to accomplish this:

```
- name: delete branch bad
  command: git branch -D badfeature
  args:
    chdir: /srv/app
  register: gitout
  failed_when:
    - gitout.rc != 0
    - not gitout.stderr is search('branch.*not found')
  changed_when: gitout.rc == 0
```

Now, if we run our task when the branch still does not exist, we'll see the following output:

*Controlling Task Conditions*

Note how the `changed` key now has the value `false`.

Just for the sake of completeness, we'll change the scenario so that the branch does exist and run it again. To create the branch, simply run `git branch badfeature` from the `/srv/app` directory. Now, we can execute our playbook once again to see the output, which is as follows:

```
~/src/mastery> ansible-playbook -i mastery-hosts error.yaml -v
Using /etc/ansible/ansible.cfg as config file

PLAY [error handling] ***********************************************************

TASK [delete branch bad] ********************************************************
changed: [localhost] => {"changed": true, "cmd": ["git", "branch", "-D", "badfea
ture"], "delta": "0:00:00.003880", "end": "2019-02-18 20:46:25.513992", "failed_
when_result": false, "rc": 0, "start": "2019-02-18 20:46:25.510112", "stderr": "
", "stderr_lines": [], "stdout": "Deleted branch badfeature (was 6d7301c).", "st
dout_lines": ["Deleted branch badfeature (was 6d7301c)."]}

PLAY RECAP **********************************************************************
localhost                  : ok=1    changed=1    unreachable=0    failed=0

~/src/mastery>
```

This time, our output is different; it's registering a change, and the `stdout` data shows the branch being deleted.

## Special handling of the command family

A subset of the command family of modules (`command`, `shell`, and `script`) has a pair of special arguments that will influence whether the task work has already been done, and thus, whether or not a task will result in a change. The options are `creates` and `removes`. These two arguments expect a file path as a value. When Ansible attempts to execute a task with the `creates` or `removes` arguments, it will first check whether the referenced file path exists.

If the path exists and the `creates` argument was used, Ansible will consider that the work has already been completed and will return `ok`. Conversely, if the path does not exist and the `removes` argument is used, then Ansible will again consider the work to be complete, and it will return `ok`. Any other combination will cause the work to actually happen. The expectation is that whatever work the task is doing will result in either the creation or removal of the file that is referenced.

The convenience of `creates` and `removes` saves developers from having to do a two-task combo. Let's create a scenario where we want to run the script `frobitz` from the `files/` subdirectory of our project root. In our scenario, we know that the `frobitz` script will create a path, `/srv/whiskey/tango`. In fact, the source of `frobitz` is the following:

```
#!/bin/bash
rm -rf /srv/whiskey/tango
mkdir -p /srv/whiskey/tango
```

We don't want this script to run twice as it can be destructive to any existing data. Replacing the existing tasks in our `error.yaml` playbook, the two-task combo will look like this:

```
- name: discover tango directory
  stat: path=/srv/whiskey/tango
  register: tango
- name: run frobitz
  script: files/frobitz --initialize /srv/whiskey/tango
  when: not tango.stat.exists
```

Assuming that the file already exists, the output will be as follows:

[ 165 ]

*Controlling Task Conditions*

If the `/srv/whiskey/tango` path did not exist, the stat module would have returned far less data, and the `exists` key would have a value of `false`. Thus, our `frobitz` script would have been run.

Now, we'll use `creates` to reduce this down to a single task:

```
- name: run frobitz
  script: files/frobitz
  args:
    creates: /srv/whiskey/tango
```

> The `script` module is actually an `action_plugin`, which will be discussed in Chapter 9, *Extending Ansible*.

This time, our output will be slightly different:

```
~/src/mastery> ansible-playbook -i mastery-hosts error.yaml -v
Using /etc/ansible/ansible.cfg as config file

PLAY [error handling] ********************************************************

TASK [run frobitz] ***********************************************************
skipping: [localhost] => {"changed": false, "msg": "/srv/whiskey/tango exists, matching creates option"}

PLAY RECAP *******************************************************************
localhost                  : ok=0    changed=0    unreachable=0    failed=0

~/src/mastery>
```

On this occasion, we simply skipped running the script altogether as the directory already existed before the playbook was even run. This saves time during the playbook execution and also prevents any potentially destructive actions that might occur from running a script.

> **TIP**: Making good use of `creates` and `removes` will keep your playbooks concise and efficient.

## Suppressing a change

Sometimes, it can be desirable to completely suppress changes. This is often used when executing a command in order to gather data. The command execution isn't actually changing anything; instead, it's just gathering info, like the `setup` module. Suppressing changes on such tasks can be helpful for quickly determining whether a playbook run resulted in any actual change in the fleet.

To suppress change, simply use `false` as an argument to the `changed_when` task key. Let's extend one of our previous examples to discover the active `iscsi` sessions to suppress changes:

```
- name: discover iscsi sessions
  command: /sbin/iscsiadm -m session
  register: sessions
  failed_when:
    - sessions.rc != 0
    - not sessions.stderr is
      search('No active sessions')
  changed_when: false
```

Now, no matter what comes in the return data, Ansible will treat the task as `ok` rather than changed:

```
~/src/mastery> ansible-playbook -i mastery-hosts error.yaml

PLAY [error handling] **********************************************************

TASK [discover iscsi sessions] *************************************************
ok: [localhost]

PLAY RECAP *********************************************************************
localhost                  : ok=1    changed=0    unreachable=0    failed=0

~/src/mastery>
```

Thus, there are only two possible states to this task now—`failed` and `ok`. We have actually negated the possibility of a `changed` task result.

# Error recovery

While error conditions can be narrowly defined, there will be times when real errors happen. Ansible provides a method to react to true errors, a method that allows running additional tasks when an error occurs, defining specific tasks that always execute even if there was an error, or even both. This method is the blocks feature.

The blocks feature, introduced with Ansible version 2.0, provides some additional structure to play task listings. Blocks can group tasks together into a logical unit, which can have task controls applied to the unit as a whole. In addition, a `block` of tasks can have optional `rescue` and `always` sections.

## Using the rescue section

The `rescue` section of a `block` defines a logical unit of tasks that will be executed should an actual failure be encountered within a `block`. As Ansible performs the tasks within a `block`, from top to bottom, when an actual failure is encountered, execution will jump to the first task of the `rescue` section of the `block` if it exists. Then, tasks are performed from top to bottom until either the end of the rescue section is reached, or another error is encountered.

After the `rescue` section completes, task execution continues with whatever comes after the `block`, as if there were no errors. This provides a way to gracefully handle errors, allowing `cleanup` tasks to be defined so that a system is not left in a completely broken state, and the rest of a play can continue. This is far cleaner than a complex set of task-registered results and task conditionals based on error status.

To demonstrate this, let's create a new task set inside a `block`. This task set will have an unhandled error in it that will cause execution to switch to the `rescue` section, where we'll perform a `cleanup` task.

We'll also provide a task after the `block` to ensure execution continues. We'll reuse the `error.yaml` playbook:

```yaml
---
- name: error handling
  hosts: localhost
  gather_facts: false

  tasks:
  - block:
      - name: delete branch bad
        command: git branch -D badfeature
        args:
          chdir: /srv/app

      - name: this task is lost
        debug:
          msg: "I do not get seen"
```

The two tasks listed in the `block` section are executed in the order in which they are listed. Should one of them result in a `failed` result, the following code shown in the `rescue block` will be executed:

```yaml
    rescue:
      - name: cleanup task
        debug:
          msg: "I am cleaning up"

      - name: cleanup task 2
        debug:
          msg: "I am also cleaning up"
```

Finally, this task is executed regardless of the earlier tasks. Note how the lower indentation level means it gets run at the same level as the `block`, rather than as part of the `block` structure:

```yaml
  - name: task after block
    debug:
      msg: "Execution goes on"
```

## Controlling Task Conditions

When this play executes, the first task will result in an error, and the second task will be passed over. Execution continues with the `cleanup` tasks, as we can see in this screenshot:

```
~/src/mastery> ansible-playbook -i mastery-hosts error.yaml -v
Using /etc/ansible/ansible.cfg as config file

PLAY [error handling] ************************************************************

TASK [delete branch bad] *********************************************************
fatal: [localhost]: FAILED! => {"changed": true, "cmd": ["git", "branch", "-D", "badfeature"], "delta": "0:00:00.006281", "end": "2019-02-19 13:28:34.334423", "msg": "non-zero return code", "rc": 1, "start": "2019-02-19 13:28:34.328142", "stderr": "error: branch 'badfeature' not found.", "stderr_lines": ["error: branch 'badfeature' not found."], "stdout": "", "stdout_lines": []}

TASK [cleanup task] **************************************************************
ok: [localhost] => {
    "msg": "I am cleaning up"
}

TASK [cleanup task 2] ************************************************************
ok: [localhost] => {
    "msg": "I am also cleaning up"
}

TASK [task after block] **********************************************************
ok: [localhost] => {
    "msg": "Execution goes on"
}

PLAY RECAP ***********************************************************************
localhost                  : ok=3    changed=0    unreachable=0    failed=1

~/src/mastery>
```

Not only was the `rescue` section executed, but the rest of the play completed as well, and the whole `ansible-playbook` execution was considered successful.

# Using the always section

In addition to `rescue`, we can also use another section, named `always`. This section of a `block` will always be executed irrespective of whether there were errors. This feature is handy for ensuring that the state of a system is always left functional, irrespective of whether a `block` of tasks was successful. As some tasks of a `block` may be skipped due to an error, and a `rescue` section is only executed when there is an error, the `always` section provides the guarantee of task execution in every instance.

Let's extend our previous example and add an `always` section to our `block`:

```
always:
  - name: most important task
    debug:
      msg: "Never going to let you down"
```

Rerunning our playbook, we see the additional task displayed:

*Controlling Task Conditions*

To verify that the `always` section does indeed always execute, we can alter the play so that the Git task is considered successful. The first part of this modified playbook is shown in the following snippet:

```
---
- name: error handling
  hosts: localhost
  gather_facts: false

  tasks:
  - block:
      - name: delete branch bad
        command: git branch -D badfeature
        args:
          chdir: /srv/app
        register: gitout
        failed_when:
          - gitout.rc != 0
          - not gitout.stderr is search('branch.*not found')
```

Note the changed `failed_when` condition, which will enable the `git` command to run without being considered a failure. The rest of the playbook (which should, by now, have been built up in the previous examples) remains unchanged.

This time, when we execute the playbook, our `rescue` section is skipped over, our previously masked-by-error task is executed, and our `always` block is still executed:

```
~/src/mastery> ansible-playbook -i mastery-hosts error.yaml -v
Using /etc/ansible/ansible.cfg as config file

PLAY [error handling] ********************************************************

TASK [delete branch bad] *****************************************************
changed: [localhost] => {"changed": true, "cmd": ["git", "branch", "-D", "badfea
ture"], "delta": "0:00:00.003121", "end": "2019-02-19 13:32:09.989143", "failed_
when_result": false, "msg": "non-zero return code", "rc": 1, "start": "2019-02-1
9 13:32:09.986022", "stderr": "error: branch 'badfeature' not found.", "stderr_l
ines": ["error: branch 'badfeature' not found."], "stdout": "", "stdout_lines":
[]}

TASK [this task is lost] *****************************************************
ok: [localhost] => {
    "msg": "I do not get seen"
}

TASK [most important task] ***************************************************
ok: [localhost] => {
    "msg": "Never going to let you down"
}

TASK [task after block] ******************************************************
ok: [localhost] => {
    "msg": "Execution goes on"
}

PLAY RECAP *******************************************************************
localhost                  : ok=4    changed=1    unreachable=0    failed=0

~/src/mastery>
```

Note also that our previously lost task is now executed, as the failure condition for the `delete branch bad` task was changed such that it no longer fails in this play. In a similar manner, our `rescue` section is no longer needed, and all other tasks (including the `always` section) complete as expected.

# Handling unreliable environments

So far in this chapter, we have focused on gracefully handling errors, and changing the default behavior of Ansible with respect to changes and failures. This is all well and good for tasks, but what about if you are running Ansible in an unreliable environment? For example, poor or transient connectivity might used to reach the managed hosts, or hosts might be down on a regular basis for some reason. The latter example might be a dynamically scaled environment that could be scaled up in times of high load and scaled back when demand is low to save on resources.

Luckily, a new playbook keyword, `ignore_unreachable`, was introduced that handles exactly these cases, and ensures that all tasks are attempted on our inventory even for hosts that get marked as unreachable during the execution of a task. This is best explained by means of an example, so let's reuse the `error.yaml` playbook to create such a case:

```yaml
---
- name: error handling
  hosts: all
  gather_facts: false

  tasks:
  - name: delete branch bad
    command: git branch -D badfeature
    args:
      chdir: /srv/app
  - name: important task
    debug:
      msg: It is important we attempt this task!
```

We are going to try to delete the `badfeature` branch from a Git repository on two remote hosts as defined in our inventory. These hosts do not exist, of course; they are fictitious, and so we know they will get marked as `unreachable` as soon as the first task is attempted. In spite of this, there is a second task that absolutely must be attempted if at all possible. Let's run the playbook as it is and see what happens:

```
~/src/mastery> ansible-playbook -i mastery-hosts error.yaml -v
Using /etc/ansible/ansible.cfg as config file

PLAY [error handling] ********************************************************

TASK [delete branch bad] *****************************************************
fatal: [mastery.example.name]: UNREACHABLE! => {"changed": false, "msg": "Failed
 to connect to the host via ssh: ssh: connect to host 192.168.10.25 port 22: Con
nection timed out\r\n", "unreachable": true}
fatal: [backend.example.name]: UNREACHABLE! => {"changed": false, "msg": "Failed
 to connect to the host via ssh: ssh: Could not resolve hostname backend.example
.name: Name or service not known\r\n", "unreachable": true}
        to retry, use: --limit @/home/jfreeman/src/mastery/error.retry

PLAY RECAP *******************************************************************
backend.example.name       : ok=0    changed=0    unreachable=1    failed=0
mastery.example.name       : ok=0    changed=0    unreachable=1    failed=0

~/src/mastery>
```

Note that `important task` was never attempted—the play was aborted after the first task since the hosts were unreachable. However, let's use our newly discovered flag to change this behavior. Change the code so that it looks like the code here:

```
---
- name: error handling
  hosts: all
  gather_facts: false

  tasks:
  - name: delete branch bad
    command: git branch -D badfeature
    args:
      chdir: /srv/app
    ignore_unreachable: true
  - name: important task
    debug:
      msg: It is important we attempt this task!
```

## Controlling Task Conditions

This time, note that even though the hosts were unreachable on the first attempt, our second task is still executed:

```
~/src/mastery> ansible-playbook -i mastery-hosts error.yaml -v
Using /etc/ansible/ansible.cfg as config file

PLAY [error handling] ************************************************

TASK [delete branch bad] *********************************************
fatal: [mastery.example.name]: UNREACHABLE! => {"changed": false, "msg": "Failed to connect to the host via ssh: ssh: connect to host 192.168.10.25 port 22: Connection timed out\r\n", "skip_reason": "Host mastery.example.name is unreachable", "unreachable": true}
fatal: [backend.example.name]: UNREACHABLE! => {"changed": false, "msg": "Failed to connect to the host via ssh: ssh: Could not resolve hostname backend.example.name: Name or service not known\r\n", "skip_reason": "Host backend.example.name is unreachable", "unreachable": true}

TASK [important task] ************************************************
ok: [mastery.example.name] => {
    "msg": "It is important we attempt this task!"
}
ok: [backend.example.name] => {
    "msg": "It is important we attempt this task!"
}

PLAY RECAP ***********************************************************
backend.example.name       : ok=1    changed=0    unreachable=1    failed=0
mastery.example.name       : ok=1    changed=0    unreachable=1    failed=0

~/src/mastery>
```

This is useful if, like the `debug` command, it might run locally, or perhaps it is vital and should be attempted even if connectivity was down on the first attempt. So far in this chapter, you have learned about the tools Ansible provides to handle a variety of error conditions with grace. Next, we will proceed to look at controlling the flow of tasks using loops—an especially important tool for making code concise and preventing repetition.

# Iterative tasks with loops

Loops deserve a special mention in this chapter. So far, we have focused on controlling the flow of a playbook in a top-to-bottom fashion—we have changed the various conditions that might be evaluated as the playbook runs, and we have also focused on creating concise efficient code. What happens, however, if you have a single task, but need to run it against a list of data; for example, creating several user accounts, or directories, or indeed something more complex.

Looping changed in Ansible 2.5—prior to this, loops were generally created with keywords such as `with_items`. Although some backward compatibility remains, it is advisable to move to the newer `loop` keyword instead.

Let's take a simple example—we need to create two directories. Create `loop.yaml` as follows:

```yaml
---
- name: looping demo
  hosts: localhost
  gather_facts: false

  tasks:
  - name: create a directory
    file:
      path: /srv/whiskey/alpha
      state: directory
  - name: create another directory
    file:
      path: /srv/whiskey/beta
      state: directory
```

When we run this, as expected, our two directories get created:

## Controlling Task Conditions

However, you can see this code is repetitive and inefficient. Instead, we could change it to something like this:

```yaml
---
- name: looping demo
  hosts: localhost
  gather_facts: false

  tasks:
  - name: create a directory
    file:
      path: "{{ item }}"
      state: directory
    loop:
      - /srv/whiskey/alpha
      - /srv/whiskey/beta
```

Note the use of the special variable `item`, which is now used to define the path from the `loop` items at the bottom of the task. Now, when we run this code, the output looks somewhat different:

```
~/src/mastery> ansible-playbook -i mastery-hosts loop.yaml

PLAY [looping demo] ************************************************************

TASK [create a directory] ******************************************************
changed: [localhost] => (item=/srv/whiskey/alpha)
changed: [localhost] => (item=/srv/whiskey/beta)

PLAY RECAP *********************************************************************
localhost                  : ok=1    changed=1    unreachable=0    failed=0

~/src/mastery>
```

The two directories were still created exactly as before, but this time within a single task. This makes our playbooks much more concise and efficient. Ansible offers many more powerful looping options, including nested loops and the ability to create loops that will carry on until a given criterion is met (often referred to as `do until` loops), as opposed to a specific limited set of data. Full details of these are available in the Ansible documentation here: https://docs.ansible.com/ansible/latest/user_guide/playbooks_loops.html.

# Summary

In this chapter, you learned that it is possible to define specifically how Ansible perceives a failure or a change when a specific task is run, how to use blocks to gracefully handle errors and perform `cleanup`, and how to write tight efficient code using loops.

As a result, you should now be able to alter any given task to provide specific conditions under which Ansible will fail it or consider a change successful. This is incredibly valuable when running shell commands, as we have demonstrated in this chapter, and also serves when defining specialized use cases for existing modules. You should also now be able to organize your Ansible tasks into blocks, ensuring that if failures do occur, recovery actions can be taken that would otherwise not need to be run. Finally, you should now be able to write tight, efficient Ansible playbooks using loops, removing the need for repetitive code and lengthy inefficient playbooks.

In the next chapter, we'll explore the use of roles for organizing tasks, files, variables, and other content.

# 7
# Composing Reusable Ansible Content with Roles

For many projects, a simple, single Ansible playbook may suffice. As time goes on and projects grow, additional playbooks and variable files are added, and task files may be split. Other projects within an organization may want to reuse some of the content, and either the projects get added to the directory tree or the desired content may get copied among multiple projects. As the complexity and size of the scenario grows, something more than a loosely organized handful of playbooks, task files, and variable files is highly desired. Creating such a hierarchy can be daunting and may explain why many Ansible implementations start off simple and only become more organized once the scattered files become unwieldy and a hassle to maintain. Making the migration can be difficult and may require rewriting significant portions of playbooks, which can further delay reorganization efforts.

In this chapter, we will cover the best practices for composable, reusable, and well-organized content within Ansible. Lessons learned in this chapter will help developers design Ansible content that grows well with the project, avoiding the need for difficult redesign work later. The following is an outline of what we will cover:

- Task, handler, variable, and playbook inclusion concepts
- Roles (structures, defaults, and dependencies)
- Designing top-level playbooks to utilize roles
- Sharing roles across projects (dependencies via Galaxy; Git-like repos)

# Technical requirements

Check out the following video to see the Code in Action:

http://bit.ly/2HKOvtS

# Task, handler, variable, and playbook inclusion concepts

The first step to understanding how to efficiently organize an Ansible project structure is to master the concept of including files. The act of including files allows content to be defined in a topic-specific file that can be included into other files one or more times within a project. This inclusion feature supports the concept of **Don't Repeat Yourself** (DRY).

## Including tasks

Task files are YAML files that define one or more tasks. These tasks are not directly tied to any particular play or playbook; they exist purely as a list of tasks. These files can be referenced by playbooks or other task files by way of the include operator. This operator takes a path to a task file, and as we learned in Chapter 1, *The System Architecture and Design of Ansible*, the path can be relative to the file referencing it.

To demonstrate how to use the include operator to include tasks, let's create a simple play that includes a task file with some debug tasks within it. First, let's write our playbook file, and we'll call it includer.yaml:

```yaml
---
- name: task inclusion
  hosts: localhost
  gather_facts: false

  tasks:
  - name: non-included task
    debug:
      msg: "I am not included"

  - include: more-tasks.yaml
```

Next, we'll create more-tasks.yaml in the same directory that holds includer.yaml:

```yaml
---
- name: included task 1
  debug:
    msg: "I am the first included task"

- name: included task 2
  debug:
    msg: "I am the second included task"
```

Now we can execute our playbook to observe the output:

```
~/src/mastery> ansible-playbook -i mastery-hosts includer.yaml

PLAY [task inclusion] **********************************************************

TASK [non-included task] *******************************************************
ok: [localhost] => {
    "msg": "I am not included"
}

TASK [included task 1] *********************************************************
ok: [localhost] => {
    "msg": "I am the first included task"
}

TASK [included task 2] *********************************************************
ok: [localhost] => {
    "msg": "I am the second included task"
}

PLAY RECAP *********************************************************************
localhost                  : ok=3    changed=0    unreachable=0    failed=0

~/src/mastery>
```

We can clearly see our tasks from the `include` file execution. Because the `include` operator was used within the play's tasks section, the included tasks were executed within that play. In fact, if we were to add a task to the play after the `include` operator, we would see that the order of execution follows as if all the tasks from the included file existed at the spot the `include` operator was used:

```
tasks:
- name: non-included task
  debug:
     msg: "I am not included"

- include: more-tasks.yaml

- name: after-included tasks
  debug:
     msg: "I run last"
```

If we run our modified playbook, we will see the task order we expect:

```
~/src/mastery> ansible-playbook -i mastery-hosts includer.yaml

PLAY [task inclusion] ****************************************************

TASK [non-included task] *************************************************
ok: [localhost] => {
    "msg": "I am not included"
}

TASK [included task 1] ***************************************************
ok: [localhost] => {
    "msg": "I am the first included task"
}

TASK [included task 2] ***************************************************
ok: [localhost] => {
    "msg": "I am the second included task"
}

TASK [after-included tasks] **********************************************
ok: [localhost] => {
    "msg": "I run last"
}

PLAY RECAP ***************************************************************
localhost                  : ok=4    changed=0    unreachable=0    failed=0

~/src/mastery>
```

By breaking these tasks into their own file, we could include them multiple times or in multiple playbooks. If we ever have to alter one of the tasks, we only have to alter a single file, no matter how many places this file gets referenced.

## Passing variable values to included tasks

Sometimes, we want to split out a set of tasks but have those tasks act slightly differently depending on variable data. The `include` operator allows us to define and override variable data at the time of inclusion. The scope of the definition is only within the included task file (and any other files that file may itself include).

To illustrate this capability, let's create a new scenario in which we need to touch a couple of files, each in their own directory path. Instead of writing two file tasks for each file (one to create the directory and another to touch the file), we'll create a task file with each task that will use variable names in the tasks. Then, we'll include the task file twice, each time passing different data in. First, we'll do this with the `files.yaml` task file:

```yaml
---
- name: create leading path
  file:
    path: "{{ path }}"
    state: directory

- name: touch the file
  file:
    path: "{{ path + '/' + file }}"
    state: touch
```

Next, we'll modify our `includer.yaml` playbook to include the task file we've just created, passing along variable data for the `path` and `file` variables:

```yaml
---
- name: touch files
  hosts: localhost
  gather_facts: false

  tasks:
  - include: files.yaml
    vars:
      path: /tmp/foo
      file: herp

  - include: files.yaml
    vars:
      path: /tmp/foo
      file: derp
```

> Variable definitions provided when including files can either be in the inline format of `key=value` or in the illustrated YAML format of `key: value` inside a `vars` hash.

# Composing Reusable Ansible Content with Roles

When we run this playbook, we'll see four tasks get executed: the two tasks from within `files.yaml` twice. The second set should result in only one change, as the path is the same for both sets:

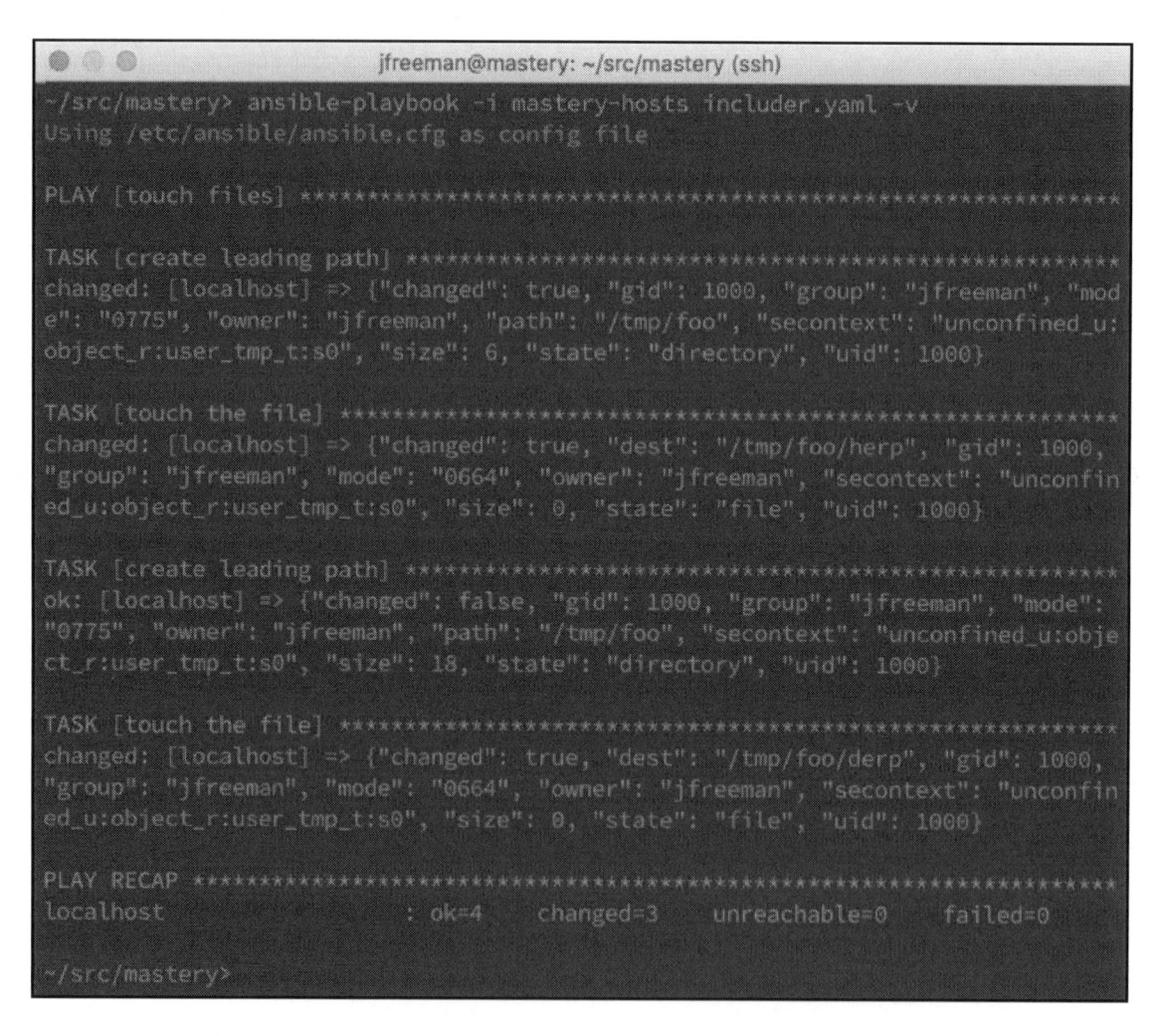

```
~/src/mastery> ansible-playbook -i mastery-hosts includer.yaml -v
Using /etc/ansible/ansible.cfg as config file

PLAY [touch files] ************************************************************

TASK [create leading path] ****************************************************
changed: [localhost] => {"changed": true, "gid": 1000, "group": "jfreeman", "mode": "0775", "owner": "jfreeman", "path": "/tmp/foo", "secontext": "unconfined_u:object_r:user_tmp_t:s0", "size": 6, "state": "directory", "uid": 1000}

TASK [touch the file] *********************************************************
changed: [localhost] => {"changed": true, "dest": "/tmp/foo/herp", "gid": 1000, "group": "jfreeman", "mode": "0664", "owner": "jfreeman", "secontext": "unconfined_u:object_r:user_tmp_t:s0", "size": 0, "state": "file", "uid": 1000}

TASK [create leading path] ****************************************************
ok: [localhost] => {"changed": false, "gid": 1000, "group": "jfreeman", "mode": "0775", "owner": "jfreeman", "path": "/tmp/foo", "secontext": "unconfined_u:object_r:user_tmp_t:s0", "size": 18, "state": "directory", "uid": 1000}

TASK [touch the file] *********************************************************
changed: [localhost] => {"changed": true, "dest": "/tmp/foo/derp", "gid": 1000, "group": "jfreeman", "mode": "0664", "owner": "jfreeman", "secontext": "unconfined_u:object_r:user_tmp_t:s0", "size": 0, "state": "file", "uid": 1000}

PLAY RECAP ********************************************************************
localhost                  : ok=4    changed=3    unreachable=0    failed=0

~/src/mastery>
```

As can be seen here, the code to create the leading path and the file is being reused, just with different values each time, making our code really efficient to maintain.

## Passing complex data to included tasks

When wanting to pass complex data to included tasks, such as a list or hash, an alternative syntax can be used when including the file. Let's repeat the last scenario, only this time instead of including the task file twice, we'll include it once and pass a hash of the paths and files in. First, we'll recreate the `files.yaml` file:

```
---
- name: create leading path
  file:
    path: "{{ item.value.path }}"
    state: directory
  with_dict: "{{ files }}"

- name: touch the file
  file:
    path: "{{ item.value.path + '/' + item.key }}"
    state: touch
  with_dict: "{{ files }}"
```

Now we'll alter our `includer.yaml` playbook to provide the `files` hash in a single `include` statement:

```
---
- name: touch files
  hosts: localhost
  gather_facts: false

  tasks:
  - include: files.yaml
    vars:
      files:
        herp:
          path: /tmp/foo
        derp:
          path: /tmp/foo
```

[ 187 ]

## Composing Reusable Ansible Content with Roles

If we run this new playbook and task file, we should see similar but slightly different output, the end result of which is the `/tmp/foo` directory already in place and the two `herp` and `derp` files being created as empty files (touched) within:

```
~/src/mastery> ansible-playbook -i mastery-hosts includer.yaml -v
Using /etc/ansible/ansible.cfg as config file

PLAY [touch files] *************************************************************

TASK [create leading path] *****************************************************
changed: [localhost] => (item={'value': {u'path': u'/tmp/foo'}, 'key': u'herp'})
 => {"changed": true, "gid": 1000, "group": "jfreeman", "item": {"key": "herp",
"value": {"path": "/tmp/foo"}}, "mode": "0775", "owner": "jfreeman", "path": "/t
mp/foo", "secontext": "unconfined_u:object_r:user_tmp_t:s0", "size": 6, "state":
 "directory", "uid": 1000}
ok: [localhost] => (item={'value': {u'path': u'/tmp/foo'}, 'key': u'derp'}) => {
"changed": false, "gid": 1000, "group": "jfreeman", "item": {"key": "derp", "val
ue": {"path": "/tmp/foo"}}, "mode": "0775", "owner": "jfreeman", "path": "/tmp/f
oo", "secontext": "unconfined_u:object_r:user_tmp_t:s0", "size": 6, "state": "di
rectory", "uid": 1000}

TASK [touch the file] **********************************************************
changed: [localhost] => (item={'value': {u'path': u'/tmp/foo'}, 'key': u'herp'})
 => {"changed": true, "dest": "/tmp/foo/herp", "gid": 1000, "group": "jfreeman",
 "item": {"key": "herp", "value": {"path": "/tmp/foo"}}, "mode": "0664", "owner"
: "jfreeman", "secontext": "unconfined_u:object_r:user_tmp_t:s0", "size": 0, "st
ate": "file", "uid": 1000}
changed: [localhost] => (item={'value': {u'path': u'/tmp/foo'}, 'key': u'derp'})
 => {"changed": true, "dest": "/tmp/foo/derp", "gid": 1000, "group": "jfreeman",
 "item": {"key": "derp", "value": {"path": "/tmp/foo"}}, "mode": "0664", "owner"
: "jfreeman", "secontext": "unconfined_u:object_r:user_tmp_t:s0", "size": 0, "st
ate": "file", "uid": 1000}

PLAY RECAP *********************************************************************
localhost                  : ok=2    changed=2    unreachable=0    failed=0

~/src/mastery>
```

Using this manner of passing in a hash of data allows for the growth of the set of things created without having to grow the number of `include` statements in the main playbook.

## Conditional task includes

Similar to passing data into included files, conditionals can also be passed into included files. This is accomplished by attaching a `when` statement to the `include` operator. This conditional does not cause Ansible to evaluate the test to determine whether the file should be included; rather, it instructs Ansible to add the conditional to each and every task within the included file (and any other files the said file may include).

> It is not possible to conditionally include a file. Files will always be included; however, a task conditional can be applied to every task within.

Let's demonstrate this by modifying our first example that includes simple debug statements. We'll add a conditional and pass along some data for the conditional to use. First, let's modify the `includer.yaml` playbook:

```
---
- name: task inclusion
  hosts: localhost
  gather_facts: false

  tasks:
  - include: more-tasks.yaml
    when: item | bool
    vars:
      a_list:
        - true
        - false
```

Next, let's modify `more-tasks.yaml` to loop over the `a_list` variable in each task:

```
---
- name: included task 1
  debug:
    msg: "I am the first included task"
  with_items: "{{ a_list }}"

- name: include task 2
  debug:
    msg: "I am the second included task"
  with_items: "{{ a_list }}"
```

[ 189 ]

Composing Reusable Ansible Content with Roles

Now let's run the playbook and see our new output:

```
~/src/mastery> ansible-playbook -i mastery-hosts includer.yaml -v
Using /etc/ansible/ansible.cfg as config file

PLAY [task inclusion] ****************************************************

TASK [included task 1] ***************************************************
ok: [localhost] => (item=True) => {
    "msg": "I am the first included task"
}
skipping: [localhost] => (item=False) => {"item": false}

TASK [include task 2] ****************************************************
ok: [localhost] => (item=True) => {
    "msg": "I am the second included task"
}
skipping: [localhost] => (item=False) => {"item": false}

PLAY RECAP ***************************************************************
localhost                  : ok=2    changed=0    unreachable=0    failed=0

~/src/mastery>
```

We can see a skipped iteration per task, the iteration where the item evaluated to a Boolean false. It's important to remember that all hosts will evaluate all included tasks. There is no way to influence Ansible to not include a file for a subset of hosts. At most, a conditional can be applied to every task within an `include` hierarchy so that included tasks may be skipped. One method to include tasks based on host facts is to utilize the `group_by` action plugin to create dynamic groups based on host facts. Then, you can give the groups their own plays to include specific tasks. This is an exercise left up to the reader.

## Tagging included tasks

When including task files, it is possible to tag all the tasks within the file. The `tags` key is used to define one or more tags to apply to all the tasks within the `include` hierarchy. The ability to tag at include time can keep the task file itself un-opinionated about how the tasks should be tagged and can allow for a set of tasks to be included multiple times but with different data and tags passed along.

> Tags can be defined at the `include` statement or at the play itself to cover all includes (and other tasks) in a given play.

Let's create a simple demonstration to illustrate how tags can be used. We'll start by editing our `includer.yaml` file to create a playbook that includes a task file twice, each with a different tag name and different variable data:

```
---
- name: task inclusion
  hosts: localhost
  gather_facts: false

  tasks:
  - include: more-tasks.yaml
    vars:
      data: first
    tags: first

  - include: more-tasks.yaml
    vars:
      data: second
    tags: second
```

Now we'll update `more-tasks.yaml` to do something with the data being provided:

```
---
- name: included task
  debug:
    msg: "My data is {{ data }}"
```

[ 191 ]

*Composing Reusable Ansible Content with Roles*

If we run this playbook without selecting tags, we'll see this task run twice:

```
~/src/mastery> ansible-playbook -i mastery-hosts includer.yaml -v
Using /etc/ansible/ansible.cfg as config file

PLAY [task inclusion] **********************************************************

TASK [included task] ***********************************************************
ok: [localhost] => {
    "msg": "My data is first"
}

TASK [included task] ***********************************************************
ok: [localhost] => {
    "msg": "My data is second"
}

PLAY RECAP *********************************************************************
localhost                  : ok=2    changed=0    unreachable=0    failed=0

~/src/mastery>
```

Now if we select which tag to run, say, the second tag, by altering our `ansible-playbook` arguments, we should see only that occurrence of the included task being run:

```
~/src/mastery> ansible-playbook -i mastery-hosts includer.yaml -v --tags second
Using /etc/ansible/ansible.cfg as config file

PLAY [task inclusion] **********************************************************

TASK [included task] ***********************************************************
ok: [localhost] => {
    "msg": "My data is second"
}

PLAY RECAP *********************************************************************
localhost                  : ok=1    changed=0    unreachable=0    failed=0

~/src/mastery>
```

Our example used the `--tags` command-line argument to indicate which tagged tasks to run. A different argument, `--skip-tags`, allows the expressing of the opposite, which tagged tasks to not run.

## Task includes with loops

Task inclusions can be combined with loops as well. When adding a `loop` instance to a task inclusion (or a `with_` loop if using a version of Ansible earlier than 2.5), the tasks inside the file will be executed with the `item` variable, which holds the place of the current loop's value. The entire `include` file will be executed repeatedly until the loop runs out of items. Let's update our example play to demonstrate this:

```yaml
---
- name: task inclusion
  hosts: localhost
  gather_facts: false

  tasks:
  - include: more-tasks.yaml
    loop:
       - one
       - two
```

We also need to update our `more-tasks.yaml` file to make use of the loop `item`:

```yaml
---
- name: included task 1
  debug:
    msg: "I am the first included task with {{ item }}"
- name: included task 2
  debug:
    msg: "I am the second included task with {{ item }}"
```

Composing Reusable Ansible Content with Roles

When executed, we can tell that tasks 1 and 2 are executed a single time for each `item` in the loop:

```
~/src/mastery> ansible-playbook -i mastery-hosts includer.yaml -v
Using /etc/ansible/ansible.cfg as config file

PLAY [task inclusion] **********************************************************

TASK [include] *****************************************************************
included: /home/jfreeman/src/mastery/more-tasks.yaml for localhost => (item=one)
included: /home/jfreeman/src/mastery/more-tasks.yaml for localhost => (item=two)

TASK [included task 1] *********************************************************
ok: [localhost] => {
    "msg": "I am the first included task with one"
}

TASK [included task 2] *********************************************************
ok: [localhost] => {
    "msg": "I am the second included task with one"
}

TASK [included task 1] *********************************************************
ok: [localhost] => {
    "msg": "I am the first included task with two"
}

TASK [included task 2] *********************************************************
ok: [localhost] => {
    "msg": "I am the second included task with two"
}

PLAY RECAP *********************************************************************
localhost                  : ok=6    changed=0    unreachable=0    failed=0

~/src/mastery>
```

Looping on inclusion is a powerful concept, but it does introduce one problem. What if there were tasks inside the included file that have their own loops? There will be a collision of the `item` variable, creating unexpected outcomes. For this reason, the `loop_control` feature was added to Ansible in version 2.1. Among other things, this feature provides a method to name the variable used for the loop, instead of the default of `item`. Using this, we can distinguish between the `item` instance that comes outside the inclusion from any `item` variables used inside the include. To demonstrate this, we'll add a `loop_var` loop control to our outer `include`:

```yaml
---
- name: task inclusion
  hosts: localhost
  gather_facts: false

  tasks:
    - include: more-tasks.yaml
      loop:
        - one
        - two
      loop_control:
        loop_var: include_item
```

Inside `more-tasks.yaml`, we'll have a task with its own loop, making use of `include_item` and the local `item`:

```yaml
---
- name: included task 1
  debug:
    msg: "I combine {{ item }} and {{ include_item }}"
  with_items:
    - a
    - b
```

# Composing Reusable Ansible Content with Roles

When executed, we see that task 1 is executed twice per inclusion loop and that the two `loop` variables are used:

```
~/src/mastery> ansible-playbook -i mastery-hosts includer.yaml -v
Using /etc/ansible/ansible.cfg as config file

PLAY [task inclusion] ************************************************

TASK [include] *******************************************************
included: /home/jfreeman/src/mastery/more-tasks.yaml for localhost
included: /home/jfreeman/src/mastery/more-tasks.yaml for localhost

TASK [included task 1] ***********************************************
ok: [localhost] => (item=a) => {
    "msg": "I combine a and one"
}
ok: [localhost] => (item=b) => {
    "msg": "I combine b and one"
}

TASK [included task 1] ***********************************************
ok: [localhost] => (item=a) => {
    "msg": "I combine a and two"
}
ok: [localhost] => (item=b) => {
    "msg": "I combine b and two"
}

PLAY RECAP ***********************************************************
localhost                  : ok=4    changed=0    unreachable=0    failed=0

~/src/mastery>
```

Other loop controls exist as well, such as `label`, which will define what is shown on the screen in the task output for the `item` value (useful for preventing large data structures from cluttering the screen) and `pause`, providing the ability to `pause` for a defined number of seconds between each loop.

## Including handlers

**Handlers** are essentially tasks. They're a set of potential tasks triggered by way of notifications from other tasks. As such, handler tasks can be included just as regular tasks can. The `include` operator is legal within the `handlers` block.

Unlike with task inclusions, variable data cannot be passed along when including handler tasks. However, it is possible to attach a conditional to a handler inclusion, to apply the conditional to every handler within the file.

Let's create an example to demonstrate this. First, we'll create a playbook that has a task that will always change, and that includes a handler task file and attaches a conditional to that inclusion:

```yaml
---
- name: touch files
  hosts: localhost
  gather_facts: false

  tasks:
  - name: a task
    debug:
      msg: "I am a changing task"
    changed_when: true
    notify: a handler

  handlers:
  - include: handlers.yaml
    when: foo | default('true') | bool
```

> When evaluating a variable that may be defined outside a playbook, it's best to use the `bool` filter to ensure that strings are properly converted to their Boolean meaning.

Next, we'll create `handlers.yaml` to define our handler task:

```yaml
---
- name: a handler
  debug:
    msg: "handling a thing"
```

If we execute this playbook without providing any further data, we should see our handler trigger:

```
~/src/mastery> ansible-playbook -i mastery-hosts includer.yaml -v
Using /etc/ansible/ansible.cfg as config file

PLAY [touch files] ************************************************************

TASK [a task] *****************************************************************
changed: [localhost] => {
    "msg": "I am a changing task"
}

RUNNING HANDLER [a handler] ***************************************************
ok: [localhost] => {
    "msg": "handling a thing"
}

PLAY RECAP ********************************************************************
localhost                  : ok=2    changed=1    unreachable=0    failed=0

~/src/mastery>
```

Now let's run the playbook again; this time, we'll define `foo` as `extra-var` and set it to `false` in our `ansible-playbook` execution arguments:

```
~/src/mastery> ansible-playbook -i mastery-hosts includer.yaml -v -e foo=false
Using /etc/ansible/ansible.cfg as config file

PLAY [touch files] ************************************************************

TASK [a task] *****************************************************************
changed: [localhost] => {
    "msg": "I am a changing task"
}

RUNNING HANDLER [a handler] ***************************************************
skipping: [localhost] => {}

PLAY RECAP ********************************************************************
localhost                  : ok=1    changed=1    unreachable=0    failed=0

~/src/mastery>
```

This time, since `foo` evaluates to `false`, our included handler gets skipped.

# Including variables

Variable data can also be separated into loadable files. This allows for the sharing of variables across multiple plays or playbooks or the inclusion of variable data that lives outside the project directory (such as secret data). Variable files are simple YAML-formatted files providing keys and values. Unlike task inclusion files, variable inclusion files cannot include more files.

Variables can be included in three different ways: via `vars_files`, via `include_vars`, or via `--extra-vars` (`-e`).

## vars_files

The `vars_files` key is a play directive. It defines a list of files to read from to load variable data. These files are read and parsed at the time the playbook itself is parsed. Just as with including tasks and handlers, the path is relative to the file referencing the file.

Here is an example play that loads variables from a file:

```yaml
---
- name: vars
  hosts: localhost
  gather_facts: false

  vars_files:
  - variables.yaml

  tasks:
  - name: a task
    debug:
      msg: "I am a {{ varname }}"
```

Now we need to create `variables.yaml` in the same directory as our playbook:

```yaml
---
varname: derp
```

Running the playbook will show that the name variable value is properly sourced from the `variables.yaml` file:

```
~/src/mastery> ansible-playbook -i mastery-hosts includer.yaml -v
Using /etc/ansible/ansible.cfg as config file

PLAY [vars] ***********************************************************

TASK [a task] *********************************************************
ok: [localhost] => {
    "msg": "I am a derp"
}

PLAY RECAP ************************************************************
localhost                  : ok=1    changed=0    unreachable=0    failed=0

~/src/mastery>
```

This is, of course, a very simple example, but it demonstrates clearly the ease of importing variables from a separate file.

## Dynamic vars_files inclusion

In certain scenarios, it may be desirable to parameterize the variable files to be loaded. It is possible to do this by using a variable as part of the filename; however, the variable must have a value defined at the time the playbook is parsed, just like when using variables in task names. Let's update our example play to load a variable file based on the data provided at execution time:

```
---
- name: vars
  hosts: localhost
  gather_facts: false

  vars_files:
    - "{{ varfile }}"

  tasks:
  - name: a task
    debug:
      msg: "I am a {{ varname }}"
```

Now when we execute the playbook, we'll provide the value for `varfile` with the `-e` argument:

```
~/src/mastery> ansible-playbook -i mastery-hosts includer.yaml -v -e varfile=variables.yaml
Using /etc/ansible/ansible.cfg as config file

PLAY [vars] ************************************************************

TASK [a task] **********************************************************
ok: [localhost] => {
    "msg": "I am a derp"
}

PLAY RECAP *************************************************************
localhost                  : ok=1    changed=0    unreachable=0    failed=0

~/src/mastery>
```

In addition to the variable value needing to be defined at execution time, the file to be loaded must also exist at execution time. This rule applies even if the file is generated by the Ansible playbook itself. Let's suppose that an Ansible playbook consists of four plays. The first play generates a YAML variable file. Then, further down, the fourth play references this file in a `vars_file` directive. Although it might initially appear as though this would work, the file does not exist at the point of execution (that is, when `ansible-playbook` is first run), and hence an error will be reported.

## include_vars

The second method to include variable data from files is the `include_vars` module. This module will load variables as a task action and will be done for each host. Unlike most modules, this module is executed locally on the Ansible host; therefore, all paths are still relative to the play file itself. Because the variable loading is done as a task, evaluation of variables in the filename happens when the task is executed. Variable data in the `file name` can be host-specific and defined in a preceding task. Additionally, the file itself does not have to exist at execution time; it can be generated by a preceding task as well. This is a very powerful and flexible concept that can lead to very dynamic playbooks if used properly.

## Composing Reusable Ansible Content with Roles

Before getting ahead of ourselves, let's demonstrate a simple usage of `include_vars` by modifying our existing play to load the variable file as a task:

```yaml
---
- name: vars
  hosts: localhost
  gather_facts: false

  tasks:
    - name: load variables
      include_vars: "{{ varfile }}"

    - name: a task
      debug:
        msg: "I am a {{ varname }}"
```

Execution of the playbook remains the same and our output differs only slightly from previous iterations:

```
~/src/mastery> ansible-playbook -i mastery-hosts includer.yaml -v -e varfile=var
iables.yaml
Using /etc/ansible/ansible.cfg as config file

PLAY [vars] **********************************************************

TASK [load variables] ************************************************
ok: [localhost] => {"ansible_facts": {"varname": "derp"}, "ansible_included_var_files": ["/home/jfreeman/src/mastery/variables.yaml"], "changed": false}

TASK [a task] ********************************************************
ok: [localhost] => {
    "msg": "I am a derp"
}

PLAY RECAP ***********************************************************
localhost                  : ok=2    changed=0    unreachable=0    failed=0

~/src/mastery>
```

Just like with other tasks, looping can be done to load more than one file in a single task. This is particularly effective when using the special `with_first_found` loop to iterate through a list of increasingly more generic filenames until a file is found to be loaded.

Let's demonstrate this by changing our play to use gathered host facts to try and load a variable file specific to the distribution, specific to the distribution family, or, finally, a default file:

```yaml
---
- name: vars
  hosts: localhost
  gather_facts: true

  tasks:
  - name: load variables
    include_vars: "{{ item }}"
    with_first_found:
      - "{{ ansible_distribution }}.yaml"
      - "{{ ansible_os_family }}.yaml"
      - variables.yaml

  - name: a task
    debug:
      msg: "I am a {{ varname }}"
```

Execution should look very similar to previous runs, only this time we'll see a fact-gathering task, and we will not pass along extra variable data in the execution:

```
~/src/mastery> ansible-playbook -i mastery-hosts -c local includer.yaml -v
Using /etc/ansible/ansible.cfg as config file

PLAY [vars] **********************************************************

TASK [Gathering Facts] ***********************************************
ok: [localhost]

TASK [load variables] ************************************************
ok: [localhost] => (item=/home/jfreeman/src/mastery/variables.yaml) => {"ansible
_facts": {"varname": "derp"}, "ansible_included_var_files": ["/home/jfreeman/src
/mastery/variables.yaml"], "changed": false, "item": "/home/jfreeman/src/mastery
/variables.yaml"}

TASK [a task] ********************************************************
ok: [localhost] => {
    "msg": "I am a derp"
}

PLAY RECAP ***********************************************************
localhost                  : ok=3    changed=0    unreachable=0    failed=0

~/src/mastery>
```

[ 203 ]

We can also see from the output which file was found to load. In this case, `variables.yaml` was loaded, as the other two files did not exist. This practice is commonly used to load variables that are operating system-specific to the host in question. Variables for a variety of operating systems can be written out to appropriately named files. By utilizing the `ansible_distribution` variable, which is populated by fact gathering, variable files that use `ansible_distribution` values as part of their name can be loaded by way of a `with_first_found` argument. A default set of variables can be provided in a file that does not use any variable data as a failsafe.

## extra-vars

The final method to load variable data from a file is to reference a file path with the `--extra-vars` (or `-e`) argument to `ansible-playbook`. Normally, this argument expects a set of `key=value` data; however, if a file path is provided and prefixed with the `@` symbol, Ansible will read the entire file to load variable data. Let's alter one of our earlier examples, where we used `-e`, and instead of defining a variable directly on the command line, we'll include the variable file we've already written out:

```
---
- name: vars
  hosts: localhost
  gather_facts: false

  tasks:
  - name: a task
    debug:
      msg: "I am a {{ varname }}"
```

When we provide a path after the `@` symbol, the path is relative to the current working directory, regardless of where the playbook itself lives. Let's execute our playbook and provide a path to `variables.yaml`:

```
~/src/mastery> ansible-playbook -i mastery-hosts includer.yaml -v -e @variables.yaml
Using /etc/ansible/ansible.cfg as config file

PLAY [vars] ************************************************************

TASK [a task] **********************************************************
ok: [localhost] => {
    "msg": "I am a derp"
}

PLAY RECAP *************************************************************
localhost                  : ok=1    changed=0    unreachable=0    failed=0

~/src/mastery>
```

Here, we can see that once again our `variables.yaml` file was included successfully, only, as you can see from the previous code, it is not even mentioned in the playbook itself—we were able to load it in its entirety through the -e flag.

> When including a variable file with the `--extra-vars` argument, the file must exist at `ansible-playbook` execution time.

Variable inclusion is incredibly powerful in Ansible—but what about playbooks themselves? Here, things are a bit different, and as the chapter progresses, we will look at how to make effective use of reusable tasks and playbook code, thus encouraging good programming practices with Ansible.

## Including playbooks

Playbook files can include other whole playbook files. This construct can be useful to tie together a few independent playbooks into a larger, more comprehensive playbook. Playbook inclusion is a bit more primitive than task inclusion. You cannot perform variable substitution when including a playbook, you cannot apply conditionals, and you cannot apply tags, either. The playbook files to be included must exist at the time of execution as well.

# Composing Reusable Ansible Content with Roles

Prior to Ansible 2.4, playbook inclusion was achieved using the `include` keyword—however, this is deprecated and will be removed in Ansible 2.8, and so it should not be used. Instead, you should now use `import_playbook`. This is a play-level directive—it cannot be used as a task. However, it is very easy to use. Let's define a simple example to demonstrate this. First, let's create a playbook that will be included, called `includeme.yaml`:

```
---
- name: include playbook
  hosts: localhost
  gather_facts: false

  tasks:
  - name: an included playbook task
    debug:
      msg: "I am in the included playbook"
```

As you will no doubt recognize by now, this is a complete standalone playbook and we could run it in isolation:

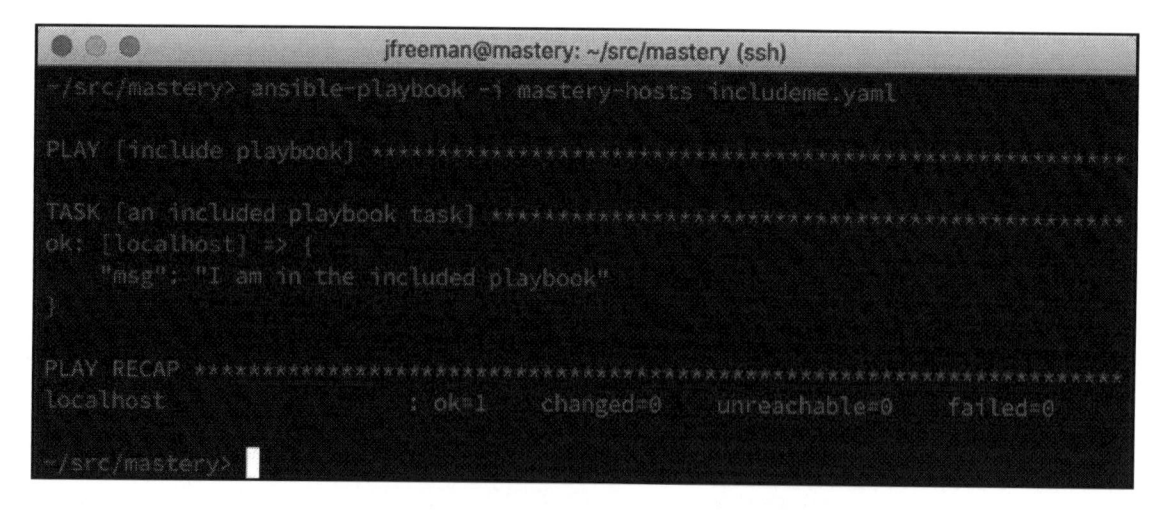

```
~/src/mastery> ansible-playbook -i mastery-hosts includeme.yaml

PLAY [include playbook] **********************************************

TASK [an included playbook task] *************************************
ok: [localhost] => {
    "msg": "I am in the included playbook"
}

PLAY RECAP ***********************************************************
localhost                  : ok=1    changed=0    unreachable=0    failed=0

~/src/mastery>
```

However, we can also import this into another playbook. Modify the original `includer.yaml` playbook so that it looks like this:

```
---
- name: include playbook
  hosts: localhost
  gather_facts: false

  tasks:
```

[ 206 ]

```yaml
    - name: a task
      debug:
        msg: "I am in the main playbook"

    - name: include a playbook
      import_playbook: includeme.yaml
```

When we run this, we can see that both debug messages are displayed, and the imported playbook is run after the initial task, which is the sequence we defined in the original playbook:

```
~/src/mastery> ansible-playbook -i mastery-hosts includer.yaml

PLAY [include playbook] ************************************************

TASK [a task] **********************************************************
ok: [localhost] => {
    "msg": "I am in the main playbook"
}

PLAY [include playbook] ************************************************

TASK [an included playbook task] ***************************************
ok: [localhost] => {
    "msg": "I am in the included playbook"
}

PLAY RECAP *************************************************************
localhost                  : ok=2    changed=0    unreachable=0    failed=0

~/src/mastery>
```

In this way, it is very easy to reuse whole playbooks without needing to restructure them into the format of roles or otherwise. Note, however, that this feature is subject to active development in Ansible, so it is recommended that you always refer to the documentation to ensure you can achieve the results you are looking for.

# Roles

With a functional understanding of the inclusion of variables, tasks, handlers, and playbooks, we can move on to the more advanced topic of **roles**. Roles move beyond the basic structure of a few playbooks and a few broken out files to reference. Roles provide a framework for fully independent, or interdependent, collections of variables, tasks, files, templates, and modules. Each role is typically limited to a particular theme or a desired end result, with all the necessary steps to reach that result either within the role itself or in other roles listed as dependencies. Roles themselves are not playbooks. There is no way to directly execute a role. Roles have no setting for which host the role will apply to. Top-level playbooks are the glue that binds the hosts from your inventory to roles that should be applied to those hosts.

## Role structure

Roles have a structured layout on the filesystem. This structure exists to provide automation around including tasks, handlers, variables, modules, and role dependencies. The structure also allows for the easy reference of files and templates from anywhere within the role.

Roles all live in a subdirectory of a playbook directory structure in the `roles/` directory. This is, of course, configurable by way of the `roles_path` general configuration key, but let's stick to the defaults. Each role is itself a directory tree. The role name is the directory name within `roles/`. Each role can have a number of subdirectories with special meanings that are processed when a role is applied to a set of hosts.

A role may contain all these elements, or as few as just one of them. Missing elements are simply ignored. Some roles exist just to provide common handlers across a project. Other roles exist as a single dependency point that in turn just depends on numerous other roles.

## Tasks

The task file is the main part of a role. If `roles/<role_name>/tasks/main.yaml` exists, all the tasks therein and any other files it includes will be embedded in the play and executed.

## Handlers

Similar to tasks, handlers are automatically loaded from `roles/<role_name>/handlers/main.yaml`, if the file exists. These handlers can be referenced by any task within the role, or by any tasks within any other role that lists this role as a dependency.

## Variables

There are two types of variables that can be defined in a role. There are role variables, loaded from `roles/<role_name>/vars/main.yaml`, and there are role defaults, loaded from `roles/<role_name>/defaults/main.yaml`. The difference between `vars` and `defaults` has to do with precedence order. Refer to Chapter 1, *The System Architecture and Design of Ansible*, for a detailed description of the order. Role defaults are the lowest order variables. Literally any other definition of a variable will take precedence over a role default. Role defaults can be thought of as placeholders for actual data, a reference of what variables a developer may be interested in defining with site-specific values. Role variables, on the other hand, have a higher order of precedence. Role variables can be overridden, but generally they are used when the same dataset is referenced more than once within a role. If the dataset is to be redefined with site-local values, then the variable should be listed in the role defaults rather than the role variables.

## Modules and plugins

A role can include custom modules as well as plugins. While the Ansible project is quite good at reviewing and accepting submitted modules, there are certain cases where it may not be advisable or even legal to submit a custom module upstream. In those cases, delivering the module with the role may be a better option. Modules can be loaded from `roles/<role_name>/library/` and can be used by any task in the role, or any later role. Modules provided in this path will override any other copies of the same module name anywhere else on the filesystem, which can be a way to distribute added functionality to a core module before the functionality has been accepted upstream and released with a new version of Ansible.

Likewise, plugins are often used to tweak Ansible behavior in a way that makes sense for a particular environment and are unsuitable for upstream contribution. Plugins can be distributed as part of a role, which may be easier than explicitly installing plugins on every host that will act as an Ansible control host.

*Composing Reusable Ansible Content with Roles*

Plugins will automatically be loaded if found inside of a role, in one of the following subdirectories:

- `action_plugins`
- `lookup_plugins`
- `callback_plugins`
- `connection_plugins`
- `filter_plugins`
- `strategy_plugins`
- `cache_plugins`
- `test_plugins`
- `shell_plugins`

## Dependencies

Roles can express a dependency upon another role. It is a common practice for sets of roles to all depend on a common role for tasks, handlers, modules, and so on. Those roles may depend upon only having to be defined once. When Ansible processes a role for a set of hosts, it will first look for any dependencies listed in `roles/<role_name>/meta/main.yaml`. If any are defined, those roles will be processed and the tasks within will be executed (after checking for any dependencies listed within, too) until all dependencies have been completed before starting on the initial role tasks. We will describe role dependencies in more depth later in this chapter.

## Files and templates

Task and handler modules can reference files relatively within `roles/<role_name>/files/`. The filename can be provided without any prefix and will be sourced from `roles/<role_name>/files/<file_name>`. Relative prefixes are allowed as well, in order to access files within subdirectories of `roles/<role_name>/files/`. Modules such as `template`, `copy`, and `script` may take advantage of this.

Similarly, templates used by the `template` module can be referenced relatively within `roles/<role_name>/templates/`. This sample code uses a relative path to load the `derp.j2` template from the full `roles/<role_name>/templates/herp/derp.j2` path:

```
- name: configure herp
  template:
```

```
          src: herp/derp.j2
          dest: /etc/herp/derp.j2
```

In this way, it is easy to organize files within the standard role directory structure, and still access them easily from within the role without having to type in long and complex paths.

## Putting it all together

To illustrate what a full role structure might look like, here is an example role by the name of demo:

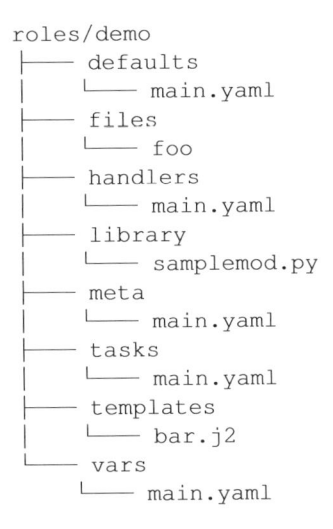

```
roles/demo
├── defaults
│   └── main.yaml
├── files
│   └── foo
├── handlers
│   └── main.yaml
├── library
│   └── samplemod.py
├── meta
│   └── main.yaml
├── tasks
│   └── main.yaml
├── templates
│   └── bar.j2
└── vars
    └── main.yaml
```

When creating a role, not every directory or file is required. Only the files that exist will be processed. Thus, our example of your role does not require or use handlers; the entire handlers part of the tree could simply be left out.

## Role dependencies

As stated before, roles can depend on other roles. These relationships are called dependencies and they are described in a role's meta/main.yaml file. This file expects a top-level data hash with a key of dependencies; the data within is a list of roles:

```
---
dependencies:
  - role: common
  - role: apache
```

In this example, Ansible will fully process the `common` role first (and any dependencies it may express) before continuing with the `apache` role and then finally starting on the role's tasks.

Dependencies can be referenced by name without any prefix if they exist within the same directory structure or live within the configured `roles_path`. Otherwise, full paths can be used to locate roles:

```
role: /opt/ansible/site-roles/apache
```

When expressing a dependency, it is possible to pass along data to the dependency. The data can be variables, tags, or even conditionals.

## Role dependency variables

Variables that are passed along when listing a dependency will override values for matching variables defined in `defaults/main.yaml` or `vars/main.yaml`. This can be useful for using a common role, such as an `apache` role, as a dependency while providing site-specific data such as what ports to open in the firewall or what `apache` modules to enable. Variables are expressed as additional keys to the role listing. Thus, continuing our hypothetical example, consider that we need to pass some variables to both the `common` and `apache` role dependencies we discussed:

```
---
dependencies:
  - role: common
    simple_var_a: True
    simple_var_b: False
  - role: apache
    complex_var:
      key1: value1
      key2: value2
    short_list:
      - 8080
      - 8081
```

When providing dependency variable data, two names are reserved and should not be used as role variables: `tags` and `when`. The former is used to pass tag data into a role, and the latter is used to pass a conditional into the role.

[ 212 ]

# Tags

Tags can be applied to all the tasks found within a dependency role. This functions much in the same way as tags being applied to included task files, as described earlier in this chapter. The syntax is simple: the `tags` key can be a single item or a list. To demonstrate, let's further expand our theoretical example by adding some tags:

```
---
dependencies:
  - role: common
    simple_var_a: True
    simple_var_b: False
    tags: common_demo
  - role: apache
    complex_var:
      key1: value1
      key2: value2
    short_list:
      - 8080
      - 8081
    tags:
      - apache_demo
      - 8080
      - 8181
```

As with adding tags to the included task files, all the tasks found within a dependency (and any dependency within that hierarchy) will gain the provided tags.

# Role dependency conditionals

While it is not possible to prevent the processing of a dependency role with a conditional, it is possible to skip all the tasks within a dependency role hierarchy by applying a conditional to a dependency. This mirrors the functionality of task inclusion with conditionals as well. The `when` key is used to express the conditional. Once again, we'll grow our example by adding a dependency to demonstrate the syntax:

```
---
dependencies:
  - role: common
    simple_var_a: True
    simple_var_b: False
    tags: common_demo
  - role: apache
    complex_var:
      key1: value1
```

```
      key2: value2
    short_list:
      - 8080
      - 8081
    tags:
      - apache_demo
      - 8080
      - 8181
    when: backend_server == 'apache'
```

In this example, the `apache` role will always be processed, but tasks within the role will only be run when the `backend_server` variable contains the `apache` string.

## Role application

Roles are not plays. They do not possess any opinions about which hosts the role tasks should run on, what connection methods to use, whether to operate serially, or any other play behaviors described in Chapter 1, *The System Architecture and Design of Ansible*. Roles must be applied inside a play within a playbook, where all these opinions can be expressed.

To apply a role within a play, the `roles` operator is used. This operator expects a list of roles to apply to the hosts in the play. Much like describing role dependencies, when describing roles to apply, data can be passed along, such as variables, tags, and conditionals. The syntax is exactly the same.

To demonstrate applying roles within a play, let's create a simple role and apply it to a simple playbook. First, let's build the role named `simple`, which will have a single `debug` task in `roles/simple/tasks/main.yaml` that prints the value of a role default variable defined in `roles/simple/defaults/main.yaml`. First, let's create the task file (in the `tasks/` subdirectory):

```
---
- name: print a variable
  debug:
    var: derp
```

Next, we'll write our default file with a single variable, `derp`:

```
---
derp: herp
```

*Chapter 7*

To execute this role, we'll write a playbook with a single play to apply the role. We'll call our playbook `roleplay.yaml`, and it'll live at the same directory level as the `roles/` directory:

```yaml
---
- hosts: localhost
  gather_facts: false

  roles:
    - role: simple
```

> If no data is provided with the role, an alternative syntax that just lists the roles to apply can be used, instead of the hash. However, for consistency, I feel it's best to always use the same syntax within a project.

We'll reuse our `mastery-hosts` inventory from earlier chapters and execute the playbook:

```
~/src/mastery> ansible-playbook -i mastery-hosts roleplay.yaml

PLAY [localhost] ****************************************************************

TASK [simple : print a variable] ************************************************
ok: [localhost] => {
    "derp": "herp"
}

PLAY RECAP **********************************************************************
localhost                  : ok=1    changed=0    unreachable=0    failed=0

~/src/mastery>
```

Thanks to the magic of roles, the `derp` variable value was automatically loaded from the role defaults. Of course, we can override the default value when applying the role. Let's modify our playbook and supply a new value for `derp`:

```yaml
---
- hosts: localhost
  gather_facts: false

  roles:
    - role: simple
      derp: newval
```

[ 215 ]

This time when we execute, we'll see `newval` as the value for `derp`:

```
~/src/mastery> ansible-playbook -i mastery-hosts roleplay.yaml

PLAY [localhost] ****************************************************************

TASK [simple : print a variable] ************************************************
ok: [localhost] => {
    "derp": "newval"
}

PLAY RECAP **********************************************************************
localhost                  : ok=1    changed=0    unreachable=0    failed=0

~/src/mastery>
```

Multiple roles can be applied within a single play. The `roles:` key expects a list value. Just add more roles to apply more roles (the next example is theoretical and left as an exercise for the reader):

```
---
- hosts: localhost
  gather_facts: false

  roles:
  - role: simple
    derp: newval
  - role: second_role
    othervar: value
  - role: third_role
  - role: another_role
```

This playbook will load a total of four roles—`simple`, `second_role`, `third_role`, and `another_role`—and each will be executed in the sequence in which they are listed.

## Mixing roles and tasks

Plays that use roles are not limited to just roles. These plays can have `tasks` of their own, as well as two other blocks of tasks: `pre_tasks` and `post_tasks`. The order in which these are executed is not dependent upon which order these sections are listed in the play itself; instead, there is a strict order to block execution within a play. See *Chapter 1, The System Architecture and Design of Ansible,* for details on the playbook order of operations.

Handlers for a play are flushed at multiple points. If there is a `pre_tasks` block, handlers are flushed after all `pre_tasks` are executed. Then, the `roles` and `tasks` blocks are executed (roles first, then tasks, regardless of the order they are written in the playbook), after which handlers will be flushed again. Finally, if a `post_tasks` block exists, handlers will be flushed once again after all `post_tasks` have executed. Of course, handlers can be flushed at any time with the `meta: flush_handlers` call. Let's expand on our `roleplay.yaml` to demonstrate all the different times handlers can be triggered:

```yaml
---
- hosts: localhost
  gather_facts: false

  pre_tasks:
  - name: pretask
    debug:
      msg: "a pre task"
    changed_when: true
    notify: say hi

  roles:
  - role: simple
    derp: newval

  tasks:
  - name: task
    debug:
      msg: "a task"
    changed_when: true
    notify: say hi
  post_tasks:
  - name: posttask
    debug:
      msg: "a post task"
    changed_when: true
    notify: say hi

  handlers:
  - name: say hi
    debug:
      msg: "hi"
```

We'll also modify our simple role's tasks to notify the `say hi` handler as well:

```yaml
---
- name: print a variable
  debug:
    var: derp
```

# Composing Reusable Ansible Content with Roles

```
        changed_when: true
        notify: say hi
```

> ℹ️ This only works because the `say hi` handler has been defined in the play that is calling the `simple` role. If the handler is not defined, an error will occur. It's best practice to only notify handlers that exist within the same role or any role marked as a dependency.

Running our playbook should result in the `say hi` handler being called a total of three times: once for `pre_tasks`, once for `roles` and `tasks`, and once for `post_tasks`:

```
~/src/mastery> ansible-playbook -i mastery-hosts roleplay.yaml

PLAY [localhost] ****************************************************************

TASK [pretask] ******************************************************************
changed: [localhost] => {
    "msg": "a pre task"
}

RUNNING HANDLER [say hi] ********************************************************
ok: [localhost] => {
    "msg": "hi"
}

TASK [simple : print a variable] ************************************************
changed: [localhost] => {
    "derp": "newval"
}

TASK [task] *********************************************************************
changed: [localhost] => {
    "msg": "a task"
}

RUNNING HANDLER [say hi] ********************************************************
ok: [localhost] => {
    "msg": "hi"
}

TASK [posttask] *****************************************************************
changed: [localhost] => {
    "msg": "a post task"
}

RUNNING HANDLER [say hi] ********************************************************
ok: [localhost] => {
    "msg": "hi"
}

PLAY RECAP **********************************************************************
localhost                  : ok=7    changed=4    unreachable=0    failed=0

~/src/mastery>
```

While the order in which `pre_tasks`, `roles`, `tasks`, and `post_tasks` are written into a play does not impact the order in which those sections are executed, it's best practice to write them in the order that they will be executed. This is a visual cue to help remember the order and to avoid confusion when reading the playbook later.

## Role includes and imports

With Ansible version 2.2, a new action plugin was made available as a technical preview, `include_role`. Then, in Ansible Version 2.4, this concept was further developed by the addition of the `import_role` plugin.

These plugins are used in a task to include and execute an entire role directly from a task. The difference between the two is subtle but important—the `include_role` plugin is considered dynamic, meaning the code is processed during runtime when the task referencing it is encountered. The `import_role` plugin, on the other hand, is considered static, meaning all imports are pre-processed at the time the playbook is initially parsed. This has various impacts on their use in playbooks—for example, `import_role` cannot be used in loops, while `include_role` can.

> Full details of the tradeoffs between importing and including can be found in the official Ansible documentation here: https://docs.ansible.com/ansible/latest/user_guide/playbooks_reuse.html.

As both of these plugins are currently considered a technical preview at the time of writing, they are not guaranteed to exist in their current form in future Ansible releases. Thus, reliance on this functionality should be avoided unless you absolutely need it for a specific purpose.

## Role sharing

One of the advantages of using roles is the ability to share the role across plays, playbooks, entire project spaces, and even across organizations. Roles are designed to be self-contained (or to clearly reference dependent roles) so that they can exist outside of a project space where the playbook that applies the role lives. Roles can be installed in shared paths on an Ansible host, or they can be distributed via source control.

# Ansible Galaxy

**Ansible Galaxy** (https://galaxy.ansible.com/) is a community hub for finding and sharing Ansible roles. Anybody can visit the website to browse the roles and reviews; plus, users who create a login can provide reviews of the roles they've tested. Roles from Galaxy can be downloaded using the `ansible-galaxy` utility provided with Ansible.

The `ansible-galaxy` utility can connect to and install roles from the Ansible Galaxy website. This utility will default to installing roles into `/etc/ansible/roles`. If `roles_path` is configured, or if a runtime path is provided with the `--roles-path` (or `-p`) option, the roles will be installed there instead. If any roles have been installed to the `roles_path` or the provided path, `ansible-galaxy` can list those and show information about those as well. To demonstrate the usage of `ansible-galaxy`, let's use it to install a role for installing and managing Docker on Ubuntu from Ansible Galaxy into the roles directory we've been working with. Installing roles from Ansible Galaxy requires `username.rolename`, as multiple users may have uploaded roles with the same name. In this case, we want the `docker_ubuntu` role from the user `angstwad`:

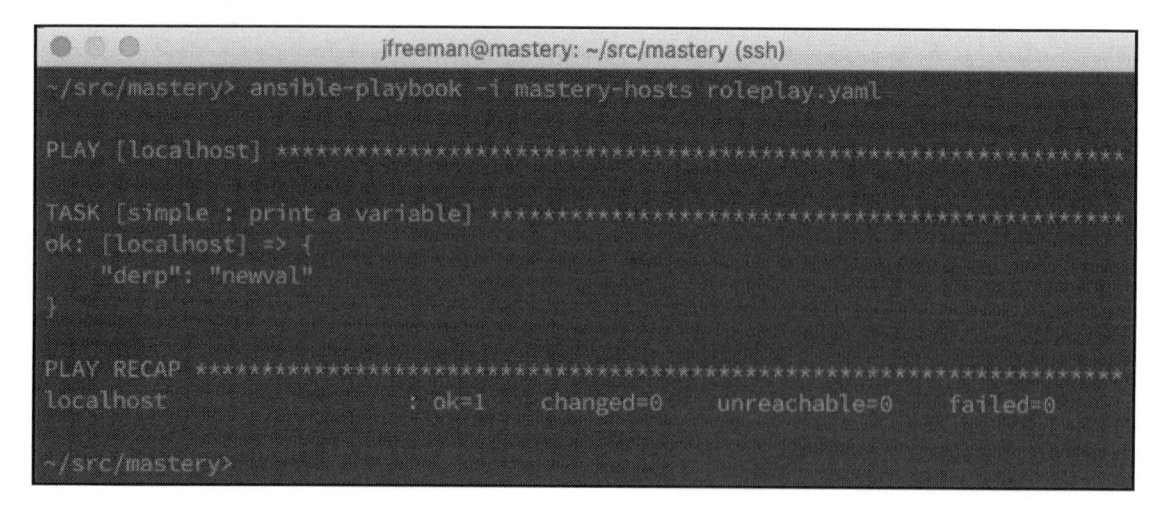

```
~/src/mastery> ansible-playbook -i mastery-hosts roleplay.yaml

PLAY [localhost] ********************************************************

TASK [simple : print a variable] ****************************************
ok: [localhost] => {
    "derp": "newval"
}

PLAY RECAP **************************************************************
localhost                  : ok=1    changed=0    unreachable=0    failed=0

~/src/mastery>
```

Now we can make use of this role by referencing `angstwad.docker_ubuntu` in a play or another role's dependencies block. We can also list it and gain information about it using the `ansible-galaxy` utility:

```
~/src/mastery> ansible-galaxy list -p roles/
- angstwad.docker_ubuntu, v3.8.0
~/src/mastery> ansible-galaxy info -p roles/ angstwad.docker_ubuntu | head -n 25


Role: angstwad.docker_ubuntu
	description: A comprehensive and (ideally) sane way to install Docker on Ubuntu 14.04+
	active: True
	commit: 6edfac43340df6983b04926ec48d9aa5fba0b00f
	commit_message: Permit to provide proxies for installation
	commit_url: https://api.github.com/repos/angstwad/docker.ubuntu/git/commits/6edfac43340df6983b04926ec48d9aa5fba0b00f
	company:
	created: 2014-01-28T03:13:44.951696Z
	dependencies: []
	download_count: 180443
	forks_count: 210
	galaxy_info:
		author: Paul Durivage
		categories: ['development', 'packaging', 'system']
		license: Apache v2.0
		min_ansible_version: 2.3
		platforms: [{'name': 'Debian', 'versions': ['jessie', 'stretch']}, {'name': 'Ubuntu', 'versions': ['trusty', 'xenial', 'zesty']}]
	github_branch: master
	github_repo: docker.ubuntu
	github_user: angstwad
	id: 292
	imported: 2018-12-18T12:52:09.717829-05:00
	install_date: Thu Feb 21 11:09:49 2019
	installed_version: v3.8.0
~/src/mastery>
```

*Composing Reusable Ansible Content with Roles*

The output was capped at `25` lines, to avoid displaying the entire information set and `README.md` contents. Some of the data being displayed by the `info` command lives within the role itself, in the `meta/main.yaml` file. Previously, we've only seen dependency information in this file, and it may not have made much sense to name the directory `meta`, but now we see that other metadata lives in this file as well:

```
~/src/mastery> cat roles/angstwad.docker_ubuntu/meta/main.yml
---
galaxy_info:
  author: Paul Durivage
  description: A comprehensive and (ideally) sane way to install Docker on Ubuntu 14.04+
  license: Apache v2.0
  min_ansible_version: 2.3
  platforms:
    - name: Debian
      versions:
        - jessie
        - stretch
    - name: Ubuntu
      versions:
        - trusty
        - xenial
        - zesty
  categories:
    - development
    - packaging
    - system
dependencies: []
  # List your role dependencies here, one per line. Only
  # dependencies available via galaxy should be listed here.
  # Be sure to remove the '[]' above if you add dependencies
  # to this list.
~/src/mastery>
```

The `ansible-galaxy` utility can also help with the creation of new roles. The `init` method will create a skeleton directory tree for the role, as well as populate the `meta/main.yaml` file with placeholders for Galaxy-related data. The `init` method takes a variety of options, as shown in the `help` output:

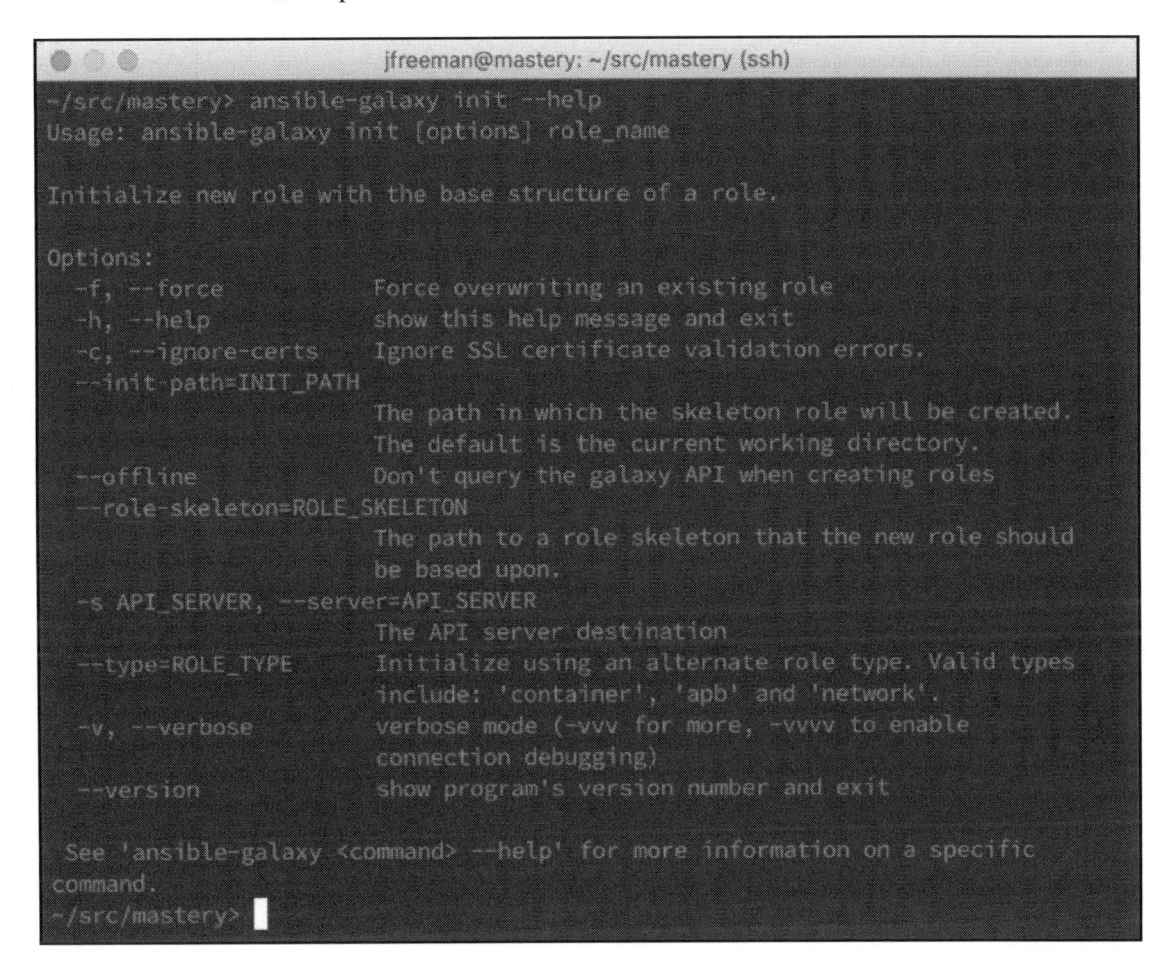

```
~/src/mastery> ansible-galaxy init --help
Usage: ansible-galaxy init [options] role_name

Initialize new role with the base structure of a role.

Options:
  -f, --force           Force overwriting an existing role
  -h, --help            show this help message and exit
  -c, --ignore-certs    Ignore SSL certificate validation errors.
  --init-path=INIT_PATH
                        The path in which the skeleton role will be created.
                        The default is the current working directory.
  --offline             Don't query the galaxy API when creating roles
  --role-skeleton=ROLE_SKELETON
                        The path to a role skeleton that the new role should
                        be based upon.
  -s API_SERVER, --server=API_SERVER
                        The API server destination
  --type=ROLE_TYPE      Initialize using an alternate role type. Valid types
                        include: 'container', 'apb' and 'network'.
  -v, --verbose         verbose mode (-vvv for more, -vvvv to enable
                        connection debugging)
  --version             show program's version number and exit

See 'ansible-galaxy <command> --help' for more information on a specific
command.
~/src/mastery>
```

*Composing Reusable Ansible Content with Roles*

Let's demonstrate this capability by creating a new role in our working directory named `autogen`:

```
~/src/mastery> ansible-galaxy init --init-path roles/ autogen
- autogen was created successfully
~/src/mastery> tree roles/autogen
roles/autogen
├── defaults
│   └── main.yml
├── files
├── handlers
│   └── main.yml
├── meta
│   └── main.yml
├── README.md
├── tasks
│   └── main.yml
├── templates
├── tests
│   ├── inventory
│   └── test.yml
└── vars
    └── main.yml

8 directories, 8 files
~/src/mastery>
```

Note that where we have used the -p switch in the past for specifying the local `roles/` directory, we have to use the `--init-path` switch instead with the `init` command. For roles that are not suitable for Ansible Galaxy, such as roles dealing with in-house systems, `ansible-galaxy` can install directly from a Git URL. Instead of just providing a role name to the `install` method, a full Git URL with an optional version can be provided instead. For example, if we wanted to install the `foowhiz` role from our internal Git server, we could simply do the following:

```
~/src/mastery> ansible-galaxy install -p /opt/ansible/roles git+git@git.internal.site:ansible-roles/foowhiz
```

Without version information, the `master` branch will be used. Without name data, the name will be determined from the URL itself. To provide a version, append a comma and the version string that Git can understand, such as a tag or branch name, such as `v1`:

```
~/src/mastery> ansible-galaxy install -p /opt/ansible/roles git+git@git.internal.site:ansible-roles/foowhiz,v1
```

A name for the role can be added with another comma followed by the name string. If you need to supply a name but do not wish to supply a version, an empty slot is still required for the version:

```
~/src/mastery> ansible-galaxy install -p /opt/ansible/roles git+git@git.internal.site:ansible-roles/foowhiz,,foo-whiz-common
```

Roles can also be installed directly from tarballs as well, by providing a URL to the tarball in lieu of a full Git URL or a role name to fetch from Ansible Galaxy.

When you need to install many roles for a project, it's possible to define multiple roles to download and install in a YAML-formatted file that ends with .yaml (or .yml). The format of this file allows you to specify multiple roles from multiple sources and retain the ability to specify versions and role names. In addition, the source control method can be listed (currently, only `git` and `hg` are supported):

```
---
- src: <name or url>
  version: <optional version>
  name: <optional name override>
  scm: <optional defined source control mechanism>
```

To install all the roles within a file, use the `--roles-file` (`-r`) option with the `install` method:

```
~/src/mastery> ansible-galaxy install -r foowhiz-reqs.yaml
```

In this manner, it is very easy to gather all your role dependencies prior to running your playbooks, and whether the roles you need are publicly available on Ansible Galaxy or held in your own internal source-control management system, this simple step can greatly speed along playbook deployment while supporting code reuse.

## Summary

Ansible provides the capability to divide content logically into separate files. This capability helps project developers to not repeat the same code over and over again. Roles within Ansible take this capability a step further and wrap some magic around the paths to the content. Roles are tunable, reusable, portable, and shareable blocks of functionality. Ansible Galaxy exists as a community hub for developers to find, rate, and share roles. The `ansible-galaxy` command-line tool provides a method to interact with the Ansible Galaxy site or other role-sharing mechanisms. These capabilities and tools help with the organization and utilization of common code.

In this chapter, you learned all about inclusion concepts relating to tasks, handlers, variables, and even entire playbooks. Then you expanded on this knowledge by learning about roles—their structure, setting default variable values, and handling role dependencies. You then proceeded to learn about designing playbooks to utilize roles effectively, and applying options such as tags that roles otherwise lack. Finally, you learned about sharing roles across projects using repositories such as Git and Ansible Galaxy.

In the next chapter, we'll cover useful and effective troubleshooting techniques to help you when your Ansible deployments run into trouble.

# 8
# Troubleshooting Ansible

Ansible is simple, but powerful. The simplicity of Ansible means that its operation is easy to understand and follow. Being able to understand and follow this is critically important when debugging unexpected behavior. In this chapter, we will explore the various methods that can be employed to examine, introspect, modify, and otherwise debug the operation of Ansible. In this chapter, we will look at the following topics:

- Playbook logging and verbosity
- Variable introspection
- Playbook debugging
- Ansible console
- Debugging local code execution
- Debugging remote code execution

## Technical requirements

Check out the following video to see the Code in Action:

```
http://bit.ly/2Fsi4ij
```

## Playbook logging and verbosity

Increasing the verbosity of Ansible output can solve many problems. From invalid module arguments to incorrect connection commands, increased verbosity can be critical in pinpointing the source of an error. Playbook logging and verbosity was briefly discussed in `Chapter 2`, *Protecting Your Secrets with Ansible,* with regard to protecting secret values while executing playbooks. This section will cover verbosity and logging in further detail.

## Verbosity

When executing playbooks with `ansible-playbook`, the output is displayed on standard out. With the default level of verbosity, very little information is displayed. As a play is executed, `ansible-playbook` will print a **PLAY** header with the name of the play. Then, for each task, a **task** header is printed with the name of the task. As each host executes the task, the name of the host is displayed along with the task state, which can be `ok`, `fatal`, or `changed`. No further information about the task is displayed, such as the module being executed, the arguments provided to the module, or the return data from the execution. While this is fine for well-established playbooks, I tend to want a little more information about my plays. In a few of the earlier examples in this book, we used higher levels of verbosity, up to level of two (-vv), so that we can see the location of the task and return data. There are five total levels of verbosity:

- **None**: The default level
- **One (-v)**: Where the return data and conditional information is displayed
- **Two (-vv)**: For task location and handler notification information
- **Three (-vvv)**: Provides details of the connection attempts and task invocation information
- **Four (-vvvv)**: Pass along extra verbosity options to the connection plugins (such as passing -vvv to the `ssh` commands)

Increasing the verbosity can help pinpoint where errors might be occurring, as well as providing extra insight into how Ansible is performing its operations.

As we mentioned in `Chapter 2`, *Protecting Your Secrets with Ansible*, verbosity beyond level one can leak sensitive data to standard out and log files, so care should be taken when using increased verbosity in a potentially shared environment.

## Logging

While the default is for `ansible-playbook` to log to standard out, the amount of output may be greater than the buffer of the Terminal emulator being used; therefore, it may be necessary to save all the output to a file. While various shells provide some mechanism to redirect output, a more elegant solution is to direct `ansible-playbook` to log to a file. This is accomplished by way of either a `log_path` definition in the `ansible.cfg` file, or by setting `ANSIBLE_LOG_PATH` as an environment variable. The value of either should be the path to a file. If the path does not exist, Ansible will attempt to create the file. If the file does exist, Ansible will append to the file, allowing consolidation of multiple `ansible-playbook` execution logs.

The use of a log file is not mutually exclusive with logging to standard output. Both can happen at the same time, and the verbosity level that's provided has an effect on both, simultaneously.

## Variable introspection

A common set of problems that are encountered when developing Ansible playbooks is the improper use, or invalid assumption, of the value of variables. This is particularly common when registering the results of one task in a variable, and later using that variable in a task or template. If the desired element of the result is not accessed properly, the end result will be unexpected, or perhaps even harmful.

To troubleshoot improper variable usage, inspection of the variable value is the key. The easiest way to inspect a variable's value is with the debug module. The debug module allows for displaying free form text on screen, and like with other tasks, the arguments to the module can take advantage of the Jinja2 template syntax as well. Let's demonstrate this usage by creating a sample play that executes a task, registers the result, and then shows the result in a debug statement using the Jinja2 syntax to render the variable:

```
---
- name: variable introspection demo
  hosts: localhost
  gather_facts: false

  tasks:
    - name: do a thing
      uri:
        url: https://derpops.bike
      register: derpops

    - name: show derpops
      debug:
        msg: "derpops value is {{ derpops }}"
```

# Troubleshooting Ansible

When we run this play, we'll see a displayed value for `derpops`, as shown in the following screenshot:

```
~/src/mastery> ansible-playbook -i mastery-hosts vintro.yaml -v
Using /etc/ansible/ansible.cfg as config file

PLAY [variable introspection demo] *********************************************

TASK [do a thing] **************************************************************
ok: [localhost] => {"accept_ranges": "bytes", "access_control_allow_origin": "*"
, "age": "382", "cache_control": "max-age=600", "changed": false, "connection":
"close", "content_length": "8338", "content_type": "text/html; charset=utf-8", "
cookies": {}, "cookies_string": "", "date": "Mon, 25 Feb 2019 15:17:21 GMT", "et
ag": "\"5c2179e7-2092\"", "expires": "Mon, 25 Feb 2019 15:20:59 GMT", "last_modi
fied": "Tue, 25 Dec 2018 00:29:27 GMT", "msg": "OK (8338 bytes)", "redirected":
false, "server": "GitHub.com", "status": 200, "url": "https://derpops.bike", "va
ry": "Accept-Encoding", "via": "1.1 varnish", "x_cache": "HIT", "x_cache_hits":
"1", "x_fastly_request_id": "7b55b3984cba19b6f4215d8027c67d706b920e49", "x_githu
b_request_id": "B196:22BE:839AD6:ABB800:5C740583", "x_served_by": "cache-lcy1924
9-LCY", "x_timer": "S1551107841.147987,VS0,VE0"}

TASK [show derpops] ************************************************************
ok: [localhost] => {
    "msg": "derpops value is {u'content_length': u'8338', u'cookies': {}, u'via'
: u'1.1 varnish', u'vary': u'Accept-Encoding', u'x_timer': u'S1551107841.147987,
VS0,VE0', u'x_fastly_request_id': u'7b55b3984cba19b6f4215d8027c67d706b920e49', u
'x_cache_hits': u'1', 'failed': False, u'etag': u'\"5c2179e7-2092\"', u'msg': u'
OK (8338 bytes)', u'accept_ranges': u'bytes', u'cache_control': u'max-age=600',
u'status': 200, u'x_github_request_id': u'B196:22BE:839AD6:ABB800:5C740583', u'e
xpires': u'Mon, 25 Feb 2019 15:20:59 GMT', u'x_served_by': u'cache-lcy19249-LCY'
, u'access_control_allow_origin': u'*', u'last_modified': u'Tue, 25 Dec 2018 00:
29:27 GMT', u'content_type': u'text/html; charset=utf-8', u'date': u'Mon, 25 Feb
 2019 15:17:21 GMT', u'url': u'https://derpops.bike', u'age': u'382', u'changed'
: False, u'server': u'GitHub.com', u'x_cache': u'HIT', u'connection': u'close',
u'redirected': False, u'cookies_string': u''}"
}

PLAY RECAP *********************************************************************
localhost                  : ok=2    changed=0    unreachable=0    failed=0

~/src/mastery>
```

The debug module has a different option that may be useful as well. Instead of printing a free form string to debug template usage, the module can simply print the value of any variable. This is done using the `var` argument instead of the `msg` argument. Let's repeat our example, but this time, we'll use the `var` argument, and we'll access just the `server` subelement of the `derpops` variable, as follows:

```
---
- name: variable introspection demo
  hosts: localhost
  gather_facts: false

  tasks:
    - name: do a thing
      uri:
        url: https://derpops.bike
      register: derpops

    - name: show derpops
      debug:
        var: derpops.server
```

Running this modified play will show just the `server` portion of the `derpops` variable, as shown in the following screenshot:

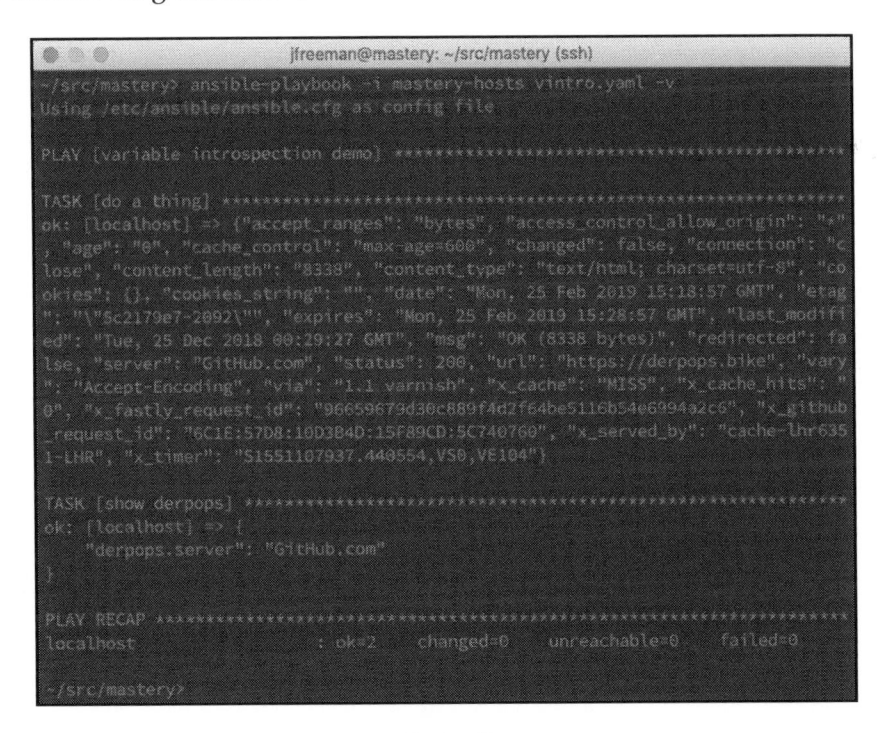

```
~/src/mastery> ansible-playbook -i mastery-hosts vintro.yaml -v
Using /etc/ansible/ansible.cfg as config file

PLAY [variable introspection demo] ************************************************

TASK [do a thing] ****************************************************************
ok: [localhost] => {"accept_ranges": "bytes", "access_control_allow_origin": "*"
, "age": "0", "cache_control": "max-age=600", "changed": false, "connection": "c
lose", "content_length": "8338", "content_type": "text/html; charset=utf-8", "co
okies": {}, "cookies_string": "", "date": "Mon, 25 Feb 2019 15:18:57 GMT", "etag
": "\"5c2179e7-2092\"", "expires": "Mon, 25 Feb 2019 15:28:57 GMT", "last_modifi
ed": "Tue, 25 Dec 2018 00:29:27 GMT", "msg": "OK (8338 bytes)", "redirected": fa
lse, "server": "GitHub.com", "status": 200, "url": "https://derpops.bike", "vary
": "Accept-Encoding", "via": "1.1 varnish", "x_cache": "MISS", "x_cache_hits": "
0", "x_fastly_request_id": "96659679d30c889f4d2f64be5116b54e6994a2c6", "x_github
_request_id": "6C1E:57D8:10D3B4D:15F89CD:5C740760", "x_served_by": "cache-lhr635
1-LHR", "x_timer": "S1551107937.440554,VS0,VE104"}

TASK [show derpops] **************************************************************
ok: [localhost] => {
    "derpops.server": "GitHub.com"
}

PLAY RECAP ***********************************************************************
localhost                  : ok=2    changed=0    unreachable=0    failed=0

~/src/mastery>
```

*Troubleshooting Ansible*

In our example that used the `msg` argument to `debug`, the variable needed to be expressed inside curly brackets, but when using `var`, it did not. This is because `msg` expects a string, and so Ansible needs to render the variable as a string via the template engine. However, `var` expects a single unrendered variable.

## Variable subelements

Another frequent mistake in playbooks is to improperly reference a subelement of a complex variable. A complex variable is one that is more than simply a string; it is either a list or a hash. Often, the wrong subelement will be referenced, or the element will be improperly referenced, expecting a different type.

While lists are fairly easy to work with, hashes present some unique challenges. A hash is an unordered key-value set of potentially mixed types, which could also be nested. A hash can have one element that is a single string, while another element can be a list of strings, and a third element can be another hash with further elements inside it. Knowing how to properly access the right subelement is critical to success.

For example, let's modify our previous play a bit more. This time, we'll allow Ansible to gather facts, and then we'll show the value of `ansible_python`:

```
---
- name: variable introspection demo
  hosts: localhost

  tasks:
    - name: show a complex hash
      debug:
        var: ansible_python
```

The output is shown in the following screenshot:

```
~/src/mastery> ansible-playbook -i mastery-hosts vintro.yaml -v
Using /etc/ansible/ansible.cfg as config file

PLAY [variable introspection demo] ***********************************************

TASK [Gathering Facts] ***********************************************************
ok: [localhost]

TASK [show a complex hash] *******************************************************
ok: [localhost] => {
    "ansible_python": {
        "executable": "/usr/bin/python2",
        "has_sslcontext": true,
        "type": "CPython",
        "version": {
            "major": 2,
            "micro": 5,
            "minor": 7,
            "releaselevel": "final",
            "serial": 0
        },
        "version_info": [
            2,
            7,
            5,
            "final",
            0
        ]
    }
}

PLAY RECAP ***********************************************************************
localhost                  : ok=2    changed=0    unreachable=0    failed=0

~/src/mastery>
```

Using `debug` to display the entire complex variable is a great way to learn all the names of the subelements.

## Troubleshooting Ansible

This variable has elements that are strings, along with elements that are lists of strings. Let's access the last item in the list of flags, as follows:

```
---
- name: variable introspection demo
  hosts: localhost

  tasks:
    - name: show a complex hash
      debug:
        var: ansible_python.version_info[-1]
```

The output is shown in the following screenshot:

```
~/src/mastery> ansible-playbook -i mastery-hosts vintro.yaml -v
Using /etc/ansible/ansible.cfg as config file

PLAY [variable introspection demo] ********************************************

TASK [Gathering Facts] ********************************************************
ok: [localhost]

TASK [show a complex hash] ****************************************************
ok: [localhost] => {
    "ansible_python.version_info[-1]": "0"
}

PLAY RECAP ********************************************************************
localhost                  : ok=2    changed=0    unreachable=0    failed=0

~/src/mastery>
```

Because flags is a list, we can use the **list index method** to select a specific item from the list. In this case, -1 will give us the very last item in the list.

[ 234 ]

# Subelements versus Python object method

A less common but confusing gotcha comes from a quirk of the Jinja2 syntax. Complex variables within Ansible playbooks and templates can be referenced in two ways. The first style is to reference the base element by the name, followed by a bracket, and the subelement within quotes inside the brackets. This is the **standard subscript syntax**. For example, to access the herp subelement of the derp variable, we will use the following:

```
{{ derp['herp'] }}
```

The second style is a convenience method that Jinja2 provides, which is to use a period to separate the elements. This is called **dot notation**, and is as follows:

```
{{ derp.herp }}
```

There is a subtle difference in how these styles work, and it has to do with Python objects and object methods. As Jinja2 is, at its heart, a Python utility, variables in Jinja2 have access to their native Python methods. A string variable has access to Python string methods, a list has access to list methods, and a dictionary has access to dictionary methods. When using the first style, Jinja2 will first search the element for a subelement of the provided name. If none are found, Jinja2 will then attempt to access a Python method of the provided name. However, the order is reversed when using the second style; first, a Python object method is searched for, and if not found, then a subelement is searched for. This difference matters when there is a name collision between a subelement and a method. Imagine a variable named derp, which is a complex variable. This variable has a subelement named keys. Using each style to access the keys element will result in different values. Let's build a playbook to demonstrate this:

```
---
- name: sub-element access styles
  hosts: localhost
  gather_facts: false
  vars:
    - derp:
        keys:
          - c
          - d
  tasks:
    - name: subscript style
      debug:
        var: derp['keys']
    - name: dot notation style
      debug:
        var: derp.keys
```

When running this play, we can clearly see the difference between the two styles. The first style successfully references the keys subelement, while the second style references the keys method of Python dictionaries:

```
~/src/mastery> ansible-playbook -i mastery-hosts objmethod.yaml

PLAY [sub-element access styles] ************************************************

TASK [subscript style] **********************************************************
ok: [localhost] => {
    "derp['keys']": [
        "c",
        "d"
    ]
}

TASK [dot notation style] *******************************************************
ok: [localhost] => {
    "derp.keys": "<built-in method keys of dict object at 0x7fbde6ae4050>"
}

PLAY RECAP **********************************************************************
localhost                  : ok=2    changed=0    unreachable=0    failed=0

~/src/mastery>
```

Generally, it's best to avoid using subelement names that conflict with Python object methods. However, if that's not possible, the next best thing to do is to be aware of the difference in subelement reference styles, and choose the appropriate one.

# Debugging code execution

Sometimes, the logging and inspection of variable data is not enough to troubleshoot a problem. When this happens, it can be necessary to interactively debug the playbook, or to dig deeper into the internals of Ansible code. There are two main sets of Ansible code: the code that runs locally on the Ansible host, and the module code that runs remotely on the target host.

# Playbook debugging

Playbooks can be interactively debugged by using an execution strategy that was introduced in Ansible 2.1, the debug strategy. If a play uses this strategy, when an error state is encountered an interactive debugging session starts. This interactive session can be used to display variable data, display task arguments, update task arguments, update variables, redo task execution, continue execution, or exit the debugger.

Let's demonstrate this with a play that has a successful task, followed by a task with an error, followed by a final successful task. We'll reuse the playbook we've been using, but update it a bit, as shown in the following code:

```
---
- name: sub-element access styles
  hosts: localhost
  gather_facts: false
  strategy: debug

  vars:
    - derp:
        keys:
          - c
          - d

  tasks:
    - name: subscript style
      debug:
        var: derp['keys']

    - name: failing task
      debug:
        msg: "this is {{ derp['missing'] }}"

    - name: final task
      debug:
        msg: "my only friend the end"
```

Upon execution, Ansible will encounter an error in our failing task and present the (debug) prompt, as shown in the following screenshot:

```
~/src/mastery> ansible-playbook -i mastery-hosts objmethod.yaml

PLAY [sub-element access styles] ******************************************

TASK [subscript style] ****************************************************
ok: [localhost] => {
    "derp['keys']": [
        "c",
        "d"
    ]
}

TASK [failing task] *******************************************************
fatal: [localhost]: FAILED! => {"msg": "The task includes an option with an unde
fined variable. The error was: 'dict object' has no attribute 'missing'\n\nThe e
rror appears to have been in '/home/jfreeman/src/mastery/objmethod.yaml': line 1
8, column 7, but may\nbe elsewhere in the file depending on the exact syntax pro
blem.\n\nThe offending line appears to be:\n\n\n    - name: failing task\n
^ here\n"}
[localhost] TASK: failing task (debug)>
```

From this prompt, we can display the task and the arguments to the task by using the `p` command, as follows:

```
[localhost] TASK: failing task (debug)> p task
TASK: failing task
[localhost] TASK: failing task (debug)> p task.args
{u'msg': u"this is {{ derp['missing'] }}"}
[localhost] TASK: failing task (debug)>
```

We can also change the playbook on the fly to try different arguments or variable values. Let's define the missing key of the `derp` variable, and then retry the execution. All of the variables are within the top-level `vars` dictionary. We can directly set the variable data using Python syntax and the `task_vars` command, and then retry with the `r` command:

```
[localhost] TASK: failing task (debug)> task_vars['derp']['missing'] = "the end"

[localhost] TASK: failing task (debug)> r
ok: [localhost] => {
    "msg": "this is the end"
}

TASK [final task] *********************************************************
ok: [localhost] => {
    "msg": "my only friend the end"
}

PLAY RECAP ****************************************************************
localhost                  : ok=2    changed=0    unreachable=0    failed=0

~/src/mastery>
```

The debug execution strategy is a handy tool for quickly iterating through different task argument and variable combinations to figure out the correct path forward. However, because errors result in interactive consoles, the debug strategy is inappropriate for automated executions of playbooks, as there is no human on the console to manipulate the debugger.

> **TIP**
> Changing data within the debugger will not save the changes to backing files. Always remember to update playbook files to reflect discoveries that are made during debugging.

## Debugging local code

The local Ansible code is the lion's share of the code that comes with Ansible. All the playbook, play, role, and task parsing code lives locally. All of the task result processing code and transport code lives locally. All of the code, except for the assembled module code that is transported to the remote host lives locally.

Local Ansible code can be broken down into three major sections: inventory, playbook, and executor. Inventory code deals with parsing inventory data from host files, dynamic inventory scripts, or combinations of the two, in directory trees. Playbook code is used to parse the playbook YAML code into Python objects within Ansible. Executor code is the core API and deals with forking processes, connecting to hosts, executing modules, handling results, and most other things. Learning the general area to start debugging comes with practice, but the general areas that are described here are a starting point.

*Troubleshooting Ansible*

As Ansible is written in Python, the tool for debugging local code execution is the Python debugger, `pdb`. This tool allows us to insert breakpoints inside the Ansible code and interactively walk through the execution of the code, line by line. This is very useful for examining the internal state of Ansible as the local code executes. There are many books and websites that cover the usage of `pdb`, and these can be found with a simple web search for an introduction to Python `pdb`, so we will not repeat them here. The basics are to edit the source file to be debugged, insert a new line of code to create a breakpoint, and then execute the code. Code execution will stop where the breakpoint was created, and a prompt will be provided to explore the code state.

## Debugging inventory code

Inventory code deals with finding inventory sources, reading or executing the discovered files, parsing the inventory data into inventory objects, and loading variable data for the inventory. To debug how Ansible will deal with an inventory, a breakpoint must be added inside `inventory/__init__.py` or one of the other files within the `inventory/` subdirectory. This directory will be located on the local filesystem wherever Ansible has been installed. On a Linux system, this is typically stored in the `/usr/lib/python2.7/site-packages/ansible/inventory/` path. This path may be inside a Python virtual environment if Ansible has been installed that way. To discover where Ansible is installed, simply type `which ansible` from the command line. This command will show you where the Ansible executable is installed, and may indicate a Python virtual environment. For this book, Ansible has been installed using the operating system Python distribute, with the Ansible binaries located in `/usr/bin/`.

To discover the path to the Ansible Python code, simply type `python -c "import ansible; print(ansible)"`. On my system, this shows `<module 'ansible' from '/usr/lib/python2.7/site-packages/ansible/__init__.pyc'>`, from which we can deduce that the inventory subdirectory is located at `/usr/lib/python2.7/site-packages/ansible/inventory`.

The inventory directory has been restructured in recent releases of Ansible, and in version 2.7, we need to look in `inventory/manager.py`. Here, there is a class definition for the `Inventory` class. This is the inventory object that will be used throughout a playbook run, and it is created when `ansible-playbook` parses the options provided to it for an inventory source. The `__init__` method of the `Inventory` class does all the inventory discovery, parsing, and variable loading. To troubleshoot an issue in those three areas, a breakpoint should be added within the `__init__()` method. A good place to start would be after all of the class variables are given an initial value, and just before any data is processed.

In version 2.7.5.0 of Ansible, this would be line 143 of `inventory/manager.py`, where the `parse_sources` function is called.

We can skip down to the `parse_sources` function definition on line `195` to insert our breakpoint. To insert a breakpoint, we must first import the `pdb` module and then call the `set_trace()` function, as follows:

```
''' sets up loaded inventory plugins for usage '''

display.vvvv('setting up inventory plugins')

for name in C.INVENTORY_ENABLED:
    plugin = inventory_loader.get(name)
    if plugin:
        self._inventory_plugins.append(plugin)
    else:
        display.warning('Failed to load inventory plugin, skipping %s' % name)

if not self._inventory_plugins:
    raise AnsibleError("No inventory plugins available to generate inventory, make sure you have at least one whitelisted.")

def parse_sources(self, cache=False):
    ''' iterate over inventory sources and parse each one to populate it'''
    import pdb; pdb.set_trace()
    self._setup_inventory_plugins()

    parsed = False
    # allow for multiple inventory parsing
    for source in self._sources:

        if source:
            if ',' not in source:
                source = unfrackpath(source, follow=False)
            parse = self.parse_source(source, cache=cache)
            if parse and not parsed:
                parsed = True

    if parsed:
        # do post processing
```

*Troubleshooting Ansible*

To start debugging, save the source file and then execute `ansible-playbook` as normal. When the breakpoint is reached, the execution will stop and a `pdb` prompt will be displayed:

```
~/src/mastery> ansible-playbook -i mastery-hosts objmethod.yaml
> /usr/lib/python2.7/site-packages/ansible/inventory/manager.py(196)parse_source
s()
-> self._setup_inventory_plugins()
(Pdb)
```

From here, we can issue any number of debugger commands, such as the `help` command, as follows:

```
~/src/mastery> ansible-playbook -i mastery-hosts objmethod.yaml
> /usr/lib/python2.7/site-packages/ansible/inventory/manager.py(196)parse_source
s()
-> self._setup_inventory_plugins()
(Pdb) help

Documented commands (type help <topic>):
========================================
EOF    bt         cont       enable   jump   pp       run      unt
a      c          continue   exit     l      q        s        until
alias  cl         d          h        list   quit     step     up
args   clear      debug      help     n      r        tbreak   w
b      commands   disable    ignore   next   restart  u        whatis
break  condition  down       j        p      return   unalias  where

Miscellaneous help topics:
==========================
exec  pdb

Undocumented commands:
======================
retval  rv

(Pdb)
```

The `where` and `list` commands can help us determine where we are in the stack, and where we are in the code:

```
(Pdb) where
  /usr/bin/ansible-playbook(118)<module>()
-> exit_code = cli.run()
  /usr/lib/python2.7/site-packages/ansible/cli/playbook.py(104)run()
-> loader, inventory, variable_manager = self._play_prereqs(self.options)
  /usr/lib/python2.7/site-packages/ansible/cli/__init__.py(786)_play_prereqs()
-> inventory = InventoryManager(loader=loader, sources=options.inventory)
  /usr/lib/python2.7/site-packages/ansible/inventory/manager.py(145)__init__()
-> self.parse_sources(cache=True)
> /usr/lib/python2.7/site-packages/ansible/inventory/manager.py(196)parse_source
s()
-> self._setup_inventory_plugins()
(Pdb) list
191                 raise AnsibleError("No inventory plugins available to genera
te inventory, make sure you have at least one whitelisted.")
192
193         def parse_sources(self, cache=False):
194             ''' iterate over inventory sources and parse each one to populat
e it'''
195             import pdb; pdb.set_trace()
196  ->         self._setup_inventory_plugins()
197
198             parsed = False
199             # allow for multiple inventory parsing
200             for source in self._sources:
201
(Pdb)
```

The `where` command shows us that we're in `inventory/manager.py` in the `parse_sources()` method. The next frame up is the same file, the `__init__()` function. Before that is a different file, the `playbook.py` file, and the function in that file is `run()`. This line calls to `ansible.inventory.InventoryManager` to create the inventory object. Before that is the original file, `ansible-playbook`, calling `cli.run()`.

The `list` command shows the source code around our current point of execution, five lines before, and five lines after.

From here, we can guide `pdb` through the function line by line with the `next` command. And, if we choose to, we can trace into other function calls with the `step` command. We can also `print` variable data to inspect values, as shown in the following screenshot:

```
                    ansible-playbook -i mastery-hosts objmethod.yaml (ssh)
192
193             def parse_sources(self, cache=False):
194                 ''' iterate over inventory sources and parse each one to populat
e it'''
195                 import pdb; pdb.set_trace()
196  ->             self._setup_inventory_plugins()
197
198                 parsed = False
199                 # allow for multiple inventory parsing
200                 for source in self._sources:
201
(Pdb) p self._sources
[u'/home/jfreeman/src/mastery/mastery-hosts']
(Pdb)
```

We can see that the `self._sources` variable has a full path of our `mastery-hosts` inventory file, which is the string we gave `ansible-playbook` for our inventory data. We can continue to walk through or jump around, or just use the `continue` command to run until the next breakpoint or the completion of the code.

## Debugging playbook code

Playbook code is responsible for loading, parsing, and executing playbooks. The main entry point for playbook handling is `playbook/__init__.py`, inside of which lives the PlayBook class. A good starting point for debugging playbook handling is line 77:

```
        cur_basedir = self._loader.get_basedir()
        self._loader.set_basedir(self._basedir)

        self._file_name = file_name

        # dynamically load any plugins from the playbook directory
        for name, obj in get_all_plugin_loaders():
            if obj.subdir:
                plugin_path = os.path.join(self._basedir, obj.subdir)
                if os.path.isdir(plugin_path):
                    obj.add_directory(plugin_path)
        import pdb; pdb.set_trace()
        try:
            ds = self._loader.load_from_file(os.path.basename(file_name))
        except UnicodeDecodeError as e:
            raise AnsibleParserError("Could not read playbook (%s) due to encoding issues: %s" % (file_name, to_native(e)))

        if not isinstance(ds, list):
            # restore the basedir in case this error is caught and handled
            self._loader.set_basedir(cur_basedir)
            raise AnsibleParserError("playbooks must be a list of plays", obj=ds)
)
```

Putting a breakpoint here will allow us to trace through finding the playbook file and parsing it. Specifically, by stepping into the `self._loader.load_from_file()` function call, we will be able to follow the parsing in action.

The PlayBook class `load()` function just does the initial parsing. Other classes within other directories are used for the execution of plays and tasks. A particularly interesting directory is the `executor/` directory, which holds files with classes to execute playbooks, plays, and tasks. The `run()` function within the `PlaybookExecutor` class that's defined in the `executor/playbook_executor.py` file will loop through all of the plays in the playbook and execute the plays, which will, in turn, execute the individual tasks. This is the function to walk through if facing an issue related to play parsing, play or task callbacks, tags, play host selection, serial operation, handler running, or anything in-between.

## Debugging executor code

Executor code in Ansible is the connector code that binds together inventory data, playbooks, plays, tasks, and connection methods. While each of those other code bits can be individually debugged, how they interact can be examined within executor code.

The executor classes are defined in various files within `executor/` and the `PlaybookExecutor` class. This class handles executing all of the plays and tasks within a given playbook. The class creation function, `__init__()`, creates a series of placeholder attributes, as well as setting some default values, while the `run()` function is where most of the fun happens.

Debugging can often take you from one file to another, jumping around the code base. For example, in the `__init__()` function of the `PlaybookExecutor` class, there is code to cache whether or not the default SSH executable supports `ControlPersist`. `ControlPersist` is the feature of SSH that keeps sockets to remote hosts open for a period of time for fast reuse. Let's put a breakpoint here and follow the code:

```
            self._options = options
            self.passwords = passwords
            self._unreachable_hosts = dict()

            if options.listhosts or options.listtasks or options.listtags or options.syntax:
                self._tqm = None
            else:
                self._tqm = TaskQueueManager(inventory=inventory, variable_manager=variable_manager, loader=loader, options=options, passwords=self.passwords)

            # Note: We run this here to cache whether the default ansible ssh
            # executable supports control persist.  Sometime in the future we may
            # need to enhance this to check that ansible_ssh_executable specified
            # in inventory is also cached.  We can't do this caching at the point
            # where it is used (in task_executor) because that is post-fork and
            # therefore would be discarded after every task.
            import pdb; pdb.set_trace()
            check_for_controlpersist(C.ANSIBLE_SSH_EXECUTABLE)

        def run(self):
            '''
            Run the given playbook, based on the settings in the play which
            may limit the runs to serialized groups, etc.
```

Now, we can run our `objmethod.yml` playbook again to get into a debugging state:

```
~/src/mastery> ansible-playbook -i mastery-hosts objmethod.yaml
> /usr/lib/python2.7/site-packages/ansible/executor/playbook_executor.py(69)__in
it__()
-> check_for_controlpersist(C.ANSIBLE_SSH_EXECUTABLE)
(Pdb)
```

We'll need to step into the function to follow the execution. Stepping into the function will take us to a different file, as follows:

```
(Pdb) step
--Call--
> /usr/lib/python2.7/site-packages/ansible/utils/ssh_functions.py(31)check_for_c
ontrolpersist()
-> def check_for_controlpersist(ssh_executable):
(Pdb)
```

From here, we can use `list` to see the code in our new file:

```
(Pdb) list
 26
 27
 28     _HAS_CONTROLPERSIST = {}
 29
 30
 31  -> def check_for_controlpersist(ssh_executable):
 32         try:
 33             # If we've already checked this executable
 34             return _HAS_CONTROLPERSIST[ssh_executable]
 35         except KeyError:
 36             pass
(Pdb)
```

[ 247 ]

# Troubleshooting Ansible

Walking a few more lines down, we come to a block of code that will execute an `ssh` command and check the output to determine whether `ControlPersist` is supported:

```
(Pdb) l
 37
 38            b_ssh_exec = to_bytes(ssh_executable, errors='surrogate_or_strict')
 39            has_cp = True
 40            try:
 41                cmd = subprocess.Popen([b_ssh_exec, '-o', 'ControlPersist'], std
out=subprocess.PIPE, stderr=subprocess.PIPE)
 42                (out, err) = cmd.communicate()
 43                if b"Bad configuration option" in err or b"Usage:" in err:
 44                    has_cp = False
 45            except OSError:
 46                has_cp = False
 47
(Pdb)
```

Let's walk through the next couple of lines and then print out what the value of `err` is. This will show us the result of the `ssh` execution and the whole string that Ansible will be searching within:

```
                    ansible-playbook -i mastery-hosts objmethod.yaml (ssh)
> /usr/lib/python2.7/site-packages/ansible/utils/ssh_functions.py(39)check_for_c
ontrolpersist()
-> has_cp = True
(Pdb) n
> /usr/lib/python2.7/site-packages/ansible/utils/ssh_functions.py(40)check_for_c
ontrolpersist()
-> try:
(Pdb) n
> /usr/lib/python2.7/site-packages/ansible/utils/ssh_functions.py(41)check_for_c
ontrolpersist()
-> cmd = subprocess.Popen([b_ssh_exec, '-o', 'ControlPersist'], stdout=subproces
s.PIPE, stderr=subprocess.PIPE)
(Pdb) n
> /usr/lib/python2.7/site-packages/ansible/utils/ssh_functions.py(42)check_for_c
ontrolpersist()
-> (out, err) = cmd.communicate()
(Pdb) n
> /usr/lib/python2.7/site-packages/ansible/utils/ssh_functions.py(43)check_for_c
ontrolpersist()
-> if b"Bad configuration option" in err or b"Usage:" in err:
(Pdb) p err
'command-line line 0: Missing ControlPersist argument.\r\n'
(Pdb)
```

As we can see, the search string is not within the `err` variable, so the value of `has_cp` remains as the default of `True`.

> **A quick note on forks and debugging**: When Ansible uses multiprocessing for multiple forks, debugging becomes difficult. A debugger may be attached to one fork and not another, which will make it very difficult to debug the code. Unless specifically debugging the multiprocessing code, it's a best practice to stick to a single fork.

## Debugging remote code

The remote code is the code that Ansible transports to a remote host to execute it. This is typically module code, or in the case of `action_plugins`, other snippets of code. Using the debugging method we discussed in the previous section to debug module execution will not work, as Ansible simply copies the code over and then executes it. There is no Terminal attached to the remote code execution, and thus there is no way to attach it to a debugging prompt, that is, without editing the module code.

To debug module code, we need to edit the module code itself to insert a debugger breakpoint. Instead of directly editing the installed module file, create a copy of the file in a `library/` directory relative to the playbooks. This copy of the module code will be used instead of the installed file, which makes it easy to temporarily edit a module without disrupting other users of modules on the system.

Unlike other Ansible code, module code cannot be directly debugged with `pdb`, because the module code is assembled and then transported to a remote host. Thankfully, there is a solution in the form of a slightly different debugger named `rpdb` the Remote Python Debugger. This debugger has the ability to start a listening service on a provided port to allow remote connections into the Python process. Connecting to the process remotely will allow debugging the code line by line, just as we did with other Ansible code.

To demonstrate how this debugger works, first, we're going to need a remote host. For this example, we're using a remote host by the name of `debug.example.com`, and setting the IP address to a host that is already set up and waiting. Next, we need a playbook to execute a module that we'd like to debug:

```
---
- name: remote code debug
  hosts: debug.example.com
  gather_facts: false
  become: true

  tasks:
```

*Troubleshooting Ansible*

```
    - name: a remote module execution
      systemd:
        name: nginx
        state: stopped
        enabled: no
```

We will also need a new inventory file to reference our new test host—as I don't have DNS set up for this host, I'm using the special `ansible_host` variable in the inventory to tell Ansible which IP address to connect to `debug.example.com` on:

```
debug.example.com ansible_host=192.168.81.154
```

> **TIP**
> Don't forget to set up SSH authentication between your two hosts—I'm using an SSH key so that I don't need to type in a password every time I run `ansible-playbook`.

This play simply calls the `systemd` module to ensure that the `nginx` service is stopped and will not start up on boot. As we stated previously, we need to make a copy of the service module and place it in `library/`. The location of the service module to copy from will vary based on the way Ansible is installed. Typically, this module will be located in the `modules/core/system/` subdirectory of where the Ansible Python code lives, like `/usr/lib/python2.7/site-packages/ansible/modules/system/systemd.py` on my system. Then, we can edit it to put in our breakpoint, as follows:

```
# initialize
module = AnsibleModule(
    argument_spec=dict(
        name=dict(type='str', aliases=['service', 'unit']),
        state=dict(type='str', choices=['reloaded', 'restarted', 'started', 'stopped']),
        enabled=dict(type='bool'),
        force=dict(type='bool'),
        masked=dict(type='bool'),
        daemon_reload=dict(type='bool', default=False, aliases=['daemon-reload']),
        user=dict(type='bool'),
        scope=dict(type='str', choices=['system', 'user', 'global']),
        no_block=dict(type='bool', default=False),
    ),
    supports_check_mode=True,
    required_one_of=[['state', 'enabled', 'masked', 'daemon_reload']],
    mutually_exclusive=[['scope', 'user']],
)
import rpdb; rpdb.set_trace(addr="0.0.0.0")
systemctl = module.get_bin_path('systemctl', True)
```

We'll put the breakpoint just before the `systemctl` variable value gets created, near line 318. First, the `rpdb` module must be imported (meaning that the `rpdb` Python library needs to exist on the remote host), and then the breakpoint needs to be created with `set_trace()`.

> **TIP**
> On CentOS 7 and other EL7 variants like the host that was used in the demo, `rpdb` can be installed using the following command: **sudo yum install python2-rpdb**.

Unlike the regular debugger, this function will open a port and listen for external connections. By default, the function will listen for connections to port `4444` on the address `127.0.0.1`. However, that address is not exposed over the network, so in my example, I've instructed `rpdb` to listen on address `0.0.0.0`, which is effectively every address on the host. Now, we can run this playbook to set up the server that will wait for a client connection:

```
~/src/mastery> ansible-playbook -i mastery-debug rpdb.yaml -vv
ansible-playbook 2.7.5
  config file = /etc/ansible/ansible.cfg
  configured module search path = [u'/home/jfreeman/.ansible/plugins/modules', u'/usr/share/ansible/plugins/modules']
  ansible python module location = /usr/lib/python2.7/site-packages/ansible
  executable location = /usr/bin/ansible-playbook
  python version = 2.7.5 (default, Oct 30 2018, 23:45:53) [GCC 4.8.5 20150623 (Red Hat 4.8.5-36)]
Using /etc/ansible/ansible.cfg as config file

PLAYBOOK: rpdb.yaml *********************************************************
1 plays in rpdb.yaml

PLAY [remote code debug] ****************************************************
META: ran handlers

TASK [a remote module execution] ********************************************
task path: /home/jfreeman/src/mastery/rpdb.yaml:8
```

*Troubleshooting Ansible*

Now that the server is running, we can connect to it from another Terminal. Connecting to the running process can be accomplished with the telnet program:

```
~/src/mastery> telnet 192.168.81.154 4444
Trying 192.168.81.154...
Connected to 192.168.81.154.
Escape character is '^]'.
> /tmp/ansible_systemd_payload_YU1b6V/__main__.py(318)main()
-> systemctl = module.get_bin_path('systemctl', True)
(Pdb)
```

From this point on, we can debug as normal. The commands we used before still exist, such as `list` to show where in the code the current frame is:

```
(Pdb) list
313             supports_check_mode=True,
314             required_one_of=[['state', 'enabled', 'masked', 'daemon_reload']
],
315             mutually_exclusive=[['scope', 'user']],
316         )
317         import rpdb; rpdb.set_trace(addr="0.0.0.0")
318  ->     systemctl = module.get_bin_path('systemctl', True)
319
320         ''' Set CLI options depending on params '''
321         if module.params['user'] is not None:
322             # handle user deprecation, mutually exclusive with scope
323             module.deprecate("The 'user' option is being replaced by 'scope'
", version='2.11')
(Pdb)
```

Using the debugger, we can walk through the `systemd` module to track how it determines the path to the underlying tool, trace which commands are executed on the host, determine how a change is computed, and so on. The entire file can be stepped through, including any other external libraries the module may make use of, allowing for the debugging of other non-module code on the remote host as well.

If the debugging session allows the module to exit cleanly, the playbook's execution will return as normal. However, if the debugging session is disconnected before the module completes, the playbook will error, as shown in the following screenshot:

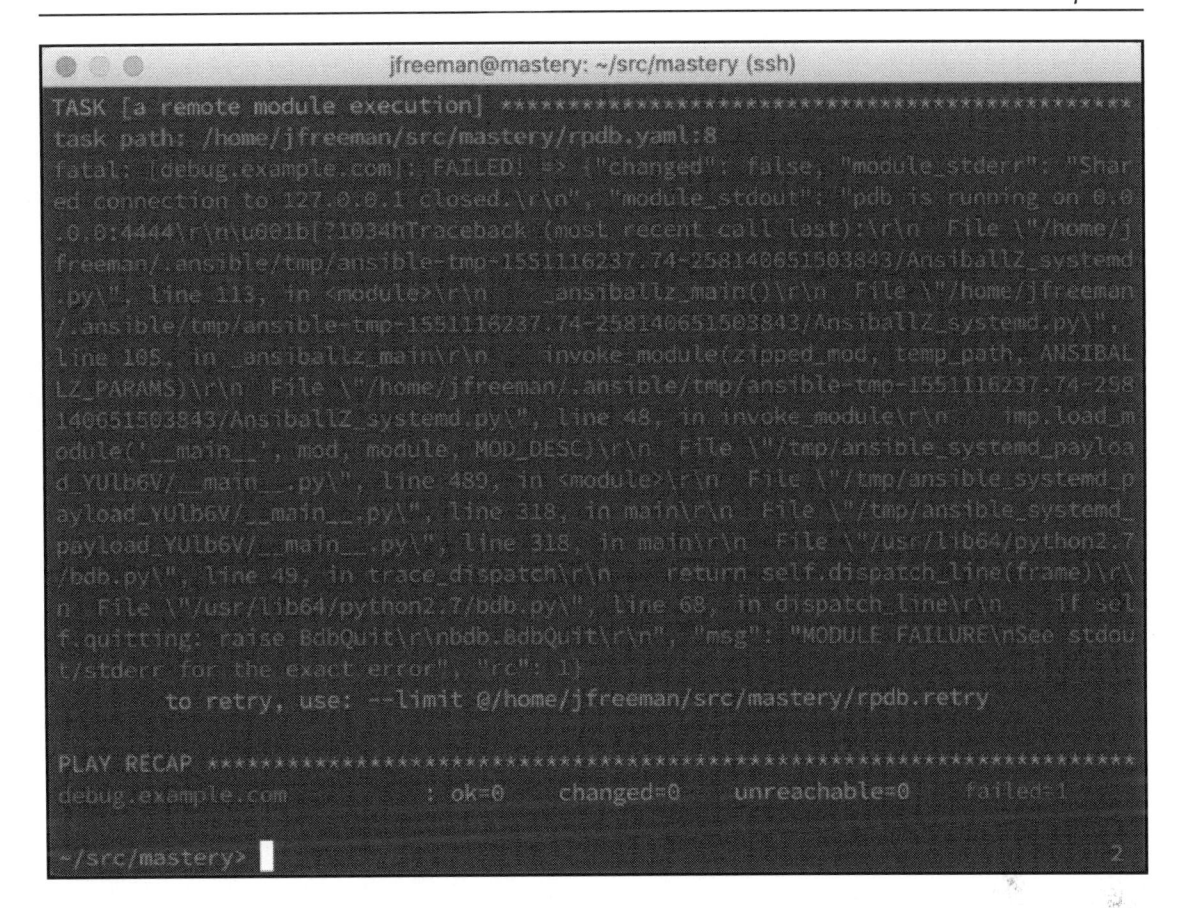

[Terminal screenshot showing an Ansible task failure with pdb traceback output, ending with PLAY RECAP: debug.example.com : ok=0 changed=0 unreachable=0 failed=1]

Because of this side effect, it is best to not exit the debugger early, and instead issue a continue command when your debugging is finished.

## Debugging the action plugins

Some modules are actually action plugins. These are tasks that will execute some code locally before transporting code to the remote host. Some example action plugins include copy, fetch, script, and template. The source to these plugins can be found in `plugins/action/`. Each plugin will have its own file in this directory that can be edited to have breakpoints inserted in order to debug the code that's executed, prior to (or in lieu of) sending code to the remote host. Debugging these is typically done with `pdb`, since most of the code is executed locally.

## Summary

Ansible is a piece of software, and software breaks; it's not a matter of if, but when. Invalid input, improper assumptions, and unexpected environments are all things that can lead to a frustrating situation when tasks and plays are not performing as expected. Introspection and debugging are troubleshooting techniques that can quickly turn frustration into elation when a root cause is discovered.

In this chapter, we learned about how to get Ansible to log its actions to a file, and how to change the verbosity level of Ansible's output. We then learned how to inspect variables to ensure their values are in line with your expectations, before we moved on to debugging Ansible code in detail. Furthermore, we walked through the process of inserting breakpoints into core Ansible code, and executed both local and remote Python debugging sessions using standard Python tools.

In the next chapter, we will learn how to extend the functionality of Ansible by writing our own modules, plugins, and inventory sources.

# 9
# Extending Ansible

It must be said that **Ansible** takes the "kitchen sink" approach to functionality and tries to provide, out of the box, every piece of functionality you might ever need. There are over 2,000 modules available for use within Ansible at the time of writing—1,200 more than when the last edition of this book was published! In addition to these, there is a rich plugin and filter architecture with numerous callback plugins, lookup plugins, filter plugins, and dynamic inventory plugins included.

In spite of this, there will always be cases where Ansible doesn't quite perform the tasks required, especially in large and complex environments, or ones where bespoke in-house systems have been developed. Luckily, the design of Ansible, coupled with its open source nature, makes it easy for anyone to extend it by developing their own features. It is also easy to contribute code back to the wider community, which in turn can help others to adopt Ansible more easily.

This chapter will explore the following ways in which new capabilities can be added to Ansible:

- Developing modules
- Developing plugins
- Developing dynamic inventory plugins
- Contributing code to the Ansible project

## Technical requirements

Check out the following video to see the Code in Action:

```
http://bit.ly/2OpCThn
```

# Developing modules

Modules are the workhorse of Ansible. They provide just enough abstraction so that playbooks can be stated simply and clearly. There are over 100 modules maintained by the core Ansible development team, covering clouds, commands, databases, files, networks, packaging, source control, system, utilities, web infrastructure, and so on. In addition, there are nearly 2,000 other modules maintained by community contributors that expand functionality in many of these categories. The real magic happens inside the module code, which takes in the arguments passed to it and works to establish the desired outcome.

Modules in Ansible are the pieces of code that get transported to the remote host to be executed. They can be written in any language that the remote host can execute; however, Ansible provides some very useful shortcuts for writing modules in Python.

## The basic module construct

A module exists to satisfy a need—the need to do a piece of work on a host. Modules usually, but not always, expect input, and will return some sort of output. Modules also strive to be idempotent, allowing the rerunning of the module over and over again without having a negative impact. In Ansible, the input is in the form of command-line arguments to the module, and the output is delivered as JSON to `STDOUT`.

Input is generally provided in the space-separated `key=value` syntax, and it's up to the module to deconstruct these into usable data. If you're using Python, there are convenience functions to manage this, and if you're using a different language, then it is up to the module code to fully process the input.

The output is JSON formatted. Convention dictates that in a successful scenario, the JSON output should have at least one key, changed, which is a Boolean, to indicate whether the module execution resulted in a change. Additional data can be returned as well, which may be useful to define specifically what changed, or provide important information back to the playbook for later use. Additionally, host facts can be returned in the JSON data to automatically create host variables based on the module execution results. We will see more on this later, in the section entitled *Providing fact data*.

## Custom modules

Ansible provides an easy mechanism to utilize custom modules other than those that come with Ansible. As we learned in Chapter 1, *The System Architecture and Design of Ansible*, Ansible will search many locations to find a requested module. One such location, and indeed the first location, is the library/ subdirectory of the path where the top-level playbook resides. This is where we will place our custom module so that we can use it in our example playbook.

Modules can also be embedded within roles to deliver the added functionality that a role may depend upon. These modules are only available to the role that contains it or any other roles or tasks executed after the role containing the module. To deliver a module with a role, place the module in the library/ subdirectory of the role's root.

## Example – Simple module

To demonstrate the ease of writing Python-based modules, let's create a simple module. The purpose of this module will be to remotely copy a source file to a destination file, a simple task that we can build up from. To start our module, we need to create the module file. For easy access to our new module, we'll create the file in the library/ subdirectory of the working directory we've already been using. We'll call this module remote_copy.py, and to start it off, we'll need to put in a sha-bang line to indicate that this module is to be executed with Python:

```
#!/usr/bin/python
#
```

For Python-based modules, the convention is to use /usr/bin/python as the listed executable. When executed on a remote system, the configured Python interpreter for the remote host is used to execute the module, so fret not if your Python doesn't exist in this path. Next, we'll import a Python library we'll use later in the module, called shutil:

```
import shutil
```

Now we're ready to create our main function. The main function is essentially the entry point to the module, where the arguments to the module will be defined and where the execution will start. When creating modules in Python, we can take some shortcuts in this main function to bypass a lot of boilerplate code and get straight to the argument definitions.

*Extending Ansible*

We do this by creating an `AnsibleModule` object and giving it an `argument_spec` dictionary for the arguments:

```
def main():
    module = AnsibleModule(
        argument_spec = dict(
            source=dict(required=True, type='str'),
            dest=dict(required=True, type='str')
        )
    )
```

In our module, we're providing two arguments. The first argument is `source`, which we'll use to define the source file for the copy. The second argument is `dest`, the destination for the copy. Both of these arguments are marked as required, which will raise an error when executed if one of the two is not provided. Both arguments are of the type `string`. The location of the `AnsibleModule` class has not yet been defined, as that happens later in the file.

With a module object at our disposal, we can now create the code that will do the actual work on the remote host. We'll make use of `shutil.copy` and our provided arguments to accomplish the copy:

```
shutil.copy(module.params['source'],
            module.params['dest'])
```

The `shutil.copy` function expects a source and a destination, which we've provided by accessing `module.params`. The `module.params` dictionary holds all of the parameters for the module. Having completed the copy, we are now ready to return the results to Ansible. This is done via another `AnsibleModule` method, `exit_json`. This method expects a set of `key=value` arguments and will format it appropriately for a JSON return. Since we're always performing a copy, we will always return a change for simplicity's sake:

```
module.exit_json(changed=True)
```

This line will exit the function, and thus the module. This function assumes a successful action and will exit the module with the appropriate return code for success: 0. We're not done with our module's code though; we still have to account for the `AnsibleModule` location. This is where a bit of magic happens, where we tell Ansible what other code to combine with our module to create a complete work that can be transported:

```
from ansible.module_utils.basic import *
```

That's all it takes! That one line gets us access to all of the basic `module_utils`, a decent set of helper functions and classes. There is one last thing we should put into our module: a couple of lines of code telling the interpreter to execute the `main()` function when the module file is executed:

```
if __name__ == '__main__':
    main()
```

Now our module file is complete and we can test it with a playbook. We'll call our playbook `simple_module.yaml` and store it in the same directory as the `library/` directory, where we've just written our module file. We'll run the play on `localhost` for simplicity's sake and use a couple of filenames in `/tmp` for the source and destination. We'll also use a task to ensure that we have a source file to begin with:

```
---
- name: test remote_copy module
  hosts: localhost
  gather_facts: false

  tasks:
  - name: ensure foo
    file:
      path: /tmp/rcfoo
      state: touch

  - name: do a remote copy
    remote_copy:
      source: /tmp/rcfoo
      dest: /tmp/rcbar
```

*Extending Ansible*

To run this playbook, we'll reference our `mastery-hosts` file. If the `remote_copy` module file is written to the correct location, everything will work just fine, and the screen output will look as follows:

```
~/src/mastery> ansible-playbook -i mastery-hosts simple_module.yaml -v
Using /etc/ansible/ansible.cfg as config file

PLAY [test remote_copy module] ************************************************

TASK [ensure foo] *************************************************************
changed: [localhost] => {"changed": true, "dest": "/tmp/rcfoo", "gid": 1000, "group": "jfreeman", "mode": "0664", "owner": "jfreeman", "secontext": "unconfined_u:object_r:user_tmp_t:s0", "size": 0, "state": "file", "uid": 1000}

TASK [do a remote copy] *******************************************************
changed: [localhost] => {"changed": true}

PLAY RECAP ********************************************************************
localhost                  : ok=2    changed=2    unreachable=0    failed=0

~/src/mastery>
```

Our first task touches the `/tmp/rcfoo` path to ensure that it exists, and then our second task makes use of `remote_copy` to copy `/tmp/rcfoo` to `/tmp/rcbar`. Both tasks are successful, resulting in a change each time.

## Documenting a module

No module should be considered complete unless it contains documentation regarding how to operate it. Documentation for a module exists within the module itself, in special variables called DOCUMENTATION, EXAMPLES, and RETURN.

The DOCUMENTATION variable contains a specially formatted string describing the module name, the version that was added to Ansible (if it is in Ansible proper), a short description of the module, a longer description, a description of the module arguments, author and license information, additional requirements, and any extra notes useful to users of the module. Let's add a DOCUMENTATION string to our module under the existing `import shutil` statement:

```
import shutil

DOCUMENTATION = '''
---
module: remote_copy
```

```
version_added: future
short_description: Copy a file on the remote host
description:
  - The remote_copy module copies a file on the remote host from a given
source to a provided destination.
options:
  source:
    description:
      - Path to a file on the source file on the remote host
    required: True
  dest:
    description:
      - Path to the destination on the remote host for the copy
    required: True
author:
  - Jesse Keating
'''
```

The format of the string is essentially YAML, with some top-level keys containing hash structures within it (the same as the `options` key). Each option has sub-elements to describe the option, indicate whether the option is required, list any aliases for the option, list static choices for the option, or indicate a default value for the option. With this string saved to the module, we can test our formatting to ensure that the documentation will render correctly. This is done via the `ansible-doc` tool, with an argument to indicate where to search for the modules. If we run it from the same place as our playbook, the command will be `ansible-doc -M library/ remote_copy`, and the output will be as follows:

```
~/src/mastery> ansible-doc -M library/ remote_copy | cat -
> REMOTE_COPY    (/home/jfreeman/src/mastery/library/remote_copy.py)

        The remote_copy module copies a file on the remote host from a
        given source to a provided destination.

OPTIONS (= is mandatory):

= dest
        Path to the destination on the remote host for the copy


= source
        Path to a file on the source file on the remote host


AUTHOR: Jesse Keating
~/src/mastery>
```

*Extending Ansible*

In this example, I've piped the output into `cat` to prevent the pager from hiding the execution line. Our documentation string appears to be formatted correctly and provides the user with important information regarding the usage of the module.

The `EXAMPLES` string is used to provide one or more example uses of the module, snippets of the task code that you would use in a playbook. Let's add an example task to demonstrate the usage. This variable definition traditionally goes after the `DOCUMENTATION` definition:

```
EXAMPLES = '''
# Example from Ansible Playbooks
- name: backup a config file
  remote_copy:
    source: /etc/herp/derp.conf
    dest: /root/herp-derp.conf.bak
'''
```

With this variable defined, our `ansible-doc` output will now include the example, as we can see in the following screenshot:

```
~/src/mastery> ansible-doc -M library/ remote_copy | cat -
> REMOTE_COPY    (/home/jfreeman/src/mastery/library/remote_copy.py)

        The remote_copy module copies a file on the remote host from a
        given source to a provided destination.

OPTIONS (= is mandatory):

= dest
        Path to the destination on the remote host for the copy


= source
        Path to a file on the source file on the remote host


AUTHOR: Jesse Keating

EXAMPLES:
# Example from Ansible Playbooks
- name: backup a config file
  remote_copy:
    source: /etc/herp/derp.conf
    dest: /root/herp-derp.conf.bak

~/src/mastery>
```

The last documentation variable, RETURN, is a relatively new feature of module documentation. This variable is used to describe the return data from a module execution. Return data is often useful as a registered variable for later usage, and having documentation of what return data to expect can aid playbook development. Our module doesn't have any return data yet; so, before we can document any some, we first have to add return data. This can be done by modifying the `module.exit_json` line to add more information. Let's add the `source` and `dest` data to the return output:

```
module.exit_json(changed=True, source=module.params['source'],
                 dest=module.params['dest'])
```

Rerunning the playbook will show extra data being returned, as shown in the following screenshot:

Looking closely at the return data, we can see more data than we put in our module. This is actually a bit of a helper functionality within Ansible; when a return dataset includes a `dest` variable, Ansible will gather more information about the destination file. The extra data gathered is `gid` (group ID), `group` (group name), `mode` (permissions), `uid` (owner ID), `owner` (owner name), `size`, and `state` (file, link, or directory). We can document all of these return items in our RETURN variable, which is added after the EXAMPLES variable. Everything between the two sets of single quotes (`'''`) is returned – thus, this first part returns the file paths and ownership:

```
RETURN = '''
source:
    description: source file used for the copy
```

*Extending Ansible*

```
      returned: success
      type: string
      sample: "/path/to/file.name"
    dest:
      description: destination of the copy
      returned: success
      type: string
      sample: "/path/to/destination.file"
    gid:
      description: group ID of destination target
      returned: success
      type: int
      sample: 502
    group:
      description: group name of destination target
      returned: success
      type: string
      sample: "users"
    uid:
      description: owner ID of destination target
      returned: success
      type: int
      sample: 502
    owner:
      description: owner name of destination target
      returned: success
      type: string
      sample: "fred"
```

Continuing this part of the module definition file, this section returns the details about the file size, state, and permissions:

```
    mode:
      description: permissions of the destination target
      returned: success
      type: int
      sample: 0644
    size:
      description: size of destination target
      returned: success
      type: int
      sample: 20
    state:
      description: state of destination target
      returned: success
      type: string
      sample: "file"
'''
```

[ 264 ]

Each returned item is listed with a description, the cases when the item would be in the return data, the type of item it is, and a sample of the value. The RETURN string is essentially repeated verbatim in the `ansible-doc` output, as shown in the following (abbreviated) example:

```
~/src/mastery> ansible-doc -M library/ remote_copy | cat -
> REMOTE_COPY    (/home/jfreeman/src/mastery/library/remote_copy.py)

        The remote_copy module copies a file on the remote host from a
        given source to a provided destination.

OPTIONS (= is mandatory):

= dest
        Path to the destination on the remote host for the copy


= source
        Path to a file on the source file on the remote host



AUTHOR: Jesse Keating

EXAMPLES:
# Example from Ansible Playbooks
- name: backup a config file
  remote_copy:
    source: /etc/herp/derp.conf
    dest: /root/herp-derp.conf.bak

RETURN VALUES:


source:
  description: source file used for the copy
  returned: success
  type: string
  sample: "/path/to/file.name"
dest:
  description: destination of the copy
  returned: success
  type: string
  sample: "/path/to/destination.file"
```

In this way, we have built up a module that contains its own documentation – incredibly useful for others if we are contributing it to the community, or even for ourselves when we come back to it after a period of time.

*Extending Ansible*

## Providing fact data

Similar to data returned as part of a module `exit`, a module can directly create facts for a host by returning data in a key named `ansible_facts`. Providing facts directly from a module eliminates the need to register the return of a task with a subsequent `set_fact` task. To demonstrate this usage, let's modify our module to return the `source` and `dest` data as facts. Because these facts will become top-level host variables, we'll want to use more descriptive fact names than `source` and `dest` – replace the current `module.exit_json` line in our module with the code listed:

```
facts = {'rc_source': module.params['source'],
         'rc_dest': module.params['dest']}

module.exit_json(changed=True, ansible_facts=facts)
```

We'll also add a task to our playbook to use one of the facts in a `debug` statement:

```
- name: show a fact
  debug:
    var: rc_dest
```

Now, running the playbook will show the new return data plus the use of the variable:

```
~/src/mastery> ansible-playbook -i mastery-hosts simple_module.yaml -v
Using /etc/ansible/ansible.cfg as config file

PLAY [test remote_copy module] ************************************************

TASK [ensure foo] *************************************************************
changed: [localhost] => {"changed": true, "dest": "/tmp/rcfoo", "gid": 1000, "gr
oup": "jfreeman", "mode": "0664", "owner": "jfreeman", "secontext": "unconfined_
u:object_r:user_tmp_t:s0", "size": 0, "state": "file", "uid": 1000}

TASK [do a remote copy] *******************************************************
changed: [localhost] => {"ansible_facts": {"rc_dest": "/tmp/rcbar", "rc_source":
 "/tmp/rcfoo"}, "changed": true}

TASK [show a fact] ************************************************************
ok: [localhost] => {
    "rc_dest": "/tmp/rcbar"
}

PLAY RECAP ********************************************************************
localhost                  : ok=3    changed=2    unreachable=0    failed=0

~/src/mastery>
```

[ 266 ]

If our module does not return facts (and our previous version of remote_copy.py didn't), we will have to register the output and use set_fact to create the fact for us, as shown in the following code:

```
- name: do a remote copy
  remote_copy:
     source: /tmp/rcfoo
     dest: /tmp/rcbar
  register: mycopy

- name: set facts from mycopy
  set_fact:
     rc_dest: "{{ mycopy.dest }}"
```

Although it is useful to be able to do this, when designing our own modules, it is better to have the module define the facts required. If this is not done, then the previous register and the set_fact code would need to be repeated for every use of our module in a playbook!

## The check mode

Since the early days of its existence, Ansible has supported **check mode**, a mode of operation that will pretend to make changes to a system without actually changing the system. Check mode is useful for testing whether a change will actually happen, or whether a system state has drifted since the last Ansible run. Check mode depends on modules to support it and return data as if it had actually completed the change. Supporting check mode in our module requires two changes; the first is to indicate that the module supports check mode, and the second is to detect when check mode is active and return data before execution.

### Supporting check mode

To indicate that a module supports check mode, an argument has to be set when creating the module object. This can be done before or after the argument_spec variable is defined in the module object; here, we will do it after it is defined:

```
module = AnsibleModule(
    argument_spec = dict(
        source=dict(required=True, type='str'),
        dest=dict(required=True, type='str')
    ),
    supports_check_mode=True
)
```

*Extending Ansible*

If you're modifying your existing code, don't forget to add the comma after the `argument_spec` dictionary definition, as shown in the preceding code.

## Handling check mode

Detecting when check mode is active is very easy. The module object will have a `check_mode` attribute, which will be set to Boolean value `true` when check mode is active. In our module, we want to detect whether check mode is active before performing the copy. We can simply move the copy action into an `if` statement to avoid copying when check mode is active. No further changes to the module are necessary beyond this:

```
if not module.check_mode:
    shutil.copy(module.params['source'],
                module.params['dest'])
```

Now, we can run our playbook and add the -C argument to our execution. This argument engages check mode. We'll also test to ensure that the playbook did not actually create and copy the files. Let's take a look at the following screenshot:

[ 268 ]

Although the module output looks as though it created and copied files, we can see that the files referenced did not exist before execution and still do not exist after execution.

## Developing plugins

Plugins are another way of extending or modifying the functionality of Ansible. While modules are executed as tasks, plugins are utilized in a variety of other places. Plugins are broken down into a few types, based on where they would plug into the Ansible execution. Ansible ships some plugins for each of these areas, and end users can create their own to extend the functionality of these specific areas.

## Connection-type plugins

Any time Ansible makes a connection to a host to perform a task, a connection plugin is used. Ansible ships with a few connection plugins, including `ssh`, `docker`, `chroot`, `local`, and `smart`. Additional connection mechanisms can be utilized by Ansible to connect to remote systems by creating a connection plugin, which may be useful if faced with connecting to some new type of system, such as a network switch, or perhaps your refrigerator some day. Creating connection plugins is a bit beyond the scope of this book; however, the easiest way to get started is to read through the existing plugins that ship with Ansible and pick one to modify as necessary. The existing plugins can be found in `plugins/connection/` wherever the Ansible Python libraries are installed on your system, such as `/usr/lib/python2.7/site-packages/ansible/plugins/connection` on my system.

## Shell plugins

Much like connection plugins, Ansible makes use of **shell plugins** to execute things in a shell environment. Each shell has subtle differences that Ansible cares about in order to properly execute commands, redirect output, discover errors, and other such interactions. Ansible supports a number of shells, including `sh`, `csh`, `fish`, and `powershell`. We can add more shells by implementing a new shell plugin.

*Extending Ansible*

## Lookup plugins

**Lookup plugins** are how Ansible accesses outside data sources from the host system and implements language features, such as looping constructs (`loop` or `with_*`). A lookup plugin can be created to access data from an existing data store, or to create a new looping mechanism. The existing lookup plugins can be found in `plugins/lookup/`. Lookup plugins can be added to introduce new ways of looping over content, or for looking up resources in external systems.

## Vars plugins

Constructs to inject variable data exist in the form of **vars plugins**. Data such as `host_vars` and `group_vars` are implemented via plugins. While it's possible to create new variable plugins, most often, it is better to create a custom inventory source or a fact module instead.

## Fact-caching plugins

Recently (as of version 1.8), Ansible gained the ability to cache facts between playbook runs. Where facts are cached depends on the configured cache plugin that is used. Ansible includes plugins to cache facts in `memory` (not actually cached between runs): `memcached`, `redis`, and `jsonfile`. Creating a **fact-caching plugin** can enable additional caching mechanisms.

## Filter plugins

While Jinja2 includes a number of filters, Ansible has made filters pluggable to extend the Jinja2 functionality. Ansible includes a number of filters that are useful for Ansible operations, and users of Ansible can add more. Existing plugins can be found in `plugins/filter/`.

To demonstrate the development of a filter plugin, we will create a simple filter plugin to do a silly thing to text strings. We will create a filter that will replace any occurrence of the words `the cloud` with the string `somebody else's computer`. We'll define our filter in a file within a new directory, `filter_plugins/`, in our existing working directory. The name of the file doesn't matter, as we'll define the name of the filter within the file; so, let's name our file `filter_plugins/sample_filter.py`.

First, we need to define the function that will perform the translation, and provide the code to translate the strings:

```
def cloud_truth(a):
    return a.replace("the cloud", "somebody else's computer")
```

Next, we'll need to construct a `FilterModule` object and define our filter within it. This object is what Ansible will load, and Ansible expects there to be a `filters` function within the object that returns a set of filter names to functions within the file:

```
class FilterModule(object):
    '''Cloud truth filters'''
    def filters(self):
        return {'cloud_truth': cloud_truth}
```

Now we can use this filter in a playbook, which we'll call `simple_filter.yaml`:

```
---
- name: test cloud_truth filter
  hosts: localhost
  gather_facts: false
  vars:
    statement: "I store my files in the cloud"
  tasks:
  - name: make a statement
    debug:
      msg: "{{ statement | cloud_truth }}"
```

Now, let's run our playbook and see our filter in action:

```
~/src/mastery> ansible-playbook -i mastery-hosts simple_filter.yaml

PLAY [test cloud_truth filter] ************************************************

TASK [make a statement] *******************************************************
ok: [localhost] => {
    "msg": "I store my files in somebody else's computer"
}

PLAY RECAP ********************************************************************
localhost                  : ok=1    changed=0    unreachable=0    failed=0

~/src/mastery>
```

Our filter worked, and it turned the words `the cloud` into `somebody else's computer`. This is a silly example without any error handling, but it clearly demonstrates our capability to extend Ansible and Jinja2's filter capabilities.

*Extending Ansible*

> Although the name of the file containing a filter definition can be whatever the developer wants, a best practice is to name it after the filter itself so that it can easily be found in the future, potentially by other collaborators. This example did not follow this, to demonstrate that the file name is not attached to the filter name.

## Callback plugins

**Callbacks** are places in Ansible execution that can be plugged into for added functionality. There are expected callback points that can be registered against to trigger custom actions at those points. Here is a list of possible points to trigger functionality at the time of writing:

- v2_on_any
- v2_runner_on_failed
- v2_runner_on_ok
- v2_runner_on_skipped
- v2_runner_on_unreachable
- v2_runner_on_no_hosts
- v2_runner_on_async_poll
- v2_runner_on_async_ok
- v2_runner_on_async_failed
- v2_runner_on_file_diff
- v2_playbook_on_start
- v2_playbook_on_notify
- v2_playbook_on_no_hosts_matched
- v2_playbook_on_no_hosts_remaining
- v2_playbook_on_task_start
- v2_playbook_on_cleanup_task_start
- v2_playbook_on_handler_task_start
- v2_playbook_on_vars_prompt
- v2_playbook_on_setup
- v2_playbook_on_import_for_host
- v2_playbook_on_not_import_for_host
- v2_playbook_on_play_start
- v2_playbook_on_stats

- v2_on_file_diff
- v2_playbook_on_include
- v2_runner_item_on_ok
- v2_runner_item_on_failed
- v2_runner_item_on_skipped
- v2_runner_retry

As an Ansible run reaches each of these states, any plugins that have code to run at these points will be executed. This provides the tremendous ability to extend Ansible without having to modify the base code.

Callbacks can be utilized in a variety of ways: to change how things are displayed on screen, to update a central status system of progress, to implement a global locking system, or nearly anything imaginable. It's the most powerful way to extend the functionality of Ansible. To demonstrate our ability to develop a callback plugin, we'll create a simple plugin that will print something silly on the screen as a playbook executes:

1. First, we'll need to make a new directory to hold our callback. The location Ansible will look for is `callback_plugins/`. Unlike the `filter` plugin earlier, we do need to name our callback plugin file carefully, as it will also have to be reflected in an `ansible.cfg` file.
2. We'll name ours `callback_plugins/shrug.py`. Inside this file, we'll need to create a `CallbackModule` class, subclassed from `CallbackModule`, defined in the `default` callback plugin found in `ansible.plugins.callback.default`, since we only need to change one aspect of the normal output.
3. Within this class, we define variable values to indicate that it is a 2.0 version callback, and that it is an `stdout` type of callback, finally, that it has the name `shrug`.
4. Also within this class, we define one or more of the callback points we'd like to plug into in order to make something happen.
5. We only have to define the points we want to plug in. In our case, we'll plug into the `v2_on_any` point so that our plugin runs at every callback spot:

   ```
   from ansible.plugins.callback import default
   class CallbackModule(default.CallbackModule):
     CALLBACK_VERSION = 2.0
     CALLBACK_TYPE = 'stdout'
     CALLBACK_NAME = 'shrug'
     def v2_on_any(self, *args, **kwargs):
       msg = '\xc2\xaf\\_(\xe3\x83\x84)_/\xc2\xaf'
       self._display.display(msg.decode('utf-8') * 8)
   ```

# Extending Ansible

6. As this callback is `stdout_callback`, we'll need to create an `ansible.cfg` file and, within it, indicate that the `shrug stdout` callback should be used. The `ansible.cfg` file can be found in `/etc/ansible/` or in the same directory as the playbook:

   ```
   [defaults]
   stdout_callback = shrug
   ```

7. That's all we have to write into our callback. Once it's saved, we can rerun our previous playbook, which exercised our `sample_filter`, but this time we'll see something different on the screen:

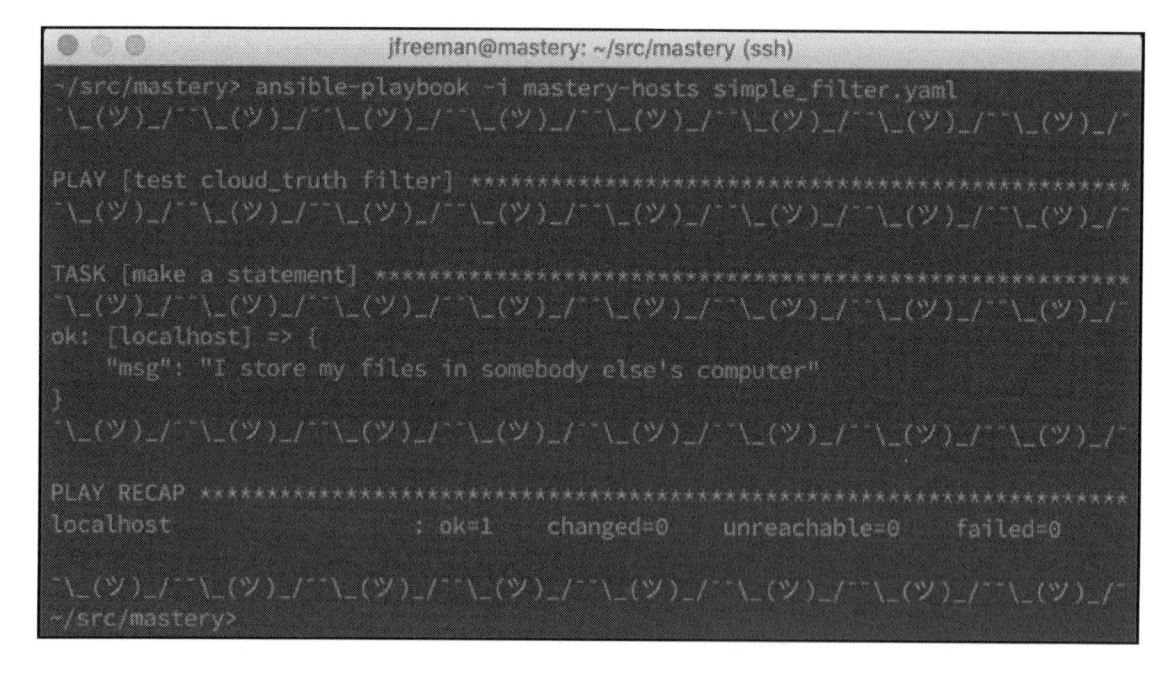

```
~/src/mastery> ansible-playbook -i mastery-hosts simple_filter.yaml
¯\_(ツ)_/¯ ¯\_(ツ)_/¯ ¯\_(ツ)_/¯ ¯\_(ツ)_/¯ ¯\_(ツ)_/¯ ¯\_(ツ)_/¯ ¯\_(ツ)_/¯ ¯\_(ツ)_/¯

PLAY [test cloud_truth filter] ************************************************
¯\_(ツ)_/¯ ¯\_(ツ)_/¯ ¯\_(ツ)_/¯ ¯\_(ツ)_/¯ ¯\_(ツ)_/¯ ¯\_(ツ)_/¯ ¯\_(ツ)_/¯ ¯\_(ツ)_/¯

TASK [make a statement] *******************************************************
¯\_(ツ)_/¯ ¯\_(ツ)_/¯ ¯\_(ツ)_/¯ ¯\_(ツ)_/¯ ¯\_(ツ)_/¯ ¯\_(ツ)_/¯ ¯\_(ツ)_/¯ ¯\_(ツ)_/¯
ok: [localhost] => {
    "msg": "I store my files in somebody else's computer"
}
¯\_(ツ)_/¯ ¯\_(ツ)_/¯ ¯\_(ツ)_/¯ ¯\_(ツ)_/¯ ¯\_(ツ)_/¯ ¯\_(ツ)_/¯ ¯\_(ツ)_/¯ ¯\_(ツ)_/¯

PLAY RECAP ********************************************************************
localhost                  : ok=1    changed=0    unreachable=0    failed=0

¯\_(ツ)_/¯ ¯\_(ツ)_/¯ ¯\_(ツ)_/¯ ¯\_(ツ)_/¯ ¯\_(ツ)_/¯ ¯\_(ツ)_/¯ ¯\_(ツ)_/¯ ¯\_(ツ)_/¯
~/src/mastery>
```

This is very silly, but it demonstrates the ability to plug into various points of a playbook execution. We chose to display a series of shrugs on screen, but we could have just as easily interacted with some internal audit and control system to record actions, or to report progress to an IRC or Slack channel.

## Action plugins

**Action plugins** exist to hook into the task construct without actually causing a module to be executed, or to execute code locally on the Ansible host before executing a module on the remote host. A number of action plugins are included with Ansible and can be found in `plugins/action/`. One such action plugin is the `template` plugin used in place of a `template` module. When a playbook author writes a `template` task, that task will actually call the `template` plugin to do the work. The plugin, among other things, will render the template locally before copying the content to the remote host. Because actions have to happen locally, the work is done by an action plugin. Another action plugin we should be familiar with is the `debug` plugin, which we've used heavily in this book to print content. Creating a custom action plugin is useful when trying to accomplish both local work and remote work in the same task.

## Distributing plugins

Much like distributing custom modules, there are standard places to store custom plugins alongside playbooks that expect to use plugins. The default locations for plugins are the locations that are shipped with the Ansible code install, subdirectories within `~/.ansible/plugins/`, and subdirectories of the project root (the place where the top-level playbook is stored). Plugins can be distributed within the same subdirectories of a role as well. To utilize plugins from any other location, we need to define the location to find the plugin for the plugin type in an `ansible.cfg` file.

When distributing plugins inside the project root, each plugin type gets its own top-level directory:

- `action_plugins/`
- `cache_plugins/`
- `callback_plugins/`
- `connection_plugins/`
- `shell_plugins/`
- `lookup_plugins/`
- `vars_plugins/`
- `filter_plugins/`

*Extending Ansible*

As with other Ansible constructs, the first plugin with a given name found will be used, and just as with modules, the paths relative to the project root are checked first, allowing a local override of an existing plugin. Simply place the filter file into the appropriate subdirectory, and it will automatically get used when referenced.

# Developing dynamic inventory plugins

**Inventory plugins** are bits of code that will create inventory data for an Ansible execution. In many environments, the simple `ini` file-style inventory source and variable structure is not sufficient to represent the actual infrastructure being managed. In such cases, a dynamic inventory source is desired, one that will discover the inventory and data at runtime at every execution of Ansible. A number of these dynamic sources ship with Ansible, primarily to operate Ansible with the infrastructure built into one cloud computing platform or another. A short, incomplete list of dynamic inventory plugins that ship with Ansible (there are now over 20) includes the following:

- `apache-libcloud`
- `cobbler`
- `console_io`
- `digital_ocean`
- `docker`
- `ec2`
- `gce`
- `libvirt_lxc`
- `linode`
- `openshift`
- `openstack`
- `rax`
- `vagrant`
- `vmware`
- `windows_azure`

An inventory plugin is essentially an executable script. Ansible calls the script with set arguments (`--list` or `--host <hostname>`) and expects JSON formatted output on STDOUT. When the `--list` argument is provided, Ansible expects a list of all the groups to be managed. Each group can list host membership, child group membership, and group variable data. When the script is called with the `--host <hostname>` argument, Ansible expects host-specific data to be returned (or an empty JSON dictionary).

Using a dynamic inventory source is easy. A source can be used directly by referring to it with the `-i` (`--inventory-file`) option to `ansible` and `ansible-playbook`, by putting the plugin file inside the directory referred to by either the inventory path in `ansible.cfg`.

Before creating an inventory plugin, we must understand the expected format for when `--list` or `--host` is used with our script.

## Listing hosts

When the `--list` argument is passed to an inventory script, Ansible expects the JSON output data to have a set of top-level keys. These keys are named for the groups in the inventory. Each group gets its own key. The structure within a group key varies depending on what data needs to be represented in the group. If a group just has hosts and no group-level variables, the data within the key can simply be a list of host names. If the group has variables or children (a group of groups), then the data needs to be a hash, which can have one or more keys named `hosts`, `vars`, or `children`. The `hosts` and `children` subkeys have a list value, a list of the hosts that exist in the group, or a list of the child groups. The `vars` subkey has a hash value, where each variable's name and value is represented by a key and value.

## Listing host variables

When the `--host <hostname>` argument is passed to an inventory script, Ansible expects the JSON output data to simply be a hash of the variables, where each variable name and value is represented by a key and a value. If there are no variables for a given host, an empty hash is expected.

# Extending Ansible

## Simple inventory plugin

To demonstrate developing an inventory plugin, we'll create one that simply prints the same host data we've been using in our `mastery-hosts` file. Integrating with a custom asset management system or an infrastructure provider is a bit beyond the scope of this book, so we'll simply code the systems into the plugin itself. We'll write our inventory plugin to a file in the top level of our project root named `mastery-inventory.py` and make it executable. We'll use Python for this file, to handle execution arguments and JSON formatting with ease:

1. First, we'll need to add a `sha-bang` line to indicate that this script is to be executed with Python:

    ```
    #!/usr/bin/env python
    #
    ```

2. Next, we'll need to import a couple of Python modules that we will need later in our plugin:

    ```
    import json
    import argparse
    ```

3. Now we'll create a Python dictionary to hold all of our groups. Some of our groups just have hosts, while others have variables or children. We'll format each group accordingly:

    ```
    inventory = {}
    inventory['web'] = {'hosts': ['mastery.example.name'],
                        'vars': {'http_port': 80,
                                 'proxy_timeout': 5}}
    inventory['dns'] = {'hosts': ['backend.example.name']}
    inventory['database'] = {'hosts': ['backend.example.name'],
                             'vars': {'ansible_ssh_user':
    'database'}}
    inventory['frontend'] = {'children': ['web']}
    inventory['backend'] = {'children': ['dns', 'database'],
                            'vars': {'ansible_ssh_user': 'blotto'}}
    inventory['errors'] = {'hosts': ['scsihost']}
    inventory['failtest'] = {'hosts': ["failer%02d" % n for n in
                             range(1,11)]}
    ```

[ 278 ]

4. To create our `failtest` group (you'll see this in action in the next chapter), which in our inventory file will be represented as `failer[01:10]`, we use a Python list comprehension to produce the list for us, formatting the items in the list just the same as our `ini`-formatted inventory file. Every other group entry is self-explanatory.

5. Our original inventory also had an `all` group variable, which provided a default variable, `ansible_ssh_user`, to all groups (which groups could override), which we'll define here and make use of later in the file:

   ```
   allgroupvars = {'ansible_ssh_user': 'otto'}
   ```

6. Next, we need to enter the host-specific variables in their own dictionary. Only one node in our original inventory had host-specific variables – we'll also add a new host, `scsihost`, to develop our example further:

   ```
   hostvars = {}
   hostvars['mastery.example.name'] = {'ansible_ssh_host':
   '192.168.10.25'}
   hostvars['scsihost'] = {'ansible_ssh_user': 'jfreeman'}
   ```

7. With all our data defined, we can now move on to the code that will handle argument parsing. This is done via the `argparse` module we imported earlier in the file:

   ```
   parser = argparse.ArgumentParser(description='Simple
   Inventory')
   parser.add_argument('--list', action='store_true', help='List
   all hosts')
   parser.add_argument('--host', help='List details of a host')
   args = parser.parse_args()
   ```

8. After parsing the arguments, we can deal with either the `--list` or `--host` actions. If a list is requested, we simply print a JSON representation of our inventory. This is where we'll take into account the `allgroupvars` data; the default `ansible_ssh_user` for each group. We'll loop through each group, create a copy of the `allgroupvars` data, update that data with any data that may already exist in the group, then replace the group's variable data with the newly updated copy. Finally, we'll print out the end result:

   ```
   if args.list:
       for group in inventory:
           ag = allgroupvars.copy()
           ag.update(inventory[group].get('vars', {}))
           inventory[group]['vars'] = ag
       print(json.dumps(inventory))
   ```

# Extending Ansible

9. Finally, we'll handle the `--host` action by building up a dictionary of all variables applicable to the host passed to this script using an approximation of the precedence order used in Ansible when parsing an `ini` format inventory. This code is iterative, and the nested loops would not be efficient in a production environment, but for the purposes of this example, it serves. The output is the JSON formatted variable data for the provided host, or an empty hash if there is no host-specific variable data for the provided host:

```python
elif args.host:
    hostfound = False
    agghostvars = allgroupvars.copy()
    for group in inventory:
        if args.host in inventory[group].get('hosts', {}):
            hostfound = True
            for childgroup in inventory:
                if group in inventory[childgroup].get('children', {}):
                    agghostvars.update(inventory[childgroup].get('vars', {}))
    for group in inventory:
        if args.host in inventory[group].get('hosts', {}):
            hostfound = True
            agghostvars.update(inventory[group].get('vars', {}))
    if hostvars.get(args.host, {}):
        hostfound = True
        agghostvars.update(hostvars.get(args.host, {}))
    if not hostfound:
        agghostvars = {}
    print(json.dumps(agghostvars))
```

Now our inventory is ready to test! We can execute it directly and pass the `--help` argument we get for free using `argparse`. This will show us the usage of our script based on the `argparse` data we provided earlier in the file:

```
~/src/mastery> ./mastery-inventory.py --help
usage: mastery-inventory.py [-h] [--list] [--host HOST]

Simple Inventory

optional arguments:
  -h, --help   show this help message and exit
  --list       List all hosts
  --host HOST  List details of a host
~/src/mastery>
```

> **TIP:** Don't forget to make the dynamic inventory script executable – for example: `chmod +x mastery-inventory.py`.

If we pass `--list`, we'll get the output of all our groups, along with all the hosts in each group and all associated inventory variables:

```
~/src/mastery> ./mastery-inventory.py --list
{"web": {"hosts": ["mastery.example.name"], "vars": {"ansible_ssh_user": "otto", "http_port": 80, "proxy_timeout": 5}}, "errors": {"hosts": ["scsihost"], "vars": {"ansible_ssh_user": "otto"}}, "frontend": {"children": ["web"], "vars": {"ansible_ssh_user": "otto"}}, "database": {"hosts": ["backend.example.name"], "vars": {"ansible_ssh_user": "database"}}, "failtest": {"hosts": ["failer01", "failer02", "failer03", "failer04", "failer05", "failer06", "failer07", "failer08", "failer09", "failer10"], "vars": {"ansible_ssh_user": "otto"}}, "dns": {"hosts": ["backend.example.name"], "vars": {"ansible_ssh_user": "otto"}}, "backend": {"children": ["dns", "database"], "vars": {"ansible_ssh_user": "blotto"}}}
~/src/mastery>
```

Similarly if we run this Python script with the `--host` argument and a hostname we know is in the inventory, we'll see the host variables for the hostname that was passed. If we pass a group name, nothing should be returned, as the script only returns data for valid individual hostnames:

```
~/src/mastery> ./mastery-inventory.py --host mastery.example.name
{"ansible_ssh_host": "192.168.10.25", "ansible_ssh_user": "otto", "http_port": 80, "proxy_timeout": 5}
~/src/mastery> ./mastery-inventory.py --host web
{}
~/src/mastery>
```

Now we're ready to use our inventory file with Ansible. Let's make a new playbook (`inventory_test.yaml`) to display the hostname and the `ssh` username data:

```
---
- name: test the inventory
  hosts: all
  gather_facts: false

  tasks:
```

## Extending Ansible

```
    - name: hello world
      debug:
        msg: "Hello world, I am {{ inventory_hostname }}.
              My username is {{ ansible_ssh_user }}"
```

There is one more thing we have to do before we can use our new inventory plugin. By default (and as a security feature), most of Ansible's inventory plugins are disabled. To ensure our dynamic inventory script will run, open the applicable `ansible.cfg` file in an editor and look for the `enable_plugins` line in the `[inventory]` section. As a minimum, it should look like the following (though you may choose to enable more plugins if you wish):

```
[inventory]
enable_plugins = ini, script
```

To use our new inventory plugin with this playbook, we simply refer to the plugin file with the `-i` argument. Because we are using the all hosts group in our playbook, we'll also limit the run to a few groups to save screen space:

```
~/src/mastery> time ansible-playbook -i mastery-inventory.py inventory_test.yaml
--limit backend,frontend,errors

PLAY [test the inventory] **********************************************

TASK [hello world] *****************************************************
ok: [scsihost] => {
    "msg": "Hello world, I am scsihost. My username is jfreeman"
}
ok: [backend.example.name] => {
    "msg": "Hello world, I am backend.example.name. My username is database"
}
ok: [mastery.example.name] => {
    "msg": "Hello world, I am mastery.example.name. My username is otto"
}

PLAY RECAP *************************************************************
backend.example.name       : ok=1    changed=0    unreachable=0    failed=0
mastery.example.name       : ok=1    changed=0    unreachable=0    failed=0
scsihost                   : ok=1    changed=0    unreachable=0    failed=0


real    1.17s
user    0.97s
sys     0.28s
~/src/mastery>
```

*Chapter 9*

As you can see, we get the hosts we expect, and we get the default `ssh` user for `master.example.name.backend.example.name` and `scsihost` each show their host-specific `ssh` username.

## Optimizing script performance

With this inventory script, when Ansible starts, it will execute the script once with `--list` to gather the group data. Then, Ansible will execute the script again with `--host <hostname>` for each host it discovered in the first call. With our script, this takes very little time, as there are very few hosts, and our execution is very fast. However, in an environment with a large number of hosts or a plugin that takes a while to run, gathering the inventory data can be a lengthy process. Fortunately, there is an optimization that can be made in the return data from a `--list` call that will prevent Ansible from rerunning the script for every host. The host-specific data can be returned all at once inside the group data return, inside a top-level key named _meta, which has a subkey named hostvars that contains a hash of all the hosts that have host variables and the variable data itself. When Ansible encounters a _meta key in the `--list` return, it'll skip the `--host` calls and assume that all of the host-specific data was already returned, potentially saving a significant amount of time! Let's modify our inventory script to return host variables inside _meta, and create an error condition inside the `--host` option to show that `--host` is not being called:

1. First, we'll add the _meta key to the inventory dictionary after all of the hostvars have been built up using the same algorithm as before, and just before argument parsing:

```
hostvars['scsihost'] = {'ansible_ssh_user': 'jfreeman'}

agghostvars = dict()
for outergroup in inventory:
    for grouphost in inventory[outergroup].get('hosts', {}):
        agghostvars[grouphost] = allgroupvars.copy()
        for group in inventory:
            if grouphost in inventory[group].get('hosts', {}):
                for childgroup in inventory:
                    if group in inventory[childgroup].get('children', {}):
                        agghostvars[grouphost].update(inventory[childgroup].get('vars', {}))
        for group in inventory:
            if grouphost in inventory[group].get('hosts', {}):
                agghostvars[grouphost].update(inventory[group].get('vars', {}))
                agghostvars[grouphost].update(hostvars.get(grouphost,
```

[ 283 ]

*Extending Ansible*

```
            {}))

            inventory['_meta'] = {'hostvars': agghostvars}

            parser = argparse.ArgumentParser(description='Simple
            Inventory')
```

Next, we'll change the `--host` handling to raise an exception:

```
            elif args.host:
                raise StandardError("You've been a bad boy")
```

2. Now, we'll rerun the `inventory_test.yaml` playbook to ensure that we're still getting the right data:

```
~/src/mastery> time ansible-playbook -i mastery-inventory.py inventory_test.yaml
  --limit backend,frontend,errors

PLAY [test the inventory] ******************************************************

TASK [hello world] *************************************************************
ok: [scsihost] => {
    "msg": "Hello world, I am scsihost. My username is jfreeman"
}
ok: [mastery.example.name] => {
    "msg": "Hello world, I am mastery.example.name. My username is otto"
}
ok: [backend.example.name] => {
    "msg": "Hello world, I am backend.example.name. My username is database"
}

PLAY RECAP *********************************************************************
backend.example.name       : ok=1    changed=0    unreachable=0    failed=0
mastery.example.name       : ok=1    changed=0    unreachable=0    failed=0
scsihost                   : ok=1    changed=0    unreachable=0    failed=0


real    0.69s
user    0.57s
sys     0.18s
~/src/mastery>
```

3. Just to be sure, we'll manually run the inventory plugin with the `--hosts` argument to show the exception:

```
~/src/mastery> ./mastery-inventory.py --host scsihost
Traceback (most recent call last):
  File "./mastery-inventory.py", line 52, in <module>
    raise StandardError("You've been a bad boy")
StandardError: You've been a bad boy
~/src/mastery>
```

With this optimization, our simple playbook using our inventory module now runs nearly twice as fast, just because of the gained efficiency in inventory parsing.

# Contributing to the Ansible project

Not all modifications need to be for local site requirements. Ansible users will often identify an enhancement that could be made to the project that others would benefit from. These enhancements can be contributed back to the Ansible project. Contributions could be in the form of updates to an existing module or core Ansible code, updates to documentation, new modules or plugins, or simply testing proposed contributions from other community members.

## Contribution submissions

The Ansible project uses GitHub (https://github.com) to manage code repositories, issues, and other aspects of the project. The Ansible organization (https://github.com/ansible) is where the code repositories can be found. The main repository is the ansible repository (https://github.com/ansible/ansible), where the core Ansible code, the modules, and the documentation can be found. This is the repository that should be cloned in order to develop a contribution.

> The Ansible project uses a development branch named `devel` instead of the traditional name of `master`. Most contributions target the `devel` branch, or a stable release branch.

*Extending Ansible*

## The Ansible repository

The Ansible repository has a number of files and folders at its root. The files are mostly high-level documentation files, code licenses, or continuous integration test platform configurations.

Of the directories, a few are worth noting:

- `bin`: Source for the various ansible core executables
- `contrib`: Source for contributed inventory and vault plugins
- `docs`: Source for API documentation, the `https://docs.ansible.com` website, and the main pages
- `hacking`: Guides and utilities for hacking on the Ansible source
- `lib/ansible`: The core Ansible source code
- `test`: Unit and integration test code

Contributions to Ansible will likely occur in one of those folders.

## Executing tests

Before any submission can be accepted by Ansible, the change must pass tests. These tests fall into three categories: unit tests, integration tests, and code-style tests. Unit tests cover very narrow aspects of source code functions, while integration tests take a more holistic approach and ensure the desired functionality happens. Code-style tests examine the syntax used, as well as whitespace and other style aspects.

Before any tests can be executed, the shell environment must be prepared to work with the Ansible code checkout. A shell environment file exists to set the required variables, which can be activated with this command:

```
$ source ./hacking/env-setup
```

Ensuring tests are passing before modifications are made can save a lot of debugging time later.

## Unit tests

All of the unit tests are located within the directory tree starting at test/units. These tests should all be self-contained and do not require access to external resources. Running the tests is as simple as executing make tests from the root of the Ansible source checkout. This will test much of the code base, including the module code.

> Executing the tests may require the installation of additional software. When using a Python virtualenv to manage Python software installations, it's best to create a new venv to use for testing Ansible–one that does not have Ansible installed in it.

To target a specific set of tests to run, the pytest (sometimes accessed as py.test) utility can be called directly, with a path provided to a directory or a specific file to test. In this example, just the parsing unit tests are executed:

```
~/src/ansible> py.test test/units/parsing                                devel
========================= test session starts =========================
platform linux2 -- Python 2.7.5 -- py-1.4.32 -- pytest-2.7.0
rootdir: /home/jfreeman/src/ansible, inifile: tox.ini
collected 301 items / 1 errors

test/units/parsing/test_ajson.py .
test/units/parsing/test_dataloader.py ..........................
test/units/parsing/test_metadata.py ...................
test/units/parsing/test_splitter.py ..................F..................
.F
test/units/parsing/test_unquote.py ................
test/units/parsing/utils/test_addresses.py ..
test/units/parsing/utils/test_jsonify.py ....
test/units/parsing/utils/test_yaml.py ..
test/units/parsing/vault/test_vault.py ...............................
...................................F.............F........
test/units/parsing/vault/test_vault_editor.py ..................
test/units/parsing/yaml/test_dumper.py .
test/units/parsing/yaml/test_loader.py ..................
test/units/parsing/yaml/test_objects.py ..............
```

As can be seen in the screenshot, the py.test utility is running through the defined unit tests and will report any errors it finds, aiding you greatly in checking any code you might be planning to submit.

## Integration tests

Ansible integration tests are tests designed to validate playbook functionality. Testing is executed by playbooks as well, making things a bit recursive. The tests are broken down into a few main categories:

- Non-destructive
- Destructive
- Cloud
- Windows
- Network

A more detailed explanation of the test categories can be found in the `README.md` file found at `test/integration/README.md`.

> Many of the integration tests require `ssh` to the localhost to be functional. Be sure that `ssh` works, ideally without a password prompt. Remote hosts can be used by altering the inventory file used for tests (`test/integration/inventory`).

As with unit tests, individual integration tests can be executed, using the `ansible-test` utility located at `test/runner/ansible-test`. This is particularly important, as many of the integration tests require external resources, such as computer cloud accounts. Each directory in `test/integration/targets` is a target that can be tested individually. For example, to test ping functionality, use the `ping` target:

```
~/src/ansible> test/runner/ansible-test integration -v ping                    devel
Run command: /usr/bin/python setup.py egg_info
Running ping integration test role
Run command: ansible-playbook ping-jMkQVB.yml -i inventory -e @integration_ ...
Using /home/jfreeman/.ansible/test/tmp/ping-_wIQos-ANSIBLE/test/integration/inte
gration.cfg as config file
 [WARNING]: The `junit_xml` python module is not installed. Disabling the
`junit` callback plugin.


PLAY [testhost] ****************************************************************

TASK [Gathering Facts] *********************************************************
ok: [testhost]

TASK [ping : ping the test] ****************************************************
ok: [testhost] => {"changed": false, "ping": "pong"}

TASK [ping : assert the ping worked] *******************************************
ok: [testhost] => {
    "changed": false,
    "msg": "All assertions passed"
}

TASK [ping : ping with data] ***************************************************
ok: [testhost] => {"changed": false, "ping": "testing"}

TASK [ping : assert the ping worked with data] *********************************
ok: [testhost] => {
    "changed": false,
    "msg": "All assertions passed"
}

TASK [ping : ping with data=crash] *********************************************
An exception occurred during task execution. To see the full traceback, use -vvv
. The error was: Exception: boom
fatal: [testhost]: FAILED! => {"changed": false, "module_stderr": "Traceback (mo
st recent call last):\n  File \"/home/jfreeman/.ansible/tmp/ansible-tmp-15512017
81.83-81175392184685/AnsiballZ_ping.py\", line 128, in <module>\n    _ansiballz_
main()\n  File \"/home/jfreeman/.ansible/tmp/ansible-tmp-1551201781.83-811753922
84685/AnsiballZ_ping.py\", line 120, in _ansiballz_main\n    invoke_module(zippe
d_mod, temp_path, ANSIBALLZ_PARAMS)\n  File \"/home/jfreeman/.ansible/tmp/ansibl
e-tmp-1551201781.83-81175392184685/AnsiballZ_ping.py\", line 63, in invoke_modul
e\n    imp.load_module('__main__', mod, module, MOD_DESC)\n  File \"/tmp/ansible
_ping_payload_HFcgUz/__main__.py\", line 86, in <module>\n  File \"/tmp/ansible_
ping_payload_HFcgUz/__main__.py\", line 75, in main\nException: boom\n", "module
_stdout": "", "msg": "MODULE FAILURE\nSee stdout/stderr for the exact error", "r
c": 1}
...ignoring

TASK [ping : assert the ping failed with data=boom] ****************************
ok: [testhost] => {
    "changed": false,
    "msg": "All assertions passed"
}

PLAY RECAP *********************************************************************
testhost                   : ok=7    changed=0    unreachable=0    failed=0    s
kipped=0    rescued=0    ignored=1
```

*Extending Ansible*

Note there is even a test in this suite designed to fail—and that, at the end, we see `ok=7` and `failed=0`, meaning all tests passed. A large set of POSIX-compatible non-destructive integration tests run by continuous integration systems on proposed changes to Ansible can be executed with the following:

```
$ test/runner/ansible-test integration -v posix/ci/
```

> At the time of writing, a number of the `posix/ci` tests do not pass on macOS. Executing these tests in a recent Fedora environment is recommended.

## Code-style tests

A third category of Ansible tests is the code-style category. These tests examine the syntax used in the Python files, ensuring a cohesive look across the code base. The code style enforced is defined by PEP8, a style guide for Python. More information is available in `test/sanity/pep8/README.md`. This style is enforced via the `pep8` make target. If there are no errors, this target does not output any text; however, the return code can be verified. A return code of `0` means there were no errors:

```
~/src/ansible> make pep8                                            devel
bin/ansible-test sanity --test pep8 --python 2.7
Sanity check using pep8
~/src/ansible> echo $?                                              devel
0
~/src/ansible>                                                      devel
```

> Additional Python modules might be required to run these tests – the method for installing these will vary from system to system, and could typically be through use of the `pip` tool. On my CentOS 7 test system, I had to run the following command to be able to run this test: **sudo yum install python2-packaging python2-pycodestyle**.

If a Python file does have a `pep8` violation, the output will reflect the violation:

```
~/src/ansible> make pep8                                                devel!
bin/ansible-test sanity --test pep8 --python 2.7
Sanity check using pep8
ERROR: Found 11 pep8 issue(s) which need to be resolved:
ERROR: lib/ansible/modules/cloud/openstack/os_zone.py:184:1: W293 blank line con
tains whitespace
ERROR: lib/ansible/modules/cloud/openstack/os_zone.py:185:9: E101 indentation co
ntains mixed spaces and tabs
ERROR: lib/ansible/modules/cloud/openstack/os_zone.py:185:9: W191 indentation co
ntains tabs
ERROR: lib/ansible/modules/cloud/openstack/os_zone.py:185:15: E111 indentation i
s not a multiple of four
ERROR: lib/ansible/modules/cloud/openstack/os_zone.py:185:15: E113 unexpected in
dentation
ERROR: lib/ansible/modules/cloud/openstack/os_zone.py:186:1: E101 indentation co
ntains mixed spaces and tabs
ERROR: lib/ansible/modules/cloud/openstack/os_zone.py:186:1: W191 indentation co
ntains tabs
ERROR: lib/ansible/modules/cloud/openstack/os_zone.py:186:4: E113 unexpected ind
entation
ERROR: lib/ansible/modules/cloud/openstack/os_zone.py:187:1: E101 indentation co
ntains mixed spaces and tabs
ERROR: lib/ansible/modules/cloud/openstack/os_zone.py:187:48: E127 continuation
line over-indented for visual indent
ERROR: lib/ansible/modules/cloud/openstack/os_zone.py:188:48: E127 continuation
line over-indented for visual indent
ERROR: The 1 sanity test(s) listed below (out of 1) failed. See error output abo
ve for details.
pep8
make: *** [pep8] Error 1
~/src/ansible> echo $?                                                2 devel!
2
~/src/ansible>                                                          devel!
```

`pep8` errors will indicate an error code, which can be looked up for detailed explanations and guidance.

## Making a pull request

With passing tests, a submission can be made. The Ansible project uses GitHub pull requests to manage submissions. To create a pull request, your changes must be committed and pushed to GitHub. Developers use a fork of the Ansible repository under their own account to push proposed changes to.

*Extending Ansible*

Once pushed, a pull request can be opened using the GitHub website. This will create the pull request, which will start continuous integration tests and notify reviewers of a new submission. Further information about GitHub pull requests can be found at `https://help.github.com/categories/collaborating-with-issues-and-pull-requests/`.

Once the pull request is open, reviewers will comment on the pull request, either asking for more information, suggesting changes, or approving of the change. For new module submissions, there is an extensive checklist to follow, which can be found at `http://docs.ansible.com/ansible/dev_guide/developing_modules_checklist.html`.

Submissions that are found acceptable and merged will be made generally available in the next release of Ansible. The latest details about the Ansible release process can be found at `http://docs.ansible.com/ansible/dev_guide/developing_releases.html`.

# Summary

Ansible is a great tool; however, sometimes, it doesn't offer all the functionality you might desire. Not every bit of functionality is appropriate to support the main project, nor is it possible to integrate with custom proprietary data sources. For these reasons, there are facilities within Ansible to extend its functionality. Creating and using custom modules is made easy by the shared module base code. Many different types of plugins can be created and used with Ansible to affect operations in a variety of ways. Inventory sources beyond what Ansible supports can still be used with relative ease and efficiency.

In this chapter, you learned about developing your own modules and including them in your playbooks. You then learned about extending Ansible through plugins, and we went into specific details about creating dynamic inventory plugins. Finally, you learned how to contribute code back to the Ansible project to enhance the code for everyone in the community. In summary, you learned that, in all cases, there are mechanisms to provide modules, plugins, and inventory sources alongside the playbooks and roles that depend on the enhanced functionality, making it seamless to distribute. This enables an almost infinite amount of expansion or customization of Ansible to your requirements, and the ability to easily contribute these back to the wider community if desired.

In `Chapter 11`, *Infrastructure Provisioning*, we will explore the use of Ansible in creating the infrastructure to be managed.

# Section 3: Orchestration with Ansible

In this section, we will explore the real-world usage of Ansible to coordinate and manage systems and services, whether on-premise or in the cloud.

The following chapters are included in this section:

Chapter 10, *Minimizing Downtime with Rolling Deployments*

Chapter 11, *Infrastructure Provisioning*

Chapter 12, *Network Automation*

# 10
# Minimizing Downtime with Rolling Deployments

Ansible is well-suited to the task of upgrading or deploying applications in a live service environment. Of course, application deployments and upgrades can be approached with a variety of different strategies. The best approach depends on the application itself, the capabilities of the infrastructure the application runs on, and any promised service level agreements with the users of the application. Whatever the approach, it is vital that the application deployment or upgrade is controlled, predictable, and repeatable, in order to ensure that users experience a stable service while automated deployments occur in the background. The last thing that anyone wants is an outage caused by unexpected behavior from their automation tool; an automation tool should be trustworthy, not an additional risk factor.

Although there is a myriad of choices, some deployment strategies are more common than others, and in this chapter, we'll walk through a couple of the more common ones. In doing so, we will showcase the Ansible features that will be useful within those strategies. We'll also discuss a couple of other deployment considerations that are common across both deployment strategies. To achieve this, we will delve into the details of the following subjects, in the context of a rolling Ansible deployment:

- In-place upgrades
- Expanding and contracting
- Failing fast
- Minimizing disruptive actions
- Serializing single tasks

## Technical requirements

Check out the following video to see the Code in Action:

`http://bit.ly/2CGJvDp`

## In-place upgrades

The first type of deployment that we'll cover is in-place upgrades. This style of deployment operates on an infrastructure that already exists, in order to upgrade the existing application. This model is a traditional model that was used when the creation of a new infrastructure was a costly endeavor, in terms of both time and money.

A general design pattern to minimize the downtime during this type of upgrade is to deploy the application across multiple hosts, behind a load balancer. The load balancer will act as a gateway between users of the application and the servers that run the application. Requests for the application will come to the load balancer, and, depending on the configuration, the load balancer will decide which backend server to direct the requests to.

To perform a rolling in-place upgrade of an application deployed with this pattern, each server (or a small subset of the servers) will be disabled at the load balancer, upgraded, and then re-enabled to take on new requests. This process will be repeated for the remaining servers in the pool, until all servers have been upgraded. As only a portion of the available application servers are taken offline to be upgraded, the application as a whole remains available for requests. Of course, this assumes that an application can perform well with mixed versions running at the same time.

Let's build a playbook to upgrade a fictional application. Our fictional application will run on servers `foo-app01` through `foo-app08`, which exist in the `foo-app` group. These servers will have a simple website that's served via the `nginx` web server, with the content coming from a `foo-app` Git repository, defined by the `foo-app.repo` variable. A load balancer server, `foo-lb`, running the `haproxy` software, will front these app servers.

In order to operate on a subset of our `foo-app` servers, we need to employ the serial mode. This mode changes how Ansible will execute a play. By default, Ansible will execute the tasks of a play across each host in the order that the tasks are listed. Ansible executes each task of the play on every host before it moves on to the next task in the play. If we were to use the default method, our first task would remove every server from the load balancer, which would result in the complete outage of our application. Instead, the serial mode lets us operate on a subset, so that the application as a whole stays available, even if some of the members are offline. In our example, we'll use a serial amount of 2, in order to keep the majority of the application members online:

```
---
- name: Upgrade foo-app in place
  hosts: foo-app
  serial: 2
```

> Ansible 2.2 introduced the concept of `serial` batches: a list of numbers that can increase the number of hosts addressed serially each time through the play. This allows the size of the hosts addressed to increase as the confidence increases. Where a batch of numbers is provided to the `serial` keyword, the last number provided will be the size of any remaining batch, until all hosts in the inventory have been completed.

Now, we can start to create our tasks. The first task will be to disable the host from the load balancer. The load balancer runs on the `foo-lb` host; however, we're operating on the `foo-app` hosts. Therefore, we need to delegate the task by using the `delegate_to` task operator. This operator redirects where Ansible will connect to in order to execute the task, but it keeps all of the variable contexts of the original host. We'll use the `haproxy` module to disable the current host from the `foo-app` backend pool:

```
  tasks:
  - name: disable member in balancer
    haproxy:
      backend: foo-app
      host: "{{ inventory_hostname }}"
      state: disabled
    delegate_to: foo-lb
```

# Minimizing Downtime with Rolling Deployments

With the host disabled, we can now update the `foo-app` content. We'll use the `git` module to update the content path with the desired version, defined as `foo-version`. We'll add a `notify` handler to this task to reload the `nginx` server if the content update results in a change. This can be done every time, but we're using this as an example usage of `notify`:

```
- name: pull stable foo-app
  git:
    repo: "{{ foo-app.repo }}"
    dest: /srv/foo-app/
    version: "{{ foo-version }}"
  notify:
    - reload nginx
```

Our next step would be to re-enable the host in the load balancer; however, if we did that task next, we'd put the old version back in place, as our notified handler hasn't run yet. So, we need to trigger our handlers early, by way of the `meta: flush_handlers` call, which you learned about in Chapter 9, *Extending Ansible*:

```
- meta: flush_handlers
```

Now, we can re-enable the host in the load balancer. We can just enable it right away and rely on the load balancer to wait until the host is healthy before sending requests to it. However, because we are running with a reduced number of available hosts, we need to ensure that all of the remaining hosts are healthy. We can make use of a `wait_for` task to wait until the `nginx` service is once again serving connections. The `wait_for` module will wait for a condition on either a port or a file path. In our example, we will wait for port 80 and the condition that the port should be in. If it is started (the default), that means it is accepting connections:

```
- name: ensure healthy service
  wait_for:
    port: 80
```

Finally, we can re-enable the member within `haproxy`. Once again, we'll delegate the task to `foo-lb`:

```
- name: enable member in balancer
  haproxy:
    backend: foo-app
    host: "{{ inventory_hostname }}"
    state: enabled
  delegate_to: foo-lb
```

[ 298 ]

Of course, we still need to define our `reload nginx` handler:

```
handlers:
- name: reload nginx
  service:
    name: nginx
    state: restarted
```

This playbook, when run, will now perform a rolling in-place upgrade of our application.

# Expanding and contracting

An alternative to the in-place upgrade strategy is the **expand and contract** strategy. This strategy has become popular of late, thanks to the self-service nature of on-demand infrastructures, such as cloud computing or virtualization pools. The ability to create new servers on demand from a large pool of available resources means that every deployment of an application can happen on brand new systems. This strategy avoids a host of issues, such as a build up of cruft on long-running systems, like the following:

- Configuration files that are no longer managed by Ansible being left behind
- Runaway processes consuming resources in the background
- Changes being made to the server manually by human beings without updating the Ansible playbooks

Starting fresh each time also removes the differences between an initial deployment and an upgrade. The same code path can be used, reducing the risk of surprises when upgrading an application. This type of installation can also make it extremely easy to roll back if the new version does not perform as expected. In addition to this, as new systems are created to replace old systems, the application does not need to go into a degraded state during the upgrade.

Let's re-approach our previous upgraded playbook with the expand and contract strategy. Our pattern will be to create new servers, deploy our application, verify our application, add new servers to the load balancer, and remove old servers from the load balancer. Let's start by creating new servers. For this example, we'll make use of an OpenStack compute cloud to `launch` new instances:

```
---
- name: Create new foo servers
  hosts: localhost

  tasks:
  - name: launch instances
```

# Minimizing Downtime with Rolling Deployments

```
      os_server:
        name: foo-appv{{ version }}-{{ item }}
        image: foo-appv{{ version }}
        flavor: 4
        key_name: ansible-prod
        security_groups: foo-app
        auto_floating_ip: false
        state: present
        auth:
          auth_url: https://me.openstack.blueboxgrid.com:5001/v2.0
          username: jlk
          password: FAKEPASSWORD
          project_name: mastery
      register: launch
      loop: "{{ range(1, 8 + 1, 1)|list }}"
```

In this task, we're looping over a count of 8, using the new `loop` with `range` syntax that was introduced in Ansible 2.5. Each loop in the `item` variable will be replaced by a number. This allows us to create eight new server instances with names based on the version of our application and the number of the loop. We're also assuming a prebuilt image to use, so that we do not need to do any further configuration on the instance. In order to use the servers in future plays, we need to add their details to the inventory. To accomplish this, we register the results of the run in the `launch` variable, which we'll use to create runtime inventory entries:

```
    - name: add hosts
      add_host:
        name: "{{ item.openstack.name }}"
        ansible_ssh_host: "{{ item.openstack.private_v4 }}"
        groups: new-foo-app
      with_items: launch.results
```

This task will create new inventory items with the same names as those of our server instance. To help Ansible know how to connect, we'll set `ansible_ssh_host` to the IP address that our cloud provider assigned to the instance (this is assuming that the address is reachable by the host running Ansible). Finally, we'll add the hosts to the `new-foo-app` group. As our `launch` variable comes from a task with a loop, we need to iterate over the results of that loop by accessing the results key. This allows us to loop over each `launch` action to access the data specific to that task.

Next, we'll operate on the servers to ensure that the new service is ready for use. We'll use `wait_for` again, just like we did earlier, as a part of a new play on our `new-foo-app` group:

```
- name: Ensure new app
  hosts: new-foo-app
  tasks:
    - name: ensure healthy service
      wait_for:
        port: 80
```

Once they're all ready to go, we can reconfigure the load balancer to make use of our new servers. For the sake of simplicity, we will assume a template for the `haproxy` configuration that expects hosts in a `new-foo-app` group, and the end result will be a configuration that knows all about our new hosts and forgets about our old hosts. This means that we can simply call a template task on the load balancer system itself, rather than attempting to manipulate the running state of the balancer:

```
- name: Configure load balancer
  hosts: foo-lb
  tasks:
  - name: haproxy config
    template:
      dest: /etc/haproxy/haproxy.cfg
      src: templates/etc/haproxy/haproxy.cfg

  - name: reload haproxy
    service:
      name: haproxy
      state: reloaded
```

Once the new configuration file is in place, we can issue a reload of the `haproxy` service. This will parse the new configuration file and start a new listening process for new incoming connections. The existing connections will eventually close, and the old processes will terminate. All new connections will be routed to the new servers running our new application version.

This playbook can be extended to decommission the old version of the servers, or that action may happen at a different times when it has been decided that a rollback to the old version capability is no longer necessary.

The expand and contract strategy can involve more tasks, and even separate playbooks for creating a golden image set, but the benefits of a fresh infrastructure for every release far outweigh the extra tasks or added complexity of creation followed by deletion.

## Failing fast

When performing an upgrade of an application, it may be desirable to fully stop the deployment at any sign of an error. A partially upgraded system with mixed versions may not work at all, so continuing with part of the infrastructure while leaving the failed systems behind can lead to big problems. Fortunately, Ansible provides a mechanism to decide when to reach a fatal error scenario.

By default, when Ansible is running through a playbook and encounters an error, it will remove the failed host from the list of play hosts and continue with the tasks or plays. Ansible will stop executing either when all the requested hosts for a play have failed, or when all the plays have been completed. To change this behavior, there are a couple of play controls that can be employed. Those controls are `any_errors_fatal` and `max_fail_percentage`.

## The any_errors_fatal option

This setting instructs Ansible to consider the entire operation fatal, and to stop executing immediately if any host encounters an error. To demonstrate this, we'll add a new group to our `mastery-hosts` inventory, using a pattern that will expand up to 10 new hosts:

```
[failtest]
failer[01:10]
```

Then, we'll create a play on this group with `any_errors_fatal` set to `true`. We'll also turn off fact gathering, since these hosts do not exist:

```
---
- name: any errors fatal
  hosts: failtest
  gather_facts: false
  any_errors_fatal: true
```

We want a task that will fail for one of the hosts, but not the others. Then, we'll want a second task as well, just to demonstrate how it will not run:

```
tasks:
- name: fail last host
  fail:
    msg: "I am last"
  when: inventory_hostname == play_hosts[-1]
- name: never run
  debug:
    msg: "I should never be run"
  when: inventory_hostname == play_hosts[-1]
```

Now, when we execute, we'll see one host fail, but the entire play will stop after the first task:

```
~/src/mastery> ansible-playbook -i mastery-hosts failtest.yaml

PLAY [any errors fatal] ****************************************************

TASK [fail last host] ******************************************************
skipping: [failer01]
skipping: [failer02]
skipping: [failer03]
skipping: [failer04]
skipping: [failer05]
skipping: [failer06]
skipping: [failer07]
skipping: [failer08]
skipping: [failer09]
fatal: [failer10]: FAILED! => {"changed": false, "msg": "I am last"}

NO MORE HOSTS LEFT *********************************************************
        to retry, use: --limit @/home/jfreeman/src/mastery/failtest.retry

PLAY RECAP *****************************************************************
failer01                   : ok=0    changed=0    unreachable=0    failed=0
failer02                   : ok=0    changed=0    unreachable=0    failed=0
failer03                   : ok=0    changed=0    unreachable=0    failed=0
failer04                   : ok=0    changed=0    unreachable=0    failed=0
failer05                   : ok=0    changed=0    unreachable=0    failed=0
failer06                   : ok=0    changed=0    unreachable=0    failed=0
failer07                   : ok=0    changed=0    unreachable=0    failed=0
failer08                   : ok=0    changed=0    unreachable=0    failed=0
failer09                   : ok=0    changed=0    unreachable=0    failed=0
failer10                   : ok=0    changed=0    unreachable=0    failed=1

~/src/mastery>
```

We can see that just one host failed; however, Ansible reported NO MORE HOSTS LEFT (implying that all hosts failed) and aborted the playbook before getting to the next play.

## The max_fail_percentage option

This setting allows play developers to define a percentage of hosts that can fail before the whole operation is aborted. At the end of each task, Ansible will perform a calculation to determine the number of hosts targeted by the play that have reached a failure state, and if that number is greater than the number allowed, Ansible will abort the playbook. This is similar to any_errors_fatal; in fact, any_errors_fatal just internally expresses a max_fail_percentage parameter of 0, where any failure is considered fatal. Let's edit our play from the preceding and remove any_errors_fatal, replacing it with the max_fail_percentage parameter set to 20:

```
---
- name: any errors fatal
  hosts: failtest
  gather_facts: false
  max_fail_percentage: 20
```

By making that change, our play should complete both tasks without aborting:

```
~/src/mastery> ansible-playbook -i mastery-hosts failtest.yaml

PLAY [any errors fatal] ********************************************************

TASK [fail last host] **********************************************************
skipping: [failer01]
skipping: [failer02]
skipping: [failer03]
skipping: [failer04]
skipping: [failer06]
skipping: [failer05]
skipping: [failer07]
skipping: [failer08]
skipping: [failer09]
fatal: [failer10]: FAILED! => {"changed": false, "msg": "I am last"}

TASK [never run] ***************************************************************
skipping: [failer01]
skipping: [failer03]
skipping: [failer04]
skipping: [failer02]
skipping: [failer06]
skipping: [failer08]
skipping: [failer05]
skipping: [failer07]
ok: [failer09] => {
    "msg": "I should never be run"
}
        to retry, use: --limit @/home/jfreeman/src/mastery/failtest.retry

PLAY RECAP *********************************************************************
failer01                   : ok=0    changed=0    unreachable=0    failed=0
failer02                   : ok=0    changed=0    unreachable=0    failed=0
failer03                   : ok=0    changed=0    unreachable=0    failed=0
failer04                   : ok=0    changed=0    unreachable=0    failed=0
failer05                   : ok=0    changed=0    unreachable=0    failed=0
failer06                   : ok=0    changed=0    unreachable=0    failed=0
failer07                   : ok=0    changed=0    unreachable=0    failed=0
failer08                   : ok=0    changed=0    unreachable=0    failed=0
failer09                   : ok=1    changed=0    unreachable=0    failed=0
failer10                   : ok=0    changed=0    unreachable=0    failed=1

~/src/mastery>
```

Now, if we change the condition on our first task so that we fail on over 20 percent of the hosts, we'll see the playbook abort early:

```
- name: fail last host
  fail:
    msg: "I am last"
  when: inventory_hostname in play_hosts[0:3]
```

We're setting up three hosts to fail, which will give us a failure rate of greater than 20 percent. The `max_fail_percentage` setting is the maximum allowed, so our setting of 20 would allow 2 out of the 10 hosts to fail. With three hosts failing, we will see a fatal error before the second task:

```
~/src/mastery> ansible-playbook -i mastery-hosts failtest.yaml

PLAY [any errors fatal] ****************************************************

TASK [fail last host] ******************************************************
fatal: [failer01]: FAILED! => {"changed": false, "msg": "I am last"}
skipping: [failer04]
fatal: [failer03]: FAILED! => {"changed": false, "msg": "I am last"}
skipping: [failer05]
fatal: [failer02]: FAILED! => {"changed": false, "msg": "I am last"}
skipping: [failer06]
skipping: [failer07]
skipping: [failer08]
skipping: [failer09]
skipping: [failer10]

NO MORE HOSTS LEFT *********************************************************

NO MORE HOSTS LEFT *********************************************************
        to retry, use: --limit @/home/jfreeman/src/mastery/failtest.retry

PLAY RECAP *****************************************************************
failer01                   : ok=0    changed=0    unreachable=0    failed=1
failer02                   : ok=0    changed=0    unreachable=0    failed=1
failer03                   : ok=0    changed=0    unreachable=0    failed=1
failer04                   : ok=0    changed=0    unreachable=0    failed=0
failer05                   : ok=0    changed=0    unreachable=0    failed=0
failer06                   : ok=0    changed=0    unreachable=0    failed=0
failer07                   : ok=0    changed=0    unreachable=0    failed=0
failer08                   : ok=0    changed=0    unreachable=0    failed=0
failer09                   : ok=0    changed=0    unreachable=0    failed=0
failer10                   : ok=0    changed=0    unreachable=0    failed=0

~/src/mastery>
```

With this combination of parameters, we can easily set up and control `fail fast` conditions on a group of hosts, which is incredibly valuable if our goal is to maintain the integrity of an environment during an Ansible deployment.

## Forcing handlers

Normally, when Ansible fails a host, it stops executing anything on that host. This means that any pending handlers will not be run. This can be undesirable, and there is a play control that will force Ansible to process pending handlers for failed hosts. This play control is `force_handlers`, which must be set to the Boolean `true`.

Let's modify our preceding example a little, in order to demonstrate this functionality. We'll remove our `max_fail_percentage` parameter and add a new first task. We need to create a task that will return successfully with a change. This is possible with the `debug` module, using the `changed_when` task control, as the `debug` module will never register a change otherwise. We'll revert our `fail` task conditional to our original ones, as well:

```
---
- name: any errors fatal
  hosts: failtest
  gather_facts: false

  tasks:
  - name: run first
    debug:
      msg: "I am a change"
    changed_when: true
    when: inventory_hostname == play_hosts[-1]
    notify: critical handler
  - name: change a host
    fail:
      msg: "I am last"
    when: inventory_hostname == play_hosts[-1]
```

[ 307 ]

# Minimizing Downtime with Rolling Deployments

Our third task remains unchanged, but we will define our critical handler:

```yaml
  - name: never run
    debug:
      msg: "I should never be run"
    when: inventory_hostname == play_hosts[-1]

  handlers:
    - name: critical handler
      debug:
        msg: "I really need to run"
```

Let's run this new play to show the default behavior of the handler not being executed. In the interest of reduced output, we'll limit execution to just one of the hosts. Note that, although the handler is referenced in the play output, it is not actually run, as evidenced by the lack of any debug message:

```
~/src/mastery> ansible-playbook -i mastery-hosts failtest.yaml --limit failer01:
failer01

PLAY [any errors fatal] ********************************************************

TASK [run first] ***************************************************************
changed: [failer01] => {
    "msg": "I am a change"
}

TASK [change a host] ***********************************************************
fatal: [failer01]: FAILED! => {"changed": false, "msg": "I am last"}

RUNNING HANDLER [critical handler] *********************************************
        to retry, use: --limit @/home/jfreeman/src/mastery/failtest.retry

PLAY RECAP *********************************************************************
failer01                   : ok=1    changed=1    unreachable=0    failed=1

~/src/mastery>
```

Now, we add the `force_handlers` play control and set it to `true`:

```yaml
---
- name: any errors fatal
  hosts: failtest
```

```
gather_facts: false
force_handlers: true
```

This time, when we run the playbook, we should see the handler run, even for the failed hosts:

```
~/src/mastery> ansible-playbook -i mastery-hosts failtest.yaml --limit failer01:
failer01

PLAY [any errors fatal] ***************************************************

TASK [run first] **********************************************************
changed: [failer01] => {
    "msg": "I am a change"
}

TASK [change a host] ******************************************************
fatal: [failer01]: FAILED! => {"changed": false, "msg": "I am last"}

RUNNING HANDLER [critical handler] ****************************************
ok: [failer01] => {
    "msg": "I really need to run"
}
        to retry, use: --limit @/home/jfreeman/src/mastery/failtest.retry

PLAY RECAP ****************************************************************
failer01                   : ok=2    changed=1    unreachable=0    failed=1

~/src/mastery>
```

> Forcing handlers can be a runtime decision, as well, using the `--force-handlers` command-line argument on `ansible-playbook`. It can also be set globally, as a parameter in `ansible.cfg`.

Forcing handlers to run can be really useful for repeated playbook runs. The first run may result in some changes, but if a fatal error is encountered before the handlers are flushed, those handler calls will be lost. Repeated runs will not result in the same changes, so the handler will never run without manual interaction. Forcing handlers to execute attempts to ensure that those handler calls are not lost.

# Minimizing disruptions

During deployment, there are often tasks that can be considered disruptive or destructive. These tasks may include restarting services, performing database migrations, and so on. Disruptive tasks should be clustered together to minimize the overall impact on an application, while destructive tasks should only be performed once.

# Delaying a disruption

Restarting services for a new code version is a very common requirement. When viewed in isolation, a single service can be restarted whenever the code and configuration for the application has changed, without concern for the overall distributed system health. Typically, a distributed system will have roles for each part of the system, and each role will essentially operate in isolation on the hosts targeted to perform those roles. When deploying an application for the first time, there is no existing uptime of the whole system to worry about, so services can be restarted at will. However, during an upgrade, it may be desirable to delay all service restarts until every service is ready, to minimize interruptions.

The reuse of role code is strongly encouraged, as opposed to designing a completely separate upgrade code path. To accommodate a coordinated reboot, the role code for a particular service needs protection around the service restart. A common pattern is to put a conditional statement on the disruptive tasks that check a variable's value. When performing an upgrade, the variable can be defined at runtime to trigger this alternative behavior. This variable can also trigger a coordinated restart of services at the end of the main playbook once all of the roles have completed, in order to cluster the disruption and minimize the total outage.

Let's create a fictional application upgrade that involves two roles with simulated service restarts. We'll call these roles `microA` and `microB`:

```
roles/microA
├── handlers
│   └── main.yaml
└── tasks
    └── main.yaml
roles/microB
├── handlers
│   └── main.yaml
└── tasks
    └── main.yaml
```

For both of these roles, we'll have a simple debug task that simulates the installation of a package. We'll notify a handler to simulate the restart of a service; and, to ensure that the handler will trigger, we'll force the task to always register as changed. The following are the contents of `roles/microA/tasks/main.yaml`:

```yaml
---
- name: install microA package
  debug:
    msg: "This is installing A"
  changed_when: true
  notify: restart microA
```

The contents of `roles/microB/tasks/main.yaml` are as follows:

```yaml
---
- name: install microB package
  debug:
    msg: "This is installing B"
  changed_when: true
  notify: restart microB
```

The handlers for these roles will be debug actions as well, and we'll attach a conditional to the handler task to only restart if the upgrade variable evaluates to the Boolean `false`. We'll also use the default filter to give this variable a default value of `false`. The contents of `roles/microA/handlers/main.yaml` are as follows:

```yaml
---
- name: restart microA
  debug:
    msg: "microA is restarting"
  when: not upgrade | default(false) | bool
```

The contents of `roles/microB/handlers/main.yaml` are as follows:

```yaml
---
- name: restart microB
  debug:
    msg: "microB is restarting"
  when: not upgrade | default(false) | bool
```

*Minimizing Downtime with Rolling Deployments*

For our top-level playbook, we'll create four plays. The first two plays will apply each of the micro roles, and the last two plays will do the restarts. The last two plays will only be executed if performing an upgrade; so, they will make use of the upgrade variable as a condition. Let's take a look at the following code snippet (called `micro.yaml`):

```yaml
---
- name: apply microA
  hosts: localhost
  gather_facts: false

  roles:
  - role: microA

- name: apply microB
  hosts: localhost
  gather_facts: false

  roles:
  - role: microB

- name: restart microA
  hosts: localhost
  gather_facts: false

  tasks:
  - name: restart microA for upgrade
    debug:
      msg: "microA is restarting"
    when: upgrade | default(false) | bool

- name: restart microB
  hosts: localhost
  gather_facts: false

  tasks:
  - name: restart microB for upgrade
    debug:
      msg: "microB is restarting"
    when: upgrade | default(false) | bool
```

If we execute this playbook without defining the `upgrade` variable, we will see the execution of each role, and the handlers within. The final two plays will have skipped tasks:

```
~/src/mastery> ansible-playbook -i mastery-hosts micro.yaml

PLAY [apply microA] ************************************************************

TASK [microA : install microA package] *****************************************
changed: [localhost] => {
    "msg": "This is installing A"
}

RUNNING HANDLER [microA : restart microA] **************************************
ok: [localhost] => {
    "msg": "microA is restarting"
}

PLAY [apply microB] ************************************************************

TASK [microB : install microB package] *****************************************
changed: [localhost] => {
    "msg": "This is installing B"
}

RUNNING HANDLER [microB : restart microB] **************************************
ok: [localhost] => {
    "msg": "microB is restarting"
}

PLAY [restart microA] **********************************************************

TASK [restart microA for upgrade] **********************************************
skipping: [localhost]

PLAY [restart microB] **********************************************************

TASK [restart microB for upgrade] **********************************************
skipping: [localhost]

PLAY RECAP *********************************************************************
localhost                  : ok=4    changed=2    unreachable=0    failed=0

~/src/mastery>
```

# Minimizing Downtime with Rolling Deployments

Now, let's execute the playbook again; this time, we'll define the upgrade as `true` at runtime:

```
~/src/mastery> ansible-playbook -i mastery-hosts micro.yaml -e upgrade=true

PLAY [apply microA] ************************************************************

TASK [microA : install microA package] *****************************************
changed: [localhost] => {
    "msg": "This is installing A"
}

RUNNING HANDLER [microA : restart microA] **************************************
skipping: [localhost]

PLAY [apply microB] ************************************************************

TASK [microB : install microB package] *****************************************
changed: [localhost] => {
    "msg": "This is installing B"
}

RUNNING HANDLER [microB : restart microB] **************************************
skipping: [localhost]

PLAY [restart microA] **********************************************************

TASK [restart microA for upgrade] **********************************************
ok: [localhost] => {
    "msg": "microA is restarting"
}

PLAY [restart microB] **********************************************************

TASK [restart microB for upgrade] **********************************************
ok: [localhost] => {
    "msg": "microB is restarting"
}

PLAY RECAP *********************************************************************
localhost                  : ok=4    changed=2    unreachable=0    failed=0

~/src/mastery>
```

This time, we can see that our handlers are skipped, but the final two plays have tasks that execute. In a real-world scenario, where many more things are happening in the `microA` and `microB` roles (and, potentially, other micro-service roles on other hosts), the difference could be of many minutes or more. Clustering the restarts at the end can reduce the interruption period significantly.

# Running destructive tasks only once

Destructive tasks come in many flavors. They can be one-way tasks that are extremely difficult to roll back, one-time tasks that cannot be rerun easily, or race condition tasks that, if performed in parallel, would result in catastrophic failure. For these reasons and more, it is essential that these tasks be performed only once, from a single host. Ansible provides a mechanism to accomplish this by way of the `run_once` task control.

The `run_once` task control will ensure that the task only executes a single time from a single host, regardless of how many hosts happen to be in a play. While there are other methods to accomplish this goal, such as using a conditional to make the task execute only on the first host of a play, the `run_once` control is the most simple and direct way to express this desire. Additionally, any variable data registered from a task controlled by `run_once` will be made available to all hosts of the play, not just the host that was selected by Ansible to perform the action. This can simplify later retrieval of the variable data.

Let's create an example playbook to demonstrate this functionality. We'll reuse our `failtest` hosts that were created in an earlier example, in order to have a pool of hosts, and we'll select two of them by using a host pattern. We'll do a `debug` task set to `run_once` and register the results, then we'll access the results in a different task with a different host:

```
---
- name: run once test
  hosts: failtest[0:1]
  gather_facts: false

  tasks:
  - name: do a thing
    debug:
      msg: "I am groot"
    register: groot
    run_once: true

  - name: what is groot
    debug:
      var: groot
    when: inventory_hostname == play_hosts[-1]
```

When we run this play, we'll pay special attention to the hostnames listed for each task operation:

```
~/src/mastery> ansible-playbook -i mastery-hosts runonce.yaml

PLAY [run once test] ****************************************************

TASK [do a thing] *******************************************************
ok: [failer01] => {
    "msg": "I am groot"
}

TASK [what is groot] ****************************************************
skipping: [failer01]
ok: [failer02] => {
    "groot": {
        "changed": false,
        "failed": false,
        "msg": "I am groot"
    }
}

PLAY RECAP **************************************************************
failer01                   : ok=1    changed=0    unreachable=0    failed=0
failer02                   : ok=1    changed=0    unreachable=0    failed=0

~/src/mastery>
```

We can see that the `do a thing` task is executed on the `failer01` host, while the `what is groot` task, which examines the data from the `do a thing` task, operates on the `failer02` host.

## Serializing single tasks

Certain applications that run multiple copies of a service may not react well to all of those services being restarted at once. Typically, when upgrading this type of application, a `serial` play is used. However, if the application is of a large enough scale, serializing the entire play may be wildly inefficient. A different approach can be used, which is to serialize only the sensitive tasks (often the handlers to restart services).

To serialize a specific handler task, we can make use of a built-in variable, `play_hosts`. This variable holds the list of hosts that should be used for a given task as a part of the play. It is kept up to date with hosts that have failed or are unreachable. Using this variable, we can construct a loop to iterate over each host that could potentially run a handler task. Instead of using the `item` in the module arguments, we'll use the `item` in a `when` conditional and a `delegate_to` directive. In this manner, handler tasks that get notified within the playbook can be delegated to a host in the aforementioned loop, rather than the original host. However, if we just use this as the list for a `loop` directive, we'll end up executing the task for every host, for each of the hosts that trigger a handler. That's obviously unwanted, so we can use a task directive, `run_once`, to change the behavior. The `run_once` directive instructs Ansible to only execute the task for one host, instead of for every host that it would normally target. Combining `run_once` and our `loop` of `play_hosts` creates a scenario where Ansible will run through the loop only once. Finally, we want to wait a small amount of time between each loop, so that the restarted service can become functional before we restart the next one. We can make use of a `loop_control` of `pause` (introduced in Ansible version 2.2) to insert a pause between each iteration of the loop.

To demonstrate how this serialization will work, we'll write a play using a few hosts from our `failtest` group, with a task that creates a change and registers the output, so that we can check this output in the handler task we `notify`, called `restart groot`. We then create the serialized handler task itself at the bottom of the playbook:

```yaml
---
- name: parallel and serial
  hosts: failtest[0:3]
  gather_facts: false

  tasks:
  - name: do a thing
    debug:
      msg: "I am groot"
    changed_when: inventory_hostname in play_hosts[0:2]
    register: groot
    notify: restart groot

  handlers:
  - name: restart groot
    debug:
      msg: "I am groot?"
    loop: "{{ play_hosts }}"
    delegate_to: "{{ item }}"
    run_once: true
    when: hostvars[item]['groot']['changed'] | bool
```

```
      loop_control:
        pause: 2
```

Upon execution of this playbook, we can see the handler notification (thanks to double verbosity, -vv), and in the handler task, we can see the loop, conditional, and delegation:

If you have tried this code out for yourself, you will notice the delay between each handler run, just as we specified in the `loop_control` part of the task.

## Summary

Deployment and upgrade strategies are a matter of taste. Each strategy comes with distinct advantages and disadvantages. Ansible does not declare an opinion about which is better, and therefore, it is well-suited to perform deployments and upgrades regardless of the strategy. Ansible provides features and design patterns that facilitate a variety of styles with ease. Understanding the nature of each strategy and how Ansible can be tuned for that strategy will empower you to decide on and design deployments for each of your applications. Task controls and built-in variables provide methods to efficiently upgrade large-scale applications, while treating specific tasks carefully.

In this chapter, you learned how to use Ansible to perform in-place upgrades, and some different methodologies for these, including techniques such as expanding and contracting an environment. You learned about failing fast to ensure that playbooks don't cause extensive damage if an early part of a play goes wrong, and how to minimize both disruptive and destructive actions. Finally, you learned about serializing single tasks for the purpose of minimizing disruption to running services, by taking nodes out of service in a minimal controlled manner. This ensures that the service remains operational while maintenance work (such as an upgrade) occurs behind the scenes.

In the next chapter, we'll go into detail about using Ansible to work with cloud infrastructure providers and container systems, in order to create an infrastructure to manage.

# 11
# Infrastructure Provisioning

Almost everything in data centers is becoming software defined, from networks to the server infrastructure on which our software runs. **Infrastructure as a Service (IaaS)** providers offer APIs for programmatically managing images, servers, networks, and storage components. These resources are often expected to be created just-in-time, in order to reduce costs and increase efficiency.

As a result, a great deal of effort has gone into the cloud provisioning aspect of Ansible since the last edition of this book, with more than 30 infrastructure providers catered for in the official Ansible release. These range from open source solutions such as OpenStack and oVirt to proprietary providers such as VMware and cloud providers such as AWS, GCP, and Azure.

There are more use cases than we can cover in this chapter, but nonetheless, we will explore the following ways in which Ansible can interact with a variety of these services:

- Managing an on-premise cloud infrastructure
- Managing a public cloud infrastructure
- Interacting with Docker containers
- Making use of Ansible containers

## Technical requirements

Check out the following video to see the Code in Action:

```
http://bit.ly/2Ft2Qty
```

# Managing cloud infrastructures

The cloud is a popular but vague term, used to describe IaaS. There are many types of resources that can be provided by a cloud, although the most commonly discussed are compute and storage. Ansible is capable of interacting with numerous cloud providers, in order to discover, create, or otherwise manage resources within them. Note that although we will focus on the compute and storage resources in this chapter, Ansible has a modules for interacting with many more cloud resource types, such as load balancers, and even cloud role-based access controls.

One such cloud provider that Ansible can interact with is OpenStack (an open source cloud operating system), and this is a likely solution for those with a need for on-premise IaaS functionality. A suite of services provides interfaces to manage compute, storage, and networking services, plus many other supportive services. There is not a single provider of OpenStack; instead, many public and private cloud providers build their products with OpenStack, and thus although the providers may themselves be disparate, they provide the same APIs and software interfaces so that Ansible can automate tasks with ease in these environments.

Ansible has supported OpenStack services since very early in the project. That initial support has grown to include over forty modules, with support for managing the following:

- Compute
- Bare-metal compute
- Compute images
- Authentication accounts
- Networks
- Object storage
- Block storage

In addition to performing **create, read, update, and delete** (**CRUD**) actions on the preceding types of resources, Ansible also includes the ability to use OpenStack (and other clouds) as an inventory source, and we touched on this earlier, in Chapter 1, *The System Architecture and Design of Ansible*. Each execution of `ansible` or `ansible-playbook` that utilizes an OpenStack cloud as an inventory source will get on-demand information about what compute resources exist, and various facts about those compute resources. Since the cloud service is already tracking these details, this can reduce overheads by eliminating the manual tracking of resources.

To demonstrate Ansible's ability to manage and interact with cloud resources, we'll walk through two scenarios: a scenario to create and then interact with new compute resources, and a scenario that will demonstrate using OpenStack as an inventory source.

## Creating servers

The OpenStack compute service provides an API for creating, reading, updating, and deleting of virtual machine servers. Through this API, we'll be able to create the server for our demonstration. After accessing and modifying the server through SSH, we'll also use the API to delete the server. This self-service ability is a key feature of cloud computing.

Ansible can be used to manage these servers by using the various `os_server` modules:

- `os_server`: This module is used to create and delete virtual servers.
- `os_server_facts`: This module is used to gather facts about a server.
- `os_server_actions`: This module is used to perform various actions on a server.
- `os_server_group`: This module is used to create and delete server groups.
- `os_server_volume`: This module is used to attach or detach block storage volumes from a server.
- `os_server_metadata`: This module is used to create, update, and delete metadata for virtual servers.

*Infrastructure Provisioning*

## Booting virtual servers

For our demonstration, we will use `os_server`. We'll need to provide authentication details about our cloud, such as the auth URL and our login credentials. In addition to this, we will need to set up our Ansible host with the correct prerequisite software for this module to function. As we discussed earlier in the book when addressing dynamic inventories, Ansible sometimes requires additional software or libraries on the host in order to function. In fact, it is a policy of the Ansible developers to not ship cloud libraries with Ansible itself, as they would rapidly become out of date, and different operating systems would require different versions.

You can always find the software dependencies in the Ansible documentation for each module, so it is worth checking this when using a module for the first time (especially a cloud provider module). The Ansible host used for the demos throughout this book is based on CentOS 7, and in order for the `os_server` module to function, I had to run the following command first:

```
sudo pip install openstacksdk decorator==4.0
```

The exact software and version will depend on our host operating system, and may change with newer Ansible releases. There may be native packages available for your operating system, too—it is worth spending a few minutes checking this before proceeding.

Once the prerequisite modules are in place, we can proceed with the server creation. For this, we'll need a flavor, an image, a network, and a name. You will also need a key, and this will need to be defined in the OpenStack GUI (or CLI) before proceeding. Naturally, these details may be different for each OpenStack cloud. For this demo, I am using a single, all-in-one VM based on devstack, and I am using defaults as much as possible, to make it easy to follow.

I'll name our playbook `boot-server.yaml`. Our play starts with a name and uses `localhost` as the host pattern. As we do not rely on any local facts, I'll turn fact gathering off, as well:

```
---
- name: boot server
  hosts: localhost
  gather_facts: false
```

To create the server, I'll use the `os_server` module and provide the `auth` details relevant to an OpenStack cloud that I have access to, as well as a flavor, image, network, and name. Note the `key_name`, which indicates the SSH public key from the keypair you would have created for yourself in OpenStack prior to writing this playbook (as discussed previously in this chapter). This SSH public key is integrated into the `Fedora 29` image we are using when it is first booted on OpenStack so that we can subsequently gain access to it over SSH. I also uploaded a `Fedora 29` image for demonstration purposes in this chapter, as it allows for greater manipulation than the default Cirros image that is included with OpenStack distributions. These images can be freely downloaded, ready-made, from `https://alt.fedoraproject.org/cloud/`. Finally, as you'd expect, I've obfuscated my password:

```
  tasks:
    - name: boot the server
      os_server:
        auth:
          auth_url: "http://devstack.example.com/identity/v3"
          username: "admin"
          password: "password"
          project_name: "demo"
          project_domain_name: "default"
          user_domain_name: "default"
        flavor: "ds1G"
        image: "Fedora 29"
        key_name: "mastery-key"
        network: "private"
        name: "mastery1"
```

> Authentication details can be written to an external file, which will be read by the underlying module code. This module code uses `os-client-config`, a standard library for managing OpenStack credentials. Alternatively, they can be stored in an Ansible Vault, as we described in Chapter 2, *Protecting Your Secrets with Ansible*, and then passed to the module as variables.

## Infrastructure Provisioning

Running this play as-is will simply create the server, and nothing more. I can use the previously created `mastery-hosts` as an inventory source, as I'm only using `localhost` from it:

```
~/src/mastery> ansible-playbook -i mastery-hosts boot-server.yaml -vv
ansible-playbook 2.7.5
  config file = /etc/ansible/ansible.cfg
  configured module search path = [u'/home/jfreeman/.ansible/plugins/modules', u
'/usr/share/ansible/plugins/modules']
  ansible python module location = /usr/lib/python2.7/site-packages/ansible
  executable location = /usr/bin/ansible-playbook
  python version = 2.7.5 (default, Oct 30 2018, 23:45:53) [GCC 4.8.5 20150623 (R
ed Hat 4.8.5-36)]
Using /etc/ansible/ansible.cfg as config file

PLAYBOOK: boot-server.yaml *****************************************************
1 plays in boot-server.yaml

PLAY [boot server] *************************************************************
META: ran handlers

TASK [boot the server] *********************************************************
task path: /home/jfreeman/src/mastery/boot-server.yaml:7
changed: [localhost] => {"changed": true, "id": "9bfbc66e-63f4-4822-8b10-49fed7e
17c0c", "openstack": {"OS-DCF:diskConfig": "MANUAL", "OS-EXT-AZ:availability_zon
e": "nova", "OS-EXT-SRV-ATTR:hypervisor_hostname": "devstack.example.com", "OS-E
XT-SRV-ATTR:instance_name": "instance-00000003", "OS-EXT-SRV-ATTR:user_data": nu
ll, "OS-EXT-STS:power_state": 1, "OS-EXT-STS:task_state": null, "OS-EXT-STS:vm_s
tate": "active", "OS-SCH-HNT:scheduler_hints": null, "OS-SRV-USG:launched_at": "
2019-03-04T16:52:35.000000", "OS-SRV-USG:terminated_at": null, "accessIPv4": "17
2.24.4.46", "accessIPv6": "fdfd:e9e0:14e1:0:f816:3eff:feba:353b", "addresses": {
"private": [{"OS-EXT-IPS-MAC:mac_addr": "fa:16:3e:ba:35:3b", "OS-EXT-IPS:type":
"fixed", "addr": "fdfd:e9e0:14e1:0:f816:3eff:feba:353b", "version": 6}, {"OS-EXT
-IPS-MAC:mac_addr": "fa:16:3e:ba:35:3b", "OS-EXT-IPS:type": "fixed", "addr": "10
.0.0.5", "version": 4}, {"OS-EXT-IPS-MAC:mac_addr": "fa:16:3e:ba:35:3b", "OS-EXT
-IPS:type": "floating", "addr": "172.24.4.46", "version": 4}]}, "adminPass": "9V
```

I've truncated the output, as there is a lot of data returned from the module. Most importantly, we get data regarding the IP addresses of the host. This particular cloud uses a floating IP to provide public access to the server instance, which we can see the value for by registering the output and then debug printing the value of `openstack.accessIPv4`:

```
          tasks:
            - name: boot the server
              os_server:
                auth:
                  auth_url: "http://devstack.example.com/identity/v3"
                  username: "admin"
                  password: "password"
                  project_name: "demo"
                  project_domain_name: "default"
                  user_domain_name: "default"
                flavor: "ds1G"
                image: "Fedora 29"
                key_name: "mastery-key"
                network: "private"
                name: "mastery1"
              register: newserver

            - name: show floating ip
              debug:
                var: newserver.openstack.accessIPv4
```

This time, when executing, the first task does not result in a change, as the server that we want already exists:

```
~/src/mastery> ansible-playbook -i mastery-hosts boot-server.yaml

PLAY [boot server] ************************************************************

TASK [boot the server] ********************************************************
ok: [localhost]

TASK [show floating ip] *******************************************************
ok: [localhost] => {
    "newserver.openstack.accessIPv4": "172.24.4.46"
}

PLAY RECAP ********************************************************************
localhost                  : ok=2    changed=0    unreachable=0    failed=0

~/src/mastery>
```

*Infrastructure Provisioning*

The output shows an IP address of `172.24.4.46`. I can use that information to connect to my newly created cloud server.

## Adding to runtime inventory

Booting a server isn't all that useful by itself. The server exists to be used, and will likely need some configuration to become useful. While it's possible to have one playbook to create resources and a completely different playbook to manage configuration, we can also do it all from the same playbook. Ansible provides a facility to add hosts to the inventory as a part of a play, which will allow for the use of those hosts in subsequent plays.

Working from the previous example, we have enough information to add the new host to the runtime inventory, by way of the `add_host` module:

```
- name: add new server
  add_host:
    name: "mastery1"
    ansible_ssh_host: "{{ newserver.openstack.accessIPv4 }}"
    ansible_ssh_user: "fedora"
```

I know that this image has a default user of `fedora`, so I set a host variable accordingly, along with setting the IP address as the connection address.

> This example is also glossing over any required security group configuration in OpenStack, and any accepting of the SSH host key. Additional tasks can be added to manage these things.

With the server added to our inventory, we can do something with it. Let's imagine a scenario in which we want to use this cloud resource to convert an image file, using `ImageMagick` software. To accomplish this, we'll need a new play to make use of the new host. I know that this particular `fedora` image does not contain Python, so we need to add Python and the Python bindings for `dnf` (so we can use the `dnf` module) as our first task, using the `raw` module:

```
- name: configure server
  hosts: mastery1
  gather_facts: false

  tasks:
    - name: install python
      raw: "sudo dnf install -y python python2-dnf"
```

Next, we'll need the `ImageMagick` software, which we can install by using the `dnf` module:

```
- name: install imagemagick
  dnf:
    name: "ImageMagick"
  become: "yes"
```

Running the playbook at this point will show the changed tasks for our new host; note that this time, we must give `ansible-playbook` the location of our private key file from OpenStack, so that it can authenticate to the `fedora` image:

```
~/src/mastery> ansible-playbook -i mastery-hosts boot-server.yaml --private-key mastery-key

PLAY [boot server] *********************************************************

TASK [boot the server] *****************************************************
ok: [localhost]

TASK [show floating ip] ****************************************************
ok: [localhost] => {
    "newserver.openstack.accessIPv4": "172.24.4.46"
}

TASK [add new server] ******************************************************
changed: [localhost]

PLAY [configure server] ****************************************************

TASK [install python] ******************************************************
changed: [mastery1]

TASK [install imagemagick] *************************************************
changed: [mastery1]

PLAY RECAP *****************************************************************
localhost                  : ok=3    changed=1    unreachable=0    failed=0
mastery1                   : ok=2    changed=2    unreachable=0    failed=0

~/src/mastery>
```

[ 329 ]

*Infrastructure Provisioning*

We can see Ansible reporting two changed tasks on the host `mastery1`, which we just created in the first play. This host does not exist in the `mastery-hosts` inventory file.

We have turned off verbose reporting here, too, as the output would otherwise be very cumbersome to wade through; however, given that we have the private key file for our OpenStack instance, we can manually log in and check the results of our playbook:

```
~/src/mastery> ssh -i mastery-key fedora@172.24.4.46
Last login: Mon Mar  4 17:36:27 2019 from 192.168.81.154
[fedora@mastery1 ~]$ rpm -qa --last | head
libgs-9.26-1.fc29.x86_64                          Mon 04 Mar 2019 05:36:50 PM UTC
ImageMagick-libs-6.9.9.38-3.fc29.x86_64           Mon 04 Mar 2019 05:36:50 PM UTC
ImageMagick-6.9.9.38-3.fc29.x86_64                Mon 04 Mar 2019 05:36:50 PM UTC
adobe-mappings-pdf-20180407-2.fc29.noarch         Mon 04 Mar 2019 05:36:49 PM UTC
urw-base35-fonts-20170801-11.fc29.noarch          Mon 04 Mar 2019 05:36:48 PM UTC
pango-1.42.4-2.fc29.x86_64                        Mon 04 Mar 2019 05:36:48 PM UTC
librsvg2-2.44.13-1.fc29.x86_64                    Mon 04 Mar 2019 05:36:48 PM UTC
libidn-1.35-3.fc29.x86_64                         Mon 04 Mar 2019 05:36:48 PM UTC
jbig2dec-libs-0.14-3.fc29.x86_64                  Mon 04 Mar 2019 05:36:48 PM UTC
harfbuzz-1.8.7-1.fc29.x86_64                      Mon 04 Mar 2019 05:36:48 PM UTC
[fedora@mastery1 ~]$
```

From here, we could extend our second play to upload a source image file by using `copy`, then perform a command by using `ImageMagick` on the host to convert the image. Another task can be added to fetch the converted file back down by using the `slurp` module, or the modified file can be uploaded to a cloud-based object store. Finally, a last play can be added to delete the server itself.

The entire lifespan of the server, from creation to configuration to use, and finally, to removal, can all be managed with a single playbook. The playbook can be made dynamic by reading runtime variable data, in order to define what file should be uploaded/modified and where it should be stored, essentially turning the playbook into a reusable program. Although somewhat simplistic, hopefully this gives you a clear idea of how powerful Ansible is for working with infrastructure service providers.

# Using OpenStack inventory sources

Our previous example imagined a single-use, short-lived cloud server. What if we want to create and use long-lived cloud servers, instead? Walking through the tasks of creating them and adding them to the temporary inventory each time we want to touch them seems inefficient. Manually recording the server details into a static inventory also seems inefficient, and also error-prone. Thankfully, there is a better way: using the cloud itself as a dynamic inventory source.

Ansible ships with a number of dynamic inventory scripts for cloud providers, as we discussed in `Chapter 1`, *The System Architecture and Design of Ansible*. We'll continue our examples here with OpenStack. To recap, the Ansible source repository holds these contributed scripts in `contrib/inventory/`, and the OpenStack script is `contrib/inventory/openstack_inventory.py`, with an associated configuration file at `contrib/inventory/openstack.yml`. To make use of this script, simply copy the `.py` file to the playbook directory that expects to use it, or to a path accessible to all users/playbooks on the system that will be executing Ansible. For our example, I'll copy it to the playbook directory.

The configuration file needs a bit more consideration. This file holds authentication details for the OpenStack cloud(s) to connect to. That makes this file sensitive, and it should only be made visible to the users that require access to this information. In addition, the inventory script will attempt to load the configuration from the standard paths used by `os-client-config` ( https://docs.openstack.org/developer/os-client-config/ ), the underlying authentication code. This means that the configuration for this inventory source can live in the following:

- `clouds.yaml`, in the current working directory when executing the inventory script
- `~/.config/openstack/clouds.yaml`
- `/etc/openstack/clouds.yaml`
- `/etc/openstack/openstack.yaml`
- `/etc/openstack/openstack.yml`

# Infrastructure Provisioning

The first file that's found will be used. For our example, I'll use a `clouds.yaml` file in the playbook directory alongside the script itself, in order to isolate configuration from any other paths.

The `help` output for the script shows a few possible arguments; however, the ones that Ansible will use are `--list` and `--host`:

```
~/src/mastery> ./openstack_inventory.py --help
usage: openstack_inventory.py [-h] [--cloud CLOUD] [--private] [--refresh]
                              [--debug] (--list | --host HOST)

OpenStack Inventory Module

optional arguments:
  -h, --help     show this help message and exit
  --cloud CLOUD  Cloud name (default: None)
  --private      Use private address for ansible host
  --refresh      Refresh cached information
  --debug        Enable debug output
  --list         List active servers
  --host HOST    List details about the specific host
~/src/mastery>
```

The first is used to get a list of all of the servers visible to the account used, and the second would be used to get host variable data from each, except that this inventory script returns all of the host variables with the `--list` call. Returning the data with the host list is a performance enhancement, as we discussed earlier in the book, eliminating the need to call the OpenStack APIs for each and every host returned.

The output from `--list` is quite long; here are the first few lines:

```
~/src/mastery> ./openstack_inventory.py --list
{
  "_meta": {
    "hostvars": {
      "mastery1": {
        "ansible_host": "172.24.4.46",
        "ansible_ssh_host": "172.24.4.46",
        "openstack": {
          "OS-DCF:diskConfig": "MANUAL",
          "OS-EXT-AZ:availability_zone": "nova",
          "OS-EXT-SRV-ATTR:hypervisor_hostname": "devstack.example.com",
          "OS-EXT-SRV-ATTR:instance_name": "instance-00000004",
          "OS-EXT-SRV-ATTR:user_data": null,
          "OS-EXT-STS:power_state": 1,
          "OS-EXT-STS:task_state": null,
          "OS-EXT-STS:vm_state": "active",
          "OS-SCH-HNT:scheduler_hints": null,
          "OS-SRV-USG:launched_at": "2019-03-04T17:20:33.000000",
          "OS-SRV-USG:terminated_at": null,
          "accessIPv4": "172.24.4.46",
          "accessIPv6": "fdfd:e9e0:14e1:0:f816:3eff:feb0:91ec",
          "addresses": {
            "private": [
              {
                "OS-EXT-IPS-MAC:mac_addr": "fa:16:3e:b0:91:ec",
                "OS-EXT-IPS:type": "fixed",
                "addr": "fdfd:e9e0:14e1:0:f816:3eff:feb0:91ec",
                "version": 6
              },
              {
                "OS-EXT-IPS-MAC:mac_addr": "fa:16:3e:b0:91:ec",
                "OS-EXT-IPS:type": "fixed",
                "addr": "10.0.0.22",
                "version": 4
              },
```

*Infrastructure Provisioning*

The configured account only has one visible server, which has a UUID of `63338332-de64-4200-bb60-c74a92fcba82`, the instance that we booted in a previous example. We see this instance listed in the `ds1G` and `Fedora 29` groups, for example. The first group is for all of the servers running with the `ds1G` flavor, and the second is for all servers running from our `Fedora 29` image. These groupings happen automatically within the inventory plugin, and may vary according to the OpenStack setup that you use. The tail end of the output will show the other groups provided by the plugin:

```
            "vm_state": "active",
            "volumes": []
          }
        }
      }
    },
    "_nova": [
      "mastery1"
    ],
    "devstack": [
      "mastery1"
    ],
    "devstack_": [
      "mastery1"
    ],
    "devstack__nova": [
      "mastery1"
    ],
    "flavor-ds1G": [
      "mastery1"
    ],
    "image-Fedora 29": [
      "mastery1"
    ],
    "instance-63338332-de64-4200-bb60-c74a92fcba82": [
      "mastery1"
    ],
    "nova": [
      "mastery1"
    ]
}
~/src/mastery>
```

*Chapter 11*

> **TIP**: Note that for the preceding groupings to appear, `expand_hostvars: True` must be set in the `clouds.yml` file.

Some of the additional groups are as follows:

- `devstack`: All servers running on our `devstack` instance
- `flavor-ds1G`: All servers that use the `ds1G` flavor
- `image-Fedora 29`: All servers that use the `Fedora 29` image
- `instance-63338332-de64-4200-bb60-c74a92fcba82`: A group named after the instance itself
- `nova`: All servers running under the `nova` service

There are many groups provided, each with a potentially different slice of the servers found by the inventory script. These groups make it easy to target just the right instances with plays. The hosts are defined as the UUIDs of the servers. As these are unique by nature, and also quite long, they are unwieldy as a target within a play. This makes groups all the more important.

To demonstrate using this script as an inventory source, we'll recreate the previous example, skipping over the creation of the server and just writing the second play by using an appropriate group target. We'll name this playbook `configure-server.yaml`:

```
---
- name: configure server
  hosts: all
  gather_facts: false
  remote_user: fedora

  tasks:
    - name: install python
      raw: "sudo dnf install -y python python2-dnf"

    - name: install imagemagick
      dnf:
        name: "ImageMagick"
      become: "yes"
```

The default user of this image is `fedora`; however, that information isn't readily available via the OpenStack APIs, and thus, it is not reflected in the data that our inventory script provides. We can simply define the user to use at the play level.

[ 335 ]

# Infrastructure Provisioning

This time, the host pattern is set to `all`, as we only have one host on our demo OpenStack server at this time; however, in real life it's unlikely that you would be so open in your host targeting in Ansible.

The rest of the play is unchanged, and the output should look similar to previous executions:

```
~/src/mastery> ansible-playbook -i openstack_inventory.py configure-server.yaml
--private-key mastery-key

PLAY [configure server] *********************************************************

TASK [install python] ***********************************************************
changed: [mastery1]

TASK [install imagemagick] ******************************************************
ok: [mastery1]

PLAY RECAP **********************************************************************
mastery1                   : ok=2    changed=1    unreachable=0    failed=0

~/src/mastery>
```

This output differs from the last time that the `boot-server.yaml` playbook was executed in only a few ways. First, the `mastery1` instance is not created or booted. We're assuming that the servers we want to interact with have already been created and are running. Secondly, we have pulled the inventory for this playbook run directly from the OpenStack server itself, using a dynamic inventory script, rather than creating one in the playbook using `add_host`. Otherwise, the output is the same.

As servers get added or removed over time, each execution of the inventory plugin will discover what servers are there at the moment of playbook execution. This can save a significant amount of time over attempting to maintain an accurate list of servers in static inventory files.

# Managing a public cloud infrastructure

The management of public cloud infrastructures with Ansible is no more difficult than the management of OpenStack with it, as we covered earlier. In general, for any IaaService provider supported by Ansible, there is a three-step process to getting it working:

1. Establish the Ansible modules available to support the cloud provider.
2. Install any prerequisite software or libraries on the Ansible host.
3. Define the playbook and run it against the infrastructure provider.

There are dynamic inventory scripts readily available for most providers, too, and we have already demonstrated two in this book:

- `ec2.py` was discussed in Chapter 1, *The System Architecture and Design of Ansible*.
- `openstack_inventory.py` was demonstrated earlier in this chapter.

Let's take a look at **Amazon Web Services (AWS)**, and specifically, their EC2 offering. We can boot up a new server from an image of our choosing, using exactly the same high-level process that we did with OpenStack earlier. However, as I'm sure you will have guessed by now, we have to use an Ansible module that offers specific EC2 support. Let's build up the playbook. First of all, our initial play will once again run from the local host, as this will be making the calls to EC2 to boot up our new server:

```
---
- name: boot server
  hosts: localhost
  gather_facts: false
```

Next, we will use the `ec2` module in place of the `os_server` module to boot up our desired server. This code is really just an example; normally, just like with our `os_server` example, you would not include the secret keys in the playbook, but would store them in a vault somewhere:

```
  - name: boot the server
    ec2:
      access_key: XXXXXXXXXXXXXXXX
      secret_key: xxxxxxxxxxxxxxxxxxxxxxxxxxxxxxxx
      keypair: mastery-key
      group: default
      type: t2.medium
      image: "ami-000848c4d7224c557"
      region: eu-west-2
      instance_tags: "{'ansible_group':'mastery_server', 'Name':'mastery1'}"
```

```
        exact_count: 1
        count_tag:
          ansible_group: "mastery_server"
        wait: true
        user_data: |
          #!/bin/bash
          sudo dnf install -y python python2-dnf
    register: newserver
```

> **TIP**: The `ec2` module requires the Python `boto` library to be installed on the Ansible host; the method for this will vary between operating systems, but on our CentOS 7 demo host, it was installed using the `sudo yum install python-boto` command.

The preceding code is intended to perform the same job as our `os_server` example, and while it looks similar at a high level, there are many differences. Hence, it is essential to read the module documentation whenever working with a new module, in order to understand precisely how to use it. Of specific interest, do note the following:

- The `ec2` module creates a new virtual machine every time it is run, unless you set the `exact_count` parameter in conjunction with the `count_tags` parameter (mentioning a tag set in the `instance_tags` line).
- The `user_data` field can be used to send post-creation scripts to the new VM; this is incredibly useful when initial configuration is needed immediately, lending itself to `raw` commands. In this case, we use it to install the Python prerequisites required to install `ImageMagick` later on.

Next, we can obtain the public IP address of our newly created server by using the `newserver` variable that we registered in the last task. However, note the different variable structure, as compared to the way that we accessed this information when using the `os_server` module (again, always refer to the documentation):

```
    - name: show floating ip
      debug:
        var: newserver.tagged_instances[0].public_ip
```

Another key difference between the `ec2` module and the `os_server` one is that `ec2` does not wait for SSH connectivity to become available before completing; thus, we must define a task specifically for this purpose to ensure that our playbook doesn't fail later on due to a lack of connectivity:

```
- name: Wait for SSH to come up
  wait_for_connection:
    timeout: 320
```

Once this task has completed, we will know that our host is alive and responding to SSH, so we can proceed to using `add_host` to add this new host to the inventory, and then install `ImageMagick` just like we did before (the image used here is the same `Fedora 29` cloud-based image used in the OpenStack example):

```
    - name: add new server
      add_host:
        name: "mastery1"
        ansible_ssh_host: "{{ newserver.tagged_instances[0].public_ip }}"
        ansible_ssh_user: "fedora"

- name: configure server
  hosts: mastery1
  gather_facts: false

  tasks:
    - name: install imagemagick
      dnf:
        name: "ImageMagick"
      become: "yes"
```

## Infrastructure Provisioning

Putting all of this together and running the playbook should result in something like the following screenshot. Note that I have turned SSH host key checking off, to prevent the SSH transport agent from asking about adding the host key on the first run, which would cause the playbook to hang and wait for user intervention, something that we don't want here:

```
~/src/mastery> ANSIBLE_HOST_KEY_CHECKING=False ansible-playbook -i mastery-hosts boot-ec2-server.yaml --private-key mastery-key.pem

PLAY [boot server] ****************************************************************

TASK [boot the server] ************************************************************
changed: [localhost]

TASK [show floating ip] ***********************************************************
ok: [localhost] => {
    "newserver.tagged_instances[0].public_ip": "18.130.230.217"
}

TASK [Wait for SSH to come up] ****************************************************
 [WARNING]: Reset is not implemented for this connection

ok: [localhost]

TASK [add new server] *************************************************************
changed: [localhost]

PLAY [configure server] ***********************************************************

TASK [install imagemagick] ********************************************************
changed: [mastery1]

PLAY RECAP ************************************************************************
localhost                  : ok=4    changed=2    unreachable=0    failed=0
mastery1                   : ok=1    changed=1    unreachable=0    failed=0

~/src/mastery>
```

As we have seen here, we can achieve the same result on a different cloud provider, using only a subtly different playbook. The key here is to read the documentation that comes with each module and ensure that both the parameters and return values are correctly referenced.

We could apply this methodology to Azure, Google Cloud, or any of the other cloud providers that Ansible ships with support for. If we wanted to repeat this example on Azure, then we would need to use the `azure_rm_virtualmachine` module. The documentation for this module states that we need Python 2.7 or newer (this is already a part of our CentOS 7 demo machine), and the `azure` Python module, version 2.0.0 or higher. On CentOS 7, there was no RPM for the latter dependency, so it was installed using the commands (the first installs the `azure` Python module, and the second installs the Ansible support for Azure):

```
sudo pip install azure
sudo pip install ansible[azure]
```

With these prerequisites satisfied, we can build up our playbook again. Note that with Azure, multiple authentication methods are possible. For the sake of simplicity, I am using the Azure Active Directory credentials that I created for this demo; however, to enable this, I had to also install the official Azure CLI utility, and log in using the following:

```
az login
```

This ensures that your Ansible host is trusted by Azure. In practice, you would set up a service principal that removes the need for this; however, doing so is beyond the scope of this book. To continue with this example, we set up the header of our playbook like before:

```
---
- name: boot server
  hosts: localhost
  gather_facts: false
  vars:
    vm_password: Password123!
```

*Infrastructure Provisioning*

Note that this time, we will store a password for our new VM in a variable; normally, we would do this in a vault, but that is left as an exercise for the reader. From here, we use the `azure_rm_virtualmachine` module to boot up our new VM. To make use of a `Fedora 29` image for continuity with the previous examples, I've had to go to the image marketplace on Azure, which requires some additional parameters, such as `plan`, to be defined. To enable the use of this image with Ansible, I first had to find it, then accept the terms of the author to enable its use, using the `az` command-line utility with these commands:

```
az vm image list --offer fedora --all --output table
az vm image show --urn tunnelbiz:fedora:fedora29:1.0.0
az vm image accept-terms --urn tunnelbiz:fedora:fedora29:1.0.0
```

I also had to create the resource group and network that the VM would use; these are very much Azure-specific steps, and are beyond the scope of this book. However, once all of that was created, I was then able to write the following playbook code to boot up our Azure-based `Fedora 29` image:

```
tasks:
  - name: boot the server
    azure_rm_virtualmachine:
      ad_user: masteryadmin@example.com
      password: xxxxxxx
      resource_group: mastery
      name: mastery1
      admin_username: fedora
      admin_password: "{{ vm_password }}"
      vm_size: Standard_B1s
      image:
        offer: fedora
        publisher: tunnelbiz
        sku: fedora29
        version: latest
      plan:
        name: fedora29
        product: fedora
        publisher : tunnelbiz
    register: newserver
```

Like before, we obtain the public IP address of our image (note the complex variable required to access this), ensure that SSH access is working, and then use `add_host` to add the new VM to our runtime inventory:

```
  - name: show floating ip
    debug:
      var:
```

```
newserver.ansible_facts.azure_vm.properties.networkProfile.networkInterface
s[0].properties.ipConfigurations[0].properties.publicIPAddress.properties.i
pAddress

    - name: Wait for SSH to come up
      wait_for_connection:
        delay: 1
        timeout: 320

    - name: add new server
      add_host:
        name: "mastery1"
        ansible_ssh_host: "{{
newserver.ansible_facts.azure_vm.properties.networkProfile.networkInterface
s[0].properties.ipConfigurations[0].properties.publicIPAddress.properties.i
pAddress }}"
        ansible_ssh_user: "fedora"
        ansible_ssh_pass: "{{ vm_password }}"
        ansible_become_pass: "{{ vm_password }}"
```

Azure allows for either password- or key-based authentication for SSH on Linux VMs; we're using password-based here for simplicity. Also, note the newly utilized `ansible_become_pass` connection variable, as the `Fedora 29` image that we are using will prompt for a password when `sudo` is used, potentially blocking execution. Finally, with this work complete, we install `ImageMagick`, like before:

```
- name: configure server
  hosts: mastery1
  gather_facts: false

  tasks:
    - name: install python
      raw: "dnf install -y python python2-dnf"
      become: "yes"

    - name: install imagemagick
      dnf:
        name: "ImageMagick"
      become: "yes"
```

*Infrastructure Provisioning*

Let's take a look at this in action:

```
~/src/mastery> ANSIBLE_HOST_KEY_CHECKING=False ansible-playbook -i mastery-hosts boot-azure-server.yaml

PLAY [boot server] ************************************************************

TASK [boot the server] ********************************************************
changed: [localhost]

TASK [show floating ip] *******************************************************
ok: [localhost] => {
    "newserver.ansible_facts.azure_vm.properties.networkProfile.networkInterfaces[0].properties.ipConfigurations[0].properties.publicIPAddress.properties.ipAddress": "51.145.12.101"
}

TASK [Wait for SSH to come up] ************************************************
 [WARNING]: Reset is not implemented for this connection

ok: [localhost]

TASK [add new server] *********************************************************
changed: [localhost]

PLAY [configure server] *******************************************************

TASK [install python] *********************************************************
changed: [mastery1]

TASK [install imagemagick] ****************************************************
changed: [mastery1]

PLAY RECAP ********************************************************************
localhost                  : ok=4    changed=2    unreachable=0    failed=0
mastery1                   : ok=2    changed=2    unreachable=0    failed=0

~/src/mastery>
```

The output is very similar to before, demonstrating that we can very easily perform the same actions across different cloud platforms with just a little effort in terms of learning how the various modules that we might need work. This section of the chapter is by no means definitive, given the number of platforms and operations supported by Ansible, but we hope that the information provided gives an idea of the process and steps required for getting Ansible to integrate with a new cloud platform. Next, we will look at using Ansible to interact with Docker containers.

## Interacting with Docker containers

Linux container technologies, especially Docker, have grown in popularity in recent years, and this has continued since the last edition of this book was published. Containers provide a fast path to resource isolation, while maintaining consistency of the runtime environment. They can be launched quickly and are efficient to run, as there is very little overhead involved. Utilities such as Docker provide a lot of useful tooling for container management, such as a registry of images to use as the filesystem, tooling to build the images themselves, clustering orchestration, and so on. Through its ease of use, Docker has become one of the most popular ways to manage containers.

Ansible can interact with Docker in numerous ways as well. Notably, Ansible can be used to build images, to start or stop containers, to compose multiple container services, to connect to and interact with active containers, or even to discover inventory from containers. Ansible provides a full suite of tools for working with Docker, including relevant modules, a connection plugin, and an inventory script.

To demonstrate working with Docker, we'll explore a few use cases. The first use case is building a new image to use with Docker. The second use case is launching a container from the new image and interacting with it. The last use case is using the inventory plugin to interact with an active container.

> Creating a functional Docker installation is beyond the scope of this book. The Docker website provides detailed installation and use instructions, at `https://docs.docker.com`. Ansible works best with Docker on a Linux host, so we will continue with the CentOS 7 demo machine that we have used throughout this book.

## Building images

Docker images are basically filesystems bundled with parameters to use at runtime. The filesystem is usually a small part of a Linux Userland, with enough files to start the desired process. Docker provides tooling to build these images, generally based on very small, preexisting base images. The tooling uses a `Dockerfile` as the input, which is a plain text file with directives. This file is parsed by the `docker build` command, and we can parse it via the `docker_image` module. The remaining examples will be from a CentOS 7 virtual machine using Docker version 1.13.1, with the `cowsay` and `nginx` packages added, so that running the container will provide a web server that will display something from `cowsay`.

First, we'll need a `Dockerfile`. This file needs to live in a path that Ansible can read, and we're going to put it in the same directory as my playbooks. The `Dockerfile` content will be very simple. We'll need to define a base image, a command to run to install the necessary software, some minimal configuration of software, a port to expose, and a default action for running a container with this image:

```
FROM docker.io/fedora:29

RUN dnf install -y cowsay nginx
RUN echo "daemon off;" >> /etc/nginx/nginx.conf
RUN cowsay boop > /usr/share/nginx/html/index.html

EXPOSE 80

CMD /usr/sbin/nginx
```

The build process performs the following steps:

- We're using the `Fedora 29` image from the `fedora` repository on the `Docker Hub` image registry.
- To install the necessary `cowsay` and `nginx` packages, we're using `dnf`.
- To run `nginx` directly in the container, we need to turn `daemon` mode `off` in `nginx.conf`.
- We use `cowsay` to generate content for the default web page.
- Then, we're instructing Docker to `expose` port `80` in the container, where `nginx` will listen for connections.
- Finally, the default action of this container will be to run `nginx`.

The playbook to build and use the image can live in the same directory. We'll name it `docker-interact.yaml`. This playbook will operate on `localhost`, and will have two tasks; one will be to build the image using `docker_image`, and the other will be to launch the container using `docker_container`:

```yaml
---
- name: build an image
  hosts: localhost
  gather_facts: false

  tasks:
    - name: build that image
      docker_image:
        path: .
        state: present
        name: fedora-moo

    - name: start the container
      docker_container:
        name: playbook-container
        image: fedora-moo
        ports: 8080:80
        state: started
```

Now, if you've been using AWX on the same host as this like I have, you will already have a few Docker containers running. Luckily, none of these are based on Fedora, so we can easily use the `--filter` parameters with Docker to exclude anything that doesn't have the term `fedora` in the image name, making the output easier to interpret, as shown in the following screenshots:

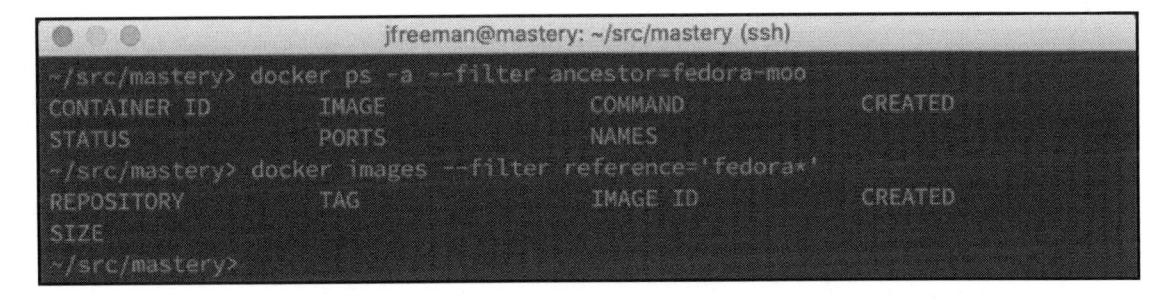

```
~/src/mastery> docker ps -a --filter ancestor=fedora-moo
CONTAINER ID        IMAGE               COMMAND             CREATED
STATUS              PORTS               NAMES
~/src/mastery> docker images --filter reference='fedora*'
REPOSITORY          TAG                 IMAGE ID            CREATED
SIZE
~/src/mastery>
```

[ 347 ]

*Infrastructure Provisioning*

Now, let's run the playbook to build the image and start a container using that image:

```
~/src/mastery> ansible-playbook -i mastery-hosts docker-interact.yaml

PLAY [build an image] **********************************************************

TASK [build that image] ********************************************************
changed: [localhost]

TASK [start the container] *****************************************************
changed: [localhost]

PLAY RECAP *********************************************************************
localhost                  : ok=2    changed=2    unreachable=0    failed=0

~/src/mastery>
```

The verbosity of this playbook execution was reduced to save screen space. Our output simply shows that the task to build the image resulted in a change, as did the task to start the container. A quick check of running containers and available images should reflect our work:

```
~/src/mastery> docker ps -a --filter ancestor=fedora-moo
CONTAINER ID        IMAGE               COMMAND                  CREATED
      STATUS              PORTS                    NAMES
cfd71ac0b9c0        fedora-moo          "/bin/sh -c /usr/s..."   49 seconds ago
      Up 48 seconds       0.0.0.0:8080->80/tcp     playbook-container
~/src/mastery> docker images --filter reference='fedora*'
REPOSITORY          TAG                 IMAGE ID            CREATED
SIZE
fedora-moo          latest              23f557565a30        53 seconds ago
533 MB
docker.io/fedora    29                  d7372e6c93c6        2 weeks ago
275 MB
~/src/mastery>
```

We can test the functionality of our container by using `curl` to access the web server, which should show us a cow saying `boop`:

[ 348 ]

```
┌─ ● ● ● ──────────── jfreeman@mastery: ~/src/mastery (ssh) ─────────┐
│ ~/src/mastery> curl http://localhost:8080                          │
│  _____                                                             │
│ < boop >                                                           │
│  -----                                                             │
│         \   ^__^                                                   │
│          \  (oo)_____                                           │
│             (__)\       )\/\                                       │
│                 ||----w |                                          │
│                 ||     ||                                          │
│ ~/src/mastery>                                                     │
└────────────────────────────────────────────────────────────────────┘
```

In this manner, we have already shown how easy it is to interact with Docker using Ansible. However, this example is still based on using a native `Dockerfile`, and, as we progress through this chapter, we'll see some more advanced Ansible usage that removes the need for this.

## Building containers without a Dockerfile

Dockerfiles are useful, but many of the actions performed inside of Dockerfiles could be completed with Ansible instead. Ansible can be used to launch a container using a base image, then interact with that container using the `docker` connection method to complete the configuration. Let's demonstrate this by repeating the previous example, but without the need for a `Dockerfile`. Instead, all of the work will be handled by an entirely new playbook named `docker-all.yaml`. The first part of this playbook starts a container from a preexisting image of `Fedora 29` from Docker Hub, and adds the resulting container details to Ansible's in-memory inventory by using `add_host`:

```
---
- name: build an image
  hosts: localhost
  gather_facts: false

  tasks:
    - name: start the container
      docker_container:
        name: playbook-container
        image: docker.io/fedora:29
        ports: 8080:80
        state: started
        command: sleep 500
```

## Infrastructure Provisioning

```yaml
    - name: make a host
      add_host:
        name: playbook-container
        ansible_connection: docker
        ansible_ssh_user: root
```

Then, using this newly added inventory host, we define a second play that runs Ansible tasks within the container that was just launched, configuring our `cowsay` service like before, but without the need for a `Dockerfile`:

```yaml
- name: do things
  hosts: playbook-container
  gather_facts: false

  tasks:
    - name: install things
      raw: dnf install -y python-dnf

    - name: install things
      dnf:
        name: ['nginx', 'cowsay']

    - name: configure nginx
      lineinfile:
        line: "daemon off;"
        dest: /etc/nginx/nginx.conf

    - name: boop
      shell: cowsay boop > /usr/share/nginx/html/index.html

    - name: run nginx
      shell: nginx &
```

## Chapter 11

The playbook consists of two plays. The first play creates the container from the base `Fedora 29` image. The `docker_container` task is given a `sleep` command to keep the container running for a period of time, as the `docker` connection plugin only works with active containers (unconfigured operating system images from Docker Hub generally exit immediately when they are run, as they have no default actions to perform). The second task of the first play creates a runtime inventory entry for the container. The inventory hostname must match the container name. The connection method is set to `docker` as well.

The second play targets the newly created host, and the first task uses the `raw` module to get the `python-dnf` package in place (which will bring the rest of `python` in), so that we can use the `dnf` module in the next task. The `dnf` module is then used to install the desired packages, namely, `nginx` and `cowsay`. Then, the `lineinfile` module is used to add a new line to the `nginx` configuration. A `shell` task uses `cowsay` to create content for `nginx` to serve. Finally, `nginx` itself is started as a background process.

Before running the playbook, let's remove any running containers from the previous example:

```
~/src/mastery> docker ps -a --filter ancestor=fedora-moo
CONTAINER ID        IMAGE              COMMAND                  CREATED
     STATUS              PORTS                  NAMES
cfd71ac0b9c0        fedora-moo         "/bin/sh -c /usr/s..."   12 minutes ago
     Up 12 minutes       0.0.0.0:8080->80/tcp   playbook-container
~/src/mastery> docker rm -f playbook-container
playbook-container
~/src/mastery> docker ps -a --filter ancestor=fedora-moo
CONTAINER ID        IMAGE              COMMAND                  CREATED
STATUS              PORTS              NAMES
~/src/mastery>
```

*Infrastructure Provisioning*

With the running container removed, we can now run our new playbook to recreate the container, bypassing the image build step:

```
~/src/mastery> ansible-playbook -i mastery-hosts docker-all.yaml

PLAY [build an image] **********************************************************

TASK [start the container] *****************************************************
changed: [localhost]

TASK [make a host] *************************************************************
changed: [localhost]

PLAY [do things] ***************************************************************

TASK [install things] **********************************************************
changed: [playbook-container]

TASK [install things] **********************************************************
changed: [playbook-container]

TASK [configure nginx] *********************************************************
changed: [playbook-container]

TASK [boop] ********************************************************************
changed: [playbook-container]

TASK [run nginx] ***************************************************************
changed: [playbook-container]

PLAY RECAP *********************************************************************
localhost                  : ok=2    changed=2    unreachable=0    failed=0
playbook-container         : ok=5    changed=5    unreachable=0    failed=0

~/src/mastery>
```

We see tasks from the first play execute on the `localhost`, and then the second play executes on the `playbook-container`. Once it's complete, we can test the web service and list the running containers to verify our work. Note the different filter this time; our container was build and run directly from the `fedora` image, without the intermediate step of creating the `fedora-moo` image:

[ 352 ]

```
~/src/mastery> curl http://localhost:8080

< boop >
  -----
        \   ^__^
         \  (oo)_____
            (__)\       )\/\
                ||----w |
                ||     ||
~/src/mastery> docker ps -a --filter ancestor=fedora:29
CONTAINER ID        IMAGE                 COMMAND              CREATED
    STATUS              PORTS              NAMES
cf30ca27104b        docker.io/fedora:29   "sleep 500"          3 minutes ago
    Up 3 minutes        0.0.0.0:8080->80/tcp   playbook-container
~/src/mastery>
```

This method of using Ansible to configure the running container has some advantages. First, you can reuse existing roles to set up an application, easily switching from cloud virtual machine targets to containers, and even to bare metal resources, if desired. Secondly, you can easily review all configuration that goes into an application, simply by reviewing the playbook content.

Another use case for this method of interaction is to use Docker containers to simulate multiple hosts, in order to verify playbook execution across multiple hosts. A container can be started with an init system as the running process, allowing for additional services to be started as if they were on a full operating system. This use case is valuable within a continuous integration environment, to validate changes to playbook content quickly and efficiently.

## Docker inventory

Similar to the OpenStack and EC2 inventory plugins detailed earlier in this book, a Docker inventory script is also available. The Docker script is located at `contrib/inventory/docker.py`, within the Ansible source repository, with an associated configuration file at `contrib/inventory/docker.yml`. To make use of this script, simply copy the `.py` file to the playbook directory that expects to use it, or to a path accessible to all users/playbooks on the system that will be executing Ansible. For our example, I'll copy it to the playbook directory. The configuration file, which can be used to define how to connect to one or more Docker daemons, does not need to be used for this example, as we'll simply be connecting to the local Docker daemon.

*Infrastructure Provisioning*

The `help` output for the script shows many possible arguments; however, the ones that Ansible will use are `--list` and `--host`:

```
~/src/mastery> ./docker.py --help
usage: docker.py [-h] [--list] [--debug] [--host HOST] [--pretty]
                 [--config-file CONFIG_FILE] [--docker-host DOCKER_HOST]
                 [--tls-hostname TLS_HOSTNAME] [--api-version API_VERSION]
                 [--timeout TIMEOUT] [--cacert-path CACERT_PATH]
                 [--cert-path CERT_PATH] [--key-path KEY_PATH]
                 [--ssl-version SSL_VERSION] [--tls] [--tls-verify]
                 [--private-ssh-port PRIVATE_SSH_PORT]
                 [--default-ip-address DEFAULT_IP_ADDRESS]

Return Ansible inventory for one or more Docker hosts.

optional arguments:
  -h, --help            show this help message and exit
  --list                List all containers (default: True)
  --debug               Send debug messages to STDOUT
  --host HOST           Only get information for a specific container.
  --pretty              Pretty print JSON output(default: False)
  --config-file CONFIG_FILE
                        Name of the config file to use. Default is docker.yml
  --docker-host DOCKER_HOST
                        The base url or Unix sock path to connect to the
                        docker daemon. Defaults to unix://var/run/docker.sock
  --tls-hostname TLS_HOSTNAME
                        Host name to expect in TLS certs. Defaults to
                        localhost
  --api-version API_VERSION
                        Docker daemon API version. Defaults to 1.24
  --timeout TIMEOUT     Docker connection timeout in seconds. Defaults to 60
  --cacert-path CACERT_PATH
                        Path to the TLS certificate authority pem file.
  --cert-path CERT_PATH
                        Path to the TLS certificate pem file.
  --key-path KEY_PATH   Path to the TLS encryption key pem file.
  --ssl-version SSL_VERSION
                        TLS version number
  --tls                 Use TLS. Defaults to False
  --tls-verify          Verify TLS certificates. Defaults to False
  --private-ssh-port PRIVATE_SSH_PORT
                        Default private container SSH Port. Defaults to 22
  --default-ip-address DEFAULT_IP_ADDRESS
                        Default container SSH IP address. Defaults to
                        127.0.0.1
~/src/mastery>
```

If the previously built container is still running when this script is executed to list hosts, it should appear in the output (`grep` has been used to make this more obvious in the screenshot):

```
~/src/mastery> ./docker.py --list --pretty | grep -C2 playbook-container
            }
        },
        "playbook-container": {
            "ansible_ssh_host": "",
            "ansible_ssh_port": 0,
--
            "docker_mountlabel": "system_u:object_r:svirt_sandbox_file_t:s0:c519,c726",
            "docker_mounts": [],
            "docker_name": "/playbook-container",
            "docker_networksettings": {
                "Bridge": "",
--
    ],
    "cf30ca27104b7": [
        "playbook-container"
    ],
    "cf30ca27104b771cdce2ad0a2057d31a5e112f920d9c3656de2d6c1072869c77": [
        "playbook-container"
    ],
    "docker_hosts": [
--
    ],
    "image_docker.io/fedora:29": [
        "playbook-container"
    ],
```

[ 355 ]

*Infrastructure Provisioning*

Like earlier, a number of groups are presented, which have the running container as a member. The two groups that were shown earlier are the short container ID and the long container ID. Many variables are also defined as a part of the output, which has been heavily truncated in the preceding screenshot. The tail end of the output reveals a few more groups:

```
        "docker_hosts": [
--
        ],
        "image_docker.io/fedora:29": [
            "playbook-container"
        ],
        "image_memcached:alpine": [
--
            "memcached"
        ],
        "playbook-container": [
            "playbook-container"
        ],
        "postgres": [
--
        ],
        "running": [
            "playbook-container",
            "awx_task",
            "awx_web",
--
        ],
        "unix://var/run/docker.sock": [
            "playbook-container",
            "awx_task",
            "awx_web",
~/src/mastery>
```

The additional groups are as follows:

- `docker_hosts`: All of the hosts running the Docker daemon that the dynamic inventory script has communicated with and queried for containers
- `image_name`: A group for each image used by discovered containers
- `container name`: A group that matches the name of the container
- `running`: A group of all the running containers
- `stopped`: A group of all the stopped containers

This inventory plugin, and the groups and data provided by it, can be used by playbooks to target various selections of containers available, in order to interact without the need for manual inventory management or the use of `add_hosts`.

## Ansible Container

Ansible Container is a set of tools that builds upon concepts introduced earlier in this chapter in order to provide a comprehensive workflow for container development, testing, and deployment. Since the last release of this book, a stable release has become available.

At the time of writing, Ansible Container does not get installed with Ansible, and it must be installed separately. It can be installed from `pypi` as the package name `ansible-container`, or it can be installed from the source repository (https://github.com/ansible/ansible-container.git). At the time of writing this book, `ansible-container` has some quite exacting requirements for the Python environment; specifically, `docker-py` must be removed, and only version 2.7.0 of the `docker` Python module can be installed. Also note there is (at the time of writing) a known issue in the interaction between the latest version of `ansible-container` and the `docker` module, and the `docker` module must be patched manually for this to work. Hopefully in future this will be fixed—however, at the time of writing this is still required.

To successfully install it on our CentOS 7 demo machine, I had to issue the following commands:

```
sudo pip uninstall docker-py
sudo pip uninstall docker
sudo pip install docker==2.7.0
sudo sed -i "s/return os.path.join(os.sep, 'run', 'secrets')/return os.path.join(os.sep, 'docker', 'secrets')/g" /usr/lib/python2.7/site-packages/container/docker/engine.py
sudo pip install -U setuptools
sudo pip install "ansible-container[docker,openshift]"
```

*Infrastructure Provisioning*

With Ansible Container, we can define one or more services to containerize. These are defined in a YAML file that closely follows the Docker Compose version 2 schema (support for the version 2 schema was added in the 0.3.0 release of `ansible-container`). Each service that's defined becomes a container and is exposed as an Ansible host. These hosts are used by a playbook file to perform all of the necessary configurations to prep the container to run the service. Additional files can be used to define any Python library requirements for modules used by the playbook, the Ansible Galaxy role dependencies of the playbook, the Ansible Galaxy metadata for sharing the project, and an Ansible configuration file used with the playbook.

The main executable of Ansible Container is `ansible-container`, which includes a number of sub-commands:

- `init`: The `init` sub-command will create the required directory structure and template files for a new Ansible Container `project` within the current directory. Optionally, it can connect to Ansible Galaxy and use a project template to pre-populate some of the files; otherwise, they will mostly be created blank.
- `build`: The `build` sub-command is used to launch the containers for each service defined, and one container with Ansible inside of it, which is used to run the playbook against the service containers. Once the playbook is finished, images are created from the configured containers.
- `run`: The `run` sub-command will launch new containers for each service using the images created during the `build` phase.
- `stop`: The `stop` sub-command will stop containers launched by a `run` sub-command.
- `push`: The `push` sub-command will upload the built images to a target Docker image registry.
- `shipit`: The `shipit` sub-command will generate Ansible content to deploy containers from built images into container orchestration platforms, such as Kubernetes or Red Hat OpenShift:

*Chapter 11*

```
~/src/mastery> ansible-container --help
usage: ansible-container [-h] [--debug] [--devel] [--engine ENGINE_NAME]
                         [--project-path BASE_PATH]
                         [--project-name PROJECT_NAME]
                         [--vars-files VARS_FILES] [--no-selinux]
                         
                         {run,help,deploy,stop,destroy,restart,init,version,buil
d,install,push,import}
                         ...

Build, orchestrate, run, and ship Docker containers with Ansible playbooks

optional arguments:
  -h, --help            show this help message and exit
  --debug               Enable debug output
  --devel               Enable developer-mode to aid in iterative development
                        on Ansible Container.
  --engine ENGINE_NAME  Select your container engine and orchestrator
  --project-path BASE_PATH, -p BASE_PATH
                        Specify a path to your project. Defaults to current
                        working directory.
  --project-name PROJECT_NAME, -n PROJECT_NAME
                        Specify an alternate name for your project. Defaults
                        to the directory it lives in.
  --vars-files VARS_FILES, --var-file VARS_FILES, --vars-file VARS_FILES
                        One or or more YAML or JSON formatted files providing
                        variables for Jinja2 style variable substitution in
```

To demonstrate Ansible Container, we'll reproduce our previous Docker service container to display `cowsay` via a web server and run it locally.

*Infrastructure Provisioning*

# Using ansible-container init

Ansible Container relies on a directory tree of content, which is created with the `init` sub-command. This content is what will be made available inside of the container used to run Ansible itself:

```
~/src/mastery> ansible-container init --help
usage: ansible-container init [-h] [--server SERVER] [--force] [project]

positional arguments:
  project              Rather than starting with a blank project, use a
                       project template from an Ansible Container project
                       downloaded from the Ansible Galaxy web site.

optional arguments:
  -h, --help           show this help message and exit
  --server SERVER, -s SERVER
                       Use a different Galaxy server URL
  --force, -f          Overrides the requirement that init be run in an empty
                       directory, for example if a virtualenv exists in the
                       directory.
~/src/mastery>
```

For this example, we'll create an `ansible/` directory and run the `init` sub-command in it:

```
~/src/mastery> mkdir ansible
~/src/mastery> cd ansible
~/src/mastery/ansible> ansible-container init
Ansible Container initialized.
~/src/mastery/ansible> tree
.
├── ansible.cfg
├── ansible-requirements.txt
├── container.yml
├── meta.yml
└── requirements.yml

0 directories, 5 files
~/src/mastery/ansible>
```

First, to define our services, we'll need to edit the `container.yml` file within the newly created `ansible/` directory. Our example only has a single service, which we'll name `cowsay`. We'll want to use the `docker.io/fedora:29` image.

As a part of the build process, `ansible-container` makes use of a container called the conductor—essentially, this is a prebuilt container image from which our target container can be built, deployed, and run. It contains, among other important things, the Ansible runtimes, associated libraries, and a Python environment, as required by Ansible. It is important that, if possible, this container matches the operating system that you are building as closely as possible; otherwise, the differing versions of Python or other libraries could cause problems. Thus, we have defined a `Fedora 29`-based conductor container by using the `conductor_base` parameter.

The build process expects `container.yml` to reference at least one role for the build process; we will create this role shortly, and we'll call it `cowsay`. This time, we'll expose port `8081`, just to differentiate it from previous examples. We'll set the command for this service to `nginx`:

```
version: "2"
services:
  cowsay:
    from: docker.io/fedora:29
    conductor_base: fedora:29
    roles:
      - cowsay
    ports:
      - "8081:80"
    command: ['nginx']
```

With the service established, we need to write the plays to configure the base image to our needs. First, we will create a skeletal role directory:

```
mkdir -p roles/cowsay/tasks/
```

Then, we will create the `roles/cowsay/tasks/main.yml` file. The tasks in this file should match the tasks that we used in a previous example, with one exception—a new `set_fact` task. When `ansible-container` builds our new container, the Python environment from the previously mentioned conductor container is mounted in `/_usr` in the target container, and is used for all tasks. This is fine until we come to using the `dnf` module, which will not run from this mounted Python environment, as it is not installed in there! To get around this, we will use `set_fact` to define the `ansible_python_interpreter` host variable, and point it at the Python environment that we installed in the first task:

```yaml
---
- name: install things
  raw: dnf install -y python-dnf

- name: use local python
  set_fact:
    ansible_python_interpreter: /usr/bin/python

- name: install things
  dnf:
    name: ['nginx', 'cowsay']

- name: configure nginx
  lineinfile:
    line: "daemon off;"
    dest: /etc/nginx/nginx.conf

- name: boop
  shell: cowsay boop > /usr/share/nginx/html/index.html
```

Unlike in the previous example, we do not need to add a task to run `nginx`; that will happen when the container is started.

## Using ansible-container build

For this example, no other files need to be modified from their initial states. We're now ready to build the images, which is done with the `build` sub-command of `ansible-container`:

*Chapter 11*

```
~/src/mastery/ansible> ansible-container build
Building Docker Engine context...
Starting Docker build of Ansible Container Conductor image (please be patient)..
.
Parsing conductor CLI args.
Docker™ daemon integration engine loaded. Build starting.        project=ansible
Building service...     project=ansible service=cowsay
PLAY [cowsay] *******************************************************************
TASK [Gathering Facts] **********************************************************
ok: [cowsay]
TASK [cowsay : install things] **************************************************
changed: [cowsay]
TASK [cowsay : use local python] ************************************************
ok: [cowsay]
TASK [cowsay : install things] **************************************************
changed: [cowsay]
TASK [cowsay : configure nginx] *************************************************
changed: [cowsay]
TASK [cowsay : boop] ************************************************************
changed: [cowsay]
PLAY RECAP **********************************************************************
cowsay                     : ok=6    changed=4    unreachable=0    failed=0
Applied role to service role=cowsay service=cowsay
Committed layer as image         image=sha256:072b6d7e5c282cd92a39ec5745dc7a5e7e4
720b2e2aa3165b31ee7b95cbe8215 service=cowsay
Build complete. service=cowsay
All images successfully built.
Conductor terminated. Cleaning up.        command_rc=0 conductor_id=4b1999639ed7ca
6efef612efd041c105d5968e5928d52f3b9b15fba023378f74 save_container=False
~/src/mastery/ansible>
```

> **TIP**
>
> If the build process fails with an error, you might have `docker-py` installed, which, at the time of writing, unfortunately breaks `ansible-container`. In addition, `ansible-container` only works with a patched version (`2.7.0`) of the `docker` Python module. The fix involves removing these modules and then reinstalling and patching the required `docker` module. Hopefully, in the future, this will no longer be required.

*Infrastructure Provisioning*

The build process will download a Docker image called the `ansible-conductor`. Ansible will be run from within this container, and used to orchestrate the changes on the target container (called `ansible-cowsay` in the following example). It'll launch a container using that image and map in the contents from the `_usr/` directory. Then, it will launch the service container and execute the playbook against it. After the playbook finishes, the configured service container will be saved as a Docker image in the local system, but not exported to the filesystem (there are native Docker commands to handle this, if it is required).

The image name comprises two parts: the first part is named after the base directory that `ansible-container` was run from (`ansible`, in this case), and the second part from the service name (`cowsay`), as we can see with `docker images`:

```
~/src/mastery/ansible> docker images
REPOSITORY                              TAG                  IMAGE ID
        CREATED             SIZE
ansible-conductor                       latest               d08d2ebf433
2       29 seconds ago      445 MB
ansible-cowsay                          20190307143506       072b6d7e5c2
8       About an hour ago   618 MB
ansible-cowsay                          latest               072b6d7e5c2
8       About an hour ago   618 MB
```

Once all of the prerequisite steps are complete, we will have a neat framework for building Docker container images without the need for a `Dockerfile`, so all of our build processes can remain in Ansible roles, adding to their portability.

## Using ansible-container run

With the image created, we can now run the service. We can launch the container manually with `docker` or write a playbook for it to launch with Ansible. Both of these approaches are entirely feasible, but require more effort than necessary, as we've already defined how this container should be launched in our `container.yml` file. We can utilize this configuration and simply use the `run` sub-command of `ansible-container`:

```
~/src/mastery/ansible> ansible-container run --help
usage: ansible-container run [-h] [-d]
                             [--vault-file VAULT_FILES [VAULT_FILES ...]]
                             [--vault-password-file VAULT_PASSWORD_FILE]
                             [--ask-vault-pass]
                             [--roles-path ROLES_PATH [ROLES_PATH ...]]
                             [--with-volumes WITH_VOLUMES [WITH_VOLUMES ...]]
                             [--volume-driver VOLUME_DRIVER]
                             [--with-variables WITH_VARIABLES [WITH_VARIABLES ..
.]]
                             [--production]
                             [service [service ...]]

positional arguments:
  service               The specific services you want to run

optional arguments:
  -h, --help            show this help message and exit
  -d, --detached        Run the application in detached mode
  --vault-file VAULT_FILES [VAULT_FILES ...]
                        A vault file to use to populate secrets
  --vault-password-file VAULT_PASSWORD_FILE
                        An optional file containing the vault password
  --ask-vault-pass      Asks for the fault file password at run time
  --roles-path ROLES_PATH [ROLES_PATH ...]
                        Specify a local path containing Ansible roles.
  --with-volumes WITH_VOLUMES [WITH_VOLUMES ...], -v WITH_VOLUMES [WITH_VOLUMES
 ...]
                        Mount one or more volumes to the Conductor. Specify
                        volumes as strings using the Docker volume format.
  --volume-driver VOLUME_DRIVER
                        Specify volume driver to use when mounting named
                        volumes to the Conductor.
  --with-variables WITH_VARIABLES [WITH_VARIABLES ...], -e WITH_VARIABLES [WITH_
VARIABLES ...]
                        Define one or more environment variables in the
                        Conductor. Format each variable as a key=value string.
  --production          Run with the production configuration.
~/src/mastery/ansible>
```

# Infrastructure Provisioning

There are a few optional arguments for the `run` sub-command. You can pick a specific service to start, attach volumes, define variables, toggle production configuration, and so on. The argument that we're interested in is the `--detached` argument, as it will run the application in the background, giving control back to the Terminal:

```
~/src/mastery/ansible> ansible-container run --detached
Parsing conductor CLI args.
Engine integration loaded. Preparing run.        engine=Docker™ daemon
Verifying service image service=cowsay
PLAY [Deploy ansible] ************************************************************
TASK [docker_service] ************************************************************
changed: [localhost]
PLAY RECAP ***********************************************************************
localhost                  : ok=1    changed=1    unreachable=0    failed=0
All services running.    playbook_rc=0
Conductor terminated. Cleaning up.    command_rc=0 conductor_id=c697eecbb6a5fd
0cbdb154d32874ac0bb50bb87ca3bdcd1a10fa8043f25d513d save_container=False
~/src/mastery/ansible>
```

The `run` sub-command will use the Ansible Container to bring up the service container(s). At this point, we should be able to see the container running in `docker ps` and communicate with the container to see what our cow has to say:

```
~/src/mastery/ansible> docker ps --filter name=cowsay
CONTAINER ID        IMAGE                              COMMAND             CREATED
                    STATUS              PORTS          NAMES
528d90e8ed4b        ansible-cowsay:20190307143506      "nginx"             About a
minute ago          Up About a minute   0.0.0.0:8081->80/tcp    ansible_cowsay_1
~/src/mastery/ansible> curl http://localhost:8081
 _____
< boop >
 ------
        \   ^__^
         \  (oo)_____
            (__)\       )\/\
                ||----w |
                ||     ||
~/src/mastery/ansible>
```

[ 366 ]

This example barely scratches the surface of what's possible with Ansible Container. The control files support templating values to make quite dynamic service arrangements, which can easily be tested locally and then pushed into a production deployment system, such as Kubernetes. More features are being added, and the functionality may change, so be sure to check the documentation before getting started with Ansible Container, at `http://docs.ansible.com/ansible-container/`.

# Summary

DevOps has pushed automation in many new directions, including the containerization of applications, and even the creation of an infrastructure itself. Cloud computing services enable self-service management of fleets of servers for running services. Ansible can easily interact with these services to provide the automation and orchestration engine.

In this chapter, you learned how to manage on-premise cloud infrastructures, such as OpenStack, using Ansible. We then extended this with examples of public cloud infrastructure provision on both AWS and Microsoft Azure. Finally, you learned how to interact with Docker using Ansible, and how to neatly package Docker service definitions using Ansible Container.

Ansible can start just about any host, except for the one that it is running on, and with proper credentials, it can create the infrastructure that it wants to manage, either for one-off actions or to deploy a new version of an application into a production container management system. The end result is that once your hardware is in place and your service providers are configured, you can manage your entire infrastructure through Ansible, if you so desire!

In the final chapter of this book, we will look at a new and rapidly growing area of automation: network provisioning with Ansible.

# 12
# Network Automation

Historically, a network consisted of mostly hardware with just a modicum of software involvement. Changing the topology of it involved installing and configuring new switches or blades in a chassis or, at the very least, re-patching some cables. Now, the scenario has changed, and the complex infrastructures built to cater for multi-tenant environments such as cloud hosting, or microservice-based deployments, require a network that is more agile and flexible. This has led to the emergence of **Software Defined Networking (SDN)**, an approach that centralizes the network configuration (where historically it was configured on a per-device basis) and results in network topology being defined as a whole, rather than as a series of component parts. It is, if you like, an abstraction layer for the network itself and thus implies that just like infrastructure as a service, networks can now be defined in code.

Since the last edition of this book was published, a great deal of work has gone into Ansible to make network automation a core proposition. Not only can you now define your infrastructure in an Ansible playbook as we described in the last chapter, but you can define the network supporting it too.

In this chapter, we will explore this area of rapidly growing importance, comprising the following topics:

- Ansible for network management
- Handling multiple device types
- Configuring Cumulus Networks switches with Ansible
- Best practices

## Technical requirements

Check out the following video to see the Code in Action:

http://bit.ly/2ujFGiz

## Ansible for network management

Core network devices, such as switches, routers, and firewalls, have long had management interfaces, especially in professional environments. Command-line interfaces have always been popular on such devices as they support scripting and hence, as you have already guessed, they lend themselves extremely well to Ansible automation.

Historically, a myriad of challenges have faced teams managing these devices, including maintaining configuration, coping with the failure/loss of a device, and obtaining support in the event of an issue. Often, companies found themselves locked in to a single network vendor (or at best a small handful) to enable the use of proprietary tools to manage the network. As with any situation where you are locked into a technology, this carries both benefits and drawbacks. Add to this the complexity of software-defined networks that are rapidly changing and evolving, and the challenge becomes even greater. In this part of this chapter, we will explore how Ansible addresses these challenges.

### Cross-platform support

As we have seen throughout this book, Ansible has been designed to make automation code portable and reusable in as many scenarios as possible. In our chapter on infrastructure management, we used almost identical playbooks to configure infrastructure on four different providers, and the examples that were given were quite simplistic; we could have improved this further through the use of roles to remove the repetition of so much code.

In short, Ansible made it possible to write playbooks that ran on multiple environments to achieve exactly the same thing with minimal effort once we had defined the first one. The same is true of networks; if you visit the network modules index in the Ansible documentation (see https://docs.ansible.com/ansible/latest/modules/list_of_network_modules.html?highlight=modules), you will find support for over 50 system types, and this grows with every release.

With such a wide (and growing) range of device support, it is easy for a network administrator to manage all of their devices from one central place, without the need for proprietary tools. However, the benefits are greater than just this.

## Configuration portability

As we have discussed already, Ansible code is highly portable. In the world of network automation, this is extremely valuable. To start with, it means that you could roll out a configuration change on a development network (or simulator) and test it, and then be able to roll out exactly the same code against a different inventory (for example, a production one) once the configuration has been deemed to have been tested successfully.

The benefits don't stop there, however. Historically, in the event of issues with a software upgrade or configuration change, the challenge of the network engineer was to engage the vendor for support and assistance successfully. This required sending sufficient detail to the vendor to enable them to at least understand the problem, and most likely want to reproduce it (especially in the case of firmware issues). When the configuration for a network is defined in Ansible, the playbooks themselves can be sent to the vendor to enable them to quickly and accurately understand the network topology and diagnose the issue. In fact, I has come across cases where network vendors are now starting to insist on Ansible playbooks with network configuration when a support ticket is raised because it empowers them to resolve the issue faster than ever before.

Effective use of ansible-vault ensures that sensitive data is kept out of the main playbooks and, hence, can easily be removed before being sent to a third party (and even if it was accidentally, it wouldn't be readable).

## Backup, restore, and version control

Although most businesses have robust change control procedures, there is no guarantee that these are followed 100% of the time, and human beings have been known to tweak configurations without accurately recording the changes they've made. Moving the network configuration to Ansible removes this issue, as the configuration is a known state defined by the playbooks that can be compared easily to the running configuration using a `check` run.

Not only is this possible, but configurations can be backed up and restored with ease. Say, for example, a switch fails and has to be replaced. If the replacement is the same type, it can be configured and brought into service rapidly by running the Ansible playbooks, perhaps limited to just the replacement switch if appropriate.

This lends itself to version control too—network configuration playbooks can be pushed to a source control repository, enabling configuration versions to be tracked, and differences over time to be easily examined.

## Automated change requests

Often, minor changes to a network might be required for the rollout of a new project—perhaps a new VLAN or VXLAN, or some previously unused ports that have been brought into service. The configuration parameters will be well-defined by a change request and/or network design, and it is probably not the best use of a highly qualified network engineer to be making simple configuration changes. Tasks such as these are typically routine, in that the configuration changes can be templated in an Ansible playbook, with variables passed to it that have been defined by the change request (for example, port numbers and VLAN membership details).

This then frees up the engineers' time for more important work, such as the design of new architectures, and new product research and testing.

In fact, coupled with the use of a package such as AWX (as we discussed earlier in this book), simple and well-tested changes could be completely automated, or passed to a frontline team to be executed safely by simply passing in the required parameters. In this way, the risk of human error is significantly reduced, regardless of the skillset of the person performing the change.

With these benefits well-established and understood, let's proceed to look at how we might start writing playbooks to handle a multi-device network.

## Handling multiple device types

In a world where we are not locked into a single vendor, it is important to know how we might handle the different network devices in an infrastructure. We established in the last chapter that for different infrastructure providers, a similar process was established for each one in terms of getting Ansible to interact with it. This can be a little different with switches, as not all command-line switch interfaces are created the same. Some, such as on a Cumulus Networks switch, use straightforward SSH connectivity, meaning that everything we have learned about in this book so far on connecting to an SSH capable device still applies. However, other devices, such as F5 BIG-IP, do not use such an interface and therefore require the module to be run from the Ansible host, and the configuration parameters to be passed to the module directly as opposed to using host variables such as `ansible_ssh_user`.

It is not expected that many of the readers of this book will have access to a wide variety of network hardware to use in the examples in this chapter. Instead, in this part of this chapter, we will go into more detail on the process to be employed when automating a new network device for the first time so that you have the knowledge to apply this to your own situation.

## Researching your modules

Your first task when working with any networking device is to understand what module you need to use with Ansible. This will be a function of two things:

- What device do you wish to automate the management of?
- What task(s) do you wish to perform on the device?

Armed with this information, you can consult the module listing in the Ansible documentation and find out if your devices and desired tasks are supported. Let's say, for example, that you have an F5 BIG-IP device, and you want to save and load configuration on this device.

A quick scan on the module listing shows that the `bigip_config` module will do just what we need, so we can proceed with the module configuration (see the next section) and then write the desired playbook around this module.

What happens if there is no module for your device, though? In this instance, you have two choices. Firstly, you could write a new module for Ansible to perform the tasks you require. This is something you could contribute back to the community, and *Chapter 9, Extending Ansible*, has all the details you need to get started on this task.

Alternatively, if you want to get something up and running quickly, remember that Ansible can send raw commands in most of the transport methods it supports. For example, in the author's lab setup, they have a TP-Link managed switch. There are no native Ansible modules for this—however, as well as a web-based GUI, this switch also has an SSH management interface. If I wanted to quickly get something up and running, I could use Ansible's `shell` or `command` modules to send raw commands over SSH to the switch. Naturally, this solution lacks elegance and makes it difficult to write playbooks that are idempotent, but nonetheless, it does enable me to get up and running quickly with Ansible and this device.

This captures the beauty of Ansible—the ease with which new devices can be managed with it with minimal effort, and how, with just a little more effort, it can be extended for the benefit of the community.

## Configuring your modules

As we have already covered the use of the `shell` and `command` modules, as well as extending Ansible, earlier in this book, we will proceed with the case where we have found a module we want to work with. As you may have noticed in some earlier chapters, although Ansible includes many modules out of the box, not all of them work straight away.

Ansible is written in Python, and, in most cases, where there are dependencies, these will be Python modules. The important thing is to review the documentation. For example, take the `bigip_config` module we selected in the last section. A quick review of the *Requirements* section of the documentation shows that this requires (at the time of writing) the Python module `f5-sdk`, version `3.0.16` or newer.

There are multiple ways to install this—some operating systems may have a native package built, and if this is available, then provided it meets the version requirements, it is perfectly fine to use this. Indeed, it may be advantageous in terms of vendor support. However, if such a package is not available, Python modules can easily be installed using the `pip` tool. Assuming this is already on your system, the installation is as simple as using the following code:

```
sudo p ip install f5-sdk
```

Also, be sure to review the *Notes* section of the documentation. Continuing with this example, we can see that it only supports BIG-IP software version 12 and newer, so if you are on an earlier version, you will have to find another route to automate your device (or upgrade the software if this is an acceptable path).

## Writing your playbooks

Once your modules are configured, and all requirements (be they Python module dependencies or device software ones) are met, it's time to start writing your playbook. This should be a simple task of following the documentation for the module. Let's suppose we want to reset the configuration on an F5 BIG-IP device. From the documentation, we can see that authentication parameters are passed to the module itself. Also, the example code shows the use of the `delegate_to` task keyword; both of these clues tell us that the module is not using the native SSH transport of Ansible, but rather one that is defined in the module itself. Thus, a playbook to reset the configuration of a single device might look something like this:

```
---
- name: reset an F5
```

```
    hosts: localhost
    gather_facts: false

    tasks:
      - name: reset my F5
        bigip_config:
          reset: yes
          save: yes
          server: lb.mastery.example.com
          user: admin
          password: mastery
          validate_certs: no
```

In this case, we are using a textbook example from the documentation to reset our configuration. Note that as our `hosts` parameter only defines `localhost`, we do not need the `delegate_to` keyword, since the `bigip_config` module will be run from `localhost` only in this playbook.

In this way, we have automated a simple, but otherwise manual and repetitive, task that might need to be performed. Running the playbook would be as simple as executing the following command:

```
ansible-playbook -i mastery-hosts reset-f5.yaml
```

Naturally, to actually test this playbook, you would have to have an F5 BIG-IP device to test against. Not everyone will have this available, so, in the next section of this chapter, we will move on to demonstrate a real-world example that everyone reading this book can work with. However, the intent of this part of this chapter has been to give you a solid overview of integrating your network devices, whatever they may be, with Ansible. Thus, it is hoped that even if you have a device that we haven't mentioned here, you understand the fundamentals of how to get it working.

# Configuring Cumulus Networks switches with Ansible

Most network devices run proprietary software that you can only obtain from the vendor when you have an active subscription in place. This can make testing or learning with this software difficult, even if an emulator for the network devices is available. Fortunately for us, Cumulus Linux exists. Cumulus Linux (from Cumulus Networks) is an open source network operating system that can run on a variety of bare metal switches, offering an open source approach to data center networking.

*Network Automation*

Even better, they offer a free version of their software that will run on the hypervisor of your choice for test and evaluation purposes called Cumulus VX. The examples in this part of this chapter are based on Cumulus VX version 3.7.3.

## Defining our inventory

A quick bit of research shows us that Cumulus VX will use the standard SSH transport method of Ansible. Furthermore, there is just one module defined for working with this system—`nclu`. No prerequisite modules are required to use this module, so we can proceed straight to defining our inventory.

By default, Cumulus VX boots up with the management interface configured to get an IP address with DHCP. It also has three other virtual switch ports for us to test and play with the configuration of. A simple inventory to get this working would look something like this:

```
[cumulus]
mastery-switch1 ansible_host=192.168.81.142

[cumulus:vars]
ansible_user=cumulus
ansible_ssh_pass=CumulusLinux!
```

Note the following:

- The IP address specified in `ansible_host` will almost certainly differ from mine—make sure you change this to the correct value for your Cumulus VX virtual machine. You might have to log in to the VM console to get the IP address.
- Normally, you would never put the password in clear text in the inventory file—however, for simplicity and to save time, we will specify the default password here. In a real-world use case, always use a Vault, or set up key-based SSH authentication.

Now, let's test connectivity with the `ping` module:

```
~/src/mastery> ansible -i switch-inventory -m ping mastery-switch1
mastery-switch1 | SUCCESS => {
    "changed": false,
    "ping": "pong"
}
~/src/mastery>
```

As we discussed earlier in this book, the Ansible ping module performs a complete end-to-end connectivity test, including authentication at the transport layer. As a result, if you received a successful test result like the one shown previously, we can proceed with confidence and write our first playbooks.

## Practical examples

The Cumulux VX image comes completely unconfigured (save for the DHCP client configuration on the management port `eth0`). It has three switch ports, that is, `swp1`, `swp2`, and `swp3`. Let's query one of those interfaces to see whether there is any existing configuration. We can use a simple playbook called `switch-query.yaml` to query `swp1`:

```
---
- name: query switch
  hosts: mastery-switch1

  tasks:
  - name: query swp1 interface
    nclu:
      commands:
        - show interface swp1
    register: interface

  - name: print interface status
    debug:
      var: interface
```

If we run this (exactly as we have run other playbooks), then we will see something like the following:

```
~/src/mastery> ansible-playbook -i switch-inventory switch-query.yaml

PLAY [query switch] ************************************************************

TASK [Gathering Facts] *********************************************************
ok: [mastery-switch1]

TASK [query swp1 interface] ****************************************************
ok: [mastery-switch1]

TASK [print interface status] **************************************************
ok: [mastery-switch1] => {
    "interface": {
        "changed": false,
        "failed": false,
        "msg": "          Name    MAC                  Speed    MTU    Mode\n----  ----  -----------------\nADMDN    swp1    00:00:01:39:34:6f    N/A     1500    NotConfigured\n\n\n\n"
    }
}

PLAY RECAP *********************************************************************
mastery-switch1            : ok=3    changed=0    unreachable=0    failed=0

~/src/mastery>
```

This confirms our initial statement about the VM image—we can see that the switch port is not configured. It is very easy to turn this VM into a simple layer 2 switch with Ansible and the `nclu` module. The following playbook, called `switch-l2-configure.yaml`, does exactly this:

```
---
- name: configure switch
  hosts: mastery-switch1

  tasks:
  - name: bring up ports swp[1-3]
    nclu:
      template: |
        {% for interface in range(1,4) %}
        add interface swp{{interface}}
        add bridge bridge ports swp{{interface}}
        {% endfor %}
      commit: true

  - name: query swp1 interface
    nclu:
      commands:
          - show interface swp1
    register: interface

  - name: print interface status
    debug:
      var: interface
```

Notice how we are using some clever inline Jinja2 templating to run a `for` loop across the three interfaces, saving the need to create repetitive and cumbersome code. These commands bring up the three switch interfaces and add them to the default layer 2 bridge.

*Network Automation*

Finally, the `commit: true` line applies these configurations immediately to the switch. Now, if we run this, we will see a different status for `swp1`:

```
~/src/mastery> ansible-playbook -i switch-inventory switch-l2-configure.yaml

PLAY [configure switch] ************************************************************

TASK [Gathering Facts] *************************************************************
ok: [mastery-switch1]

TASK [bring up ports swp[1-3]] *****************************************************
changed: [mastery-switch1]

TASK [query swp1 interface] ********************************************************
ok: [mastery-switch1]

TASK [print interface status] ******************************************************
ok: [mastery-switch1] => {
    "interface": {
        "changed": false,
        "failed": false,
        "msg": "    Name    MAC                 Speed   MTU    Mode\n--  ----  ------
-----------  -----  ----  ---------\nUP  swp1  00:00:01:39:34:6f  1G      1500   A
ccess/L2\n\nAll VLANs on L2 Port\n----------------------\n1\n\nUntagged\n---------\
n1\n\ncl-netstat counters\n-------------------\nRX_OK  RX_ERR  RX_DRP  RX_OVR  T
X_OK  TX_ERR  TX_DRP  TX_OVR\n-----  ------  ------  ------  -----  ------  ------
--  ------\n97879      0       0       0     620     0       0       0\n\nLLDP
 Details\n-----------\nLocalPort  RemotePort(RemoteHost)\n---------  -------------
----------\nswp1       swp3(cumulus)\n\nRouting\n--------\n  Interface swp1 is
up, line protocol is up\n  Link ups:      2    last: 2019/03/08 13:31:07.21\n
Link downs:    2    last: 2019/03/08 13:29:35.76\n  PTM status: disabled\n  vrf
: default\n  index 3 metric 0 mtu 1500 speed 1000\n  flags: <UP,BROADCAST,RUNNIN
G,MULTICAST>\n  Type: Ethernet\n  HWaddr: 00:00:01:39:34:6f\n  Interface Type Ot
her\n  Master (bridge) ifindex 8\n\n\n\n"
    }
}

PLAY RECAP *************************************************************************
mastery-switch1            : ok=4    changed=1    unreachable=0    failed=0

~/src/mastery>
```

Chapter 12

As we can see, the `swp1` interface is now up and part of the bridge, ready to switch traffic. Note that the task to configure the ports was marked as `changed`, since the configuration was applied for the first time here. What happens if we run the playbook again without performing any other steps on the switch? Let's see:

```
~/src/mastery> ansible-playbook -i switch-inventory switch-l2-configure.yaml

PLAY [configure switch] ************************************************

TASK [Gathering Facts] *************************************************
ok: [mastery-switch1]

TASK [bring up ports swp[1-3]] *****************************************
ok: [mastery-switch1]

TASK [query swp1 interface] ********************************************
ok: [mastery-switch1]

TASK [print interface status] ******************************************
ok: [mastery-switch1] => {
    "interface": {
        "changed": false,
        "failed": false,
        "msg": "    Name    MAC                Speed  MTU   Mode\n--  ------  -----------------  -----  ----  -------
-------  ------  -----------------\nUP  swp1    00:00:01:39:34:6f  1G     1500  A
ccess/L2\n\nAll VLANs on L2 Port\n---------------------\n1\n\nUntagged\n---------\
n1\n\ncl-netstat counters\n--------------------\n RX_OK  RX_ERR  RX_DRP  RX_OVR
TX_OK   TX_ERR  TX_DRP  TX_OVR\n------  ------  ------  ------  ------  ------  -
----  ------\n122378  0       0       0       641     0       0       0\n\nL
LDP Details\n------------\nLocalPort  RemotePort(RemoteHost)\n-----------  -------
------------------\nswp1       swp3(cumulus)\n\nRouting\n-------\n Interface swp1
 is up, line protocol is up\n  Link ups:       2    last: 2019/03/08 13:31:07.21\
n  Link downs:     2    last: 2019/03/08 13:29:35.76\n  PTM status: disabled\n
vrf: default\n  index 3 metric 0 mtu 1500 speed 1000\n  flags: <UP,BROADCAST,RUN
NING,MULTICAST>\n  Type: Ethernet\n  HWaddr: 00:00:01:39:34:6f\n  Interface Type
 Other\n  Master (bridge) ifindex 8\n\n\n\n"
    }
}

PLAY RECAP *************************************************************
mastery-switch1            : ok=4    changed=0    unreachable=0    failed=0

~/src/mastery>
```

[ 381 ]

This time, the state of this task is ok, meaning that the nclu module did not detect any changes being applied to the switch. In this way, playbooks that automate the configuration of our Cumulus Linux switch are idempotent and result in a consistent state, even when they're run multiple times. This also means that if the configuration of the switch drifts (for example, due to user intervention), it is very easy to see that something has changed. Unfortunately, the nclu module doesn't currently support the check mode of ansible-playbook, but nonetheless, it still provides a powerful way to configure and manage your switches.

Automating Cumulux Linux with Ansible really is as simple as that – further examples are beyond the scope of this book, as they would entail more advanced usage of the nclu command. Hopefully, however, by means of these simple examples, it can be seen that the automation of network infrastructure with Ansible is now no more difficult than automating anything else.

# Best practices

All the usual best practices of using Ansible apply when automating network devices with it. For example, never store passwords in the clear, and make use of ansible-vault where appropriate. In spite of this, network devices are their own special class of device when it comes to Ansible, and support for them really started to flourish from the 2.5 release of Ansible onward. As such, there are a few special best practices that deserve to be mentioned when it comes to network automation with Ansible.

## Inventory

Make good use of the inventory structure supported by Ansible when it comes to organizing your network infrastructure, and pay particular attention to grouping. Doing so will make your playbook development much easier. For example, suppose you have two switches on your network—one is a Cumulus Linux Switch, as we examined previously, and the another is a Cisco IOS-based device. Your inventory may look like this:

```
[switches:children]
ios
cumulus

[ios]
ios01 ansible_host=ios01.mastery.example.com

[cumulus]
cumulus01 ansible_host=cumulus01.mastery.example.com
```

We know that we cannot run the `nclu` module on anything other than a cumulus switch, so, with some careful use of the `when` statement, we can build tasks in playbooks to ensure that we run the correct command on the correct device. Here is a task that will only run on devices in the `cumulus` group we defined in the preceding inventory:

```yaml
- name: query swp1 interface
  nclu:
    commands:
      - show interface swp1
  register: interface
  when: inventory_hostname in groups['cumulus']
```

Similarly, good use of grouping enables us to set variables on a device basis. Although you would not put passwords in the clear into your inventory, it might be that your switches of a given type all use the same username (for example, `cumulus` in the case of Cumulus Linux devices). Alternatively, perhaps your IOS devices need specific Ansible host variables set for connectivity to work, and to achieve the privilege escalation that's required to perform configuration. Thus, we can extend our preceding inventory example by adding the following code:

```
[cumulus:vars]
ansible_user=cumulus

[ios:vars]
ansible_network_os=ios
ansible_become=yes
ansible_become_method=enable
```

Good inventory structure and variable definition will make the development of your playbooks a great deal easier, and the resulting code will be more manageable and easier to work with.

## Gathering facts

Ansible includes a number of specific fact-gathering modules for network devices, and these may well be useful for running conditional tasks, or simply reporting back data about your devices. The device-specific fact modules are not run at the start of the playbook run since, at this stage, Ansible does not know what sort of device it is communicating with. Thus, we must tell it to gather the facts for each device as appropriate.

Network Automation

There is no specific facts module for Cumulus Linux switches (although, since they are based on Linux, the standard host facts can still be gathered). Taking forward the example of our IOS device, we would specifically run this facts module in our playbook based on some unique key in our inventory. We know that, in the example inventory we defined in the last section, our Cisco IOS switches are in the `ios` group, and also have `ansible_network_os` set to `ios`. We can use either of these as a condition in a `when` statement to run the `ios_facts` module on our switches—as such, the beginning of our playbook might look like this:

```
---
- name: "gather device facts"
  hosts: all
  gather_facts: false

  tasks:
  - name: gather ios facts
    ios_facts:
    when: ansible_network_os == 'ios'
  - name: gather cumulus facts
    setup:
    when: inventory_hostname in groups['cumulus']
```

Notice that we set `gather_facts` to `false` at the beginning of this playbook. This is done in this way since the standard facts module is intended for Linux-based hosts, and would fail if run against a network device such as a Cisco IOS switch.

## Jump hosts

Finally, a word on jump hosts. It is common for network devices to be behind a bastion of jump hosts of some kind for important security reasons. Ansible provides a number of mechanisms for doing this, depending on the underlying network transport. For example, SSH connectivity (such as with Cumulus Linux switches) can make use of SSH's ability to proxy commands. There are several ways to achieve these, but the simplest is to add an additional group variable to the inventory. For example, if we can only access our Cumulus Linux switch via a host called `bastion01`, our inventory variables section would look like this:

```
[cumulus:vars]
ansible_user=cumulus
ansible_ssh_pass=CumulusLinux!
ansible_ssh_common_args='-o ProxyCommand="ssh -W %h:%p -q bastion01"'
```

The preceding proxy command assumes that password-less authentication is already configured and working for `bastion01`.

SSH Proxy commands like this would work for other `ansible_connection` modes that are used in network device management, too, including `netconf` and `network_cli`, offering support for jump hosts to handle a wide range of network devices. As ever, the best method to be sure about the way to handle a specific type of connectivity is to check the documentation for your specific network device and follow the specific guidance therein.

# Summary

As more and more of our infrastructure gets defined and managed by code, it becomes ever more important that the network layer can be automated effectively by Ansible. A great deal of work has gone into Ansible since the last release of this book in precisely this area, especially since the release of Ansible 2.5. With these advancements, it is now easy to build playbooks to automate network tasks, from simple device changes to rolling out entire network architectures through Ansible. All of the benefits of Ansible relating to code reuse, portability, and so on are all now available to those who manage network devices.

In this chapter, you learned about how Ansible enables network management. You learned effective strategies for handling different device types within your infrastructure and how to write playbooks for them, and then you expanded on this with some specific examples on Cumulus Linux. Finally, you learned about some of the best practices that must be applied when using Ansible to manage a network infrastructure.

This brings us to the conclusion of this book. I hope you have found it beneficial, and that it has given you the strategies and tools for managing everything, from small configuration changes to entire infrastructure deployments with Ansible.

# Other Books You May Enjoy

If you enjoyed this book, you may be interested in these other books by Packt:

### Learning Ansible 2 - Second Edition
Fabio Alessandro Locati

ISBN: 978-1-78646-423-1

- Set up Ansible 2 and an Ansible 2 project in a future-proof way
- Perform basic operations with Ansible 2 such as creating, copying, moving, changing, and deleting files, and creating and deleting users)
- Deploy complete cloud environments using Ansible 2 on AWS and DigitalOcean
- Explore complex operations with Ansible 2 (Ansible vault, e-mails, and Nagios)
- Develop and test Ansible playbooks
- Write a custom module and test it

Other Books You May Enjoy

## Security Automation with Ansible 2
Madhu Akula, Akash Mahajan

ISBN: 978-1-78839-451-2

- Use Ansible playbooks, roles, modules, and templating to build generic, testable playbooks
- Manage Linux and Windows hosts remotely in a repeatable and predictable manner
- See how to perform security patch management, and security hardening with scheduling and automation
- Set up AWS Lambda for a serverless automated defense
- Run continuous security scans against your hosts and automatically fix and harden the gaps
- Extend Ansible to write your custom modules and use them as part of your already existing security automation programs
- Perform automation security audit checks for applications using Ansible
- Manage secrets in Ansible using Ansible Vault

## Leave a review - let other readers know what you think

Please share your thoughts on this book with others by leaving a review on the site that you bought it from. If you purchased the book from Amazon, please leave us an honest review on this book's Amazon page. This is vital so that other potential readers can see and use your unbiased opinion to make purchasing decisions, we can understand what our customers think about our products, and our authors can see your feedback on the title that they have worked with Packt to create. It will only take a few minutes of your time, but is valuable to other potential customers, our authors, and Packt. Thank you!

# Index

## A

action plugins 275
analog-to-digital converters (ADCs) 87
Ansible Containers
  about 357, 358
  ansible-container build, using 362
  ansible-container init, using 360, 361
  ansible-container run, using 364, 366
Ansible Galaxy
  reference 220
Ansible project
  contributing to 285
  contribution submissions 285
  pull request, making 292
  repository 286
  tests, executing 286
Ansible-playbook
  executing, with encrypted files 64
Ansible
  automaton, system requirements 77
  challenges, network management 370
  configuration 10
  connecting, to Windows 81, 83
  Cumulus Networks switches, configuring 375
  reference 74, 80, 285, 370
  running, from Windows 74
  version 10
  Window tasks, automating 89
AWX
  auditing 110, 111
  basics 108
  credentials, defining 104, 105
  executing 94, 96, 98
  integrating, with playbook 98
  inventory, defining 101, 102, 103
  notifications 114
  organizations 109
  project, defining 99
  reference 95
  role-based access control (RBAC) 108
  scheduling 109
  starting with 94
  surveys 111
  template, defining 105, 107
  workflow templates 112

## B

best practices, Ansible
  fact-gathering modules 383
  jump hosts 384
built-in filters
  about 138
  count 139
  default 139
  random 139
  reference 138
  round 140

## C

callback plugins 272, 273, 274
challenges, network management
  about 370
  automated change requests 372
  backup 371
  configuration portability 371
  cross-platform support 370
  restore 371
  version control 371
change
  command family, handling 164, 166
  defining 163, 164
  suppressing 167
check mode, modules

about 267
  handling 268, 269
  supporting 267
cloud infrastructures
  managing 322, 323
  OpenStack inventory sources, using 331, 334
  servers, creating 323
code execution
  debugging 236
  local code, debugging 239
complex data
  passing, to including tasks 187, 188
conditional task includes 189, 190
configuration management database (CMDB) 17
connection-type plugins 269
control machine 43
control structures
  about 120, 122
  conditionals 120
  inline conditionals 122, 124
  loops 124
  macros 129
create, read, update, or delete (CRUD) 323
Cumulus Networks switches configuration
  best practices 382
  examples 377, 380, 382
  inventory, defining 376
custom filters, Ansible
  about 140
  base64 encoding 145
  content, searching for 146
  filters, dealing with path names 143
  filters, related to task status 140
  shuffle 142

# D

data encryption
  about 52
  by Vault 54
  encrypted files, creating 55
  encrypted files, editing 60
  existing files, encrypting 58, 60
  password rotation, on encrypted files 62
  passwords 53
  vault IDs 53

data manipulation
  about 137
  built-in filters 138
  Python object methods 149
  syntax 137
  undefined arguments, omitting 148
data sources 11
device types
  handling 372
  modules, configuring 374
  modules, researching 373
  playbook, writing 374
disruptions
  delaying 310, 311, 313, 314
  destructive tasks, running 315, 316
  minimizing 310
Docker containers
  about 345
  building, with Dockerfile 349, 352, 353
  images, building 346, 347, 349
  inventory 353, 355, 357
dynamic vars_files inclusion 200, 201

# E

encrypted data
  integrating, with 68, 69
  integrating, with plain XML 66
encrypted files, creating
  about 55
  password file, using 57
  password prompt, using 56
  password script, using 58
encrypted files
  decrypting 63, 64
  used, for executing Ansible-playbook 64
error recovery
  about 168
  always section, using 171, 172, 173
  rescue action, using 168, 170
  unreliable environments, handling 174, 176
expand and contract strategy 299, 301
external data
  accessing 43
extra variables 41
extra-vars 204, 205

## F

fact modules  41
fact-caching plugin  270
failing fast approach
  about  302
  any_errors_fatal option, using  302, 304
  handlers, forcing  307, 308, 309
  max_fail_percentage option, using  304, 306
failures
  defining  156
  error condition, defining  158
  error conditions, defining  159, 160, 162
  errors, ignoring  156, 157
filter plugins  270, 271

## H

handler include concepts  182

## I

in-place upgrades  296, 297, 298, 299
include_vars  201, 203
including handlers  197, 198
including playbooks  205, 207
including tasks
  about  182, 184
  complex data, passing to  187, 188
  tagging  191, 192
  variable values, passing to  184, 186
  with loops  193, 195, 196
including variables
  about  199
  dynamic vars_files inclusion  200, 201
  extra-vars  204, 205
  include_vars  201, 203
  vars_files key  199
infrastructure as a Service (IaaS)  321
inventories  109
inventory plugins
  about  278, 279, 280, 281, 282
  developing  276, 277
  host variables, listing  277
  hosts, listing  277
  script performance, optimizing  283, 285
inventory variables  40

inventory
  behavior inventory variables  15
  dynamic inventories  17, 18
  limiting  21, 23, 24
  ordering  13
  parsing  11
  runtime additions  20
  static inventory  12
  variable data  14

## J

Jinja2
  about  37
  documentation, reference  124
job templates  109

## L

LDAP  17
local code
  action plugins, debugging  253
  debugging  239
  executor code, debugging  246, 247, 248
  inventory code, debugging  240, 242, 243, 244
  playbook code, debugging  244, 245
  remote code, debugging  249, 251, 252, 253
lookup plugin  43, 270
loops
  about  124
  indexing  126, 128
  items, filtering  125
  used, for performing iterative tasks  177, 178

## M

macro variables
  about  129, 130
  arguments  131
  caller  134, 136
  catch_kwargs  133
  catch_varargs  134
  defaults  132
  name  130
macros
  about  129
  variables  129
magic variables

    about 42
    reference 42
 modules
    arguments 36, 37
    blacklisting 37
    check mode 267
    construct 256
    custom modules 257
    developing 256
    documenting 260, 262, 263, 265
    execution 35, 38
    fact data, providing 266, 267
    reference 35
    simple module 257, 259
    task performance 39
    transport 35, 38

# O

organization 109
os-client-config
    reference 331

# P

path names
    about 143
    basename 143
    dirname 144
    expanduser 144
play directives
    reference 30
play variables 41
playbook parsing
    about 24
    execution strategies 30
    host selection, for plays and tasks 31
    order of operations 24, 26
    play behavior directives 29
    play names 32, 34
    relative path assumptions 26
    task names 32, 34
playbook
    debugging 237, 238
    include concepts 182
    logging 227, 228
plugins

    action plugins 275
    callback plugins 272, 273, 274
    connection-type plugins 269
    developing 269
    distributing 275
    fact-caching plugins 270
    filter plugins 270
    lookup plugins 270
    shell plugins 269
    vars plugins 270
projects 109
public cloud infrastructure
    managing 337, 340, 341, 345
pull request
    request 292
Python object methods
    about 149
    float method 151
    int method 151
    list methods 150
    string methods 149

# R

rich role-based access control (RBAC) 94
role application
    about 214, 215, 216
    mixing, with including tasks 216, 219
role default 41
role dependency
    about 211
    conditionals 213
    tags 213
    variables 212
role imports 219
role includes 219
role sharing
    about 219
    Ansible Galaxy 220, 223, 225
role structure
    about 208
    dependencies 210
    files 210
    handlers 209
    modules 209
    plugins 209

tasks 208
templates 210
variables 209
role variables 40
roles 208

## S

secrets
  logging, to remote or local files 70, 72
  protecting 69
  transmitting, to remote hosts 70
servers
  creating 323
  runtime inventory, adding to 328, 330
  virtual servers, booting 324, 327
shell plugin 269
single tasks
  serializing 316, 317
Software Defined Networking (SDN) 369
Source Control Management (SCM) 99
standard subscript syntax 235
static inventory 12
structure, Ansible
  inventory 382

## T

task header 228
task include concepts 182
task variables 41
teams 108, 109
test execution, Ansible project
  code-style tests 290
  integration tests 288, 290
  unit tests 287

## U

users 108

## V

values
  comparisons 151
  logic 152
  tests 152
variable include concepts 182

variable introspection 229, 231
variable precedence
  about 43
  group priority ordering 45, 47
  hashes, merging 49, 50
  order 44
variable subelements
  about 232, 233
  versus Python object method 235, 236
variable types
  about 40
  extra variables 41
  play variables 41
  role default 41
  role variables 40
  task variables 41
variable values
  passing, to including tasks 184, 186
variable
  location 40
  types 40
vars plugins 270
vars_files key 199
verbosity 228

## W

Windows hosts
  setting up, for Ansible control 77
Windows Subsystem for Linux (WSL)
  about 74
  enabling 75
  Linux, installing 75, 76
Windows tasks
  automating, with Ansible 89
  module, extending beyond 91
  right module, selecting 89
  software, installing 91
Windows
  accounts 86
  Ansible, connecting 81, 83
  Ansible, running 74
  authentication mechanisms 83, 86
  authentication, handling 83
  builds, checking 74
  certificate validation 87

[ 395 ]

encryption, handling 83
WinRM listener

enabling 78, 80

Printed in Poland
by Amazon Fulfillment
Poland Sp. z o.o., Wrocław